The
Gallup
Poll

Public Opinion 1991

Other Gallup Poll Publications Available from Scholarly Resources

The Gallup Poll: Public Opinion Annual Series

1990 (ISBN 0-8420-2368-2)	*1983* (ISBN 0-8420-2220-1)
1989 (ISBN 0-8420-2344-5)	*1982* (ISBN 0-8420-2214-7)
1988 (ISBN 0-8420-2330-5)	*1981* (ISBN 0-8420-2200-7)
1987 (ISBN 0-8420-2292-9)	*1980* (ISBN 0-8420-2181-7)
1986 (ISBN 0-8420-2274-0)	*1979* (ISBN 0-8420-2170-1)
1985 (ISBN 0-8420-2249-X)	*1978* (ISBN 0-8420-2159-0)
1984 (ISBN 0-8420-2234-1)	*1972–77* (ISBN 0-8420-2129-9, 2 vols.)
	1935–71 (ISBN 0-394-47270-5, 3 vols.)

International Polls

The International Gallup Polls: Public Opinion, 1979
ISBN 0-8420-2180-9 (1981)

The International Gallup Polls: Public Opinion, 1978
ISBN 0-8420-2162-0 (1980)

The Gallup International Public Opinion Polls:
France, 1939, 1944–1975
2 volumes ISBN 0-394-40998-1 (1976)

The Gallup International Public Opinion Polls:
Great Britain, 1937–1975
2 volumes ISBN 0-394-40992-2 (1976)

The Gallup Poll

Public Opinion 1991

George Gallup, Jr.

SR *Scholarly Resources Inc.*
Wilmington, Delaware

ACKNOWLEDGMENTS

The preparation of this volume has involved the staff of both the Gallup Poll and Scholarly Resources Inc., and their contributions are gratefully acknowledged. I also wish to thank Professor Fred L. Israel of the City College of New York, who was the principal coordinator.

G.G., Jr.

The paper used in this publication meets the minimum requirements of the American National Standard for permanence of paper for printed library materials, Z39.48, 1984.

Scholarly Resources Inc.
104 Greenhill Avenue
Wilmington, DE 19805-1897

Library of Congress Catalog Card Number: 79-56557
International Standard Serial Number: 0195-962X
International Standard Book Number: 0-8420-2397-6

CONTENTS

DESIGN OF THE SAMPLE

The Gallup Poll gathers information both in personal interviews and in interviews conducted by telephone. Although the method for selecting households in which to conduct interviews is different, the goal is the same: to provide representative samples of adults living in the United States. In either case the standard size for Gallup Polls is 1000 interviews. More interviews are conducted in specific instances where greater survey accuracy is desired.

Design of the Sample for Personal Surveys

The design of the sample for personal (face-to-face) surveys is that of a replicated area probability sample down to the block level in the case of urban areas and to segments of townships in the case of rural areas.

After stratifying the nation geographically and by size of community according to information derived from the most recent census, over 350 different sampling locations are selected on a mathematically random basis from within cities, towns, and counties that, in turn, have been selected on a mathematically random basis.

The interviewers are given no leeway in selecting the areas in which they are to conduct their interviews. Each interviewer is given a map on which a specific starting point is marked and is instructed to contact households according to a predetermined travel pattern. At each occupied .dwelling unit, the interviewer selects respondents by following a systematic procedure that is repeated until the assigned number of interviews has been completed.

Design of the Sample for Telephone Surveys

The samples of telephone numbers used in telephone interview surveys are based on a random digit stratified probability design. The sampling procedure involves selecting listed "seed" numbers, deleting the last two digits, and randomly generating two digits to replace them. This procedure provides telephone samples that are geographically representative. The random digit aspect, since it allows for the inclusion of unlisted and unpublished numbers, protects the samples from "listing bias"—the unrepresentativeness of telephone samples that can occur if the distinctive households whose telephone numbers are unlisted or unpublished are excluded from the sample.

Weighting Procedures

After the survey data have been collected and processed, each respondent is assigned a weight so that the demographic characteristics of the total weighted sample of respondents match the latest estimates of the demographic characteristics of the adult population available from the U.S. Census Bureau. Telephone surveys are weighted to match the characteristics of the adult population living in households with access to a telephone. The weighting of personal interview data includes a factor to improve the representation of the kind of people who are less likely to be found at home.

The procedures described above are designed to produce samples approximating the adult civilian population (18 and older) living in private households (that is, excluding those in prisons, hospitals, hotels, religious and educational institutions, and those living on reservations or military bases)—and in the case of telephone surveys, households with access to a telephone. Survey percentages may be applied to census estimates of the size of these populations to project percentages into numbers of people. The manner in which the sample is drawn also produces a sample that

TABLE C

	Percentages near 50			
	750	**600**	**400**	**200**
Size of sample				
750	6			
600	7	7		
400	7	8	8	
200	10	10	10	12

*The chances are 95 in 100 that the sampling error is not larger than the figures shown.

Here is an example of how the tables would be used: Let us say that 50 percent of men respond a certain way and 40 percent of women also respond that way, for a difference of 10 percentage points between them. Can we say with any assurance that the 10-point difference reflects a real difference between men and women on the question? The sample contains approximately 600 men and 600 women.

Since the percentages are near 50, we consult Table C, and since the two samples are about 600 persons each, we look for the number in the column headed "600" that is also in the row designated "600." We find the number 7 here. This means that the allowance for error should be 7 points, and that in concluding that the percentage among men is somewhere between 3 and 17 points higher than the percentage among women, we should be wrong only about 5 percent of the time. In other words, we can conclude with considerable confidence that a difference exists in the direction observed and that it amounts to at least 3 percentage points.

If, in another case, men's responses amount to 22 percent and women's 24 percent, we consult Table B because these percentages are near 20. We look in the column headed "600" that is also in the row headed "600" and see that the number is 6. Obviously, then, the 2-point difference is inconclusive.

RECORD OF
GALLUP POLL ACCURACY

Year	Gallup Final Survey*		Election Result*	
1988	56.0%	Bush	53.9%	Bush
1984	59.0	Reagan	59.2	Reagan
1982	55.0	Democratic	55.8	Democratic
1980	47.0	Reagan	50.8	Reagan
1978	55.0	Democratic	54.0	Democratic
1976	48.0	Carter	50.0	Carter
1974	60.0	Democratic	58.9	Democratic
1972	62.0	Nixon	61.8	Nixon
1970	53.0	Democratic	54.3	Democratic
1968	43.0	Nixon	43.5	Nixon
1966	52.5	Democratic	51.9	Democratic
1964	64.0	Johnson	61.3	Johnson
1962	55.5	Democratic	52.7	Democratic
1960	51.0	Kennedy	50.1	Kennedy
1958	57.0	Democratic	56.5	Democratic
1956	59.5	Eisenhower	57.8	Eisenhower
1954	51.5	Democratic	52.7	Democratic
1952	51.0	Eisenhower	55.4	Eisenhower
1950	51.0	Democratic	50.3	Democratic

* The figure shown is the winner's percentage of the Democratic-Republican vote except in the elections of 1948, 1968, and 1976. Because the Thurmond and Wallace voters in 1948 were largely split-offs from the normally Democratic vote, they were made a part of the final Gallup Poll preelection estimate of the division of the vote. In 1968, Wallace's candidacy was supported by such a large minority that he was clearly a major candidate, and the 1968 percentages are based on the total Nixon-Humphrey-Wallace vote. In 1976, because of interest in McCarthy's candidacy and its potential effect on the Carter vote, the final Gallup Poll estimate included Carter, Ford, McCarthy, and all other candidates as a group.

1948	44.5	Truman	49.9	Truman
1946	58.0	Republican	54.3	Republican
1944	51.5	Roosevelt	53.5*	Roosevelt
1942	52.0	Democratic	48.0	Democratic
1940	52.0	Roosevelt	55.0	Roosevelt
1938	54.0	Democratic	50.8	Democratic
1936	55.7	Roosevelt	62.5	Roosevelt

*Civilian vote 53.3, Roosevelt soldier vote 0.5 = 53.8% Roosevelt. Gallup final survey based on civilian vote.

Average Deviation for 26
   National Elections ....2.2 percentage points

Average Deviation for 19
   National Elections
   Since 1950, inclusive ....1.5 percentage points

Trend in Deviation

Elections	Average Error
1936–1950	3.6
1952–1960	1.7
1962–1970	1.6
1972–1988	1.4

CHRONOLOGY

This chronology is provided to enable the reader to relate poll results to specific events, or series of events, that may have influenced public opinion.

1990

December 1–31   The Persian Gulf crisis continues to dominate world news. More than one million troops face off across the Saudi-Kuwaiti border. The United Nations establishes a January 15, 1991, deadline for an Iraqi withdrawal from Kuwait.

1991

The Persian Gulf war (Operation Desert Storm) dominates the news for the first half of the year.

Throughout 1991 state governments across the nation face increased financial shortfalls, with the alternative being either deep cuts in spending or increases in taxes. Nationally, economic news remains dismal as the country slips further into a recession.

January 1   Rhode Island's governor orders the closing of forty-five privately insured credit unions and small banks after their insurer becomes insolvent.

January 4   The Labor Department reports that the unemployment rate at the end of 1990 was at a three-year high.

Congressional leaders announce that debate will be held on U.S. policy in the Persian Gulf before the United Nations' January 15 deadline for the withdrawal of Iraqi troops from Kuwait. On January 12, Congress passes a resolution authorizing President George Bush to use military action to force Iraq from Kuwait. The resolution passes the Senate by a vote of 52 to 47 and the House by 250 to 183.

January 8 — The Federal Reserve eases monetary policy for the sixth time since July 1990, thus indicating the central bank's concern that an economic recession outweighs worries about inflation.

January 9 — Secretary of State James Baker and the Iraqi foreign minister meet in Geneva but fail to reach an agreement that would forestall war in the Persian Gulf. The stock market plunges on this news.

January 16 — An international force led by the United States launches air and missile attacks on Iraq and Iraqi-occupied Kuwait. The attack begins after the expiration of the United Nations Security Council's January 15 deadline for Iraq to withdraw from Kuwait.

January 17 — The federal Center for Disease Control confirms that a Florida dentist who died from AIDS now is believed to have infected three of his patients with the virus. This is the first case in which a health-care provider allegedly has infected patients with AIDS.

January 18 — Eastern Airlines stops flying and announces that it will liquidate its assets.

January 23 — Treasury Secretary Nicholas Brady asks Congress to appropriate at least another $80 billion toward the bailout of the nation's troubled Savings and Loan industry.

January 29–31	As the Persian Gulf war enters its third week, the first major ground battle is fought for a Saudi Arabian town near the Kuwaiti border.
February 1	The Labor Department reports that unemployment in January rose to 6.2%.
	The Federal Reserve continues to ease monetary policy by reducing interest rates, thereby causing an upward surge in stock prices.
February 4	President Bush sends Congress a $1.45-trillion budget for fiscal 1992.
February 9	Lithuania holds a plebiscite on independence from the Soviet Union. The results overwhelmingly support secession.
February 12	The dollar reaches a record low against foreign currencies.
February 20	The Commerce Department reports that January housing starts reached a nine-year low.
February 21	The parliaments of Slovenia and Croatia pass resolutions that push them toward independence from Yugoslavia.
	Throughout February the government's leading economic indicators continue to fall, a sign that the U.S. economy is entering into a recessionary period.
March 3	The Baltic states of Estonia and Latvia declare their independence from the Soviet Union.
March 4	The Federal Reserve Board orders the Bank of Credit and Commerce International (BCCI) to divest itself of all holdings in its parent company. Thus, another major banking scandal is revealed.

March 6	President Bush tells a joint session of Congress that the war is over in the Persian Gulf.
	The first units of U.S. ground troops start to come home from the Persian Gulf. For the next few months, in a national outpouring of patriotic fervor, returning troops will be greeted with emotional welcomes and parades.
March 8	The Labor Department reports that unemployment in February rose to 6.5%, a four-year high.
	The Census Bureau releases the last of its state-by-state reports on the racial and ethnic composition of the U.S. population. These data reveal a large increase in the number of minorities. The 1990 census puts the total resident population at 248.7 million, representing an increase of 22.2 million, or 9.8%, over the 1980 census count. Blacks, Hispanics, Asians, and American Indians account for more than one half of the overall increase, or about 11.5 million people.
March 28	Former President Ronald Reagan endorses federal legislation that would impose a seven-day waiting period on the purchase of handguns so that law-enforcement officials can check the background of prospective buyers.
April 3	The United Nations passes a resolution on a cease-fire in the Persian Gulf war.
April 5	The Labor Department reports that unemployment in March rose to 6.8%, setting another four-year high.
April 6	President Bush signs into law a bill that provides expanded benefits for Persian Gulf war veterans.

April 9	The Soviet Republic of Georgia votes to declare its independence from the Soviet Union.
April 17–23	U.S., French, and British soldiers cross from Turkey into northern Iraq to secure a safe zone for some 850,000 Iraqi refugees, including Kurds, who are stranded along the Iraqi-Turkish border.
April 18	President Bush issues a series of proposals designed to improve the quality of American education. These proposals represent his first major effort to carry out his campaign promise to become the "education president."
	The Commerce Department reports that the U.S. trade gap with foreign nations has reached an eight-year low. The recession is given as the prime factor in the drop in imports.
April 22	*Fortune* magazine's survey of the country's five hundred largest industrial corporations shows the effects of the recession. Aggregate profits for 1990 fell almost 12%.
April 28–May 6	The U.S. space shuttle *Discovery* carries out a military mission. The flight is the tenth launch for *Discovery* and the nation's fortieth shuttle mission.
April 30	The Federal Reserve Board cuts its basic interest rate in an attempt to stimulate economic growth. This is the second reduction in the so-called discount rate since the beginning of 1991.
May 1	The Big Three U.S. automakers, battered by the recession and foreign competition, post record losses for the first quarter of 1991.
May 3	The Labor Department reports that the nation's unemployment rate in April decreased from 6.8% to 6.6%, the first drop in the percentage since June 1990.

May 13	The Federal Reserve Board reports that U.S. mines, factories, and utilities operated at only 78.3% of capacity in April.
May 16	Housing starts rose 6.2% in April. This advance followed a 9.2% decrease in March.
May 29	President Bush proposes a ban on weapons of mass destruction in the Middle East. He had promised to make arms control in the region a part of his post-Persian Gulf war agenda.
June 7	The nation's unemployment rate in May rose from 6.6% to 6.9%.
June 10	Hundreds of thousands of spectators turn out for parades and celebrations in New York City to welcome home U.S. servicemen and women from the Persian Gulf.
June 12	Albania installs its first non-Communist government in forty-seven years.
June 17	South Africa repeals the bulk of its apartheid laws.
June 18	Members of the Federal Reserve Board tell Congress that the recession has reached its nadir and that a gradual upturn in the economy is likely to begin by the third quarter of 1991.
June 25	Slovenia and Croatia declare their independence from Yugoslavia.
June 26	According to the Commerce Department, after-tax profits of U.S. corporations fell 6.3% in the first quarter of 1991, the largest drop since the spring of 1989.
June 27	Justice Thurgood Marshall announces his retirement from the Supreme Court after twenty-four years of service.

The Commerce Department reports that consumer spending in May outpaced income.

July 1   President Bush nominates Judge Clarence Thomas to the Supreme Court.

July 5   Unemployment increased to 7% during June, according to the Labor Department.

July 8   Iraq admits to the United Nations that it has been conducting clandestine programs to produce enriched uranium, a key element in nuclear weapons.

July 10   The United States lifts sanctions on trade and investments against South Africa.

July 11   Pan American Airways, founded in 1927, announces an "orderly liquidation" of its assets.

July 17   The Defense Department issues official statistics on the U.S. casualties in the Persian Gulf war: total dead, 268; total wounded in combat, 458.

July 18–21   The Arab states accept U.S. terms for a Middle East peace conference.

July 22   Ethnic fighting escalates in Yugoslavia.

July 30–31   President Bush and Soviet President Mikhail Gorbachev hold the first post-Cold War superpower summit in Moscow.

July 31   The National Association for the Advancement of Colored People (NAACP) announces its opposition to the nomination of Thomas to the Supreme Court.

August 1   Israel gives its conditional acceptance to a Middle East peace conference.

August 2   The nation's unemployment rate decreased from 7% to 6.8% in July. Almost the entire decline occurred because 415,000 people had left the work force altogether. Some private economists say that recovery from the recession is failing.

August 8 | A radical Shiite Moslem faction in Lebanon releases two Western hostages.

August 19–21 | A group of top Soviet hard-liners, backed by the security forces, detain President Gorbachev in an attempted coup d'état, but the plotters' bid for power falls apart in the face of international condemnation and the defiance of hundreds of thousands of prodemocratic Soviets led by Boris Yeltsin, president of the Russian Republic.

August 24–27 | The Soviet republics stampede for independence as the Soviet Union breaks apart.

August 29 | The Supreme Soviet, the legislature of the Soviet Union, suspends the Communist party.

September 6 | The unemployment rate for August remained unchanged at 6.8%.

September 10 | The Senate Judiciary Committee begins its hearings on the nomination of Clarence Thomas to the Supreme Court.

September 16 | The Philippine Senate rejects a treaty that would extend the lease of the U.S. naval base at Subic Bay.

September 24 | Iraq provokes international outrage over its resistance to efforts to dismantle its arms program.

September 27 | President Bush announces a unilateral cut in nuclear arms and asks the Soviet Union to respond in kind.

September 30	Haitian President Jean-Bertrand Aristide, the nation's first freely elected president, is overthrown.
October 6–8	A former aide to Clarence Thomas publicly accuses him of sexually harassing her over a period from 1981 to 1983. The charge, made by Anita Hill, a tenured law professor at the University of Oklahoma, sparks an emotional and contentious national debate over the issue of sexual harassment.
October 11	President Bush vetoes an extension of jobless benefits for the long-term unemployed.
October 14–20	The State Department receives at least twelve million applicants for forty thousand permanent resident visas available by a lottery held under the provisions of the Immigration Act of 1990.
October 15	The Senate, after one of the most bitter and divisive confirmation battles in the 202-year history of the Supreme Court, confirms Clarence Thomas to the Court by a 52-to-48 vote.
October 23	The Federal Reserve Board announces that the nation's economy is "weak or growing slowly."
October 30	The Middle East peace conference convenes in Madrid with delegates from Israel and the Arab nations.
November 1	According to the Labor Department, unemployment rose from 6.7% in September to 6.8% in October.
November 5	In Pennsylvania, Harris Wofford (D) defeats former U.S. Attorney General Richard Thornburgh (R) in the nation's only 1991 Senate race. The results are regarded as a major upset for the Republicans. Wofford had been

appointed to the Senate earlier in the year to fill the seat left vacant by the death of Senator John Heinz.

November 15   President Bush signs into law a compromise bill providing up to twenty weeks of additional benefits for the long-term unemployed.

November 16   Former Governor Edwin Edwards (D) defeats State Representative David Duke (R) in a runoff gubernatorial election in Louisiana.

November 18   Additional hostages, including Church of England envoy Terry Waite, are freed by their radical Lebanese kidnappers.

December 1   The Ukraine declares its independence from the Soviet Union.

December 2–4   The last three American hostages held in Lebanon, including Terry Anderson, are freed.

December 4   Pan American World Airways formally ceases its operations.

December 6   The number of payroll jobs in the United States dropped sharply in November, according to the Labor Department.

December 7   The fiftieth anniversary of the Japanese attack on the U.S. naval base at Pearl Harbor in Hawaii is commemorated.

December 8   The turmoil in the Soviet Union takes a stunning turn when the leaders of three Slavic republics—Russia, the Ukraine, and Byelorussia—form a commonwealth replacing the old USSR.

December 11   William Kennedy Smith, nephew of Senator Edward Kennedy, is found not guilty of rape charges in his highly publicized trial in West Palm Beach, Florida.

December 15	This day marks the two-hundredth anniversary of the adoption of the Bill of Rights.
December 17	The White House says that the economy is still in a recession. This announcement signals a change from the administration's policy of trying to minimize the country's economic problems.
December 18	General Motors announces that it will reduce its work force by 18%.
December 25	In a speech outside the Kremlin, Gorbachev announces his resignation as president of the Soviet Union.

Interviewing Date: 12/6–9/90 (United States only)
Survey #GO 922023

Asked in thirty-seven countries plus Hong Kong: Do you think that 1991 will be a peaceful year more or less free of international disputes, a troubled year with much international discord, or remain the same?

	Peaceful	Troubled	Remain the same	No opinion
Soviet Union (Moscow)	54%	16%	18%	12%
Taiwan	37	26	12	25
South Africa	30	27	28	15
Chile (Santiago)	29	41	26	4
Switzerland	28	43	22	7
South Korea	28	33	13	26
Brazil	27	45	22	6
Costa Rica	26	33	28	13
Iceland	25	32	35	8
Argentina (Buenos Aires)	22	41	23	14
Sweden	22	36	33	9
Austria	22	34	36	8
Ireland*	21	44	23	12
Hong Kong	19	40	40	1
Turkey	18	54	12	16
Italy*	18	40	35	7
India	17	51	26	6
Mexico	17	50	29	4
Portugal*	17	45	21	17
Luxembourg*	17	41	30	12
Uruguay	17	35	35	13
Philippines	16	53	29	2
Germany*	16	43	30	11
Greece*	16	43	27	14
Spain*	15	45	24	16
Denmark*	14	57	23	6
Israel	13	34	38	15
United States	11	46	38	5
Great Britain*	9	67	17	7
New Zealand	9	50	37	4
Belgium*	8	54	32	6
France*	7	54	33	6
Japan	7	43	27	23
Netherlands*	6	66	25	3
Hungary	6	62	19	13
Australia	6	61	28	5
Finland	5	57	31	7
Canada	4	72	21	3

*Member of the European Economic Community (EEC)

Selected National Trend
(United States Only)

	Peaceful	Troubled	Remain the same	No opinion
1990	11%	46%	38%	5%
1989	37	26	32	5
1988	20	25	49	6
1987	9	35	48	9
1986	12	31	51	6
1985	15	34	43	8
1984	11	55	29	5
1983	18	32	43	7
1982	12	45	37	6
1981	15	39	38	8

So far as you are concerned, do you think 1991 will be better or worse than 1990?

	Better	Worse	Same (volunteered)	No opinion
Chile (Santiago)	51%	17%	29%	3%
Taiwan	50	19	14	17
Brazil	49	30	15	6
United States	48	42	6	4
Argentina (Buenos Aires)	47	19	23	11

Ireland*	45	20	23	12
Italy*	43	31	20	6
South Africa	43	27	18	12
Great Britain*	43	25	27	5
South Korea	43	23	28	6
Mexico	42	37	18	3
New Zealand	41	42	12	5
Denmark*	41	18	32	9
Sweden	40	17	39	4
Luxembourg*	40	12	36	12
Iceland	38	3	55	4
France*	35	28	26	11
India	34	39	18	9
Greece*	34	39	16	11
Australia	33	49	15	3
Hong Kong	31	38	17	14
Netherlands*	31	20	46	3
Portugal*	30	24	27	19
Israel	28	51	10	11
Costa Rica	27	41	19	13
Switzerland	26	24	46	4
Spain*	25	25	37	13
Germany*	25	8	57	10
Turkey	23	49	11	17
Japan	23	11	48	18
Philippines	22	55	21	2
Austria	22	9	60	9
Belgium*	20	33	38	9
Soviet Union (Moscow)	18	64	8	10
Canada	18	63	16	3
Uruguay	18	46	27	9
Finland	12	47	35	6
Hungary	2	84	6	8

*Member of the EEC

Note: A new worldwide Gallup Poll indicates that much of mankind expects troubled times ahead in 1991, in sharp contrast to the optimism that marked the beginning of 1990. Gallup conducted its annual year-end survey in Hong Kong and thirty-seven countries with a combined population of 2.46 billion—nearly one half of the world's population. In almost all of these countries, citizens are more likely to think that 1991 will be a troubled year rather than a peaceful year.

In the United States, some 46% of those interviewed say that they think the coming year will be troubled, while only 11% predict that it will be peaceful. An additional 38% forecast that 1991 will be similar to 1990. These predictions represent the least optimistic forecast by Americans since late 1983, when 55% expected trouble in the coming year.

The worldwide mood of increased pessimism holds for respondents' personal outlook as well. A surprisingly high proportion throughout the globe say that 1991 will be a worse year for them personally than was 1990, with residents of Eastern Europe the most bleak in their expectations for the coming year. Some 84% of Hungarians expect 1991 to be worse for them than 1990, while only 2% think that it will be better. Residents of Moscow also are troubled by their immediate future: 64% think that 1991 will bring harder times, while only 18% expect their lot to improve.

Americans' current personal outlook is far less grim than that of East Europeans, but their level of optimism nevertheless is down considerably from that of one year ago. Some 48% expect a better year in 1991, while 42% expect a worse one. In late 1989 optimists outnumbered pessimists in the United States by the wide margin of 49% to 27%. Across the globe, in thirty-one of the countries surveyed, the proportion of pessimists is now higher than was the case one year ago.

JANUARY 3
EASTERN EUROPE*

Interviewing Date: 12/10–23/90
Special Survey

How do you think the general economic situation in this country has changed over the last twelve months?

	Better	Worse	Same	No opinion
Poland	39%	41%	15%	5%
Czecho-slovakia	7	77	12	4
Hungary	4	84	8	4
Yugoslavia	38	41	18	3
Bulgaria	6	79	10	5

*The following data have been made available to the Gallup Poll by the International Division of the Gallup Organization. The

How does the financial situation of your household now compare to what it was twelve months ago?

	Better	Worse	Same	No opinion
Poland	19%	48%	30%	3%
Czecho-slovakia	7	61	31	1
Hungary	2	77	17	4
Yugoslavia	29	33	38	*
Bulgaria	9	62	26	3

*Less than 1%

Compared with 1990, will 1991 be a year of economic prosperity, economic difficulty, or about the same?

	Prosperity	Difficulty	Same	No opinion
Poland	32%	16%	38%	14%
Czecho-slovakia	1	88	5	6
Hungary	1	88	8	3
Yugoslavia	33	28	27	12
Bulgaria	5	68	16	11

Looking ahead to next year, 1991, do you think the number of unemployed in this country will increase, decrease, or remain the same?

	Increase	Decrease	Remain the same	No opinion
Poland	58%	15%	17%	10%
Czecho-slovakia	89	4	2	5
Hungary	93	1	2	4
Yugoslavia	55	20	16	9
Bulgaria	74	5	6	15

---

survey and the analysis were prepared by Dr. Robert Manchin, managing director and general manager of Gallup Hungary Ltd. and vice president and regional representative for Eastern Europe of the Gallup Organization Inc. Based on over 5,000 mid-December interviews in five countries with a combined population of nearly 100 million, this survey represents one of the first simultaneous soundings of public opinion ever conducted across Eastern Europe.

So far as you are concerned, do you think that in 1991 strikes and industrial disputes in this country will increase, decrease, or remain the same?

	Increase	Decrease	Remain the same	No opinion
Poland	33%	18%	25%	24%
Czecho-slovakia	69	2	15	14
Hungary	76	2	3	19
Yugoslavia	33	33	18	16
Bulgaria	29	22	33	16

So far as you are concerned, do you think 1991 will be better or worse than 1990?

	Better	Worse	Remain the same	No opinion
Poland	32%	17%	28%	23%
Czecho-slovakia	3	78	8	11
Hungary	2	84	6	8
Yugoslavia	51	21	17	11
Bulgaria	25	49	15	11

Do you think that 1991 will be a peaceful year more or less free of international disputes, a troubled year with much international discord, or remain the same?

	Peaceful	Troubled	Remain the same	No opinion
Poland	37%	16%	28%	19%
Czecho-slovakia	13	42	34	11
Hungary	6	62	19	13
Yugoslavia	37	23	33	7
Bulgaria	24	38	26	12

Note: Most East Europeans expect their life to get harder, not easier, in the coming year, according to a just-completed Gallup survey. In fact, the level of pessimism expressed is so great that it represents a significant challenge to the new political leadership of the region unless the public's low expectations are accompanied by extraordinary reserves of patience.

The survey results indicate that overwhelming majorities of Hungarians and Czechs are pessimistic about what the New Year will bring, an outlook also shared by most

Bulgarians. The most positive note is that relatively few Poles and Yugoslavs expect their economies to deteriorate further in the coming year. However, expectations of increased unemployment and labor unrest are common throughout each of the five countries surveyed.

Attempts to bring about long-term economic restructuring have resulted in short-term hardships for residents of the region. In each of the five nations surveyed, more residents say that economic conditions have deteriorated over the past year than say that they have improved. In Hungary (84%), Bulgaria (79%), and Czechoslovakia (77%), more than three fourths of those surveyed find that their country's economy has gotten worse during 1990.

Similarly, in every country except Yugoslavia, large majorities report that their own household financial situation has gotten worse rather than better over the course of the past twelve months. In Hungary, Poland, and Bulgaria, roughly one third go so far as to say that their household is now a lot worse off financially than at the end of 1989.

Moreover, East Europeans expect no quick solution to their economic woes. Looking ahead, nearly nine in ten Hungarians and Czechs (88%) say that 1991 will bring increased difficulty rather than increased prosperity, a prediction shared by 68% of Bulgarians. However, 32% of Poles and 33% of Yugoslavs expect the coming year to be relatively prosperous, while similar proportions expect economic conditions to be about the same as in 1990 (38% and 27%, respectively).

Nor is any quick payoff expected for the region's workers. Fully 93% of Hungarians expect higher levels of unemployment in 1991, as do 89% of Czechs, 74% of Bulgarians, 58% of Poles, and 55% of Yugoslavs. Even in Poland, where many expect the overall economy to improve, the forecast is that unemployment rolls will continue to grow in the coming year.

Increased labor unrest and work stoppages also are expected throughout the region, particularly by Hungarians (76%) and Czechs (69%). In Poland, where former Solidarity labor leader Lech Walesa now heads the government, more people expect an increase than a decrease in strikes (33% versus 18%). Yugoslavs and Bulgarians are uncertain about whether the coming year will bring an increase in labor unrest.

When asked what kind of year they expect 1991 to be for them personally, Yugoslavs and Poles express guarded optimism, while others in the region display considerable pessimism. Some 51% of Yugoslavs say that they expect 1991 to be better for them than 1990, while only 21% think that the reverse will be true. In Poland, most think that 1991 will be either better (32%) or the same (28%) for them as 1990, while only 17% expect it to be worse. However, the prevailing expectation is that the New Year will be worse rather than better.

JANUARY 6
FEAR OF DYING

Interviewing Date: 11/15–18/90
Survey #GO 122008

Do you think a person has the moral right to end his or her life under these circumstances:

	Yes	No	No opinion
When this person has a disease that is incurable?	58%	36%	6%
When this person is suffering great pain and has no hope of improvement?	66	29	5
When this person is an extremely heavy burden on his or her family?	33	61	6
When an otherwise healthy person wants to end his or her life?	16	80	4

When a person has a disease that cannot be cured, do you think doctors should be allowed by law to end the patient's life by some painless means if the patient and his family request it?

Yes...65%
No...31
No opinion....................................... 4

Suppose a terminally ill person wants treatment withheld so that he or she may die. Please tell me whether or not you agree with each of the following statements: The patient has the right to stop treatment:

	Agree	Dis-agree	No opinion
If the doctor agrees....	75%	22%	3%
If he or she is in great pain.........	78	18	4
If his or her family agrees.................	76	22	2
Under any circumstances.......	59	40	1
Under no circumstances.......	11	87	2

Have you, yourself, discussed with family members whether or not you should be kept on life-support systems if you are terminally ill or have a debilitating injury and are unable to communicate your wishes?

Yes...52%
No...47
No opinion....................................... 1

If you, yourself, were on life-support systems and there was no hope of recovering, would you like to remain on the life-support system or would you like treatment withheld so that you could end your life?

Remain on life-support system................ 9%
Like treatment withheld........................84
No opinion....................................... 7

Do you, yourself, have a written "living will" which states what should be done in case you have a terminal or debilitating illness or injury, with no hope of recovering?

Yes...20%
No...80
No opinion....................................... *

*Less than 1%

Asked of those who do not have a "living will": Would you like to have such a written "living will" at some point in the future?

Yes...75%
No...17
No opinion....................................... 8

Do you believe in life after death, or not?

Yes...65%
No...27
No opinion....................................... 8

Do you think there is a hell, to which people who have led bad lives without being sorry are eternally damned?

Yes...60%
No...32
No opinion....................................... 8

Do you think there is a heaven where people who have led good lives are eternally rewarded?

Yes...78%
No...15
No opinion....................................... 7

Asked of those who think there is a heaven: How would you describe your own chances of going to Heaven—excellent, good, only fair, or poor?

Excellent......................................29%
Good...49
Fair...17
Poor... 2
No opinion..................................... 3

Asked of those who think there is a hell: How would you describe your own chances of going to Hell—excellent, good, only fair, or poor?

Excellent...2%
Good.. 2
Fair...15
Poor..77
No opinion... 4

Here is a question about unusual experiences people say they have had when they have been on the verge of death or have had a "close call," such as experiences of continued life or an awareness after death. Have you, yourself, ever been on the verge of death or had a "close call" which involved any unusual experience at that time?

Yes...12%
No..88
No opinion.. *

*Less than 1%

Do you believe in reincarnation—that is, the rebirth of the soul in a new body after death—or not?

Yes...23%
No..69
No opinion.. 8

Do you fear death, or not?

Yes...23%
No..75
No opinion.. 2

	Yes	No	No opinion
By Age			
18–29 Years	33%	66%	1%
30–49 Years	25	74	1
50 Years and Over	16	83	1

How often would you say you think about your death?

Very often 7%
Somewhat often 9
Every now and again.............................47
Almost never.......................................36
No opinion... 1

Do you have a will that describes how you would like your money and estate to be handled after your death?

Yes...48%
No..51
No opinion.. 1

After your death, would you prefer to be buried or cremated?

Buried..65%
Cremated...26
No opinion.. 9

Have you made any arrangements for your burial or cremation such as purchasing a burial plot, prepaying your funeral expenses, or leaving plans for how your funeral is to be conducted?

Yes...34%
No..66
No opinion.. *

*Less than 1%

	Yes	No	No opinion
By Age			
18–29 Years	12%	88%	*
30–49 Years	24	76	*
50 Years and Over	57	43	*

*Less than 1%

Note: A new Gallup Mirror of America survey reveals that Americans in large numbers simply do not fear death or even think about it. Only 7% say that they think about death very often, and another 9% say somewhat often. Three out of four report that they do not fear death, while only 23% say that they do. The majority—about two out of three (65%)—believes in life after death, a relatively stable figure; Gallup Poll data since 1944 have measured a belief in life after death that ranges between 67% and 77%. We might assume that belief in an afterlife is one reason why there is not a prevalent fear of death among Americans, but this belief does not carry with it any immunity from worry about death. Those respondents who profess to believe in a life after death are no different from others in thinking about death and are only slightly less likely to say that they fear it.

Substantially more Americans believe in the existence of a heaven (78%) than in a hell (60%). Certainly, they are a nation of positive thinkers when it comes to assessing the probability of getting past St. Peter's gates into Heaven. Fully 78% of those who believe in Heaven say that they have an excellent or good chance of getting in. Another 17% say that they have only a fair chance, while 2% admit that they have only a poor chance.

For a small number of respondents, belief in Heaven or Hell is based on a supernatural experience. There is also another group (12%) who claim to have had a "near death" experience in which they actually felt an awareness of continuing life after coming close to death. Moreover, one fourth (23%) believes in reincarnation.

Despite the fact that respondents claim that they do not worry about dying, 34% have made "pre-need" preparations, in the argot of the funeral industry. About 57% of adults age 50 and over claim to have made plans for their own funeral, compared to only 12% of the 18-to-29-years group. And what do they want to happen to their remains when they die? Traditional burial wins out over cremation by a 65%-to-26% margin. Moreover, 48% have made out a will.

According to the recent poll, respondents believe strongly that death is preferable to living either in permanent pain or on life-support systems. They would like their lives to be ended if they ever reach such a state and want their relatives and doctors to take steps to end life should this situation occur. The public's sentiments are clear: two thirds (65%) say that a doctor should be allowed to end a patient's life if the patient and his or her family agree. What this comes down to, of course, is a form of suicide: "mercy killing" or euthanasia. The topic has become increasingly important in recent decades as the medical capability of maintaining vital functions, even in the absence of an individual's mental functioning, has vastly improved.

Now, three out of four respondents agree that a patient with a terminal disease has the right to request that treatment be withheld so that he or she can die—if the doctor agrees (75%), if the family agrees (76%), or if the patient is in great pain (78%). A majority (59%) says that a terminally ill patient has the right to end his or her own life under any circumstances, while only 11% say that such a patient never has the right to end his or her own life. And two thirds (66%) believe that an individual has the moral right to end his or her life if he or she is suffering great pain and has no hope for improvement.

However, those polled do not condone the taking of one's own life in all circumstances. Only one third (33%) says that being an extremely heavy burden on the family is grounds. And very few (16%) are willing to condone the suicide of an otherwise healthy person.

The strongest support for mercy killing or euthanasia comes when respondents themselves think about being faced with a hopeless situation. When asked directly, a dramatic 84% say that they would want treatment withheld. Only 9% say that they would want to be left on life-support systems.

These types of situations—what to do if a terminal or debilitating illness strikes—have been discussed in about one half (52%) of all American homes. Still, some people worry that the issue will arise only when they are unable to discuss it rationally—that is, when they are actually in a coma or otherwise debilitated. However, the "living will"—a statement of what should be done in the event of a terminal or debilitating illness—apparently is an idea whose time has not yet come. Only 20% say that they have a living will. Nevertheless, it does have strong appeal: 75% would like to have one at some point in the future.

JANUARY 9
PRESIDENT BUSH/PERSIAN GULF SITUATION

Interviewing Date: 1/3–6/91
Survey #GO 122011

Do you approve or disapprove of the way George Bush is handling his job as president?

Approve...58%
Disapprove..31
No opinion..11

	Approve	Dis-approve	No opinion
By Sex			
Male	66%	24%	10%
Female	52	37	11
By Ethnic Background			
White	63	27	10
Nonwhite	42	36	22
Black	27	60	13
By Education			
College Graduate	66	26	8
College Incomplete	66	27	7
High-School Graduate	58	31	11
Less Than High-School Graduate	45	38	17
By Region			
East	58	34	8
Midwest	57	34	9
South	60	24	16
West	58	33	9
By Age			
18–29 Years	59	28	13
30–49 Years	64	28	8
50 Years and Over	54	34	12
By Household Income			
$50,000 and Over	76	18	6
$30,000–$49,999	62	32	6
$20,000–$29,999	65	22	13
Under $20,000	44	40	16
By Politics			
Republicans	81	12	7
Democrats	42	45	13
Independents	55	33	12
By Religion			
Protestants	60	30	10
Catholics	61	28	11

Selected National Trend

	Approve	Dis-approve	No opinion
1990			
December 6–9	58%	33%	9%
November 15–18	54	33	13
November 1–4	58	32	10
October 25–28	54	36	10
October 18–21	53	37	10
October 11–14	56	33	11
October 3–4	66	25	9
September 27–30	67	20	13
September 14–16	73	17	10
September 10–11	76	16	8
August 30–September 2	74	17	9
August 23–26	76	16	8
August 16–19	75	16	9
August 9–12	74	16	10
July 19–22	60	25	15
July 6–8	63	24	13
June 15–17	69	17	14
June 7–10	67	18	15
May 17–20	65	20	15

How closely have you followed news about the situation involving the invasion of Kuwait by Iraq [and the sending of U.S. troops to Saudi Arabia]? Would you say you have followed it very closely, fairly closely, not too closely, or not at all closely?*

Very closely......................................41%
Fairly closely....................................47
Not too closely...................................10
Not at all closely**.............................. 2

*All questions asked after August 16–19, 1991, included the phrase in brackets.
**"No opinion"—at less than 1%—has been combined with "not at all closely."

	Very closely	Fairly closely	Not too closely	Not at all closely
By Sex				
Male	47%	43%	9%	1%
Female	35	51	10	4

By Ethnic Background

White..........41	48	8	3
Nonwhite......43	21	29	7
Black..........37	46	15	2

By Education

College Graduate.....44	49	7	*
College In-complete....44	49	6	1
High-School Graduate.....36	52	10	2
Less Than High-School Graduate.....46	34	14	6

By Region

East.............39	45	11	5
Midwest........41	52	6	1
South..........43	47	9	1
West...........39	45	13	3

By Age

18–29 Years...29	57	11	3
30–49 Years...37	51	11	1
50 Years and Over..........53	35	8	4

By Household Income

$50,000 and Over..........48	46	5	1
$30,000–$49,999.....39	53	8	*
$20,000–$29,999.....39	47	14	*
Under $20,000.....39	44	12	5

By Politics

Republicans...40	51	7	2
Democrats.....44	43	11	2
Independents..41	47	9	3

By Religion

Protestants....44	44	10	2
Catholics......42	47	8	3

By Political Ideology

Liberal..........47	43	9	1
Moderate.......44	46	10	*
Conservative..38	53	8	1

By Bush Approval

Approve........41	49	9	1
Disapprove....45	44	8	3

*Less than 1%

Selected National Trend

1990	Very closely	Fairly closely	Not too closely	Not at all closely
Dec. 13–16....44%	45%	10%	1%
Nov.8–11......35	52	11	2
Oct. 3–4........35	50	12	3
Sept. 10–11...36	48	12	4
Aug. 9–12.....40	43	12	5
Aug. 3–4.......18	39	25	18

Do you approve or disapprove of the way George Bush is handling this current situation in the Middle East involving Iraq and Kuwait?

Approve..60%
Disapprove...34
No opinion...6

	Approve	Dis-approve	No opinion
By Sex			
Male.....................70%	28%	2%
Female..................51	39	10
By Ethnic Background			
White...................64	30	6
Nonwhite..............56	36	8
Black...................25	66	9
By Education			
College Graduate......65	30	5
College Incomplete...67	27	6
High-School Graduate.............59	35	6
Less Than High-School Graduate....49	42	9
By Region			
East.....................58	35	7
Midwest................56	37	7

South 64 28 8
West 59 37 4

By Age
18–29 Years............58 37 5
30–49 Years............65 29 6
50 Years and Over.....57 35 8

By Household Income
$50,000 and Over.....77 18 5
$30,000–$49,999....64 34 2
$20,000–$29,999....59 35 6
Under $20,000........50 41 9

By Politics
Republicans............78 17 5
Democrats 49 44 7
Independents...........54 38 8

By Religion
Protestants 61 33 6
Catholics 64 30 6

By Political Ideology
Liberal..................59 38 3
Moderate................70 23 7
Conservative..........68 28 4

By Bush Approval
Approve.................86 10 4
Disapprove.............17 79 4

Selected National Trend

	Approve	Dis-approve	No opinion
1990			
December 13–16 ......63%		30%	7%
November 8–11 60		34	6
October 3–4............69		25	6
September 10–11 76		17	7
August 9–12............80		12	8
August 3–4 52		16	32

Recently, the United Nations Security Council passed a resolution that allows Iraq one final opportunity to pull out of Kuwait by January 15 or else face possible military action. If Iraq lets this deadline pass, would you favor the United States and its allies going to war with Iraq in order to drive the Iraqis out of Kuwait, or not?

Yes...62%
No...32
No opinion.......................................6

	Yes	No	No opinion
By Sex			
Male 72%		24%	4%
Female...................53		39	8
By Ethnic Background			
White....................65		29	6
Nonwhite 54		33	13
Black 34		56	10
By Education			
College Graduate 62		34	4
College Incomplete...67		29	4
High-School Graduate..............62		32	6
Less Than High-School Graduate 56		33	11
By Region			
East 59		35	6
Midwest.................58		36	6
South 65		29	6
West 66		30	4
By Age			
18–29 Years............63		32	5
30–49 Years............65		31	4
50 Years and Over.....59		32	9
By Household Income			
$50,000 and Over.....75		21	4
$30,000–$49,999....67		30	3
$20,000–$29,999....61		34	5
Under $20,000........53		41	6
By Politics			
Republicans............72		23	5
Democrats 53		40	7
Independents...........62		33	5
By Religion			
Protestants 63		31	6
Catholics 63		31	6

By Political Ideology

Liberal	60	38	2
Moderate	60	27	13
Conservative	67	28	5

By Bush Approval

Approve	76	20	4
Disapprove	41	53	6

Selected National Trend

	Yes	No	No opinion
1990			
December 13–16	59%	34%	7%
December 6–9	61	33	6
November 29– December 2	64	31	5

If the current situation in the Middle East involving Iraq and Kuwait does not change by January,* would you favor or oppose the United States going to war with Iraq in order to drive the Iraqis out of Kuwait?

Favor	52%
Oppose	39
No opinion	9

*The January 1991 question specified the 15th.

	Favor	Oppose	No opinion

By Sex

Male	64%	31%	5%
Female	42	46	12

By Ethnic Background

White	56	36	8
Nonwhite	33	48	19
Black	22	65	13

By Education

College Graduate	51	42	7
College Incomplete	61	34	5
High-School Graduate	52	41	7
Less Than High- School Graduate	45	38	17

By Region

East	50	41	9
Midwest	52	40	8
South	55	36	9
West	51	40	9

By Age

18–29 Years	54	41	5
30–49 Years	57	37	6
50 Years and Over	47	40	13

By Household Income

$50,000 and Over	64	29	7
$30,000–$49,999	59	36	5
$20,000–$29,999	55	39	6
Under $20,000	38	50	12

By Politics

Republicans	63	30	7
Democrats	42	49	9
Independents	52	39	9

By Religion

Protestants	53	38	9
Catholics	55	38	7

By Political Ideology

Liberal	49	46	5
Moderate	48	35	17
Conservative	58	36	6

By Bush Approval

Approve	67	27	6
Disapprove	28	62	10

Selected National Trend

	Favor	Oppose	No opinion
1990			
December 13–16	48%	43%	9%
December 6–9	53	40	7
November 29– December 2	53	40	7
November 15–18	37	51	12

Suppose Saddam Hussein agrees to hold a conference after January 15 for the purpose of working out a staged withdrawal from Kuwait. If so, should the United States postpone any action until that conference takes place, or should we exercise the option of military action as planned on the fifteenth?

Postpone any action............................61%
Take military action............................33
No opinion...6

	Postpone any action	Take military action	No opinion
By Sex			
Male.....................55%	42%	3%
Female...................65	26	9
By Ethnic Background			
White..................59	36	5
Nonwhite...............55	20	25
Black...................78	17	5
By Education			
College Graduate......71	25	4
College Incomplete...54	43	3
High-School Graduate..............61	34	5
Less Than High-School Graduate 56	30	14
By Region			
East.....................59	33	8
Midwest................63	32	5
South...................63	33	4
West....................56	37	7
By Age			
18–29 Years............61	36	3
30–49 Years............62	35	3
50 Years and Over.....60	30	10
By Household Income			
$50,000 and Over.....56	41	3
$30,000–$49,999....61	37	2
$20,000–$29,999....61	36	3
Under $20,000.........68	24	8
By Politics			
Republicans............58	39	3
Democrats..............67	27	6
Independents...........60	35	5

By Religion			
Protestants.............63	33	4
Catholics...............58	36	6
By Political Ideology			
Liberal.................65	32	3
Moderate................63	31	6
Conservative..........61	35	4
By Bush Approval			
Approve.................55	41	4
Disapprove.............70	24	6

What do you think is the most important problem facing this country today?*

Kuwait, Iraq...25%
Economy in general 15
Drugs; drug abuse................................. 9
Poverty; homelessness 6
Ethics, morals 5
Fear of war... 5
Other;** no opinion 55

*Multiple responses were given.
**None of the "other" replies drew more than 4%.

Note: With the UN deadline for Iraqi withdrawal from Kuwait less than one week away, Americans are increasingly likely to say that war will occur in the Persian Gulf. They also say that President George Bush should seek formal approval from Congress before he commits U.S. troops to action. However, respondents are following the situation no more closely than they have in the past (only 41% say that they are following the news from the Persian Gulf very closely, essentially the same as in the fall). Additionally, the Persian Gulf situation does not yet dominate the American agenda; it is seen as the most important problem facing the United States by only 25%.

A majority (61%) thinks that war should be postponed if the Iraqis agree to a conference about their withdrawal, even if it occurs after the January 15 deadline. Previous Gallup Polls also have shown strong approval for other possible compromises to avoid war, including the involvement or linkage of the Palestinian problem to the Persian Gulf resolution.

Nevertheless, a majority (62%) say that they will support Bush if he does initiate war after the 15th; about one third oppose such actions. Most of these measures have not changed essentially since late November. Approval of the way President Bush is handling the war, now at 60%, also has not changed significantly since December. However, there has been an increase over the last month in support for the use of force when such action is contrasted to giving sanctions more time to work.

The big divisions within the American population on support for a war in the Persian Gulf continue to be by gender and race, with men much more supportive than women and whites much more supportive than blacks. A possible war is also backed more by Republicans than Democrats, more by conservatives than liberals, and more by high-income respondents than those with lower incomes.

JANUARY 15
PRESIDENT BUSH/PERSIAN GULF SITUATION

Interviewing Date: 1/11–13/91
Survey #GO 122012

Do you approve or disapprove of the way George Bush is handling his job as president?

Approve..64%
Disapprove..25
No opinion...11

Selected National Trend

	Approve	Dis-approve	No opinion
1991			
January 3–6 ....58%		31%	11%
1990			
December 13–16 63		30	7
December 6–9..........58		33	9

How closely have you followed news about the situation involving the invasion of Kuwait by Iraq [and the sending of U.S. troops to Saudi Arabia]? Would you say you have followed it very closely, fairly closely, not too closely, or not at all closely?

Very closely......................................50%
Fairly closely....................................41
Not too closely................................. 8
Not at all closely* 1

*"No opinion"—at 1% or less—has been combined with "not at all closely."

	Very closely	Fairly closely	Not too closely	Not at all closely
By Sex				
Male 59%	35%	5%	1%
Female..........42	46	10	2
By Ethnic Background				
White..........51	41	7	1
Nonwhite 56	43	*	1
Black 42	37	16	5
By Education				
College Graduate.....57	41	2	*
College In-complete....53	42	5	*
High-School Graduate.....48	41	8	3
Less Than High-School Graduate.....43	39	14	4
By Region				
East 53	38	7	2
Midwest........47	45	7	1
South 50	37	11	2
West 52	43	4	1
By Age				
18–29 Years...40	48	10	2
30–49 Years...45	46	7	2
50 Years and Over..........63	30	6	1
By Household Income				
$50,000 and Over..........51	46	3	*

$30,000–$49,999.....55	41	3	1
$20,000–$29,999.....52	40	6	2
Under $20,000.....45	39	14	2

By Politics

Republicans...50	44	5	1
Democrats.....49	41	9	1
Independents..53	37	8	2

By Religion

Protestants....50	41	7	2
Catholics......54	39	6	1

By Political Ideology

Liberal..........55	35	8	2
Moderate.......56	38	6	*
Conservative..52	42	5	1

By Bush Approval

Approve........54	40	5	1
Disapprove....48	39	9	4

*Less than 1%

Selected National Trend

	Very closely	Fairly closely	Not too closely	Not at all closely
1991				
Jan. 3–6........41%	47%	10%	2%
1990				
Dec. 6–9 43	46	9	2
Nov. 1–4.......37	49	12	2
Oct. 3–4........35	50	12	3
Aug. 30–Sept. 2.......43	43	11	3
Aug. 3–4.......18	39	25	18

Do you approve or disapprove of the way George Bush is handling this current situation in the Middle East involving Iraq and Kuwait?

Approve..62%
Disapprove..28
No opinion...10

	Approve	Dis-approve	No opinion
By Sex			
Male 71%	22%	7%
Female...................54	34	12
By Ethnic Background			
White....................66	24	10
Nonwhite 57	33	10
Black 29	61	10
By Education			
College Graduate 65	30	5
College Incomplete...67	27	6
High-School Graduate...............61	28	11
Less Than High-School Graduate 54	28	18
By Region			
East......................59	32	9
Midwest..................62	26	12
South 63	27	10
West 64	28	8
By Age			
18–29 Years............62	35	3
30–49 Years............62	26	12
50 Years and Over.....62	26	12
By Household Income			
$50,000 and Over.....65	25	10
$30,000–$49,999....71	22	7
$20,000–$29,999....66	28	6
Under $20,000........50	35	15
By Politics			
Republicans............77	17	6
Democrats..............52	35	13
Independents...........60	30	10
By Religion			
Protestants.............64	26	10
Catholics 65	24	11
By Political Ideology			
Liberal..................52	40	8
Moderate...............67	28	5
Conservative..........71	21	8

By Bush Approval

Approve...............87	8	5
Disapprove............14	81	5

Selected National Trend

	Approve	Dis-approve	No opinion
1991			
January 3–6............60%	34%	6%
1990			
December 6–9..........57	36	7
November 1–4.........61	29	10
October 3–4............69	25	6
August 30– September 2.........74	18	8
August 9–12...........80	12	8
August 3–4.............52	16	32

Do you approve or disapprove of the U.S. decision to send U.S. troops to Saudi Arabia as a defense against Iraq?

Approve...65%
Disapprove...29
No opinion.. 6

	Approve	Dis-approve	No opinion

By Sex

Male.....................78%	19%	3%
Female..................54	38	8

By Ethnic Background

White....................70	24	6
Nonwhite...............55	38	7
Black....................30	67	3

By Education

College Graduate......70	26	4
College Incomplete...71	27	2
High-School Graduate..............62	31	7
Less Than High- School Graduate 59	30	11

By Region

East......................64	32	4
Midwest................66	27	7
South...................66	26	8
West....................66	31	3

By Age

18–29 Years............64	33	3
30–49 Years............68	27	5
50 Years and Over.....63	29	8

By Household Income

$50,000 and Over.....70	25	5
$30,000–$49,999....74	23	3
$20,000–$29,999....74	22	4
Under $20,000........51	42	7

By Politics

Republicans............77	18	5
Democrats..............58	38	4
Independents...........64	29	7

By Religion

Protestants.............66	28	6
Catholics...............71	25	4

By Political Ideology

Liberal..................60	36	4
Moderate..............71	23	6
Conservative..........73	22	5

By Bush Approval

Approve...............86	10	4
Disapprove............25	71	4

Selected National Trend

	Approve	Dis-approve	No opinion
1991			
January 3–6............64%	30%	6%
1990			
December 6–9..........63	33	4
November 1–4.........67	27	6
October 3–4............72	23	5
August 30– September 2.........74	20	6
August 9–12...........78	17	5

In view of the developments since we first sent our troops to Saudi Arabia, do you think the United States made a mistake in sending troops to Saudi Arabia, or not?

Yes...29%
No..65
No opinion.. 6

	Yes	No	No opinion
By Sex			
Male	21%	75%	4%
Female	37	55	8
By Ethnic Background			
White	25	68	7
Nonwhite	34	65	1
Black	62	35	3
By Education			
College Graduate	29	69	2
College Incomplete	27	69	4
High-School Graduate	30	63	7
Less Than High-School Graduate	33	56	11
By Region			
East	34	63	3
Midwest	26	66	8
South	26	65	9
West	33	65	2
By Age			
18–29 Years	31	65	4
30–49 Years	26	70	4
50 Years and Over	31	60	9
By Household Income			
$50,000 and Over	25	72	3
$30,000–$49,999	24	72	4
$20,000–$29,999	29	66	5
Under $20,000	37	55	8
By Politics			
Republicans	18	77	5
Democrats	39	55	6
Independents	30	64	6
By Religion			
Protestants	28	65	7
Catholics	26	70	4
By Political Ideology			
Liberal	36	60	4
Moderate	35	59	6
Conservative	23	73	4

By Bush Approval			
Approve	13	83	4
Disapprove	70	25	5

Selected National Trend

	Yes	No	No opinion
1991			
January 3–6	31%	61%	8%
1990			
December 6–9	28	66	6
November 1–4	25	67	8
October 3–4	21	71	8
August 30–September 2	16	76	8
August 9–12	17	75	8

If the current situation in the Middle East involving Iraq and Kuwait does not change by January, would you favor or oppose the United States going to war with Iraq in order to drive the Iraqis out of Kuwait?

Favor	55%
Oppose	38
No opinion	7

	Favor	Oppose	No opinion
By Sex			
Male	67%	29%	4%
Female	45	46	9
By Ethnic Background			
White	58	35	7
Nonwhite	50	46	4
Black	29	60	11
By Education			
College Graduate	56	42	2
College Incomplete	60	35	5
High-School Graduate	51	39	10
Less Than High-School Graduate	56	35	9
By Region			
East	48	47	5
Midwest	58	36	6

South 57	31	12
West 58	38	4

By Age

18–29 Years...........56	37	7
30–49 Years...........56	40	4
50 Years and Over.....54	36	10

By Household Income

$50,000 and Over.....60	36	4
$30,000–$49,999....62	34	4
$20,000–$29,999....56	36	8
Under $20,000........48	43	9

By Politics

Republicans............67	27	6
Democrats 45	47	8
Independents...........56	39	5

By Religion

Protestants 56	36	8
Catholics 56	38	6

By Political Ideology

Liberal..................46	48	6
Moderate...............62	35	3
Conservative..........63	31	6

By Bush Approval

Approve................74	21	5
Disapprove.............15	78	7

Selected National Trend

	Favor	Oppose	No opinion
1991			
January 3–6 ....52%	39%	9%
1990			
December 13–16 48	43	9
December 6–9..........53	40	7
November 29–December 2..........53	40	7
November 15–18......37	51	12

All in all, is the current situation in the Mideast worth going to war over, or not?

Yes..46%
No..44
No opinion..10

	Yes	No	No opinion
By Sex			
Male 60%	31%	9%
Female...................34	56	10
By Ethnic Background			
White....................50	41	9
Nonwhite 33	53	14
Black 21	67	12
By Education			
College Graduate 50	43	7
College Incomplete...49	44	7
High-School Graduate..............47	44	9
Less Than High-School Graduate 36	48	16
By Region			
East 41	51	8
Midwest.................47	44	9
South 49	37	14
West 48	46	6
By Age			
18–29 Years...........43	49	8
30–49 Years...........49	44	7
50 Years and Over.....46	41	13
By Household Income			
$50,000 and Over....52	39	9
$30,000–$49,999....56	40	4
$20,000–$29,999....50	41	9
Under $20,000........34	55	11
By Politics			
Republicans............58	34	8
Democrats 35	54	11
Independents...........48	46	6
By Religion			
Protestants 46	43	11
Catholics 49	43	8
By Political Ideology			
Liberal..................41	54	5
Moderate...............53	40	7
Conservative..........53	39	8

By Bush Approval

Approve................65	27	8
Disapprove..............9	85	6

Selected National Trend

	Yes	No	No opinion
1991			
January 3–6 ....47%	44%	9%
1990			
December 13–16......49	44	7
December 6–9..........47	45	8
November 29–			
December 2..........51	41	8
November 15–18......46	45	9
September 27–30 49	41	10
August 30–			
September 2.........45	44	11
August 23–26..........49	41	10

How likely do you think it is that the U.S. forces in and around Saudi Arabia will become engaged in combat?

Very likely 66%
Somewhat likely 24
Not too likely........................3
Not at all likely......................2
No opinion.............................5

By Sex

Male

Very likely 68%
Somewhat likely 23
Not too likely........................4
Not at all likely......................2
No opinion.............................3

Female

Very likely 64%
Somewhat likely 26
Not too likely........................2
Not at all likely......................2
No opinion.............................6

By Ethnic Background

White

Very likely 68%
Somewhat likely 24
Not too likely........................3
Not at all likely......................1
No opinion.............................4

Nonwhite

Very likely 59%
Somewhat likely 31
Not too likely........................5
Not at all likely......................4
No opinion.............................1

Black

Very likely 51%
Somewhat likely 27
Not too likely........................5
Not at all likely......................8
No opinion.............................9

By Education

College Graduate

Very likely 65%
Somewhat likely 27
Not too likely........................4
Not at all likely......................1
No opinion.............................3

College Incomplete

Very likely 66%
Somewhat likely 24
Not too likely........................4
Not at all likely......................3
No opinion.............................3

High-School Graduate

Very likely 69%
Somewhat likely 25
Not too likely........................1
Not at all likely......................2
No opinion.............................3

Less Than High-School Graduate

Very likely 60%
Somewhat likely 21
Not too likely.................................. 5
Not at all likely............................... 2
No opinion.......................................12

By Region

East

Very likely 64%
Somewhat likely 29
Not too likely.................................. 3
Not at all likely............................... 1
No opinion....................................... 3

Midwest

Very likely 64%
Somewhat likely 26
Not too likely.................................. 3
Not at all likely............................... 2
No opinion....................................... 5

South

Very likely 67%
Somewhat likely 21
Not too likely.................................. 3
Not at all likely............................... 3
No opinion....................................... 6

West

Very likely 69%
Somewhat likely 22
Not too likely.................................. 4
Not at all likely............................... 2
No opinion....................................... 3

By Age

18–29 Years

Very likely 72%
Somewhat likely 23
Not too likely.................................. 2
Not at all likely............................... 2
No opinion....................................... 1

30–49 Years

Very likely 69%
Somewhat likely 24
Not too likely.................................. 2
Not at all likely............................... 3
No opinion....................................... 2

50 Years and Over

Very likely 59%
Somewhat likely 26
Not too likely.................................. 5
Not at all likely............................... 1
No opinion....................................... 9

By Household Income

$50,000 and Over

Very likely 66%
Somewhat likely 27
Not too likely.................................. 4
Not at all likely............................... *
No opinion....................................... 3

$30,000–$49,999

Very likely 73%
Somewhat likely 22
Not too likely.................................. 3
Not at all likely............................... 1
No opinion....................................... 1

$20,000–$29,999

Very likely 63%
Somewhat likely 26
Not too likely.................................. 5
Not at all likely............................... 2
No opinion....................................... 4

Under $20,000

Very likely 63%
Somewhat likely 24
Not too likely.................................. 3
Not at all likely............................... 4
No opinion....................................... 6

By Politics

Republicans

Very likely	64%
Somewhat likely	27
Not too likely	3
Not at all likely	1
No opinion	5

Democrats

Very likely	66%
Somewhat likely	24
Not too likely	3
Not at all likely	3
No opinion	4

Independents

Very likely	70%
Somewhat likely	22
Not too likely	3
Not at all likely	3
No opinion	2

By Religion

Protestants

Very likely	64%
Somewhat likely	26
Not too likely	3
Not at all likely	2
No opinion	5

Catholics

Very likely	69%
Somewhat likely	23
Not too likely	3
Not at all likely	3
No opinion	2

By Political Ideology

Liberal

Very likely	69%
Somewhat likely	23
Not too likely	4
Not at all likely	1
No opinion	3

Moderate

Very likely	70%
Somewhat likely	26
Not too likely	2
Not at all likely	1
No opinion	1

Conservative

Very likely	67%
Somewhat likely	25
Not too likely	3
Not at all likely	2
No opinion	3

By Bush Approval

Approve

Very likely	70%
Somewhat likely	22
Not too likely	3
Not at all likely	1
No opinion	4

Disapprove

Very likely	59%
Somewhat likely	29
Not too likely	3
Not at all likely	4
No opinion	5

*Less than 1%

Selected National Trend

	Very, somewhat likely	Not too, not at all likely	No opinion
1991			
January 3–6	84%	10%	6%
1990			
December 13–16	84	11	5
November 15–18	76	18	6
November 1–4	76	18	6
August 23–24*	80	15	5
August 18–19*	74	22	4

*Newsweek/Gallup Poll

Recently, the United Nations Security Council passed a resolution that allows Iraq one final opportunity to pull out of Kuwait by January 15 or else face possible military action. If Iraq lets this deadline pass, would you favor the United States and its allies going to war with Iraq in order to drive the Iraqis out of Kuwait, or not?

Yes..63%
No..33
No opinion.. 4

	Yes	No	No opinion
By Sex			
Male.....................71%	26%	3%
Female...................55	40	5
By Ethnic Background			
White....................66	30	4
Nonwhite...............65	32	3
Black....................30	64	6
By Education			
College Graduate......61	36	3
College Incomplete...65	32	3
High-School Graduate..............64	32	4
Less Than High-School Graduate 57	36	7
By Region			
East......................57	38	5
Midwest................63	32	5
South 67	27	6
West.....................62	38	*
By Age			
18–29 Years............63	35	2
30–49 Years............64	32	4
50 Years and Over.....61	34	5
By Household Income			
$50,000 and Over.....68	29	3
$30,000–$49,999....69	29	2
$20,000–$29,999....62	35	3
Under $20,000.........55	38	7

By Politics			
Republicans............75	22	3
Democrats 53	43	4
Independents...........63	33	4
By Religion			
Protestants 64	32	4
Catholics 65	31	4
By Political Ideology			
Liberal...................57	41	2
Moderate................69	29	2
Conservative...........70	27	3
By Bush Approval			
Approve.................80	17	3
Disapprove.............25	73	2

*Less than 1%

Selected National Trend

	Yes	No	No opinion
1991			
January 3–6 ....62%	32%	6%
1990			
December 13–16......59	34	7
December 6–9..........61	33	6
November 29–December 2..........64	31	5

Which of the following three statements comes closest to your opinion:

A) The United States should withdraw its troops from Saudi Arabia.

B) The United States should continue to enforce sanctions and seek some form of peaceful solution to the crisis, no matter how long it takes, without initiating a war to drive Iraq out of Kuwait.

C) The United States should initiate a war to drive Iraq out of Kuwait if Iraq does not change its position within the next several months, in order to draw matters to a close.

Statement A 9%
Statement B 36

Statement C 50
No opinion......................................5

	A	B	C	No opinion
By Sex				
Male 6%	28%	62%	4%	
Female..........11	42	40	7	
By Ethnic Background				
White.............8	33	54	5	
Nonwhite 2	56	42	*	
Black 22	47	25	6	
By Education				
College				
Graduate......6	39	52	3	
College				
Incomplete ..7	31	57	5	
High-School				
Graduate.....10	38	48	4	
Less Than				
High-School				
Graduate.....13	34	46	7	
By Region				
East 8	43	45	4	
Midwest.........9	36	48	7	
South 8	28	58	6	
West 9	39	50	2	
By Age				
18–29 Years...12	34	51	3	
30–49 Years....9	34	54	3	
50 Years and				
Over...........7	38	47	8	
By Household Income				
$50,000 and				
Over...........7	35	54	4	
$30,000–				
$49,999......6	30	62	2	
$20,000–				
$29,999......7	42	48	3	
Under				
$20,000.....13	38	42	7	
By Politics				
Republicans....4	30	62	4	
Democrats 11	44	40	5	
Independents..10	33	52	5	

By Religion				
Protestants 8	35	52	5	
Catholics 7	35	53	5	
By Political Ideology				
Liberal..........13	39	46	2	
Moderate........*	38	56	6	
Conservative... 8	30	58	4	
By Bush Approval				
Approve.........3	25	68	4	
Disapprove....20	59	17	4	

*Less than 1%

Selected National Trend

	A	B	C	No opinion
1991				
Jan. 3–6.........8%	43%	45%	4%	
1990				
Dec. 13–16.....9	44	43	4	
Dec. 6–9 10	41	46	3	
Nov.29–				
Dec. 2..........9	46	42	3	

*Less than 1%

Do you approve or disapprove of the way each of the following is dealing with the Persian Gulf crisis:

Secretary of State James Baker?

Approve..71%
Disapprove..14
No opinion..15

	Approve	Dis-approve	No opinion
By Politics			
Republicans............78%	11%	11%	
Democrats 68	18	14	
Independents...........68	15	17	
By Political Ideology			
Liberal..................67	20	13	
Moderate................73	19	8	
Conservative...........78	11	11	

Democratic congressional leaders?

Approve..37%
Disapprove.......................................38
No opinion.......................................25

	Approve	Dis-approve	No opinion
By Politics			
Republicans.............23%	56%	21%
Democrats 59	20	21
Independents...........30	40	30
By Political Ideology			
Liberal...................45	34	21
Moderate................45	32	23
Conservative...........31	52	17

Republican congressional leaders?

Approve..44%
Disapprove.......................................29
No opinion.......................................27

	Approve	Dis-approve	No opinion
By Politics			
Republicans.............62%	19%	19%
Democrats 36	39	25
Independents...........38	28	34
By Political Ideology			
Liberal...................39	35	26
Moderate................46	27	27
Conservative...........53	27	20

What do you think is the primary reason the United States is prepared to go to war with Iraq? Do you think it is more to protect our supply of oil and our economic interests, or do you think it is more to stop aggression and protect other countries in the Middle East?

Protect our own interests 37%
Protect other countries in the region.........55
No opinion.......................................8

	Own interests	Other countries	No opinion
By Sex			
Male 33%	58%	9%
Female..................40	52	8
By Ethnic Background			
White...................34	58	8
Nonwhite 46	46	8
Black 50	36	14
By Education			
College Graduate 46	48	6
College Incomplete...34	58	8
High-School Graduate..............35	58	7
Less Than High-School Graduate 33	54	13
By Region			
East 37	57	6
Midwest.................39	53	8
South 34	54	12
West 37	56	7
By Age			
18–29 Years............41	49	10
30–49 Years............37	57	6
50 Years and Over.....32	58	10
By Household Income			
$50,000 and Over.....45	52	3
$30,000–$49,999...34	59	7
$20,000–$29,999...31	59	10
Under $20,000.........38	53	9
By Politics			
Republicans............27	67	6
Democrats 41	50	9
Independents...........39	52	9
By Religion			
Protestants 36	55	9
Catholics 33	62	5
By Political Ideology			
Liberal...................44	49	7
Moderate................40	53	7
Conservative...........32	61	7

Approve.................26   68   6
Disapprove............61   27   12

If Iraq were to withdraw from most of Kuwait—except for two offshore islands and some oil fields on the Iraq border— would you be less likely to support taking military action against Iraq, more likely, or would this not affect your opinion about taking military action against Iraq?

Less likely...33%
More likely...10
Not affect opinion 46
No opinion..11

Asked of those who favor going to war with Iraq: Do you favor taking military action against Iraq on January 15 or 16, or a few days after the 15th deadline, or sometime later in the month of January, or sometime after January 31?

On January 15 or 16 ....33%
A few days after the deadline 25
Later in January but before the 31st..........19
Sometime after January 31 11
United States will not strike at all/
  solution will happen before
  force is used (volunteered).....................2
No opinion..10

Do you think the United States has done all it can to solve the crisis diplomatically, or not?

Yes..60%
No..33
No opinion..7

How about Iraq? Do you think it has done all it can to solve the Gulf crisis diplomatically, or not?

Yes...4%
No..89
No opinion..7

Please tell me whether or not you feel each of the following countries and groups of countries are doing as much as they can to help to support the United States and its allies in the Persian Gulf:

	Yes	No	No opinion
Arab nations 28%		54%	18%
Japan 8		72	20
European nations......30		54	16
USSR 29		56	15

Do you think that military force is the only way that Saddam Hussein will leave Kuwait, or do you think there is still a possibility that he will leave Kuwait as a result of diplomatic means?

Only by force 55%
By diplomatic means............................38
No opinion... 7

If the United States does succeed in getting Iraq to leave Kuwait—either through military or diplomatic means—do you think our troops should stay in the region indefinitely after that point to keep the peace, or not?

Yes..33%
No..61
No opinion... 6

How worried are you that the current situation in the Persian Gulf will develop into a larger war that could spread throughout the region and other parts of the world? Would you say you are very worried, somewhat worried, not too worried, or not at all worried about that?

Very worried.......................................38%
Somewhat worried...............................34
Not too worried...................................17
Not at all worried................................. 9
No opinion... 2

From what you have heard or read, which of these do you think is the most likely action with regard to the United States and its allies taking military action against Iraq: The United States and its allies will strike militarily on January 15 or 16, or the United States will strike a few days after the 15th deadline, or sometime later in the month of January, or sometime after January 31?

On January 15 or 16 ....33%
A few days after the deadline 25
Later in January but before the 31st 19
Sometime after January 31 11
United States will not strike at all
   (volunteered)....................................2
No opinion.......................................10

Some people feel that the United States should agree to a diplomatic solution to the Gulf crisis that would link Iraqi withdrawal from Kuwait to a solution to the issue of Israeli occupation of the West Bank and a Palestinian homeland. Others believe we should continue to insist on Iraq's unconditional withdrawal from Kuwait without linking it to any other issues in the region. Which comes closer to your view?

Link withdrawal to Palestinian issue.........17%
Insist on unconditional withdrawal...........70
No opinion.......................................13

Do you think Congress has played too large a role in determining U.S. policy in this Persian Gulf crisis, too small a role, or has the role of Congress been about right?

Too large a role....................................17%
Too small a role 28
About right...47
No opinion..8

Note: The American people back President George Bush on the Persian Gulf situation at this tense point in history. A majority (65%) supports his initial decision to send U.S. troops there, and a majority (55%) also supports military action against Iraq if nothing changes by the January 15 deadline.

At the same time, almost one half (44%) believes that the current situation is not worth going to war over, and many are worried that any war in the Persian Gulf will spread throughout the entire region or beyond. As of the latest Gallup interview, one third (33%)

says that the United States can do more diplomatically, and four in ten (38%) hope that a diplomatic solution will arise to avert war.

If war does break out, the United States will begin with the support of 50% to 60% of its citizens and with the opposition of a little more than one third of the population. About three out of ten (29%), in fact, still continue to think that our involvement in the region has been a mistake from the beginning.

Whatever their attitudes, Americans expect the worst. Gallup's latest survey shows a large jump in the number of those who think that war is very likely—now at 66%, up from 46% only one week before, and 29% last August. Another 24% think that war is somewhat likely, and only 5% think it not likely.

In addition, respondents expect an immediate war. One third (33%) think that America and its allies will strike within hours after the deadline, by the 16th. Another 25% say that action will be initiated within a few days after the deadline, while only 11% think that the United States and its allies will wait until after the end of the month.

For those Americans who favor offensive action, there is no reason to wait: 57% of this group say that we should strike immediately on the 15th or 16th, and another 19% say that we should strike within a few days thereafter.

What could stop the war? Almost four out of ten (38%) believe that it still may be possible by diplomatic means to persuade Iraq to leave Kuwait. Respondents strongly agree with the administration's position of no direct linkage of a solution to the Israeli-Palestinian issue as a prerequisite to Iraqi withdrawal from Kuwait (70%). However, previous Gallup Polls have shown that a majority favors the United States agreeing to a Middle East conference discussing the Israeli situation, as a way to delay military action.

Additionally, the possibility that Iraq might partially withdraw and retain only a portion of Kuwait and two Kuwaiti islands has some, but not overwhelming, impact on respondents' thoughts about the war. One third (33%) say that they would be less likely to support taking military action in the event of this development.

More Americans think that we are prepared to go to war with Iraq in order to stop aggression and protect other countries in the Middle East (55%) than simply to protect our supply of oil and our economic interests (37%). These attitudes are related to support for a possible war—those who believe that the situation is not worth a war tend to think that the United States is involved for economic reasons. Those who think that the situation is worth going to war over are more likely to say that we are involved to deter aggression.

Approval of the way in which President Bush has been handling the crisis is now at 62%, not much different from earlier measures in January and in December but still below the levels he attained immediately after our involvement in August of last year. Secretary of State James Baker, who has been the point man on much of the diplomatic activity relating to the crisis, gets higher marks than the president: 71% approve of the job he has been doing. Both Bush and Baker get substantially higher marks than congressional leaders: only 37% approve of the job being done by the Democrats, and 44% approve of the job being done by the Republican leaders. Americans have mixed views about Congress: one half (47%) think that its involvement has been about right, while slightly over one fourth (28%) say too little and 17% say too great.

Respondents believe strongly that the United States is not getting enough support from its allies. They are particularly tough on Japan: 72% say that it has not been helping enough. Between 54% and 56% say that other Arab nations, West European nations, and the Soviet Union have not been doing enough.

They do not believe that the U.S. presence is going to be required indefinitely in the region—even after Iraq leaves Kuwait, by whatever means. Six in ten (61%) think that our troops should pull out and come home after Kuwait is liberated, while one third (33%) thinks that they will have to stay there indefinitely to keep the peace.

Iraqi leaders are calling this a "holy war." The possibility of its spreading beyond the immediate confines of Iraq, Kuwait, and Saudi Arabia is very real to many Americans—38% are very worried about the possibility of proliferation, with another 34% somewhat worried.

JANUARY 17
PRESIDENT BUSH/PERSIAN GULF SITUATION

Interviewing Date: 1/16/91 between 9:25 P.M. and 11:30 P.M. EST
Survey #GO 122002W

First of all, did you happen to see or hear President Bush's address to the nation which was completed earlier this evening?

	Yes
National	84%

Asked of those who said they had watched or heard the president's speech: As far as you are concerned, did President Bush do a satisfactory job tonight of explaining why we are taking military action against Iraq, or not?

	Yes
National	86%

Do you approve or disapprove of the way President Bush is handling the current situation in the Persian Gulf?

	Approve
National	81%

Selected National Trend

	Approve
1991	
January 11–13	62%
January 3–6	60
1990	
December 6–9	57
November 1–4	61
October 3–4	69
August 30–September 2	74
August 9–12	80
August 3–4	52

Do you approve or disapprove of the U.S. decision today to go to war with Iraq in order to drive the Iraqis out of Kuwait?

		Approve
National		79%

Now that the United States has taken military action against Iraq, do you think the fighting will continue for just a few days, a matter of weeks, several months, or a year or more?

Days	17%
Weeks	39
Months	23
Year or more	5
No opinion	16

Note: A nationwide Gallup Poll conducted within minutes of the conclusion of George Bush's address to the nation on the evening of January 16 shows that Americans' initial reactions to the president's actions in the Persian Gulf are overwhelmingly positive. Seventy-nine percent say that they approve of the U.S. decision to go to war against Iraq in order to drive the Iraqis out of Kuwait. Similarly, 81% approve of the way in which President Bush is handling the situation in the Persian Gulf.

Respondents, however, still do not necessarily believe that the military action in the Gulf region will be over in a short period of time: 39% say that war will continue for a matter of weeks, and another 23% say that it will be several months before it is over. Only 17% estimate a matter of days.

The Gallup Poll shows that President Bush's address had an amazingly high viewership; it was watched by 84% of those interviewed across the country. And he apparently achieved his objectives with the address; 86% of those who watched say that he did a satisfactory job of explaining why we are now at war. It is important to note, however, that these early reactions reflect a "rally 'round the flag" attitude often observed immediately after military actions are begun.

About the same number of respondents—80%—also approved of Bush's handling of the situation shortly after our initial movement of troops to Saudi Arabia in August. That support, however, eroded throughout the fall months. In a Gallup Poll conducted on January 11–13, only 62% approved of the way that Bush was handling the situation. Thus, the initiation of military action produced an immediate 19-percentage point jump in approval for Bush's handling of the crisis.

JANUARY 18
PERSONAL FINANCES

Interviewing Date: 1/11–13/91
Survey #GO 122012

We are interested in how people's financial situation may have changed. Would you say that you are financially better off now than you were a year ago, or are you financially worse off now?

Better	26%
Worse	33
Same (volunteered)	39
No opinion	2

	Better	Worse	Same	No opinion
By Sex				
Male	30%	31%	37%	2%
Female	23	36	40	1
By Ethnic Background				
White	27	31	40	2
Nonwhite	30	41	29	*
Black	25	50	24	1
By Education				
College Graduate	31	29	38	2
College Incomplete	30	31	38	1
High-School Graduate	26	34	39	1
Less Than High-School Graduate	17	41	38	4
By Region				
East	19	38	42	1
Midwest	29	30	39	2
South	28	32	39	1
West	31	35	32	2

By Age

	Better	Worse	Same	No opinion
18–29 Years...40	32	27	1
30–49 Years...30	34	34	2
50 Years and Over..........14	33	51	2

By Household Income

	Better	Worse	Same	No opinion
$50,000 and Over..........37	22	38	3
$30,000– $49,999.....33	29	38	*
$20,000– $29,999.....30	31	38	1
Under $20,000.....13	46	40	1

*Less than 1%

Selected National Trend

1990	Better	Worse	Same	No opinion
December 13–16.......38%	36%	26%	*
October 25–28.......38	35	26	1
October 18–21.......27	41	30	2
September.....40	27	32	1
August..........43	27	29	1
July............44	28	27	1

*Less than 1%

Looking ahead, do you expect that at this time next year you will be financially better off than now or worse off than now?

Better...41%
Worse...25
Same (volunteered)...............................21
No opinion...13

By Income

	Better	Worse	Same	No opinion
$50,000 and Over..........41%	28%	23%	8%
$30,000– $49,999.....47	24	22	7
$20,000– $29,999.....42	25	20	13
Under $20,000.....39	24	22	15

Selected National Trend

1990	Better	Worse	Same	No opinion
December 13–16.......58%	18%	17%	7%
October 25–28.......50	27	15	8
October 18–21.......41	34	16	9
September.....51	17	20	12
August..........57	16	20	7
July............58	17	18	7

Note: Just prior to the outbreak of war in the Middle East, the Gallup Business Poll shows significant improvement in some important measures of consumer confidence. Compared to last October, fewer respondents say that they are worse off financially now than one year ago, and fewer expect to be worse off one year from now.

In the current survey, 33% admit that they are worse off financially now than one year ago. Although higher than the 27% measured in last August and September, this is significantly lower than the 41% measured in mid-October, when the budget deficit and failure to balance the budget were cited as the most important problems facing the country. Moreover, 25% of consumers expect to be worse off one year from now, a more pessimistic figure than in the July through September polls.

Retail sales were especially disappointing in the fourth quarter of last year, and many economists attribute this in part to the sharp decline in consumer confidence between August and October. Gallup surveys suggest that this decline was caused more by worries about the economy and recession than by concerns about the Middle East. However, with the onset of war and with the early success of U.S. air power, many observers have begun to speculate about how a relatively quick and painless victory might affect consumer confidence and therefore the ability of the United States to pull out of recession.

In fact, there are reasons to believe that such an outcome could have a very positive impact on consumer confidence. Surveys over many years have shown that important good news of any kind often translates into improved consumer confidence, even if the news is not directly related to the economy or to people's own personal financial prospects. This is especially likely to be true if the war ends in a way that rebuilds America's self-confidence as a nation.

There is one important exception to this conclusion. Those with incomes below $20,000 per year (46%) and blacks (50%) are much more likely than all consumers (33%) to say that they are worse off now than one year ago. These groups are less likely to be impressed by good news that is not perceived as being directly related to their financial well-being.

JANUARY 21
PRESIDENT BUSH/SATISFACTION INDEX/PERSIAN GULF SITUATION

Interviewing Date: 1/17–20/91
Survey #GO 122013

Do you approve or disapprove of the way George Bush is handling his job as president?

Approve..82%
Disapprove...12
No opinion.. 6

Selected National Trend

	Approve	Dis-approve	No opinion
1991			
January 11–13	64%	25%	11%
January 3–6	58	31	11

In general, are you satisfied or dissatisfied with the way things are going in the United States at this time?

Satisfied..62%
Dissatisfied.......................................33
No opinion... 5

	Satisfied	Dis-satisfied	No opinion
By Sex			
Male	67%	30%	3%
Female	58	36	6
By Ethnic Background			
White	65	31	4
Nonwhite	66	30	4
Black	37	56	7
By Education			
College Graduate	62	34	4
College Incomplete	61	36	3
High-School Graduate	66	31	3
Less Than High-School Graduate	57	35	8
By Political Ideology			
Liberal	52	45	3
Moderate	59	34	7
Conservative	71	26	3

Selected National Trend

	Satisfied	Dis-satisfied	No opinion
1991			
January 3–6	32%	61%	7%
1990			
December 13–16	33	64	3
November 1–4	31	64	5
October 25–28	31	66	3
October 11–14	29	67	4

In general, are you satisfied or dissatisfied with the way things are going in your own personal life?

Satisfied..86%
Dissatisfied.......................................12
No opinion... 2

Selected National Trend

	Satisfied	Dis-satisfied	No opinion
1991			
January 3–6	84%	14%	2%
1990			
December 13–16	82	18	*
November 1–4	85	13	2
October 25–28	87	11	2
October 11–14	82	16	2

*Less than 1%

How closely have you followed news about the situation in the Persian Gulf region?* Would you say you have followed it very closely, fairly closely, not too closely, or not at all closely?

Very closely	70%
Fairly closely	27
Not too closely	3
Not at all closely	**

Selected National Trend

	Very closely	Fairly closely	Not too closely	Not at all closely
1991				
Jan. 11–13	50%	41%	8%	1%
Jan. 3–6	41	47	10	2
1990				
Dec. 6–9	43	46	9	2
Nov. 1–4	37	49	12	2
Oct. 3–4	35	50	12	3
Aug. 30– Sept. 2	43	43	11	3
Aug. 3–4	18	39	25	18

*The wording of the question changed in the January 17–20 survey from the original: "How closely have you followed news about the situation involving the invasion of Kuwait by Iraq?" All questions asked after August 16–19, 1990, included the phrase "and the sending of U.S. troops to Saudi Arabia."
*"No opinion"—at less than 1%—has been combined with "not at all closely."

Do you approve or disapprove of the way George Bush is handling the situation in the Persian Gulf region?*

Approve	86%
Disapprove	9
No opinion	5

Selected National Trend

	Approve	Dis-approve	No opinion
1991			
January 16**	81%	12%	7%
January 11–13	62	28	10
January 3–6	60	34	6
1990			
December 6–9	57	36	7
November 1–4	61	29	10
October 3–4	69	25	6
August 30– September 2	74	18	8
August 9–12	80	12	8
August 3–4	52	16	32

*The wording of the question changed in the January 16 survey from the original: "Do you approve or disapprove of the way George Bush is handling this current situation in the Middle East involving Iraq and Kuwait?"
**This poll was conducted in the first two hours after President Bush's speech.

In view of the developments since we first sent our troops to Saudi Arabia, do you think the United States made a mistake in sending troops to Saudi Arabia, or not?

Yes	16%
No	80
No opinion	4

Selected National Trend

	Yes	No	No opinion
1991			
January 11–13	29%	65%	6%
January 3–6	31	61	8
1990			
December 6–9	28	66	6

	Approve	Disapprove	No opinion
November 1–4	.25	67	8
October 3–4	.21	71	8
August 30– September 2	.16	76	8
August 9–12	.17	75	8

Do you approve or disapprove of the U.S. decision to go to war with Iraq in order to drive the Iraqis out of Kuwait?

Approve...80%
Disapprove..15
No opinion...5

	Approve	Dis-approve	No opinion
By Sex			
Male	.87%	11%	2%
Female	.74	18	8
By Ethnic Background			
White	.83	12	5
Nonwhite	.81	13	6
Black	.59	36	5
By Education			
College Graduate	.78	20	2
College Incomplete	.84	14	2
High-School Graduate	.82	12	6
Less Than High-School Graduate	.74	16	10
By Region			
East	.77	19	4
Midwest	.78	17	5
South	.84	10	6
West	.82	12	6
By Age			
18–29 Years	.84	13	3
30–49 Years	.85	12	3
50 Years and Over	.74	18	8
By Household Income			
$50,000 and Over	.88	11	1
$30,000–$49,999	.84	12	4
$20,000–$29,999	.84	10	6
Under $20,000	.68	24	8
By Politics			
Republicans	.91	4	5
Democrats	.70	25	5
Independents	.80	15	5
By Religion			
Protestants	.82	13	5
Catholics	.84	14	2
By Political Ideology			
Liberal	.72	24	4
Moderate	.76	16	8
Conservative	.88	9	3
By Bush Approval			
Approve	.92	5	3
Disapprove	.21	72	7

Do you approve or disapprove of the way the U.S. military is handling the situation in the Persian Gulf region?

Approve...93%
Disapprove...4
No opinion...3

Regardless of whether you approve or disapprove of the military action against Iraq, do you think the Bush administration and the U.S. military have done as well as you expected, better than you expected, or not as well as you expected in fighting the war so far?

As well as expected 43%
Better than expected.............................49
Not as well as expected...........................4
No opinion...4

How worried are you that the current situation in the Persian Gulf will develop into a larger war that could spread throughout the region and other parts of the world? Would you say you are very worried, somewhat worried, not too worried, or not at all worried about that?

Very worried..31%
Somewhat worried................................36
Not too worried....................................22
Not at all worried*.................................11

*"No opinion"—at 1% or less—has been combined with "not at all worried."

	Very worried	Some-what worried	Not too worried	Not at all worried
By Sex				
Male	19%	36%	28%	17%
Female	41	37	16	6
By Ethnic Background				
White	28	38	23	11
Nonwhite	37	36	18	9
Black	50	26	17	7
By Education				
College Graduate	35	32	21	12
College Incomplete	30	41	21	8
High-School Graduate	29	38	21	12
Less Than High-School Graduate	31	36	26	7
By Region				
East	28	37	24	11
Midwest	34	38	18	10
South	31	35	22	12
West	29	37	23	11
By Age				
18–29 Years	29	43	23	5
30–49 Years	29	39	22	10
50 Years and Over	34	30	21	15
By Household Income				
$50,000 and Over	24	36	27	13
$30,000–$49,999	29	41	21	9
$20,000–$29,999	22	40	26	12
Under $20,000	40	35	16	9
By Politics				
Republicans	23	39	26	12
Democrats	39	35	19	7
Independents	30	38	20	12

By Religion				
Protestants	30	36	23	11
Catholics	31	42	20	7
By Political Ideology				
Liberal	37	35	19	9
Moderate	35	29	18	18*
Conservative	25	39	26	10
By Bush Approval				
Approve	25	39	24	12
Disapprove	65	20	11	4

*"No opinion" here is 4%.

Selected National Trend

	Very worried	Some-what worried	Not too worried	Not at all worried
1990				
Jan. 11–13	38%	34%	17%	11%

Who do you think is currently winning the war in the Persian Gulf—the United States and its allies, Iraq, or neither side?

United States and its allies 73%
Iraq... 1
Neither side...20
No opinion... 6

Now that war has broken out with Iraq, do you personally feel any sense of danger from terrorist acts where you live and work, or not?

Yes...27%
No..73
No opinion.. *

*Less than 1%

How do you think the war in the Persian Gulf will end—in an all-out victory for the United States and its allies, in a compromise peace settlement, or in a defeat for the United States and its allies?

Victory for United States 52%
Compromise peace..............................35

Defeat for United States.........................1
No opinion......................................12

Do you think U.S. and allied troops on the ground will eventually have to become involved in combat in order to win the war with Iraq, or do you think only U.S. and allied air forces will be needed to win?

Ground troops involved.........................80%
Air forces only.................................12
No opinion......................................8

Do you think the United States should stop its military action against Iraq if Iraq pulls all of its troops out of Kuwait but Saddam Hussein remains in power in Iraq? Or do you think the United States should stop its military action only if Saddam Hussein is also removed from power?

Stop military action,
   Hussein remains in power 30%
Stop military action,
   Hussein removed from power 65
No opinion......................................5

Now that the United States has taken military action against Iraq, do you think the fighting will continue for just a few days, a matter of weeks, several months, or a year or more?

Days..4%
Weeks...39
Months..39
Year or more....................................8
No opinion......................................10

Now that the United States has taken military action against Iraq, do you think that the number of Americans killed and injured will be:

Less than 100?..................................12%
Several hundred?................................24
Up to a thousand? 16
Several thousand?...............................29
Tens of thousands?..............................4
No opinion......................................15

In general, how would you rate the job the news organizations in this country have done in covering the situation in the Mideast concerning the war with Iraq? Would you say it has been excellent, good, only fair, or poor?

Excellent.......................................63%
Good..26
Fair..8
Poor..2
No opinion......................................1

Thinking about the news coverage of the war in the Gulf, do you think:

The Bush administration and the military have been cooperative enough in providing information to the news organizations?

Yes...84%
No..11
No opinion......................................5

News organizations have done enough to respect the military's concern about the security of the operation?

Yes...72%
No..23
No opinion......................................5

News organizations have done enough to respect the privacy of the families of U.S. troops in the region?

Yes...75%
No..20
No opinion......................................5

Which of these is your main source of information about the war in the Persian Gulf—newspapers, radio, or television?

Newspapers......................................2%
Radio 8
Television......................................89
No opinion......................................1

Is there anyone in your family, or do you personally know anyone else, who is part of the U.S. military operation in the Persian Gulf region?

Yes...59%
No..40
No opinion...1

Some people think that the National Football League playoffs and the Super Bowl should be postponed as a result of the war in the Persian Gulf region. Others think that the playoffs and Super Bowl should go on as planned. Which comes closer to your view?

Postpone playoffs and
  Super Bowl....................................23%
Go on as planned................................68
No opinion...9

As a result of the beginning of the war in the Persian Gulf, have you:

	Yes	No	No opinion
Changed or canceled business or personal travel plans?	8%	92%	*
Missed work or school so you could follow the war coverage? ...	4	95	1
Stayed up later or gotten up earlier so you could follow the war coverage?	74	26	*
Canceled plans for going out, entertainment, or parties?	9	91	*
Prayed more than you usually do?	58	41	1

*Less than 1%

How effective do you think prayers can be in a situation like this one in the Persian Gulf—very effective, fairly effective, or not very effective?

Very effective....................................59%
Fairly effective..................................22
Not very effective..............................14
No opinion...5

Note: From the moment the war was announced on the evening of January 16, Americans have been remarkably supportive. Eighty percent approve of the U.S. decision to begin military action, and 86% approve of the way that President George Bush is handling the situation. These numbers are up substantially from similar measures taken just before the war began (62%). Overall job approval for Bush, now at 82%, has matched the highest levels of his administration.

Moreover, nine out of ten respondents (93%) approve of the job being done by the U.S. military. Much of this positive reaction is due to the fact that Americans are upbeat about the progress of the war: 73% think that we are winning, and 49% say that we are making better progress than expected.

However, 67% are somewhat or very worried that the conflict will develop into a larger war that could spread throughout the region, down from 72% in the previous poll. Additionally, despite early reports of the success of U.S. and allied air and missile attacks, there is little expectation that the war can be won without the involvement of ground troops. Some 80% say that ground troops eventually will be needed to win the war, while 12% think it is possible that the war can be won with air power alone. Most agree, at 65%, that the war effort must be pressed until Saddam Hussein himself is removed from power, even if Iraqi troops withdraw from Kuwait. Only 30% say that troop withdrawal alone will be sufficient to bring about a cease-fire.

The start of war immediately doubled the number of those who say they are satisfied with the way things are going in the United States, while the number who are dissatisfied dropped in half. This phenomenon may be due to two factors: The war may be taking Americans' minds off the recession and economic concerns, or the aggressive military response in the Persian Gulf may be restoring their confidence in their country as a great nation. In the first week of January, only 32% were satisfied with the way things were going in the United States, with 61% dissatisfied. Now, after the war has begun, 62% are satisfied, and only 33% dissatisfied.

The war has very personal implications for about six in ten (59%), who say they know someone who is a part of the military operation in the Persian Gulf region. Thus, almost three quarters of Americans (74%) say that they have stayed up later or risen earlier to follow news coverage of the war. Seventy percent are following events very closely, up from only 50% the weekend before the war began. And 58% have been praying more than usual.

Despite increased worries about terrorism, only 8% report changing or canceling travel plans; only 9% have canceled entertainment plans, and only 4% have missed work or school because of the war. Indeed, two thirds (68%) think that the Super Bowl in Tampa, Florida, on January 27 should go on as scheduled; only one fourth (23%) thinks that it should be postponed.

Respondents who are following the war intensely are generally pleased with the media coverage, and most approve of the way the media, the Bush administration, and the military have handled the dissemination of accurate and timely information to the public. Two thirds (63%) think that the media have been doing an excellent job in covering the war—up substantially from perceptions measured in late August, when troops were first moving into Saudi Arabia.

Respondents also are pleased with the quality of war information they have been receiving. Seven in ten (72%) think that news organizations have done enough to respect the military's concerns about the security of Operation Desert Storm, while three quarters (75%) think that the media have done enough to respect the privacy of families of U.S. troops in the Persian Gulf region. And despite grumblings from the media that information about the war is sometimes hard to come by, there is very little complaint from the public about government censorship. More than eight in ten (84%) think that the Bush administration and the military have been sufficiently cooperative in providing information to news organizations.

JANUARY 23
PRESIDENT BUSH/PERSIAN GULF SITUATION

Interviewing Date: 1/19–22/91
Survey #GO 122028

Do you approve or disapprove of the way George Bush is handling the situation in the Persian Gulf region?

Approve...84%
Disapprove...11
No opinion...5

	Approve	Dis- approve	No opinion
By Sex			
Male	89%	10%	1%
Female...................	80	12	8
By Ethnic Background			
White....................	85	11	4
Nonwhite	71	17	12
Black	81	15	4
By Education			
College Graduate	79	17	4
College Incomplete...	87	12	1
High-School Graduate..............	88	9	3
Less Than High- School Graduate	81	8	11
By Region			
East	82	12	6
Midwest.................	82	13	5
South	86	10	4
West	88	10	2
By Age			
18–29 Years............	84	10	6
30–49 Years............	88	10	2
50 Years and Over.....	81	13	6
By Household Income			
$50,000 and Over.....	87	11	2
$30,000–$49,999....	88	11	1
$20,000–$29,999....	84	11	5
Under $20,000........	80	12	8

By Politics
Republicans	96	3	1
Democrats	75	19	6
Independents	82	13	5

By Religion
Protestants	85	10	5
Catholics	86	11	3

By Political Ideology
Liberal	76	18	6
Moderate	82	14	4
Conservative	91	7	2

By Bush Approval
Approve	97	2	1
Disapprove	32	63	5

Selected National Trend

	Approve	Dis-approve	No opinion
1991			
January 17–20	86%	9%	5%
January 11–13	62	28	10

Do you approve or disapprove of the U.S. decision to go to war with Iraq in order to drive the Iraqis out of Kuwait?

Approve	79%
Disapprove	18
No opinion	3

Selected National Trend

	Approve	Dis-approve	No opinion
1991			
January 17–20	80%	15%	5%

Do you approve or disapprove of the way the U.S. military is handling the situation in the Persian Gulf region?

Approve	92%
Disapprove	6
No opinion	2

Selected National Trend

	Approve	Dis-approve	No opinion
1991			
January 17–20	93%	4%	3%

Regardless of whether you approve or disapprove of the military action against Iraq, do you think the Bush administration and the U.S. military have done as well as you expected, better than you expected, or not as well as you expected in fighting the war so far?

As well as expected	49%
Better than expected	42
Not as well as expected	6
No opinion	3

Selected National Trend

	As well as expected	Better than expected	Not as well as expected	No opinion
1991				
Jan. 17–20	43%	49%	4%	4%

Who do you think is currently winning the war in the Persian Gulf—the United States and its allies, Iraq, or neither side?

United States and its allies	66%
Iraq	*
Neither side	26
No opinion	8

*Less than 1%

Selected National Trend

	United States	Iraq	Neither side	No opinion
1991				
Jan. 17–20	73%	1%	20%	6%

Now that the United States has taken military action against Iraq, do you think the fighting will continue for just a few days, a matter of weeks, several months, or a year or more?

Days 2%
Weeks 29
Months...49
Year or more...................................12
No opinion...................................... 8

Selected National Trend

	Days	Weeks	Months	Year
1991				
Jan. 17–20*	4%	39%	39%	8%

*"No opinion" here is 10%.

How worried are you that the current situation in the Persian Gulf will develop into a larger war that could spread throughout the region and other parts of the world? Would you say you are very worried, somewhat worried, not too worried, or not at all worried about that?

Very worried.....................................32%
Somewhat worried.............................40
Not too worried.................................19
Not at all worried* 9

*"No opinion"—at 2% or less—has been combined with "not at all worried."

Selected National Trend

	Very worried	Some- what worried	Not too worried	Not at all worried
1991				
Jan. 17–20	31%	36%	22%	11%
Jan. 11–13	38	34	17	11

As you may know, Iraq has attacked the country of Israel with missiles. The U.S. government has asked Israel to refrain from striking back at Iraq because it might harm cooperation between the United States and allied Arab nations in the war. Some people think that Israel should refrain from attacking Iraq. Others think that Israel should strike back in its own self-defense. Which comes closer to your view—should Israel refrain from attacking Iraq, or not?

Yes...69%
No...25
No opinion...................................... 6

	Yes	No	No opinion
By Sex			
Male	72%	24%	4%
Female	67	25	8
By Ethnic Background			
White	71	23	6
Nonwhite	67	27	6
Black	58	40	2
By Education			
College Graduate	83	13	4
College Incomplete	73	22	5
High-School Graduate	64	30	6
Less Than High-School Graduate	60	31	9
By Region			
East	66	27	7
Midwest	71	23	6
South	68	25	7
West	74	22	4
By Age			
18–29 Years	67	30	3
30–49 Years	70	25	5
50 Years and Over	70	22	8
By Household Income			
$50,000 and Over	83	14	3
$30,000–$49,999	72	21	7
$20,000–$29,999	63	31	6
Under $20,000	63	32	5
By Politics			
Republicans	74	21	5
Democrats	65	28	7
Independents	70	25	5
By Religion			
Protestants	68	25	7
Catholics	68	27	5

By Political Ideology
Liberal....................71   26   3
Moderate................81   15   4
Conservative...........72   23   5

By Bush Approval
Approve...................71   24   5
Disapprove.............63   29   8

What do you think will happen? Do you think Israel will continue to refrain from striking back at Iraq, or not?

Yes...30%
No...56
No opinion..14

If Israel does strike back by attacking Iraq, do you think Israel should strike back at military targets only, or do you think Israel should strike back more generally at military and civilian targets throughout Iraq?

Military targets only............................73%
Military and civilian targets...................18
Neither (volunteered)............................ 1
No opinion... 8

If Israel becomes involved in the war with Iraq, do you think the war will last longer as a result, be shorter, or will it have no effect on the length of the war?

Last longer 49%
Be shorter...17
Have no effect.....................................26
No opinion... 8

Should the United States and its allies continue to urge Israel to refrain from attacking Iraq, or not?

Yes...75%
No...19
No opinion... 6

Note: A majority of Americans (69%) strongly favors Israel's continuing to refrain from retaliating against Iraq for the recent Scud missile attacks on Tel Aviv, and an even larger number (75%) want the U.S. government to continue to urge Israel to stay out of the conflict. One half (49%) worry that a retaliatory strike by Israel would only prolong the war, while only 17% believe that an Israeli attack on Iraq would shorten it.

Despite this hope for Israeli restraint, respondents are not optimistic that it will continue: 56% think that Israel will eventually strike back. If it does, then most Americans (73%) would favor the Israelis hitting only Iraqi military targets and not the civilian population.

Approval for U.S. involvement in the Persian Gulf war remains strong. About eight out of ten (79%) continue to approve of the decision to go to war, and 84% approve of the way President George Bush is handling the situation.

Some changes, however, are becoming apparent: There are slight indications that the initial euphoria over our winning the war may be waning: the number saying that we are winning dropped from 73% to 66%. Moreover, Americans are clearly readjusting their estimates of how long we will be involved. On January 16, as war began, 56% guessed that the conflict would only last a matter of days or weeks. That number declined to 43% in last weekend's poll (January 17–20) and continued to fall during the current poll (January 19–22) to 31%. However, before the war began, 20% believed that it would last a year or more (*Newsweek* Poll conducted by Gallup on January 10–11), while only 12% think so today.

JANUARY 24
PRESIDENT BUSH—TWO YEARS IN OFFICE

Special Report

The following table shows the average approval and disapproval ratings for eight elected presidents during their first and second years:

Presidential Performance Ratings*

(Percent Approval)

	First year	Second year	Point difference
Kennedy	76%	74%	-2
Eisenhower	68	66	-2
Johnson**	66	51	-15
Bush	65	66	+1
Carter	62	46	-16
Nixon	61	57	-4
Truman**	59	41	-18
Reagan	58	44	-14

(Percent Disapproval)

	First year	Second year	Point difference
Reagan	28%	46%	+18
Truman**	24	40	+16
Johnson**	21	35	+14
Carter	20	38	+18
Nixon	17	29	+12
Bush	17	23	+6
Eisenhower	15	22	+7
Kennedy	10	17	+7

*Gerald Ford, as a nonelected president, is omitted.

**First two years of elected terms (Truman, 1949–50; Johnson, 1965–66)

Note: At the halfway point of his first term as president, George Bush is one of the highest-rated chief executives in Gallup annals. Overall, the ratings for his first two years are higher than those of Harry Truman, Ronald Reagan, Jimmy Carter, Richard Nixon, and Lyndon Johnson and are on a par with Dwight Eisenhower. Only John Kennedy's ratings are substantially higher. Bush averaged a 65% approval rating during his first year and 66% during his second.

Even Kennedy, the most popular president, did not improve his ratings the second year; he and every other recent president experienced the end of the traditional "honeymoon" with the public during the second year—some remaining roughly the same (Eisenhower lost 2 points, Kennedy 2, and Nixon 4), with others declining more severely (Reagan, 14; Johnson, 15; Carter, 16; and Truman, 18).

All recent presidents also suffered rising disapproval levels during their second year in office, but here again President Bush held his own, on a par with Kennedy and Eisenhower: his average disapproval increased 6 points, about the same as Kennedy and Eisenhower. The other five elected presidents experienced double-digit increases in disapproval (Nixon, 12; Johnson, 14; Truman, 16; and both Carter and Reagan, 18) during their second year.

In Gallup's final measure (January 11–13) before the start of the war in the Persian Gulf, President Bush enjoyed 64% approval. That rating jumped to 82% in the final measurement of his second year, thus reflecting the strong tendency of Americans to rally around the person who symbolizes the nation at a time of crisis.

JANUARY 27
PRESIDENT BUSH/PERSIAN GULF SITUATION

Interviewing Date: 1/23–26/91
Survey #GO 122014

Do you approve or disapprove of the way George Bush is handling his job as president?

Approve 83%
Disapprove 13
No opinion 4

Selected National Trend

	Approve	Dis-approve	No opinion
1991			
January 19–22	80%	14%	6%
January 17–20	82	12	6
January 11–13	64	25	11
January 3–6	58	31	11

How closely have you followed news about the situation in the Persian Gulf region? Would you say you have followed it very closely, fairly closely, not too closely, or not at all closely?

Very closely......................................59%
Fairly closely....................................34
Not too closely.................................... 6
Not at all closely* 1

*"No opinion"—at less than 1%—has been combined with "not at all closely."

Selected National Trend

	Very closely	Fairly closely	Not too closely	Not at all closely
1991				
Jan. 17–20	70%	27%	3%	*
Jan. 11–13	50	41	8	1
Jan. 3–6	41	47	10	2

*Less than 1%

Do you approve or disapprove of the way George Bush is handling the situation in the Persian Gulf region?

Approve...84%
Disapprove...12
No opinion... 4

Selected National Trend

	Approve	Dis-approve	No opinion
1991			
January 19–22	84%	11%	5%
January 17–20	86	9	5
January 16	81	12	7
January 11–13	62	28	10
January 3–6	60	34	6

In view of the developments since we first sent our troops to Saudi Arabia, do you think the United States made a mistake in sending troops to Saudi Arabia, or not?

Yes...18%
No..77
No opinion... 5

	Yes	No	No opinion
By Sex			
Male	14%	83%	3%
Female	22	72	6
By Ethnic Background			
White	15	80	5
Nonwhite	20	78	2
Black	39	54	7
By Education			
College Graduate	20	78	2
College Incomplete	16	81	3
High-School Graduate	16	80	4
Less Than High-School Graduate	19	65	16
By Region			
East	19	79	2
Midwest	18	76	6
South	17	76	7
West	17	78	5
By Age			
18–29 Years	19	78	3
30–49 Years	14	84	2
50 Years and Over	20	70	10
By Household Income			
$50,000 and Over	13	85	2
$30,000–$49,999	13	83	4
$20,000–$29,999	19	78	3
Under $20,000	22	71	7
By Politics			
Republicans	9	87	4
Democrats	26	70	4
Independents	18	77	5
By Religion			
Protestants	15	79	6
Catholics	19	78	3
By Political Ideology			
Liberal	26	71	3
Moderate	16	81	3
Conservative	12	85	3

By Bush Approval

Approve...............10	86	4
Disapprove............65	32	3

Selected National Trend

1991	Yes	No	No opinion
January 17–20.........16%	80%	4%
January 11–13.........29	65	6
January 3–6 31	61	8

Do you approve or disapprove of the U.S. decision to go to war with Iraq in order to drive the Iraqis out of Kuwait?

Approve.............................81%
Disapprove..........................15
No opinion........................... 4

Selected National Trend

1991	Approve	Dis- approve	No opinion
January 19–22.........79%	18%	3%
January 17–20.........80	15	5
January 16..............79	15	6

Now that the United States has taken military action against Iraq, do you think the fighting will continue for just a few days, a matter of weeks, several months, or a year or more?

Days 2%
Weeks 12
Months..............................62
Year or more......................19
No opinion........................... 5

Selected National Trend

1991*	Days	Weeks	Months	Year
Jan. 19–22 .... 2%	29%	49%	12%
Jan. 17–20 4	39	39	8
Jan. 16 17	39	23	5

*"No opinion" for these three polls is 8% (19–22), 10% (17–20), and 16% (16).

Just your impression, do you think the United States and its allies are losing ground in the Middle East, standing still, or making progress?

Losing ground 3%
Standing still 18
Making progress...................74
No opinion........................... 5

Do you think the United States should stop its military action against Iraq if Iraq pulls all of its troops out of Kuwait or only if Saddam Hussein is also removed from power?

Stop military action,
  Iraq pulls out 28%
Stop military action,
  Hussein removed from power 67
No opinion........................... 5

Would you favor or oppose stopping allied military action for a few days in order to give the Iraqis another chance to settle diplomatically?

Favor 25%
Oppose..............................72
No opinion........................... 3

As you may know, several U.S. and allied airmen have been captured by the Iraqis. Iraq has said it will use these airmen as human shields and put them at military targets throughout Iraq. As a result of this threat to the captured airmen, do you think the U.S. and allied forces should:

Stop the air strikes against Iraq?.............. 2%
Reduce the number of air strikes? 6
Continue them at the same level?.............51
Increase the number of air strikes?...........34
No opinion........................... 7

	Stop, reduce	Continue	Increase	No opinion
By Sex				
Male 5%	52%	40%	3%
Female..........12	49	29	10

By Ethnic Background

White............7	54	32	7
Nonwhite......22	36	40	2
Black..........18	27	51	4

By Education

College Graduate......7	58	31	4
College Incomplete..6	58	32	4
High-School Graduate......9	51	35	5
Less Than High-School Graduate.....11	31	41	17

By Region

East.............10	51	36	3
Midwest.........5	54	33	8
South...........11	42	38	9
West.............8	59	27	6

By Age

18–29 Years...15	54	28	3
30–49 Years....6	54	36	4
50 Years and Over...........6	44	37	13

By Household Income

$50,000 and Over...........5	57	34	4
$30,000–$49,999......6	58	32	4
$20,000–$29,999.....10	55	30	5
Under $20,000.....11	42	40	7

By Politics

Republicans....5	56	36	3
Democrats.....13	44	32	11
Independents...8	54	34	4

By Religion

Protestants.....7	51	36	6
Catholics......10	51	31	8

By Political Ideology

Liberal..........12	51	32	5
Moderate.......10	56	31	3
Conservative...6	55	36	3

By Bush Approval

Approve.........5	54	35	6
Disapprove....26	32	37	5

The treatment of captured airmen by the Iraqis has led to talk of war crimes trials for Iraqi offenders after the Gulf war ends. Do you think the threat of war crimes trials will lead the Iraqis to treat POWs better, treat them worse, or will it not have much of an effect?

Better..7%
Worse..13
No effect..75
No opinion...5

Do you favor or oppose using tactical nuclear weapons against Iraq if it might save the lives of U.S. troops?

Favor..45%
Oppose..45
No opinion...10

	Favor	Oppose	No opinion
By Sex			
Male.....................44%	48%	8%
Female.................46	42	12
By Ethnic Background			
White...................45	45	10
Nonwhite..............45	52	3
Black...................45	45	10
By Education			
College Graduate......35	58	7
College Incomplete...44	49	7
High-School Graduate.............51	38	11
Less Than High-School Graduate....46	42	12
By Region			
East.....................42	47	11
Midwest................52	36	12
South..................47	44	9
West....................40	55	5

By Age

18–29 Years	44	51	5
30–49 Years	45	47	8
50 Years and Over	47	40	13

By Household Income

$50,000 and Over	37	58	5
$30,000–$49,999	43	48	9
$20,000–$29,999	48	40	12
Under $20,000	51	39	10

By Politics

Republicans	46	43	11
Democrats	45	48	7
Independents	46	47	7

By Religion

Protestants	47	43	10
Catholics	43	48	9

By Political Ideology

Liberal	45	48	7
Moderate	40	51	9
Conservative	47	44	9

By Bush Approval

Approve	47	43	10
Disapprove	39	58	3

How worried are you that Iraq's setting fire to oil refineries in Kuwait will lead to major ecological problems in the region—very worried, somewhat worried, not too worried, or not at all worried?

Very worried	23%
Somewhat worried	38
Not too worried	24
Not at all worried	12
No opinion	3

In the Middle East situation, are your sympathies more with the Israelis or more with the Palestinian Arabs?

Israelis	64%
Palestinian Arabs	7
Both; neither (volunteered)	19
No opinion	10

Selected National Trend

	Israelis	Palestinian Arabs	Both; neither	No opinion
Oct. 1990	48%	23%	19%	10%
Aug. 1989	50	14	15	21
Dec. 1988	46	24	16	14
May 1986	43	20	20	17

Now that Iraq has hit Israel with missiles, do you think the Israelis should strike back in their own defense, or should they hold off to avoid damaging the alliance against Iraq?

Strike back	28%
Hold off	66
No opinion	6

What do you think will happen? Do you think Israel will continue to refrain from striking back at Iraq, or not?

Yes	32%
No	60
No opinion	8

Which of the following statements better describes the way you personally feel about the antiwar demonstrations now taking place in the United States: It is a good thing that Americans who disagree with the government are speaking out on what they believe, or it is a bad thing for Americans to be demonstrating against the war when U.S. troops are fighting overseas?

Good	34%
Bad	63
No opinion	3

	Good	Bad	No opinion
By Sex			
Male	34%	63%	3%
Female	40	58	2
By Ethnic Background			
White	33	63	4
Nonwhite	32	62	6
Black	42	56	2

By Education

	Favor	Oppose	No opinion
College Graduate 47	47	6	
College Incomplete...37	59	4	
High-School Graduate 30	68	2	
Less Than High-School Graduate 20	76	4	

By Region

East 39	58	3	
Midwest..................30	66	4	
South 29	66	5	
West......................38	60	2	

By Age

18–29 Years............40	57	3	
30–49 Years............39	58	3	
50 Years and Over.....23	72	5	

By Household Income

$50,000 and Over.....43	54	3	
$30,000–$49,999...32	64	4	
$20,000–$29,999....29	66	5	
Under $20,000........31	66	3	

By Politics

Republicans............26	71	3	
Democrats 35	61	4	
Independents...........40	57	3	

By Religion

Protestants 32	65	3	
Catholics 30	66	4	

By Political Ideology

Liberal..................42	55	3	
Moderate................45	51	4	
Conservative...........27	71	2	

By Bush Approval

Approve.................30	67	3	
Disapprove.............60	38	2	

Would you favor or oppose a law to ban peace demonstrations while U.S. troops are fighting overseas?

Favor 31%			
Oppose...65			
No opinion...4			

	Favor	Oppose	No opinion

By Sex

	Favor	Oppose	No opinion
Male 31%	66%	3%
Female...................32	63	5

By Ethnic Background

White....................31	65	4
Nonwhite 27	67	6
Black 41	58	1

By Education

College Graduate 16	83	1
College Incomplete...18	79	3
High-School Graduate 38	58	4
Less Than High-School Graduate 51	39	10

By Region

East 30	66	4
Midwest..................30	67	3
South 36	57	7
West......................28	71	1

By Age

18–29 Years............33	64	3
30–49 Years............27	70	3
50 Years and Over.....34	59	7

By Household Income

$50,000 and Over.....20	79	1
$30,000–$49,999...31	65	4
$20,000–$29,999....34	62	4
Under $20,000........40	55	5

By Politics

Republicans............31	65	4
Democrats 37	59	4
Independents...........26	72	2

By Religion

Protestants 33	63	4
Catholics 32	64	4

By Political Ideology

Liberal..................29	70	1
Moderate................13	66	1
Conservative...........36	61	3

By Bush Approval

Approve..................34   63   3
Disapprove............22   76   2

Is there anyone in your immediate family who is part of the U.S. military operation in the Persian Gulf region?

Yes...16%
No...83
No opinion...1

Do you personally know anyone else who is part of the U.S. military operation in the Persian Gulf region?

Yes...63%
No...36
No opinion...1

Some people feel that this Middle Eastern war means Armageddon, the final great battle before Judgment Day, predicted in the Bible. Do you think this war is Armageddon, or not?

Yes...15%
No...74
No opinion...11

	Yes	No	No opinion
By Religion			
Protestant...............16%		74%	10%
Catholic.................13		74	13
By Importance of Religion			
Very important........19%		68%	13%
Somewhat important............11		81	8
Not very important....8		87	5

Note: As the conflict enters its second week, American support for the Persian Gulf war remains strong. The latest Gallup Poll shows that a week of fighting and the resulting intensive media coverage have solidified, rather than dissipated, the public's support for U.S. involvement and for President George Bush.

Nearly eight out of ten (77%) continue to support the decision to take military action against Iraq. Eighteen percent say that it is a mistake—unchanged from last week (January 17–20) and still about one half of the number who said that it was a mistake immediately before the war began. In addition, support for President Bush remains remarkably strong. His overall job approval is now at 83%, the highest level of his administration and as high as any president since the end of World War II. Approval of the way Bush is handling the war is even higher, at 84%.

This strong support comes at the same time that the White House has been cautioning Americans to talk about the war in terms of months rather than days or weeks. The message apparently has made an impact: six out of ten (62%) now agree that the war will last months, with another 19% saying that it will last for a year or more. These estimates are sharply higher than one week ago, when only 39% thought that the war would last months and as many thought it would be over in weeks.

Still, seven out of ten (74%) think that the United States is making progress in the war (18% say that we are standing still, while only 3% say that we are losing ground). The majority favors pressing forward rather than pausing; only 25% support the idea of a temporary cease-fire in order to pursue a negotiated settlement. Interestingly, the country is evenly split on the use of nuclear weapons in the war: 45% favor and 45% oppose using tactical nuclear weapons if they might save the lives of our own troops.

Saddam Hussein's efforts to use captured U.S. and allied fliers as human shields around military targets have strengthened rather than weakened the resolve of the American public. One third (34%) says that we should increase the number of air strikes as a result of Hussein's threats, and another one half (51%) says that we should continue the air strikes at the same level. Only 8% want them to be reduced or stopped in order to avoid hitting the POWs.

The continuing Scud missile attacks on Israel, and the resulting casualties, have not changed the opinion of two thirds of respondents (66%) that Israel should refrain from retaliating, in order to help preserve the allied coalition. About six out of ten (60%), however, continue to think that Israel ultimately will retaliate.

Moreover, the war apparently is having a positive impact on support for Israel vis-à-vis the Palestinians. Sixty-four percent now say that their sympathies in the Middle East dispute are with the Israelis rather than with the Palestinian Arabs, considerably higher than in 1989, when only 50% favored the Israelis.

The war is affecting Americans in a very real way: 16% say that they have an immediate family member serving in the Persian Gulf. Perhaps as a result, attitudes toward antiwar protestors in this country are negative: 63% say that demonstrating against the war while U.S. troops are fighting is bad, but only 31% would favor a law banning peace demonstrations while U.S. troops are fighting overseas.

Could this Persian Gulf war be the beginning of Armageddon, the final great battle before Judgment Day, as predicted in the Bible? "Yes," according to 15% of respondents, but 74% deny it and 11% are not sure.

FEBRUARY 3
PRESIDENT BUSH/PERSIAN GULF SITUATION

Interviewing Date: 1/30–2/2/91
Survey #GO 122015

Do you approve or disapprove of the way George Bush is handling his job as president?

Approve...82%
Disapprove.......................................15
No opinion..3

Selected National Trend

	Approve	Dis-approve	No opinion
1991			
January 23–26	83%	13%	4%
January 19–22	80	14	6
January 17–20	82	12	6

January 11–13	64	25	11
January 3–6	58	31	11

Do you approve or disapprove of the way George Bush is handling the situation in the Persian Gulf region?

Approve...85%
Disapprove.......................................13
No opinion..2

Selected National Trend

	Approve	Dis-approve	No opinion
1991			
January 23–26	84%	12%	4%
January 19–22	84	11	5
January 17–20	86	9	5
January 16	81	12	7
January 11–13	62	28	10
January 3–6	60	34	6

Did you happen to see or hear President Bush's State of the Union address Tuesday night [January 29]?

	Yes
National	63%

Asked of those who replied in the affirmative: As far as you are concerned, did President Bush do a good job of explaining why we are in the Persian Gulf?

	Yes
National	81%

Did you happen to see or hear the Democratic response by Senator George Mitchell after President Bush's State of the Union address Tuesday night [January 29]?

	Yes
National	33%

In view of the developments since we first sent our troops to Saudi Arabia, do you think the United States made a mistake in sending troops to Saudi Arabia, or not?

Yes...18%
No..80
No opinion..2

	Yes	No	No opinion
1991			
January 23–26.........18%		77%	5%
January 17–20.........16		80	4
January 11–13.........29		65	6
January 3–6 31		61	8

Do you approve or disapprove of the U.S. decision to go to war with Iraq in order to drive the Iraqis out of Kuwait?

Approve..80%
Disapprove..18
No opinion... 2

	Approve	Dis-approve	No opinion
1991			
January 23–26.........81%		15%	4%
January 19–22.........79		18	3
January 17–20.........80		15	5
January 16.............79		15	6

Just your impression, do you think the United States and its allies are losing ground in the Middle East, standing still, or making progress?

Losing ground 4%
Standing still 15
Making progress................................78
No opinion... 3

	Losing ground	Standing still	Making progress	No opinion
1991				
Jan. 23–26 .....3%	18%	74%	5%	

All in all, is the current situation in the Mideast worth going to war over, or not?

Yes..71%
No...24
No opinion... 5

	Yes	No	No opinion
1991			
January 11–13.........46%		44%	10%
January 3–6 47		44	9
1990			
December 13–16 49		44	7
December 6–9.........47		45	8
November 15–18......46		45	9
September 27–30 49		41	10
August 23–26.........49		41	10

Looking ahead, how likely do you think it is that each of the following will happen in the Gulf war? First, how likely is it that:

	Very, some-what likely	Not too, not at all likely	No opinion
Iraq will use chemical, biological, or nuclear weapons against the allies?..82%		14%	4%
Iran will enter the fighting in support of Iraq? 52		40	8
An Israeli attack on Iraq in response to Scud missile attacks will damage the alliance against Iraq?...................66		28	6
The situation will develop into a bloody ground war with high numbers of casualties on both sides? 83		15	2
Iraqis will unleash new major threats to the region's environment?.......84		11	5
U.S. citizens will become victims of Iraqi terrorism? 77		21	2

For each of the following, please tell me how much effect you think it had on causing the situation in the Persian Gulf— a great deal, some, not too much, or none at all:

	Great deal, some	Not too much, none at all	No opinion
U.S. policies that favored Iraq during its war with Iran?	65%	26%	9%
Not having a conservation or alternative energy policy in the United States?	60	34	6

In general, how would you rate the job news organizations in this country have done in covering the situation in the Mideast concerning Iraq and Kuwait? Would you say it has been excellent, good, only fair, or poor?

Excellent	42%
Good	37
Fair	13
Poor	7
No opinion	1

In general, do you think the amount of coverage the news media have given to the Persian Gulf war has been too much, not enough, or about right?

Too much	37%
Not enough	6
About right	55
No opinion	2

Note: Despite reports of the first U.S. ground troops killed in action in the Persian Gulf war, and despite the fact that many Americans foresee a bloody ground war and the use of chemical and nuclear weapons by Iraq, support for the war effort remains as strong as it has been since the conflict began. Respondents, however, are becoming less satisfied with the way the media are covering the military operation.

The latest Gallup Poll shows that 80% continue to support the decision to go to war, 18% think that it was a mistake to get involved, and 85% approve of President George Bush's handling of the conflict. Another 78% say that the United States and its allies are continuing to make progress in the war.

Respondents also give high marks to President Bush for his explanation, in the State of the Union address on January 29 (watched by 63% of respondents), of U.S. involvement in the war. Only 33% report watching the Democratic response given by Senator George Mitchell.

The "rally 'round the flag" effect noted immediately after the January 16 decision to go to war continues unabated. Over seven out of ten (71%) now say that the situation in the Persian Gulf is worth going to war over, a substantial increase from the 46% who said so immediately before war broke out.

This stability in support for U.S. efforts in the Persian Gulf war has occurred despite the fact that respondents are less satisfied with the way it is being handled by the media. Forty-two percent now give the media's coverage an "excellent" rating, compared to 63% in the days immediately after the war began. However, Americans may be tiring of the war coverage: 37% now say that there has been too much, while only 6% complain of too little. In late August and early September, about one month after the initial movement of troops to the region, only 18% thought that there was too much coverage by the media.

The very high levels of support for the war also continue in spite of the fact that many Americans seem resigned to several negative facets of this conflict. First, about 83% think it very or somewhat likely that a bloody ground war will occur. Second, about the same number, 84%, think that a likely outcome of the war will be Iraq's unleashing of new major threats to the region's environment. Third, 82% think that Iraq eventually will end up using chemical, biological, or nuclear weapons against the allies. Fourth, 77% say that U.S. citizens will become the victims of Iraqi terrorism. Fifth, 66% say that Israel will respond to Iraqi attacks, thus damaging the alliance. And last, 52% say that Iran will enter the war on the side of Iraq.

FEBRUARY 3
READING IN AMERICA

Interviewing Date: 12/13–16/90
Survey #GO 122010

We are trying to determine as accurately as possible just how much time people spend listening to the radio, viewing television, and reading magazines, books, and newspapers. Please tell me, as accurately as you can, the amount of time you spent yesterday—that is, morning, afternoon, and evening:

	None	Less than one hour	One to less than three hours	Three or more hours
Listening to the radio	22%	20%	33%	25%
Watching television	12	8	42	38
Reading newspapers	29	39	30	2
Reading magazines	64	22	14	*
Reading books for work, school, etc.	62	11	18	9
Reading books for pleasure or recreation	67	14	16	3

*Less than 1%

Thinking about the last seven days, have you had the chance to:

	Yes
Read a book?	52%
Read a magazine?	69
Read a newspaper?	89

Which of these two activities—watching television or reading books—is:

The most relaxing for you?

Watching television	46%
Reading books	48
Both (volunteered)	3
Neither (volunteered)	3
No opinion	*

The best way to learn for you?

Watching television	31%
Reading books	60

Both (volunteered) 6
Neither (volunteered) 2
No opinion 1

The most rewarding for you?

Watching television	33%
Reading books	61
Both (volunteered)	3
Neither (volunteered)	2
No opinion	1

The most enjoyable way to spend an evening for you?

Watching television	52%
Reading books	34
Both (volunteered)	5
Neither (volunteered)	8
No opinion	1

*Less than 1%

Thinking about how you spend your nonworking time each day, do you think that you spend too much time or too little time:

	Too much	Too little	About right	No opinion
Watching television?	49%	18%	31%	2%
Reading newspapers?	8	54	35	3
Reading magazines?	6	65	24	5
Reading books for work, school, etc.?	9	62	19	10
Reading books for pleasure or recreation?	7	73	16	4

As far as you are concerned, is reading a good use of your time or not a good use of your time?

Good use	92%
Not a good use	7
No opinion	1

Looking ahead, do you think you'll find yourself reading more in the months and years ahead, reading less, or is the amount *of reading you do probably going to stay the same?*

More.......................................45%
Less..3
Same......................................51
No opinion...............................1

Do you happen to be reading any books or novels at the present time?

	Yes
National	37%

Selected National Trend

	Yes
March 1957	17%
October 1953	17
October 1952	18
January 1949	21

During the past year, about how many books, either hardcover or paperback, did you read either all or part of the way through?

None.....................................16%
One to five...........................32
Six to ten.............................15
Eleven to fifty 27
More than fifty 7
No opinion............................3

Do you have a favorite author?

	Yes
National	39%

Asked of those who replied in the affirmative: Who is your favorite author?

Stephen King 18%
Danielle Steele.......................9
Louis L'Amour.......................4
Sidney Sheldon.......................4
James Michener 3
V. C. Andrews........................3
Charles Dickens......................2
Mark Twain............................2
Ernest Hemingway..................2
John Steinbeck........................2
William Shakespeare...............2

Tom Clancy 2
Other....................................44
No opinion............................3

Do you happen to belong to any book club at present?

	Yes
National	9%

Do you happen to have a library card?

	Yes
National	59%

Do you happen to have any bookcases or bookshelves in your home?

	Yes
National	84%

About how many books do you have in your home right now—not including text or schoolbooks? Just your best guess:

Less than 20.........................16%
20 to 49...............................20
50 to 100 27
101 to 249............................15
250 or more 16
No opinion............................6

Do you, yourself, know anyone who is illiterate?

	Yes
National	35%

Note: There are signs of a coming surge in reading in America. Almost one half of respondents (45%)—particularly young people—say that they expect to read more in the future than they do today, while only a handful (3%) expect to read less. Additionally, despite recent publicity about "aliteracy," young people are just as likely to read for pleasure as older Americans and are much more likely to be readers of books for work or school. All of this suggests a turnaround in the making. Despite television and its pervasive influence on today's young people, reading may be coming back into favor with renewed fervor.

FEBRUARY 6
FOREIGN COUNTRIES/SOVIET UNION

Interviewing Date: 1/30–2/2/91
Survey #GO 122015

I'd like your overall opinion of some foreign countries. Is your overall opinion of [country] very favorable, mostly favorable, mostly unfavorable, or very unfavorable:

Great Britain?

Very favorable	45%
Mostly favorable	45
Mostly unfavorable	3
Very unfavorable	1
No opinion	6

Israel?

Very favorable	28%
Mostly favorable	51
Mostly unfavorable	10
Very unfavorable	3
No opinion	8

Japan?

Very favorable	11%
Mostly favorable	51
Mostly unfavorable	21
Very unfavorable	9
No opinion	8

Soviet Union?

Very favorable	8%
Mostly favorable	49
Mostly unfavorable	26
Very unfavorable	9
No opinion	8

Egypt?

Very favorable	10%
Mostly favorable	56
Mostly unfavorable	12
Very unfavorable	3
No opinion	19

France?

Very favorable	17%
Mostly favorable	57
Mostly unfavorable	11
Very unfavorable	4
No opinion	11

Germany?

Very favorable	15%
Mostly favorable	60
Mostly unfavorable	13
Very unfavorable	3
No opinion	9

Iran?

Very favorable	2%
Mostly favorable	11
Mostly unfavorable	39
Very unfavorable	40
No opinion	8

Iraq?

Very favorable	*
Mostly favorable	3
Mostly unfavorable	17
Very unfavorable	73
No opinion	7

*Less than 1%

Selected National Trend
(Opinion of Soviet Union)

	Very, mostly favorable	Mostly, very un-favorable	No opinion
September 1990	58%	32%	10%
May 1990	55	32	13
August 1989	51	40	9
February 1989	62	29	9
December 1988	44	46	10

I'd like your overall opinion of Mikhail Gorbachev. Is your overall opinion of him very favorable, mostly favorable, mostly unfavorable, or very unfavorable?

Very favorable....................................14%
Mostly favorable..............................56
Mostly unfavorable............................17
Very unfavorable................................ 6
No opinion.. 7

Selected National Trend

	Very, mostly favorable	Mostly, very un- favorable	No opinion
October 1990 ....74%	17%	9%
September 1990.......70	21	9
May 1990...............68	21	11
December 1989........77	15	8
December 1988........72	21	7

Now, what are your expectations for the Soviet Union? Do you think President Gorbachev's attempts to restructure the Soviet economy are likely to succeed or likely to fail?

Succeed..46%
Fail...42
No opinion...12

Do you think relations between the United States and the Soviet Union are getting better, getting worse, or staying about the same?

Better...41%
Worse...12
Same...46
No opinion.. 1

As far as you know, is there still a "cold war" between the United States and the Soviet Union, or is the "cold war" over?

Still exists...38%
Over...56
No opinion.. 6

Selected National Trend

	Still exists	Over	No opinion
1990			
September 40%	50%	10%
May......................52	40	8

In your opinion, how likely is it that within the next five years there will be an all-out nuclear war between the United States and the Soviet Union? Do you think it is almost certain to happen, there is a good chance it will happen, there is only some chance it will happen, or there is almost no chance it will happen?

Almost certain.....................................3%
Good chance....................................... 7
Some chance 25
Almost no chance.............................62
No opinion.. 3

Note: Most Americans continue to have positive feelings toward the Soviet Union and President Mikhail Gorbachev despite the Soviet crackdown on the independence movements in Latvia and Lithuania. Almost six in ten (57%) have a favorable opinion of the USSR, statistically no change from the 58% recorded by Gallup last September. And seven in ten (70%) hold a favorable opinion of President Gorbachev, only marginally lower than the 74% reported last October.

The crackdown on the Baltic States also has had little impact on thoughts about progress in Soviet-American relations. Four in ten (41%), for example, think that the relationship between the two superpowers is getting better, while only 12% say that it is getting worse, a substantial improvement over the mid-1980s. In an October 1986 Gallup Poll, 60% thought that relations between the two countries were getting worse. Today a majority believes that the "cold war" is over (56%) and sees almost no chance of an all-out nuclear war between the two countries (62%).

While the public still likes Gorbachev, Americans are not optimistic that his economic reforms will work. Less than one half (46%) now think that his attempt to restructure the Soviet economy will succeed, while 42% expect it to fail. In June 1989, 65% thought that *perestroika* would work, while only 21% thought that it would not.

FEBRUARY 8
RECESSION/MOST IMPORTANT PROBLEM

Interviewing Date: 1/30–2/2/91
Survey #GO 122015

How much longer do you think the country's current economic recession will last?

A few more months 10%
Up to six months................................25
Up to a year.......................................32
Up to two years..................................13
Longer than that................................13
No opinion... 7

What do you think is the most important problem facing this country today?

Kuwait, Iraq; Middle East crisis;
  Persian Gulf crisis...........................37%
Economy in general 16
Poverty; homelessness 6
Federal budget deficit........................... 6
Unemployment.................................... 5
Drugs; drug abuse................................ 5
Other;* no opinion..............................25

*None of the "other" replies drew more than 3%.

Note: Americans are not optimistic about a quick end to the current economic recession. In spite of recent government pronouncements that the recession will be over by midyear, over one half of respondents (58%) say that it will last more than six months, with one quarter (26%) saying that it will last a year or longer. Only about one third (35%) believes that it will be over within six months.

Additionally, despite the predominance of the Persian Gulf war in the headlines, it is clear that the recession and other economic concerns are still very worrisome. While 37% cite the war as the number one problem facing the country, economic concerns (16%) are mentioned as the second most important problem, followed by poverty and homelessness (6%), the federal budget deficit (6%), unemployment (5%), and drugs and drug abuse (5%).

The relative predominance of the Persian Gulf war as the number one problem, however, is still not at Vietnam levels: in several different Gallup surveys in 1967 and 1968, over one half of respondents said that the Vietnam War was the most important problem facing the country.

FEBRUARY 13
PRESIDENT BUSH/PERSIAN GULF SITUATION

Interviewing Date: 2/7–10/91
Survey #GO 122016

Do you approve or disapprove of the way George Bush is handling his job as president?

Approve...79%
Disapprove..18
No opinion... 3

Selected National Trend

1991	Approve	Dis- approve	No opinion
January 30– February 2 ....82%		15%	3%
January 23–26........83		13	4
January 19–22........80		14	6
January 17–20........82		12	6
January 11–13.........64		25	11
January 3–6............58		31	11

How closely have you followed news about the situation in the Persian Gulf region? Would you say you have followed it very closely, fairly closely, not too closely, or not at all closely?

Very closely.......................................55%
Fairly closely.....................................38
Not too closely.................................... 6
Not at all closely* 1

Selected National Trend

1991	Very closely	Fairly closely	Not too closely	Not at all closely
Jan. 23–26 ....59%		34%	6%	1%
Jan. 17–20 70		27	3	**
Jan. 11–13 50		41	8	1
Jan. 3–6........41		47	10	2

*"No opinion"—at less than 1%—has been combined with "not at all closely."
**Less than 1%

Do you approve or disapprove of the way George Bush is handling the situation in the Persian Gulf region?

Approve...79%
Disapprove..17
No opinion.. 4

Selected National Trend

	Approve	Dis-approve	No opinion
1991			
January 30–			
February 2	85%	13%	2%
January 23–26	84	12	4
January 19–22	84	11	5
January 17–20	86	9	5
January 16	81	12	7
January 11–13	62	28	10
January 3–6	60	34	6

In view of the developments since we first sent our troops to Saudi Arabia, do you think the United States made a mistake in sending troops to Saudi Arabia, or not?

Yes...21%
No...76
No opinion.. 3

Selected National Trend

	Yes	No	No opinion
1991			
January 30–			
February 2	18%	80%	2%
January 23–26	18	77	5
January 17–20	16	80	4
January 11–13	29	65	6
January 3–6	31	61	8

Just your impression, do you think the United States and its allies are losing ground in the Middle East, standing still, or making progress?

Losing ground 4%
Standing still 17
Making progress...................................75
No opinion.. 4

Selected National Trend

	Losing ground	Standing still	Making progress	No opinion
1991				
Jan. 30–				
Feb. 2	4%	15%	78%	3%
Jan. 23–26	3	18	74	5

Now that the United States has taken military action against Iraq, do you think the fighting will continue for just a few days, a matter of weeks, several months, or a year or more?

Days 2%
Weeks 15
Months...63
Year or more.......................................16
No opinion.. 4

Selected National Trend

	Days	Weeks	Months	Year
1991*				
Jan. 23–26	2%	12%	62%	19%
Jan. 19–22	2	29	49	12
Jan. 17–20	4	39	39	8
Jan. 16	17	39	23	5

*"No opinion" for these four polls is 5% (23–26), 8% (19–22), 10% (17–20), and 16% (16).

Now that the United States has taken military action against Iraq, do you think that the number of Americans killed and injured will be:

Less than 100?.................................... 6%
Several hundred?..................................21
Up to a thousand? 17
Several thousand?.................................39
Tens of thousands?............................... 8
No opinion.. 9

Some people think the United States should continue the military action against Iraq only until Iraq agrees to withdraw from Kuwait, in keeping with the United Nations Security Council resolutions. Others think the United States should go beyond the UN resolutions and continue fighting until Saddam Hussein is removed from power or his war-making capability is destroyed. Which comes closer to your view?

Stop after Iraq withdraws
   from Kuwait 34%
Continue until Hussein's war-making
   capability is destroyed........................62
No opinion...4

	Stop	Continue	No opinion
By Sex			
Male 32%	66%	2%
Female...................36	59	5
By Ethnic Background			
White....................34	63	3
Nonwhite 44	51	5
Black 25	63	12
By Education			
College Graduate 51	47	2
College Incomplete...38	60	2
High-School Graduate...............29	66	5
Less Than High-School Graduate 19	75	6
By Region			
East 42	55	3
Midwest..................34	61	5
South 25	71	4
West 38	58	4
By Age			
18–29 Years............35	62	3
30–49 Years............37	60	3
50 Years and Over.....30	65	5
By Household Income			
$50,000 and Over.....50	50	*
$30,000–$49,999....36	61	3
$20,000–$29,999....27	70	3
Under $20,000.........26	69	5
By Politics			
Republicans............31	68	1
Democrats 33	64	3
Independents...........40	54	6
By Religion			
Protestants 30	66	4
Catholics 42	55	3
By Political Ideology			
Liberal...................42	55	3
Moderate................37	61	2
Conservative..........31	67	2
By Bush Approval			
Approve.................32	65	3
Disapprove............45	47	8

*Less than 1%

Do you think the U.S. and allied forces should begin a ground attack soon to drive the Iraqis out of Kuwait, or should we hold off for now and continue to rely on air power to do the job?

Begin ground attack soon 17%
Hold off, rely on air power 74
No opinion...9

Regardless of whether you personally feel we should take action now, do you think the U.S. and allied forces will soon begin a ground offensive against Iraq, or not?

Yes...82%
No..12
No opinion...6

Note: With the ground war phase of Operation Desert Storm apparently drawing near, three quarters (74%) of Americans favor continuing to rely on air power to drive Iraq from Kuwait. Only 17% opt for an immediate ground offensive. Despite these attitudes, most (82%) think that the ground offensive will occur soon.

Most respondents also favor going beyond the mandate of the United Nations Security Council resolutions that call only for driving Iraq from Kuwait. Six in ten (62%) would like to continue fighting in order to force Saddam Hussein from power or destroy his war-making capability. Only one third (34%) thinks that the U.S. and allied forces should stop military action after Iraq withdraws from Kuwait, in keeping with the UN resolutions.

Perhaps in anticipation of the U.S. and allied ground offensive, respondents are readjusting their estimates of the number of U.S. casualties. Almost one half (47%) now thinks that several thousand or more Americans will be killed or injured—up from the 33% who gave this estimate in the first days of the war.

Support for President George Bush and his handling of the war remains very high, although slightly down from the polls of the last three weeks. His overall approval rating now stands at 79%, down slightly from the stratospheric high of 83% recorded on January 23–26. Approval of Bush's handling of the Persian Gulf situation is also at 79%, down from the record high of 85% registered one week ago, on January 30–February 2. And similarly, 76% think that the decision to go to war was not a mistake, down slightly from the 80% recorded in the latter survey.

Despite this slight downturn in support, Americans still think that the U.S. and allied forces are doing their job well. Three quarters (75%) of the public believe that the United States is making progress in the war against Iraq, with only 4% thinking that we are losing ground. This progress report is essentially unchanged from two surveys conducted over the past two weeks.

FEBRUARY 14
THE "JUST WAR" CONCEPT

Interviewing Date: 2/7–10/91
Survey #GO 122016

Some people feel that war is an outmoded way of settling differences between nations. Others feel that wars are sometimes necessary to settle differences. With which point of view do you agree?

Outmoded 17%
Sometimes necessary...........................80
No opinion.. 2

Selected National Trend

	Outmoded	Sometimes necessary	No opinion
1990	48%	49%	3%
1981	50	43	7
1975	45	46	9
1971	46	43	11

Here are six statements about the U.S. involvement in the Persian Gulf war. Please tell me if you agree strongly, agree somewhat, disagree somewhat, or disagree strongly with each statement:

The good that will be achieved by the military action will clearly outweigh the harm that may be done?

Agree strongly.....................................40%
Agree somewhat.................................32
Disagree somewhat 10
Disagree strongly 13
No opinion... 5

The military action has been undertaken by responsible authorities—that is, by a recognized leader of a nation or leaders of a group of nations?

Agree strongly.....................................61%
Agree somewhat.................................26
Disagree somewhat 6
Disagree strongly 3
No opinion... 4

The military action was taken as a last resort—that is, all attempts to resolve the conflict peacefully were exhausted?

Agree strongly.....................................56%
Agree somewhat.................................21
Disagree somewhat 9
Disagree strongly 11
No opinion... 3

There is a "just" cause for taking the military action—that is, a moral reason?

Agree strongly.....................................54%
Agree somewhat.................................26
Disagree somewhat 7

Disagree strongly...............................10
No opinion...3

There is a reasonable likelihood that the military action will succeed?

Agree strongly....................................76%
Agree somewhat...................................19
Disagree somewhat 2
Disagree strongly...............................2
No opinion...1

The military action is likely to avoid harming civilians where possible?

Agree strongly....................................43%
Agree somewhat...................................28
Disagree somewhat 13
Disagree strongly...............................13
No opinion...3

As I read a list of the wars the United States has been involved in, please tell me, for each, whether you think it to be a "just" war, or not:

	Yes	No	No opinion
World War II	89%	5%	6%
World War I	76	8	16
Revolutionary War	75	9	16
Persian Gulf war	74	21	5
Civil War	70	19	11
Korean War	49	32	19
Vietnam War	25	65	10

Note: The initial reaction to the Persian Gulf war by most Americans is that it is a "just" war, on a level with such earlier conflicts as the Revolutionary War, the Civil War, and World War I, and at this stage significantly more just than the Vietnam and Korean wars. However, there is less agreement that the conflict meets all six of the historic criteria for a just war put forth by St. Augustine and other theologians.

Three quarters of respondents (74%) believe that the Gulf war is a just one. World War II was the most just of all, so considered by 89%. By contrast, only 25% consider the Vietnam War to have been just, with 49% saying that the Korean War was just.

Despite Americans' willingness to classify the Gulf war as just on a general basis, not all

agree that it meets all six of the classic criteria. This lack of agreement occurs despite the fact that significant majorities agree with each criterion on an individual basis.

About seven out of ten (72%), for example, agree that "the good that will be achieved by the military action will clearly outweigh the harm that may be done." Similarly, 71% agree that "the military action is likely to avoid harming civilians where possible," and 77% agree that the military action was taken as a last resort.

Ninety-five percent agree that "there is a reasonable likelihood that the military action will succeed," and 87% agree that the military action has been undertaken by responsible authorities. Finally, 80% agree with the sixth criterion for a just war—that there is a moral reason for taking military action.

FEBRUARY 15
IRAQI PEACE PROPOSAL

Interviewing Date: 2/15/91
Survey #GO 122031

How closely have you followed the news today about Iraq's proposal to end the war in the Gulf and President Bush's reaction to that proposal? Would you say you have followed it very closely, somewhat closely, or not at all closely?

Very closely.......................................43%
Somewhat closely...............................43
Not at all closely................................13
No opinion...1

As a result of today's developments, are you more optimistic or less optimistic that there will be a quick end to the war in the Persian Gulf?

More optimistic..................................37%
Less optimistic...................................38
No change 18
No opinion...7

As you may know, Iraq made a proposal today to pull its troops out of Kuwait under certain conditions. Do you think it was a genuine attempt to end the war, or do you think it was just an attempt by Iraq to gain political or military advantage?

Genuine attempt to end war.......................7%
Attempt to gain an advantage..................86
No opinion...7

Do you think President Bush was correct in dismissing the Iraqi proposal, or do you think he should have been more receptive to the proposal than he was?

Correct in dismissing proposal................79%
Should have been more receptive.............13
No opinion...8

Should the U.S. government have accepted Iraq's proposal in its entirety, should it have rejected it in its entirety, or should the United States have been willing to discuss certain of the conditions for Iraq's withdrawal?

Accept it in its entirety...........................1%
Reject it in its entirety...........................55
Discuss certain conditions.....................36
No opinion...8

Now I am going to read you a list of some specific conditions Iraq has put forward for its withdrawal from Kuwait. As I read each item, please tell me whether you think the United States and its allies should accept or reject it as a condition for Iraqi withdrawal from Kuwait:

A total and comprehensive cease-fire on land, air, and sea before the withdrawal would begin?

Accept...34%
Reject...60
No opinion...6

Israel must withdraw from Palestine and all occupied Arab territories or face UN sanctions?

Accept...22%
Reject...64
No opinion...14

The United States and its allies must pay for all reconstruction of war damages in Iraq?

Accept...10%
Reject...88
No opinion...2

The United Nations must abolish all boycotts, embargoes, and sanctions against Iraq?

Accept...26%
Reject...65
No opinion...9

Within one month of the cease-fire all allied forces, weapons, and equipment brought into the region must be totally withdrawn, including weapons provided to Israel?

Accept...24%
Reject...71
No opinion...5

Establish an arrangement whereby the government of Kuwait is based on the people's will rather than on the rights of the exiled emir's family?

Accept...55%
Reject...30
No opinion...15

All Iraq's foreign debt will be canceled?

Accept...11%
Reject...84
No opinion...5

The Gulf region should be declared a zone free of foreign military bases or presence?

Accept...27%
Reject...63
No opinion...10

Note: The initial reaction of the American public to Iraq's February 15 peace proposal is strongly supportive of President George Bush and the allied coalition's rejection of the proposal. At the same time, a special Gallup Poll shows that more than one third of respondents think that the United States and its allies should have been willing to discuss conditions for Iraq's withdrawal, as outlined in the proposal.

About eight in ten (79%) think that Bush's immediate dismissal of the Iraqi peace proposal was correct, and 86% endorse the contention that it was not a genuine attempt to end the war but rather an attempt by Iraq to gain political or military advantage. However, as many as 36% think that the United States and its allies should have been willing to discuss some of the conditions for withdrawal outlined in the Iraqi proposal.

Respondents are quickest to dismiss the Iraqi condition that war damage should be repaired by the United States or that Iraqi debts should be written off. Both of these are acceptable to only 10% and 11%, respectively. One third (34%) is willing to accept a total cease-fire before the withdrawal would begin. One fourth would agree that dropping sanctions (26%), removing all forces from the area (24%), and declaring the Gulf area free from any military forces from outside the region (27%) would be acceptable as conditions. One fifth (22%) would accept a condition involving Israeli withdrawal from Palestine and the occupied Arab territories.

The Iraqi proposal also included a condition that called for Kuwait's government to be determined on the basis of the people's will and not on the rights of the exiled emir's family. Some 55% agree that this would be acceptable as a condition for Iraq's withdrawal, although it may be questionable whether a true democracy in Kuwait is what Saddam Hussein has in mind.

FEBRUARY 20
PERSIAN GULF SITUATION

Interviewing Date: 2/14–17/91
Survey #GO 122017

There are several peace initiatives currently being proposed for ending the Persian Gulf war. If Saddam Hussein agrees to withdraw all Iraqi troops from Kuwait, *would you favor or oppose an immediate cease-fire by the United States and its allies?*

Favor 71%
Oppose...24
No opinion..5

Would you favor or oppose a temporary cease-fire by the United States and its allies as a show of good faith and to provide time to arrange a settlement with Saddam Hussein?

Favor 36%
Oppose...59
No opinion..5

Do you favor or oppose the U.S. use of tactical nuclear weapons in the Persian Gulf war?

Favor 28%
Oppose...66
No opinion..6

	Favor	Oppose	No opinion
By Sex			
Male 32%		65%	3%
Female..................25		67	8
By Ethnic Background			
White....................29		66	5
Nonwhite 31		64	5
Black 26		63	11
By Education			
College Graduate 23		71	6
College Incomplete...29		66	5
High-School Graduate..............28		66	6
Less Than High-School Graduate 37		57	6
By Region			
East 26		69	5
Midwest................27		70	3
South 32		61	7
West 28		65	7

By Age
18–29 Years............24	73	3
30–49 Years............27	67	6
50 Years and Over.....33	60	7

By Household Income
$50,000 and Over.....28	69	3
$30,000–$49,999....27	68	5
$20,000–$29,999....33	59	8
Under $20,000.........26	68	6

By Politics
Republicans............31	64	5
Democrats 30	63	7
Independents...........25	70	5

By Religion
Protestants 30	63	7
Catholics 30	68	2

By Political Ideology
Liberal....................26	71	3
Moderate................33	62	5
Conservative...........29	64	7

By Bush Approval
Approve.................30	65	5
Disapprove.............18	75	7

In terms of sheer destructive power, do you think tactical nuclear weapons are a lot more destructive, about as destructive, or not as destructive as the conventional weapons we are currently using?

A lot more destructive............................77%
About as destructive 10
Not as destructive 3
No opinion.......................................10

Do you favor changing U.S. policy in order to allow women to serve in combat roles, or not?

Yes..38%
No...56
No opinion.. 6

	Yes	No	No opinion
By Sex			
Male.....................43%	50%	7%
Female..................34	61	5

By Ethnic Background
White....................40	54	6
Nonwhite 40	53	7
Black 29	66	5

By Education
College Graduate 42	49	9
College Incomplete...45	50	5
High-School Graduate..............35	58	7
Less Than High-School Graduate 34	65	1

By Region
East 37	57	6
Midwest.................38	57	5
South 39	54	7
West 39	55	6

By Age
18–29 Years............49	45	6
30–49 Years............42	52	6
50 Years and Over.....28	67	5

By Household Income
$50,000 and Over.....40	55	5
$30,000–$49,999....40	55	5
$20,000–$29,999....40	54	6
Under $20,000.........38	56	6

By Politics
Republicans............40	55	5
Democrats 34	60	6
Independents...........42	51	7

By Religion
Protestants 38	57	5
Catholics 38	58	4

By Political Ideology
Liberal...................45	50	5
Moderate................50	39	11
Conservative..........34	62	4

By Bush Approval
Approve.................38	57	5
Disapprove.............40	51	9

For each of the following, please tell me if this is something you are doing more often or less often since the war began on January 16:

	More often	Less often	Same (vol.)	No opinion
Watching television news	77%	6%	17%	*
Reading daily newspaper	42	7	49	2
Listening to news on the radio	61	8	30	1

*Less than 1%

Do you think that CNN and the networks should broadcast reports and film from Iraq even though they are controlled and censored by the Iraqi government, or not?

Yes...59%
No...34
No opinion.. 7

Do you think the Bush administration and the military have been cooperative enough in providing information to the news organizations, or not?

Yes...80%
No...16
No opinion.. 4

Selected National Trend

	Yes	No	No opinion
1991			
January 17–20........	84%	11%	5%

Note: Seven out of ten Americans (71%) would support an immediate cease-fire in the Persian Gulf if Saddam Hussein agrees to withdraw all Iraqi troops from Kuwait, according to the latest Gallup Poll. In general, these polls since the war began one month ago have shown that more than three out of four respondents disagree with President George Bush's hard-line policy of no negotiations and no conditions on Iraqi troop withdrawal. They tend to favor actions that might forestall an all-out ground war. However, when given a choice in previous polls, the majority of Americans surveyed also have said that the goals of the U.S.-led coalition in the Gulf ideally should include forcing Hussein from power or destroying Iraq's war-making potential.

In the most recent poll, 36% support the idea of a temporary cease-fire designed to allow Hussein to negotiate a settlement to the war—an idea that President Bush and other coalition leaders have rejected. This is about the same percentage who, in earlier Gallup Polls, suggested that the coalition pay more attention to the proposed Iraqi peace plans and be willing to negotiate or accept certain conditions for Iraqi withdrawal.

FEBRUARY 21
VICE PRESIDENT QUAYLE

Interviewing Date: 2/14–17/91
Survey #GO 122017

Asked of registered voters: If President Bush runs for reelection in 1992, do you think he should keep Dan Quayle as his vice presidential running mate or choose someone else?

Keep Quayle......................................38%
Choose someone else 53
No opinion.. 9

Republicans and Those Who Lean Republican

Keep Quayle......................................50%
Choose someone else 43
No opinion.. 7

Asked of registered voters: If President Bush were to choose a new vice presidential running mate for 1992, which of the following would you like to see him choose?

	All voters	Republicans and those who lean Republican
Robert Dole	21%	21%
James Baker.......................	20	21
Colin Powell.......................	18	18

Dick Cheney	17	20
Jack Kemp	10	9
Other; none; no opinion	14	11

Note: Vice President Dan Quayle continues to be a potential electoral liability for George Bush, but replacing him may create as many problems as it solves. The latest Gallup Poll, consistent with previous poll results, shows that voters favor dropping Quayle from the GOP ticket in 1992 by 53% to 38%. Among Republican and Republican-leaning voters, however, opinion is closely divided: about as many favor keeping Quayle (50%) as favor replacing him with someone else (43%).

FEBRUARY 21
DEMOCRATIC PRESIDENTIAL CANDIDATES

Interviewing Date: 2/14–17/91
Survey #GO 122017

Asked of registered voters: If George Bush runs for reelection in 1992, in general are you more likely to vote for Bush or for the Democratic party's candidate for president?

Bush	54%
Democratic candidate	33
Undecided; no opinion	13

Asked of registered Democrats and those who lean Democratic: Please tell me whether you have a favorable or unfavorable opinion of each of the following Democrats who might run for president in 1992:

	Favorable	Unfavorable*
Mario Cuomo	42%	19%
George McGovern	40	31
Richard Gephardt	38	17
Jesse Jackson	36	50
Lloyd Bentsen	35	25
Albert Gore	29	18
Sam Nunn	29	17
Bill Bradley	28	11
George Mitchell	25	9
Jay Rockefeller	23	22

Douglas Wilder	14	12
Bob Kerrey	14	12
Bill Clinton	13	12

*The missing remainder for each man—adding to 100%—is "heard of," "not heard of," and "no opinion," thus not strictly part of this question.

Asked of registered Democrats and those who lean Democratic: Please tell me which one of these persons you would like to see nominated as the Democratic party's candidate for president in 1992. And who would be your second choice?

	First choice	Second choice	First & second choices combined
Cuomo	18%	6%	24%
Jackson	12	8	20
McGovern	9	7	16
Gephardt	8	7	15
Bentsen	6	10	16
Gore	6	5	11
Nunn	6	5	11
Rockefeller	5	3	8
Bradley	4	6	10
Mitchell	4	3	7
Wilder	2	2	4
Clinton	2	2	4
Kerrey	1	2	3
No opinion	17	34	–

Note: The Democratic party's prospects for recapturing the White House in 1992 are not so bleak as President George Bush's 80% current approval rating might suggest. While there is little doubt that he would be reelected today, the next presidential election is still a year and one half away, with ample time for the political climate to change. And even today, at the peak of his popularity, Bush wins support for reelection from only a bare majority of voters. In a test election against the Democratic party's yet-unknown candidate, Bush leads by 54% to 33%, with 13% expressing no preference.

To win their first presidential election since 1976, however, the Democrats must overcome an even bigger obstacle than George Bush: themselves. A new Gallup Poll focusing on 1992 suggests that the Democrats must offset certain areas of weakness to avoid losing their fourth consecutive presidential election.

• Failure to Attract Male Voters. The gender gap has yet to work to the Democrats' advantage at the presidential level because their candidates have failed to win enough votes from women to make up for the Republicans' margin of victory among men. In the current poll, Bush leads among male voters by a 2-to-1 margin (60% to 28%). Among women the vote is much more closely divided, with 49% favoring Bush and 38% favoring the Democrat.

• A Racially Divided Electorate. Blacks remain the most reliably Democratic-voting group in the population, but their numbers are too small to elect a presidential candidate on their own. And if a Democratic candidate goes too far in addressing the concerns of blacks during the campaign, he risks alienating the white majority. In the current poll, Bush has a 2-to-1 lead among white voters (59% versus 28%).

• Lack of Appeal among Younger Voters. The Democratic party has largely been replaced by the GOP as the party of the young. In the current poll, Bush wins the under-30 vote by a lopsided margin of 66% to 25%; the president also has a big lead among those age 30 to 49 (59% versus 32%). Only among those over age 50 is the Democratic party's candidate competitive; 44% prefer Bush, while 38% favor the Democrat.

• A Perception of Being Too Liberal. The loss of many conservative voters to the GOP, particularly in the South, has shifted the Democratic party to the left, while the country as a whole has drifted to the right. Unless the Democrats can attract more votes among self-described conservatives, they seem doomed to failure at the presidential level. Currently, Bush holds a 3-to-1 lead among conservatives (65% versus 24%), while the liberal vote divides about evenly between Bush (45%) and the Democratic nominee (47%).

FEBRUARY 22
PERSIAN GULF SITUATION

Interviewing Date: 2/22/91
Survey #GO 122030

How closely have you followed the news today about the Iraqi-Soviet proposal to end the war in the Gulf and President Bush's reaction to that proposal? Would you say you have followed it very closely, somewhat closely, or not at all closely?

Very closely.......................................39%
Somewhat closely...............................39
Not at all closely................................22
No opinion...*

*Less than 1%

In response to the Iraqi-Soviet proposal, President Bush has put forth a plan setting a deadline of noon tomorrow [February 23] for Iraq to begin an immediate and unconditional withdrawal from Kuwait. All things considered, do you approve or disapprove of President Bush's plan in response to the Iraqi-Soviet proposal?

Approve...84%
Disapprove...10
No opinion...6

Regardless of whether you approve or disapprove of President Bush's response, do you think President Bush should have given Saddam Hussein a longer period of time to begin the withdrawal, or not?

Yes...12%
No...84
No opinion...4

And is President Bush correct in insisting that Iraq comply with all UN resolutions relating to Iraq's withdrawal from Kuwait, or should Bush be willing to negotiate some of the conditions?

Is correct..72%
Should negotiate 22
No opinion...6

If Iraq does not meet the noon Saturday [February 23] deadline, do you think the United States and its allies should start the ground war immediately or just continue with the air attacks?

Start ground war 41%
Continue air attacks only......................46
Cease fire, stop war (volunteered).............. 2
No opinion.......................................11

All in all, do you think President Bush has been too willing to negotiate to end the war, not willing enough, or do you think he has been about right in his willingness to negotiate to end the war?

Too willing.. 4%
Not willing enough.............................11
About right...82
No opinion.. 3

Finally, do you think tonight we are on the brink of a peaceful settlement to the war, or do you think we are on the brink of the beginning of the ground war?

Peaceful settlement 19%
Beginning of the ground war...................69
Neither (volunteered)............................ 3
No opinion.. 9

Note: As the world watches and waits, a special Gallup/CNN Poll conducted on February 22 shows that the majority of Americans is convinced that we are heading for a ground war. Hours away from President George Bush's noon deadline on February 23 for Iraq's withdrawal from Kuwait, 69% say that we are on the brink of the ground war, with only 19% willing to say that we are on the brink of a peaceful settlement.

There is little doubt in the minds of the public that President Bush is pursuing the right course in his dealings with Iraq. Eighty-four percent approve of his response to the latest Iraqi-Soviet proposal. Another 84% say that Bush did the right thing in setting the deadline of noon on February 23 for Saddam Hussein to begin withdrawal; only 12% think that Hussein should have been given a longer period of time.

There is slightly more doubt about Bush's hard-line position that Iraq comply with all of the UN resolutions and withdraw without conditions. Seventy-two percent say that the president is correct in insisting on a truly unconditional withdrawal, while 22% want him

to be more willing to negotiate some of the conditions.

Thus, there emerges a picture of an American public strongly behind their president and his hard-line dealings with Iraq, despite the fact that the majority (69%) thinks that a ground war is much more imminent as the deadline approaches.

FEBRUARY 22
PRESIDENT BUSH/PERSIAN GULF SITUATION

Interviewing Date: 2/24/91
Survey #GO 122029

Do you approve or disapprove of the U.S. decision to start the ground war against the Iraqis in Kuwait?

Approve...84%
Disapprove...11
No opinion.. 5

Do you think President Bush should have waited longer to allow time for Soviet and other diplomatic efforts to end the war, or do you think he was right to start the ground war when he did?

Should have waited..............................14%
Right to start ground war 81
No opinion.. 5

Some people think that the United States and its allies should continue the military action against Iraq only until Iraq is driven from Kuwait, in keeping with the United Nations resolutions. Others feel that the United States and its allies should go beyond the UN resolutions and continue fighting until Saddam Hussein is removed from power or his war-making capability is destroyed. Which comes closer to your view?

Stop after Iraq is driven from Kuwait 24%
Continue until Hussein's war-making
  capability is destroyed.......................72
No opinion.. 4

Selected National Trend

1991	Stop	Continue	No opinion
February 7–10	34%	62%	4%

How likely do you think it is that Saddam Hussein will remain a military threat to the region after his forces are driven from Kuwait? Do you think it is very likely, somewhat likely, not too likely, or not at all likely?

Very likely 29%
Somewhat likely 23
Not too likely..................................22
Not at all likely................................21
No opinion.. 5

Note: An overwhelming majority of Americans (84%) approves of President George Bush's February 23 decision to begin the ground war against Iraq without waiting any longer for possible diplomatic solutions. Only 14% say that he should have waited longer to allow time for Soviet and other diplomatic efforts to end the war.

Respondents now are more insistent than ever that the objective of the war should be to remove Saddam Hussein from power or destroy Iraq's war-making capability—not simply to get Iraq out of Kuwait, as mandated by the UN resolutions. Seventy-two percent say that the United States and its allies should go beyond the UN resolutions. Only 24% say that the allies should fight only until Iraq is out of Kuwait. These attitudes are more hawkish than two weeks ago (February 7–10), when opinion divided 62% to 34% in favor of going beyond the UN mandate.

FEBRUARY 28
PUERTO RICO

Interviewing Date: 2/21–24/91
Special Survey; International Division of Gallup USA

Suppose that the people of the Commonwealth of Puerto Rico voted to apply for statehood. If that happened, *would you support or oppose Puerto Rico becoming the fifty-first state?*

Support..60%
Oppose..22
No opinion...18

Now, suppose that the people of Puerto Rico voted instead for complete independence from the United States. If that happened, would you support or oppose the United States granting full independence to the Commonwealth of Puerto Rico?

Support..67%
Oppose..16
No opinion...17

Note: As the prospects improve for a Puerto Rican plebiscite on the commonwealth's future status, a new Gallup survey on the mainland indicates that either statehood or independence is acceptable to the public at large.

The prospect of statehood for Puerto Rico is supported by 60% of respondents and opposed by 22%. Interestingly, the proportion of the public favoring statehood for Puerto Rico exceeds the proportion (50%) that would support statehood for Washington, DC, as cited by *U.S. News & World Report* (February 18, 1991).

However, if a Puerto Rican plebiscite showed that the populace would prefer full independence to statehood or continued commonwealth status, over two thirds (67%) of respondents say that they would support granting full independence to the island, while only 16% would oppose this move. Prior research has shown that Puerto Ricans themselves are split on the issue, with the majority favoring either statehood or a continuation of commonwealth status and with only a small minority endorsing independence.

MARCH 3
PERSIAN GULF SITUATION

Interviewing Date: 2/14–17/91
Survey #GO 122017

The following three questions were asked of those with children between the ages of 5 and 17: Have you made a special effort to talk to your child about his or her concerns about the Persian Gulf war, or not?

	Yes
National	71%

Since the war in the Persian Gulf began, which, if any, of the following has your child done:*

	Yes
Told you his or her fears or worries about the war?	49%
Had difficulty sleeping?	5
Had nightmares about the war?	4
Asked to talk to you about his or her concerns about the war?	45
None of the above; no opinion	38

*Multiple responses were given.

Since the war in the Persian Gulf began, have you limited the amount of time your child spends watching news reports about the war on television?

	Yes
National	23%

For each of the following, please tell me if this is something you are doing more often or less often since the war began on January 16:

	More often	Less often	Same (vol.)	No opinion
Watching television news	77%	6%	17%	*
Reading daily newspaper	43	7	49	1
Reading weekly news magazine	25	20	51	4
Listening to news on the radio	61	8	30	1
Going to movies or renting a video	10	33	54	3
Watching entertainment programs on television	17	35	47	1

*Less than 1%

Since the war in the Persian Gulf began, have you:*

	Yes
Talked seriously with friends about the war?	87%
Displayed yellow ribbon on clothes, around home, or on car?	52
Stayed up or gotten up earlier to follow war coverage?	50
Displayed the U.S. flag?	49
Prayed more than you usually do?	47
Become more interested in spiritual values in life?	38
Mailed letter, Valentine, or care package to someone in Gulf?	27
Bought T-shirt or item with message about the war?	19
Gone to church more often?	15
Lost sleep or had nightmares?	12
Bought map of Middle East or Persian Gulf region?	10
Signed up for cable to watch CNN's war coverage?	5
Participated in a demonstration for or against the war?	5
Bought book about Middle East or Persian Gulf region?	4
Missed work or school to follow war coverage?	3
Started seeing or increased visits to therapist such as a psychiatrist, psychologist, or social worker?	1
Bought a gas mask?	**
None of the above; no opinion	3

*Multiple responses were given.
**Less than 1%

Since the war began, have you postponed or delayed buying:*

	Yes
A new car?	8%
A new house?	6
A major appliance, home electronic item, or household furniture?	10
None of the above; no opinion	85

*Multiple responses were given.

And, since the war began, have you and your family made a special effort to spend less money and save more, or have your spending patterns not changed much?

Spend less and save more	20%
Spending patterns have not changed	78
No opinion	2

Since the war began, have you postponed or canceled:

	Yes	No	No opinion
A vacation for you or your family?	11%	85%	4%
A business trip?	4	91	5

Are you more afraid of traveling by air now than you were before the war began, or not?

Yes	44%
No	54
No opinion	2

Note: Three quarters of U.S. adults (77%) have been watching more television news; one half has displayed a yellow ribbon (52%), flown the American flag (49%), or prayed more than usual (47%). A new Gallup Mirror of America survey finds that the war in the Persian Gulf has had a major impact on many aspects of American life. The poll also shows that Operation Desert Storm has resulted in many parents spending time to talk with their children about the war (71%). And for some respondents the war has prompted less spending and increased savings (20%).

MARCH 6
PRESIDENT BUSH

Interviewing Date: 2/28–3/3/91
Survey #GO 122019

Do you approve or disapprove of the way George Bush is handling his job as president?

Approve	89%
Disapprove	8
No opinion	3

How strongly would you say you approve or disapprove? Would you say very strongly or not so strongly?

Approve	89%
Very strongly	74
Not so strongly	14
No opinion	1
Disapprove	8
Very strongly	5
Not so strongly	3
No opinion	*
No opinion	3

*Less than 1%

Do you approve or disapprove of the way George Bush is handling our foreign policy—that is, our relations with other nations?

Approve	84%
Disapprove	11
No opinion	5

Do you approve or disapprove of the way George Bush is handling our domestic problems—that is, our problems here at home?

Approve	51%
Disapprove	47
No opinion	2

Presidential Performance Ratings
(At Highest Point of Approval)

Bush .... March 1991	89%
Truman .... June 1945	87
Roosevelt.............. January 1942	84
Kennedy.................... May 1961	83
Eisenhower.......... December 1956	79
Johnson .... Feb.–March 1964	79
Carter..................... March 1977	75
Ford..................... August 1974	71
Reagan .... May 1981, May 1986	68
Nixon.............. November 1969, January 1973	67

Note: In the wake of victory in the Persian Gulf, George Bush has received the highest approval rating of any president since the Gallup Poll began to track presidents' performance in office in 1938. Eighty-nine percent of those surveyed in a new poll approve of the way that Bush is handling his job. The previous record of 87% was accorded Harry Truman after Germany's surrender in 1945.

Revealing the intensity of Bush's support, the survey shows that three quarters of all respondents (74%) strongly approve of his performance—the highest "strong" approval figure ever measured by Gallup. However, he receives much lower marks for his handling of domestic issues (51%), suggesting that his stratospheric approval levels will likely drop as the impact of the war fades.

Bush's approval rating tops the previous highs registered by such popular presidents as Franklin Roosevelt (84%, one month after the bombing of Pearl Harbor); John Kennedy (83%, immediately after the Bay of Pigs invasion); and Dwight Eisenhower (79%, immediately following his reelection to the presidency).

MARCH 7
SATISFACTION INDEX/PERSONAL FINANCES

Interviewing Date: 2/28–3/3/91
Survey #GO 122019

In general, are you satisfied or dissatisfied with the way things are going in the United States at this time?

Satisfied... 66%
Dissatisfied.. 31
No opinion.. 3

Selected National Trend

1991	Satisfied	Dis-satisfied	No opinion
February 14–17	54%	40%	6%
January 17–20	62	33	5
January 3–6	32	61	7
1990			
December 13–16	33	64	3
November 1–4	31	64	5
October 25–28	31	66	3
October 11–14	29	67	4

We are interested in how people's financial situation may have changed. Would you say that you are financially better off now than you were a year ago, or are you financially worse off now?

Better... 37%
Worse... 28
Same (volunteered)............................. 34
No opinion.. 1

Selected National Trend

1991	Better	Worse	Same	No opinion
Feb. 14–17	37%	28%	35%	*
Jan. 11–13	26	33	39	2
Jan. 3–6	35	32	32	1
1990				
Dec. 13–16	38	36	26	*
Oct. 25–28	38	35	26	1

*Less than 1%

Looking ahead, do you expect that at this time next year you will be financially better off than now or worse off than now?

Better				64%
Worse				9
Same (volunteered)				20
No opinion				7

Selected National Trend

	Better	Worse	Same	No opinion
1991				
Feb. 14–17	57%	15%	20%	8%
Jan. 11–13	41	25	21	13
Jan. 3–6	52	18	20	10
1990				
Dec. 13–16	58	18	17	7
Oct. 25–28	50	27	15	8

I am going to read you a list of institutions in American society. Please tell me how much confidence you, yourself, have in each one—a great deal, quite a lot, some, or very little:*

	Great deal	Quite a lot	Some	Very little
United States	58%	33%	8%	1%
Military	52	33	11	3
Presidency	38	34	21	5
Church and organized religion	33	26	26	12
Supreme Court	21	27	36	10
Public schools	20	24	36	17
Television	15	17	42	24
Newspapers	14	23	43	17
Banks	12	20	46	19
Organized labor	11	14	42	25
Congress	11	19	44	21
Big business	11	15	45	22
Soviet Union	5	10	45	31

*"None" (volunteered) and "no opinion"—at no more than 6%—have been omitted.

Selected National Trend
(Percent Saying "Great Deal" or "Quite a Lot")

	1990	1989	1988	1987
Military	68%	63%	58%	61%
Church and organized religion	56	52	59	61
Supreme Court	47	46	56	52
Public schools	45	43	49	50
Newspapers	39	–	36	31
Banks	36	42	49	51
Organized labor	27	–	26	26
Television	25	–	27	28
Big business	25	–	25	–
Congress	24	32	35	–

Do you approve or disapprove of the way the following people handled the situation in the Persian Gulf region: Soviet Premier Mikhail Gorbachev; Allied commander General Norman Schwarzkopf; Chairman of the Joint Chiefs of Staff General Colin Powell; Defense Secretary Dick Cheney; Secretary of State James Baker; the U.S. news media covering the war; the U.S. Congress?

	Approve	Disapprove	No opinion
Schwarzkopf	88%	5%	7%
Powell	87	4	9
Cheney	85	5	10
Baker	84	7	9
Congress	79	15	6
News media	71	27	2
Gorbachev	44	47	9

Note: The success of U.S. and allied forces in the Persian Gulf war has sharply elevated the mood of America, boosted optimism that better financial times lie ahead, and dramatically increased confidence in the U.S. military. The current level of satisfaction with the way things are going in this country matches the highest rating previously recorded by Gallup on this measure in March 1986. Two thirds of Americans (66%) now say that they are satisfied, thus continuing the sharp upswing measured immediately after the war began on January 16.

The major political and military figures involved in the war receive very high approval ratings. General Norman Schwarzkopf draws 88%, closely followed by Chairman of the

Joint Chiefs of Staff Colin Powell (87%), Secretary of Defense Dick Cheney (85%), and Secretary of State James Baker (84%). Seventy-nine percent of the public even approve of the role that the U.S. Congress played in the war. Assessment of the role of the press in covering the conflict is mixed, but still much more positive than negative. Seventy-one percent say that they approve, while 27% disapprove.

The new poll also shows that the military now receives the highest confidence ratings of any institution since Gallup began these measurements two decades ago. Fifty-two percent say that they have a great deal of confidence in the military, and another 33% have quite a lot. This represents a substantial increase from last year, when 37% replied a great deal and 31% quite a lot.

Despite criticisms aimed at the media, confidence in television actually rose by 7 percentage points to 32% from Gallup's 1990 measurement. Confidence in Congress is also up slightly, to 30%—6 percentage points over 1990. The big loser over time continues to be banks, where confidence is now at the lowest levels since 1979. The war had little effect either way on confidence in newspapers.

MARCH 13
PRESIDENT BUSH

Interviewing Date: 3/7–10/91
Survey #GO 122020

Do you approve or disapprove of the way George Bush is handling his job as president?

Approve...87%
Disapprove....................................... 8
No opinion....................................... 5

What do you think is President Bush's greatest achievement to date?

	Mar. 1991	Nov. 1990	July 1990	Feb. 1990
Persian Gulf	80%	17%	–	–
Panama	*	2	3	18
Drug war	*	3	4	9
USSR; Gorbachev	*	5	24	7
Foreign policy	4	9	9	7
Getting elected	*	1	1	3
Leadership	3	4	1	2
Eastern Europe	*	1	4	2
Abortion stand	*	*	1	1
Economy; budget	*	2	1	1
Taxes	*	1	*	1
Education	*	1	–	–
Status quo	*	1	–	–
No war	*	*	–	–
Supreme Court appointments	*	*	–	–
Other	2	9	12	9
Nothing	4	15	13	6
No opinion	5	29	27	36

*Less than 1%

Now, let me ask you about some specific problems facing the country. As I read off each one, would you tell me whether you approve or disapprove of the way President Bush is handling that problem:

Environmental issues?

Approve...52%
Disapprove.......................................38
No opinion.......................................10

Selected National Trend

	Approve	Dis-approve	No opinion
October 1990	45%	45%	10%
July 1990	42	46	12
September 1989	46	40	14

Foreign policy?

Approve...79%
Disapprove.......................................11
No opinion.......................................10

Selected National Trend

	Approve	Dis-approve	No opinion
October 1990	61%	29%	10%
July 1990	62	26	12
November 1989	65	21	14
March 1989	62	15	23

Poverty and homelessness?

Approve	27%
Disapprove	65
No opinion	8

Selected National Trend

	Approve	Dis-approve	No opinion
July 1990	30%	62%	8%
November 1989	30	59	11
August 1989	33	53	14

Education policy?

Approve	53%
Disapprove	40
No opinion	7

Selected National Trend

	Approve	Dis-approve	No opinion
July 1990	46%	41%	13%
November 1989	53	35	12

Situation in Eastern Europe?

Approve	70%
Disapprove	12
No opinion	18

Selected National Trend

	Approve	Dis-approve	No opinion
July 1990	63%	20%	17%
January 1990	73	13	14
November 1989	63	16	21

Drug problem?

Approve	50%
Disapprove	44
No opinion	6

Selected National Trend

	Approve	Dis-approve	No opinion
July 1990	46%	48%	6%
January 1990	69	24	7
November 1989	53	41	6
September 1989	72	18	10

Abortion issue?

Approve	46%
Disapprove	33
No opinion	21

Selected National Trend

	Approve	Dis-approve	No opinion
July 1990	36%	44%	20%
November 1989	38	45	17
July 1989	43	35	22

Situation in Central America?

Approve	52%
Disapprove	21
No opinion	27

Selected National Trend

	Approve	Dis-approve	No opinion
July 1990	42%	39%	19%
January 1990	66	21	13
November 1989	40	39	21
March 1989	37	33	30

Relations with the Soviet Union?

Approve	86%
Disapprove	10
No opinion	4

	Approve	Dis- approve	No opinion
October 1990	84%	11%	5%
July 1990	82	12	6
November 1989	81	11	8
March 1989	70	10	20

Savings and Loan crisis?

Approve	28%
Disapprove	56
No opinion	16

Race relations?

Approve	63%
Disapprove	26
No opinion	11

Crime?

Approve	47%
Disapprove	44
No opinion	9

Availability of health care?

Approve	34%
Disapprove	57
No opinion	9

Situation in the Middle East?

Approve	90%
Disapprove	8
No opinion	2

Energy situation in this country?

Approve	47%
Disapprove	42
No opinion	11

How would you rate President George Bush's performance on each of the following? Would you say his performance has been excellent, good, only fair, or poor on:

Making good appointments to cabinet and other positions?

Excellent	18%
Good	47
Fair	22
Poor	5
No opinion	8

1990	Excel- lent	Good	Fair	Poor	No opinion
Nov.	8%	37%	37%	11%	7%
July	5	40	36	7	12
Feb.	7	42	32	6	13

Being an efficient manager of government?

Excellent	22%
Good	52
Fair	20
Poor	4
No opinion	2

1990	Excel- lent	Good	Fair	Poor	No opinion
Nov.	7%	40%	37%	13%	3%
July	7	45	33	11	4
Feb.	10	52	28	5	5

Developing programs to address the pressing problems America faces?

Excellent	8%
Good	41
Fair	35
Poor	13
No opinion	3

1990	Excel- lent	Good	Fair	Poor	No opinion
Nov.	5%	29%	40%	23%	3%
July	4	31	42	19	4
Feb.	8	39	35	13	5

Communicating his ideas to the American public?

Excellent..35%
Good...44
Fair...15
Poor...5
No opinion..1

Selected National Trend

1990	Excellent	Good	Fair	Poor	No opinion
Nov.	12%	41%	33%	13%	1%
July	9	46	30	13	2
Feb.	16	49	26	7	2

Following through on his ideas and initiatives?

Excellent..23%
Good...51
Fair...19
Poor...5
No opinion..2

Selected National Trend

1990	Excellent	Good	Fair	Poor	No opinion
Nov.	5%	34%	38%	20%	3%
July	4	36	38	18	4
Feb.	10	45	32	7	6

Working effectively with Congress?

Excellent..18%
Good...51
Fair...23
Poor...4
No opinion..4

Selected National Trend

1990	Excellent	Good	Fair	Poor	No opinion
Nov.	5%	31%	39%	22%	3%
July	5	46	35	7	7
Feb.	7	46	34	6	7

Being a good representative or symbol of the United States?

Excellent..45%
Good...42
Fair...9
Poor...3
No opinion..1

Selected National Trend

1990	Excellent	Good	Fair	Poor	No opinion
Nov.	19%	44%	27%	9%	1%
July	22	49	22	6	1
Feb.	24	52	18	4	2

Being an inspirational leader to the American people?

Excellent..44%
Good...40
Fair...11
Poor...4
No opinion..1

Selected National Trend

1990	Excellent	Good	Fair	Poor	No opinion
Nov.	10%	37%	32%	20%	1%
July	10	45	30	13	2
Feb.	17	47	27	8	1

Here is a list of some problems and responsibilities facing the president and his administration. Do you think George Bush is making progress or is not making progress on handling each of these different problems:

Keeping the nation out of war?

Making progress...................................64%
Not making progress............................31
No opinion..5

Selected National Trend

	Making progress	Not making progress	No opinion
1990			
November	.37%	55%	8%
February	.77	17	6

Keeping America prosperous?

Making progress	60%
Not making progress	35
No opinion	5

Selected National Trend

	Making progress	Not making progress	No opinion
1990			
November	.41%	54%	5%
February	.59	33	8

Increasing respect for the United States abroad?

Making progress	87%
Not making progress	8
No opinion	5

Selected National Trend

	Making progress	Not making progress	No opinion
1990			
November	.62%	32%	6%
February	.73	21	6

Improving educational standards?

Making progress	52%
Not making progress	41
No opinion	7

Selected National Trend

	Making progress	Not making progress	No opinion
1990			
November	.42%	48%	10%
February	.48	44	8

Improving the quality of the environment?

Making progress	54%
Not making progress	38
No opinion	8

Selected National Trend

	Making progress	Not making progress	No opinion
1990			
November	.50%	43%	7%
February	.46	45	9

Improving the lot of minorities and the poor?

Making progress	38%
Not making progress	53
No opinion	9

Selected National Trend

	Making progress	Not making progress	No opinion
1990			
November	.28%	62%	10%
February	.35	54	11

Reducing the crime rate in the United States?

Making progress	41%
Not making progress	52
No opinion	7

Selected National Trend

	Making progress	Not making progress	No opinion
1990			
November	.27%	65%	8%
February	.37	54	9

Reducing the federal budget deficit?

Making progress	28%
Not making progress	63
No opinion	9

Selected National Trend

	Making progress	Not making progress	No opinion
1990			
November	24%	70%	6%
February	30	58	12

Getting the drug crisis under control?

Making progress 50%
Not making progress 46
No opinion 4

Selected National Trend

	Making progress	Not making progress	No opinion
1990			
November	47%	49%	4%
February	57	39	4

Avoiding raising taxes?

Making progress 43%
Not making progress 51
No opinion 6

Selected National Trend

	Making progress	Not making progress	No opinion
1990			
November	21%	74%	5%
February	54	36	10

Please tell me which word or phrase better describes your impression of George Bush. If you feel neither phrase describes Bush, please say so.

Sincere 87%
Insincere 7
Neither; no opinion 6

Selected National Trend

	Sincere	Insincere	Neither/no opinion
1990			
November	74%	19%	7%

July	75	18	7
February	85	9	6
1988			
August 19–21	74	15	11
August 5–7	59	26	15

Steady, reliable 88%
Undependable 6
Neither; no opinion 6

Selected National Trend

	Steady, reliable	Unde- pendable	Neither/no opinion
1990			
November	67%	23%	10%
July	72	19	9
February	83	8	9
1988			
August 19–21	73	19	8
August 5–7	59	27	14

Intelligent 83%
Only average 15
Neither; no opinion 2

Selected National Trend

	Intel- ligent	Only average	Neither/no opinion
1990			
November	65%	33%	2%
July	66	31	3
February	72	25	3
1988			
August 19–21	70	27	3
August 5–7	61	33	6

Confident 91%
Insecure 6
Neither; no opinion 3

Selected National Trend

	Confident	Insecure	Neither/no opinion
1990			
November	72%	22%	6%
July	76	18	6
February	82	12	6
1988			
August 19–21	67	25	8
August 5–7	56	32	12

Warm, friendly.....................................89%
Cold, unfriendly................................... 4
Neither; no opinion 7

Selected National Trend

	Warm, friendly	Cold, unfriendly	Neither/no opinion
1990			
November..............80%	11%	9%
July 84	7	9
February.................86	5	9
1988			
August 19–21..........65	18	17
August 5–7 49	28	23

Strong..88%
Weak.. 5
Neither; no opinion 7

Selected National Trend

	Strong	Weak	Neither/no opinion
1990			
November..............62%	22%	16%
July 63	21	16
February.................73	14	13
1988			
August 19–21..........57	28	15
August 5–7 42	39	19

A leader...88%
A follower 7
Neither; no opinion 5

Selected National Trend

	A leader	A follower	Neither/no opinion
1990			
November..............68%	20%	12%
July 67	24	9
February.................75	18	7
1988			
August 19–21..........50	39	11
August 5–7 37	52	11

An active president 91%
A passive president.............................. 6
Neither; no opinion 3

Selected National Trend

	An active president	A passive president	Neither/no opinion
1990			
November...............71%	21%	8%
July 70	22	8

Note: With victory in the Persian Gulf, President George Bush has emerged with historic approval ratings and a highly favorable image as a strong and capable leader—perhaps eradicating forever the "wimp" image that dogged him in earlier years. However, the credit given to Bush for his leadership by the public appears to be limited to foreign policy and international affairs. Thus, as Americans in the months ahead focus less on the Gulf war and more on the situation at home, there is every indication that Bush's extremely strong approval ratings (now at 87%) may decline to the levels he reached before the war.

Nearly eight in ten (79%) approve of the way he is handling foreign policy in general. Bush's ratings on this issue have increased 18 percentage points since last October. He even receives high marks for handling foreign policy in areas of the world where the United States has not taken an active role. Seven in ten (70%) approve of the way that Bush is dealing with the situation in Eastern Europe (up 7 percentage points from July 1990), and about one half (52%) approves of the way that he is handling the situation in Central America (a 10-percentage point increase from last July).

Respondents, however, are much less enthusiastic about the president's handling of the domestic challenges that this country faces. Only one in four (28%) approves of the way he is handling the Savings and Loan crisis, while only 27% approve of his handling of poverty and homelessness and only 34% approve of his failure to deal with the availability of health care. These low marks are relatively unchanged from the summer of 1990 and show that the tremendous overall boost to Bush from the events in the Persian Gulf has not translated into increased approval for his handling of issues here at home. Only about one half of respondents, for example, approves of the way the president is dealing with crime (47%), the environment (52%), the drug problem (50%), and education policy (53%).

In this latest Gallup Poll, Americans also were asked to rate the progress that the president is making on a range of issues. The public credits the president with making progress on international issues such as increasing respect for the United States abroad (87%). However, on controlling drugs (50%), improving educational standards (52%), reducing the crime rate (41%), or reducing the federal budget deficit (28%), Bush gets no more credit (and in some instances less) than he did one year ago.

His overall image as a strong leader has been improved dramatically by the Gulf war. Nearly nine in ten now think that Bush is strong (88%), sincere (87%), and steady (88%). Even more think that he is confident (91%) and active (91%). Eighty-eight percent describe Bush as a leader, while only 7% think of him as a follower. All of these positive measures have increased substantially since last November, in some instances by more than 20 percentage points.

MARCH 20
POLICE BRUTALITY

Interviewing Date: 3/14–17/91
Survey #GO 122021

Is your overall opinion of your local police department very favorable, mostly favorable, mostly unfavorable, or very unfavorable?

Very favorable.....................................29%
Mostly favorable..................................53
Mostly unfavorable..............................10
Very unfavorable................................. 6
No opinion.. 2

	Very favor-able	Mostly favor-able	Mostly unfavor-able	Very un-favor-able*
By Sex				
Male............29%	53%	10%	6%
Female..........28	53	10	8

By Ethnic Background				
White...........31	54	9	4
Black...........21	40	14	20
By Age				
18–29 Years...18	55	18	8
30–49 Years...28	56	9	5
50 Years and Over..........38	47	8	4
By Income				
$50,000 and Over..........30	56	11	2
$30,000– $49,999.....28	57	10	3
$20,000– $29,999.....26	55	11	7
Under $20,000.....32	46	10	10
By Community Size				
Large City.....22	55	16	5
Medium City ..27	58	10	4
Suburban Area..........32	52	8	6
Small Town....32	47	11	8
Rural Area......33	54	7	4

*"No opinion"—at no more than 5%—has been omitted.

How much respect do you have for the police in your area—a great deal, some, or hardly any?

Great deal 60%
Some..32
Hardly any 7
No opinion.. 1

Selected National Trend

	Great deal	Some	Hardly any	No opinion
1967............	77%	17%	4%	2%
1965............	70	22	4	4

In some places in the nation, there have been charges of police brutality. Do you think there is any police brutality in your area, or not?

	Yes
National..	35%

By Sex
Male 37%
Female...33

By Ethnic Background
White..33
Black 45

By Age
18–29 Years......................................37
30–49 Years......................................40
50 Years and Over 25

By Income
$50,000 and Over...............................38
$30,000–$49,999...............................37
$20,000–$29,999...............................38
Under $20,000...................................30

By Community Size
Large City 59
Medium City 40
Suburban Area...................................33
Small Town.......................................24
Rural Area..20

Have you seen or read anything recently about the videotaped incident in Los Angeles in which policemen were shown beating a motorist?

Yes

National...92%

How frequently do you think incidents like this happen in police departments across the country? Do you think they happen very frequently, somewhat frequently, not very frequently, or not at all?

Very frequently 22%
Somewhat frequently 46
Not very frequently 27
Not at all..2
No opinion..3

How frequently do you think incidents like this happen in your local police department in your area? Do you think they happen very frequently, somewhat frequently, not very frequently, or not at all?

Very frequently 5%
Somewhat frequently 15
Not very frequently 45
Not at all..32
No opinion..3

	Very frequently	Somewhat frequently	Not very frequently	Not at all frequently*
By Sex				
Male 5%	15%	44%	34%
Female..........4	15	46	31
By Ethnic Background				
White............3	13	47	35
Black 15	31	27	15**
By Age				
18–29 Years....5	21	47	25
30–49 Years....5	15	50	28
50 Years and Over..........4	11	38	43
By Income				
$50,000 and Over..........3	12	51	33
$30,000–$49,999......4	16	52	27
$20,000–$29,999......6	16	43	32
Under $20,000......6	14	40	35
By Community Size				
Large City 12	26	45	12
Medium City ...1	18	53	23
Suburban Area..........2	14	49	31
Small Town.....5	10	37	46
Rural Area.......1	8	46	44

*"No opinion"—at no more than 5%—has been omitted.
**"No opinion" here draws 12%.

Do you happen to know anyone who has been physically mistreated or abused by the police?

	Yes
National	20%

By Sex	Yes
Male	24%
Female	16

By Ethnic Background
White	17
Black	40

By Age
18–29 Years	30
30–49 Years	21
50 Years and Over	11

By Income
$50,000 and Over	19
$30,000–$49,999	18
$20,000–$29,999	21
Under $20,000	20

By Community Size
Large City	33
Medium City	17
Suburban Area	21
Small Town	16
Rural Area	12

Has anyone in your own household ever been physically mistreated or abused by the police?

	Yes
National	8%

By Sex	Yes
Male	10%
Female	6

By Ethnic Background
White	7
Black	18

By Age
18–29 Years	12
30–49 Years	8
50 Years and Over	5

By Income
$50,000 and Over	11
$30,000–$49,999	5
$20,000–$29,999	10
Under $20,000	7

By Community Size
Large City	11
Medium City	8
Suburban Area	7
Small Town	7
Rural Area	7

How about yourself—have you ever been physically mistreated or abused by the police?

	Yes
National	5%

Note: Two out of three Americans think that police violence similar to the recent videotaped beating in Los Angeles is a frequent occurrence across the country, but they say that such violence is much less frequent in their own communities. Even so, four times as many today think that police brutality exists in their own communities than did so in 1965—35% now compared to 9% then.

Additionally, about one in five (20%) professes to know someone who has been physically mistreated or abused by the police, and one male in ten (10%) claims that he personally has been beaten or abused.

The incident in Los Angeles, in which a motorist was severely beaten by three police officers while a dozen others watched, has caught the attention of the public. Ninety-two percent say that they saw or read about the beating, a very high awareness level for a local news event, and as many as two in three (68%) believe that incidents of this kind occur very or somewhat frequently around the country. More than one in five (22%) say that they happen very frequently, while only 2% claim that they never happen. However, when asked about such incidents in their own community, only one in five (20%) says that they occur very or somewhat frequently.

Nonwhites are more likely than whites to say that physical abuse by the police is frequent at both the national and local levels. More than three quarters of nonwhites think that incidents similar to the one in Los Angeles happen either very or somewhat frequently across the country, with four in ten (46%) saying that they happen very or somewhat frequently in their own communities.

MARCH 21
MIDDLE EAST SITUATION

Interviewing Date: 3/14–17/91
Survey #GO 122021

I'd like your overall opinion of some foreign countries. Is your overall opinion of [country] very favorable, mostly favorable, mostly unfavorable, or very unfavorable?

	Those saying "very," "mostly favorable"
Israel	69%
Egypt	66
Jordan	22
Iran	14
Iraq	7

Selected National Trend
(Israel)

	Those saying "very," "mostly favorable"
October 1990	48%
February 1990	44
August 1989	45
February–March 1989	49

How closely would you say you have followed the recent situation in the Middle East involving Israel and the Palestinians—very closely, fairly closely, or not closely?

Very closely	40%
Fairly closely	45
Not closely	14
No opinion	1

Asked of those following the Middle East situation: In the Middle East situation, are your sympathies more with the Israelis or more with the Palestinian Arabs?

Israelis	60%
Palestinian Arabs	17
Both; neither (volunteered)	16
No opinion	7

Selected National Trend

	Israelis	Palestinian Arabs	Both; neither	No opinion
Oct. 1990	48%	23%	19%	10%
Dec. 1988	46	24	16	14
May 1986	43	20	20	17

Also asked of those following the Middle East situation: Do you favor or oppose the establishment of an independent Palestinian nation within the territories occupied by Israel in the 1967 war?

Favor	46%
Oppose	31
No opinion	23

Selected National Trend

	Favor	Oppose	No opinion
October 1990	41%	32%	27%
May 1988	38	30	32

Also asked of those following the Middle East situation: Do you think there will or will not come a time when Israel and the Arab nations will be able to settle their differences and live in peace?

	Yes
National	54%

Selected National Trend

	Yes
October 1990	46%
May 1988	55

Asked of those who replied in the affirmative (54%): Do you think this will happen during the next five years, or not?

	Yes
National	23%

Selected National Trend

	Yes
October 1990	18%
May 1988	18

As far as you are concerned, should the development of a peaceful solution to the Israeli-Palestinian problem in the Middle East be a very important foreign policy goal of the United States, a somewhat important goal, not too important, or not an important goal at all?

Very important	46%
Somewhat important	41
Not too important	6
Not at all important	5
No opinion	2

As a way to bring peace to the Middle East, it has been proposed that Israel withdraw from occupied Arab lands if Arab nations in return recognize Israel's right to exist as a nation. Do you favor or oppose this proposal?

Favor	73%
Oppose	17
No opinion	10

If Israel did give up occupied Arab lands, how likely is it that this action would bring lasting peace to the Mideast?

Very likely	11%
Somewhat likely	46
Not too likely	27
Not at all likely	12
No opinion	4

Which of the following approaches do you think the United States should take with regard to the issue of the Israeli-occupied territories and the possibility of a Palestinian homeland:

Not pressure Israel at all and let Israel pursue whatever policy it thinks best?	26%
Exert diplomatic pressure on Israel to negotiate a settlement but not reduce economic and military assistance?	35
Reduce economic and military assistance if Israel does not negotiate a settlement?	18
Cut off all economic and military aid if Israel does not negotiate a settlement?	14
No opinion	7

Note: More Americans than ever side with Israel against the Palestinians, according to the latest Gallup Poll. And, although they strongly favor the idea of trading land for peace as a solution to the long-standing Israeli-Palestinian dispute, they are nevertheless pessimistic that this approach will be adopted by both sides or that, if implemented, it will result in peace.

Today, about seven in ten (69%) have a favorable opinion of Israel. Although this is down 10 percentage points from early February, when Iraqi Scud missiles were hitting the Jewish state, it is significantly higher than the 45% to 49% favorable ratings given Israel throughout 1989 and 1990.

Respondents also are more likely than before to sympathize with Israel against the Palestinian Arabs. Six in ten (60%) say that their sympathies are with the Israelis, up 12 percentage points from last October. Only 17% are sympathetic to the Palestinian cause. At the same time, the percentage who favor establishing an independent Palestinian homeland on the occupied territories has not changed substantially since last October (46% versus 41%).

An overwhelming majority (73%) favors a basis peace proposal calling for Israel to give back land it occupied in the 1967 war in return for Arab recognition of Israel's right to exist as a nation. Even if this solution could be implemented, only 57% think that a lasting peace for the region would very or somewhat likely result, while 39% say that it would be unlikely. More generally, however, there has been a slight increase in the number of those who think that a time will come when Israel and the Arabs will be able to live in peace; 54% agree now, compared to 46% last October.

Americans favor our taking a passive role in encouraging Israel to settle the crisis. Six out of ten (61%) favor only diplomatic pressure or no pressure at all on Israel. Only 18% favor reducing economic and military assistance, and 14% favor cutting off all financial and military assistance if Israel does not negotiate a settlement with the Palestinians.

MARCH 28
GUN CONTROL

Interviewing Date: 3/21–24/91
Survey #GO 122022

In general, do you feel that the laws covering the sale of firearms should be made more strict, less strict, or kept as they are now?

More strict	68%
Less strict	5
Kept as they are	25
No opinion	2

	More strict	Less strict	Kept as they are	No opinion
By Sex				
Male	59%	5%	34%	2%
Female	76	3	18	3
By Ethnic Background				
White	68	4	26	2
Black	68	8	19	5
By Region				
East	77	3	20	*
Midwest	72	3	23	2

	More strict	Less strict	Kept as they are	No opinion
South	61	6	29	4
West	63	5	29	3
By Age				
18–29 Years	62	7	30	1
30–49 Years	69	4	26	1
50 Years and Over	71	4	21	4
By Political Ideology				
Liberal	75	6	18	1
Moderate	77	2	18	3
Conservative	65	4	30	1

*Less than 1%

Selected National Trend

	More strict	Less strict	Kept as they are	No opinion
1990	78%	2%	17%	3%
1986	60	8	30	2
1981	65	3	30	2
1975	69	3	24	4

Would you favor or oppose the registration of all handguns?

Favor	80%
Oppose	17
No opinion	3

Selected National Trend

	Favor	Oppose	No opinion
1990	81%	17%	2%
1985	70	25	5
1982	66	30	4

Do you think there should or should not be a law that would ban the possession of handguns except by the police and other authorized persons?

Should	43%
Should not	53
No opinion	4

	Should	Should not	No opinion
1990	41%	55%	4%
1987	42	50	8
1980	38	51	11

Would you favor or oppose a law requiring that any person who carries a gun outside his home must have a license to do so?

Favor 88%
Oppose..11
No opinion.. 1

Selected National Trend

	Favor	Oppose	No opinion
1990	87%	12%	1%
1988	84	15	1

Would you favor or oppose a national law requiring a seven-day waiting period before a handgun could be purchased, in order to determine whether the prospective buyer has been convicted of a felony or is mentally ill?

Favor 93%
Oppose.. 7
No opinion.. *

Selected National Trend

	Favor	Oppose	No opinion
1990	95%	5%	*
1988	91	9	*

*Less than 1%

Do you have a gun in the house?

	Yes
National	46%

Selected National Trend

	Yes
1990	47%
1985	44

1980	45
1975	44
1968	50
1959	49

Asked of those who replied in the affirmative: Is it a pistol, shotgun, rifle, or what?

Pistol...55%
Shotgun...53
Rifle 55
Assault gun.. *
Other... *
No opinion.. 3

*Less than 1%

Selected National Trend

	Pistol	Shotgun	Rifle
1989	52%	60%	65%
1985	49	55	60
1975	41	58	55
1972	36	61	60

Asked of gun owners: What is the total number of guns kept in your house?

One...22%
Two 19
Three..17
Four or more.....................................36
Not sure 6

Selected National Trend

	One	Two	Three	Four or more	Not sure
1990	27%	22%	14%	31%	6%
1989	29	21	12	32	6

Note: On the eve of the tenth anniversary of the shooting of President Ronald Reagan and his press secretary James Brady, more than nine out of ten Americans (93%) support a new law that would require a seven-day waiting period before the purchase of a handgun. Congress is now considering this so-called Brady bill, named after the disabled press secretary and publicly championed by his wife Sarah over the last several years.

Respondents generally favor specific restrictions on gun ownership—such as the proposed waiting period—but resist an outright ban on gun ownership. Currently, while two thirds (68%) agree that gun control laws should be stricter than they are now, only 43% favor an outright ban on handgun ownership by private citizens. Although there have been fluctuations in both of these measures over the past ten years, support for a handgun ban has always been significantly lower than support for stricter laws regulating gun ownership.

In other gun restrictions, 88% would favor a law requiring that any person who carries a gun outside his or her home must have a license to do so. Moreover, 80% favor the registration of all handguns. Support for such registration is significantly higher now than it was in a 1982 poll, when only 66% supported the idea.

Nearly one half of all households (46%) contain at least one gun. Despite the enormous changes in our society over the past thirty years, this number has remained remarkably stable: 49% contained a gun in 1959, when Gallup began asking the question. The type of gun, however, has changed; pistols are now more prevalent, while ownership of shotguns and rifles has declined.

MARCH 28
GENERAL SCHWARZKOPF

Interviewing Date: 3/21–24/91
Survey #GO 122022

Asked of registered voters: Suppose the presidential election were being held today. If George Bush were the Republican candidate and Norman Schwarzkopf were the Democratic candidate, whom would you vote for? As of today, do you lean more to Bush, the Republican, or to Schwarzkopf, the Democrat?

Bush 65%
Schwarzkopf 28
Other; undecided................................. 7

Asked of registered Democrats and those who lean Democratic: Would you like to see General Norman Schwarzkopf become a candidate for the Democratic presidential nomination in 1992, or not?

Yes...42%
No..37
No opinion..21

Note: Is General Norman Schwarzkopf the kind of man whom the Democrats need to lead their party against a popular Republican incumbent in 1992? Whatever party leaders may think, rank-and-file Democrats do not appear to yearn for the military hero as their party's standard bearer. In the latest Gallup Poll, fewer than one half (42%) of Democratic voters say that they would like to see Schwarzkopf run for their party's presidential nomination. Considering the lack of competition—there are still no declared Democratic presidential candidates—support within the party for a Schwarzkopf candidate seems low.

APRIL 4
NORTH AMERICAN FREE-TRADE ZONE

Interviewing Date: 3/8–10/91; in Canada and Mexico, 3/6–9/91
Survey #GO 122020

Have you read or heard anything about the recent proposal to create a so-called North American free-trade zone comprised of Canada, the United States, and Mexico?

	United States	Mexico	Canada
Yes	32%	70%	79%
No	66	25	19
No opinion	2	5	2

As you may know, Canada and the United States now share a free-trade agreement which ensures that trade between the two countries is not subject to tariffs or import quotas. It has been suggested that a wider free-trade zone could be established, consisting of Canada, the United States, and Mexico. In general, do you think a North American free-trade zone consisting of these three countries would be mostly good for [respondent's country] or mostly bad for [respondent's country]?

	United States	Mexico	Canada
Mostly good for this country	72%	66%	28%
Mostly bad for this country	15	20	53
Neither good nor bad (volunteered)	3	7	6
No opinion	10	7	13

Which of the three countries—Canada, the United States, or Mexico—do you think would probably benefit most from a North American free-trade zone?

	United States	Mexico	Canada
Canada	15%	2%	5%
United States	20	52	54
Mexico	52	23	29
All of them equally (volunteered)	3	15	3
No opinion	10	8	9

Note: A new Gallup survey conducted in the United States, Canada, and Mexico shows that a strong majority of Americans (72%) and Mexicans (66%) think a proposed North American free-trade zone would, on balance, benefit their own national economy. Canadians, however, appear far less confident about their ability to compete in a region-wide free-trade zone: 53% of those polled predict that it would be mostly bad for Canada if the current U.S.-Canadian free-trade arrangement were to be expanded to include Mexico. Only 15% of Americans and 20% of Mexicans take the negative view.

Despite the fact that both Americans and Mexicans view favorably the net domestic effects of such an arrangement, each country thinks the other would be the major beneficiary. Asked which country would benefit most, Americans pick Mexico (52%), the United States (20%), and Canada (15%). Among Mexicans, however, 52% say that they think the United States would gain the most, with 23% citing Mexico and 2% Canada. Among Canadians, 54% say that the United States would be the major beneficiary, while 29% think Mexico would derive the greatest benefit; only 5% see their own country as being the big winner. In effect, each society sees the other as being in a better position to capitalize on freer cross-border trade. Nonetheless, each views such an arrangement as valuable.

Despite their strong support for a three-country free-trade agreement, relatively few Americans (32%) report having heard or read about any previous discussion of this proposal. The initiative has been front-page news in Mexico and Canada, however, where fully 70% of Mexicans and 79% of Canadians say that they are already familiar with the issue.

Previous opinion research has shown that the instincts of the American public often seem inconsistent in the area of trade policy. The principle of free trade is widely endorsed, but there is also evidence of broad support for import tariffs if these are depicted as protecting American jobs. Nevertheless, general concern over foreign imports need not necessarily translate into opposition to the North American free-trade agreement proposal. In the eyes of most Americans, the current threat to U.S. economic power comes primarily from the Pacific Rim (especially Japan), with an additional challenge likely to be posed by the post-1992 European Community (in particular, Germany).

APRIL 18
PRESIDENT BUSH

Interviewing Date: 4/11–14/91
Survey #GO 122025

Do you approve or disapprove of the way George Bush is handling his job as president?

Approve	77%
Disapprove	13
No opinion	10

Note: President George Bush's job approval rating continues to decline from the historic high (89%) recorded immediately following the Persian Gulf war. However, his current approval rating of 77% remains extremely high, not only in relation to the first year and one half of his administration (before the Iraqi crisis) but also in comparison with any president since Franklin D. Roosevelt.

APRIL 20
ENVIRONMENT

Interviewing Date: 4/11–14/91
Survey #GO 122025

Do you consider yourself to be an environmentalist, or not?

	Yes
National	78%

	Yes

By Sex

	Yes
Male	75%
Female	81

By Ethnic Background

White	79
Nonwhite	78
Black	68

By Education

College Graduate	81
College Incomplete	76
High-School Graduate	79
Less Than High-School Graduate	75

By Region

East	82
Midwest	78
South	76
West	75

By Age

18–29 Years	72
30–49 Years	80
50 Years and Over	79

By Household Income

$50,000 and Over	77
$30,000–$49,999	83
$20,000–$29,999	79
Under $20,000	76

By Political Ideology

Liberal	83
Moderate	87
Conservative	75

Selected National Trend

	Yes
1990	73%
1989	76

Asked of those who replied in the affirmative: Would you say you are a strong environmentalist, or not?

	Yes
National	37%

I'm going to read you a list of environmental problems. As I read each one, please tell me if you personally worry about this problem a great deal, a fair amount, only a little, or not at all. First, how much do you personally worry about:

Pollution of drinking water?

Great deal	67%
Fair amount	19
A little	10
Not at all	3
No opinion	1

Pollution of rivers, lakes, and reservoirs?

Great deal	67%
Fair amount	21
A little	8
Not at all	3
No opinion	1

Contamination of soil and water by toxic waste?

Great deal	62%
Fair amount	21

A little...................................11
Not at all................................5
No opinion...............................1

Air pollution?

Great deal 59%
Fair amount........................27
A little................................10
Not at all..............................4
No opinion...............................*

*Less than 1%

Ocean and beach pollution?

Great deal 53%
Fair amount........................26
A little................................14
Not at all..............................6
No opinion..............................1

Loss of natural habitats for wildlife?

Great deal 53%
Fair amount........................27
A little................................15
Not at all..............................5
No opinion...............................*

*Less than 1%

Damage to the earth's ozone layer?

Great deal 49%
Fair amount........................24
A little................................15
Not at all..............................8
No opinion..............................4

Contamination of soil and water by radioactivity from nuclear facilities?

Great deal 44%
Fair amount........................25
A little................................20
Not at all.............................10
No opinion..............................1

Loss of tropical rain forests?

Great deal 42%
Fair amount........................25

A little...................................21
Not at all................................10
No opinion..............................2

The "greenhouse effect," or global warming?

Great deal 35%
Fair amount........................27
A little................................21
Not at all.............................12
No opinion..............................5

Acid rain?

Great deal 34%
Fair amount........................30
A little................................20
Not at all.............................13
No opinion..............................3

All in all, which of the following best describes how you feel about the environmental problems facing the earth? Life on earth will continue without major environmental disruptions only if:

	April 1991	April 1990
We take additional, immediate, and drastic action concerning the environment?	57%	54%
We take some additional actions concerning the environment?	31	33
We take just about the same actions we have been taking on the environment?	8	9
No opinion	4	4

Do you think [the following group] today is too worried about the environment, not worried enough, or expresses about the right amount of concern about the environment:

The American public?

	April 1991	April 1990
Too worried	6%	7%
Not worried enough	70	72
Right amount of concern	22	19
No opinion	2	2

The government?

	April 1991	April 1990
Too worried	3%	3%
Not worried enough	73	75
Right amount of concern	20	18
No opinion	4	4

Business and industry?

	April 1991	April 1990
Too worried	1%	1%
Not worried enough	83	85
Right amount of concern	13	11
No opinion	3	3

How much progress have we made in dealing with environmental problems in this country over the last twenty-one years—that is, since 1970? Would you say we have made a great deal of progress, only some progress, or hardly any progress at all?

	April 1991	April 1990*
Great deal	18%	14%
Some	62	63
Hardly any	19	21
No opinion	1	2

*Over the last twenty years

How much optimism do you have that we will have our environmental problems well under control in twenty years—that is, by the year 2011?

	April 1991	April 1990*
Great deal	19%	18%
Some	60	58
Hardly any	18	22
No opinion	3	2

*By the year 2010

Would you favor a ban on chlorofluorocarbons and other chemicals known to damage the ozone layer even if it meant higher prices for air conditioners, refrigerators, and some other consumer products?

Yes	79%
No	12
No opinion	9

Which of the following things, if any, have you or other household members done in recent years to try to improve the quality of the environment:

	Have done
Voluntarily recycled newspapers, glass, aluminum, motor oil, or other items?	86%
Cut your household's use of energy by improving insulation or changing heating or air-conditioning system?	73
Avoided buying or using aerosol sprays?	68
Cut your household's use of water?	68
Replaced "gas-guzzling" automobile with more fuel-efficient one?	67
Contributed money to an environmental, conservation, or wildlife preservation group?	51
Specifically avoided buying a product because it was not recyclable?	49
Cut down on use of car by carpooling or taking public transportation?	46
Boycotted a company's products because of its record on the environment?	28
Used cloth rather than disposable diapers?	25
Did volunteer work for an environmental, conservation, or wildlife preservation group?	18

*Multiple responses were given.

Does your community require the sorting of glass, metal, and paper garbage so that materials can be reused or recycled, or not?

	April 1991	April 1990
Yes	41%	30%
No	57	67
No opinion	2	3

Here are two statements which people sometimes make when discussing the environment and economic growth. Which of these statements comes closer to your own point of view:

	April 1991	April 1990
Protection of the environment should be given priority, even at the risk of curbing economic growth?	71%	71%
Economic growth should be given priority, even if the environment suffers to some extent?	20	19
No opinion	9	10

A new environmental tax law has been proposed which would place fees on corporations which produce environmentally harmful products such as carbon emissions, hazardous waste, and chlorofluorocarbons. This could lower personal income taxes but might raise the cost of products to consumers. Would you favor or oppose this type of new environmental tax?

Favor	78%
Oppose	15
No opinion	7

Note: On the twenty-first anniversary of the first Earth Day, most Americans continue to be concerned about the environmental threats to the planet and say that they are taking active steps to conserve its resources. And, despite the current economic recession, seven in ten (71%) favor protecting the environment, even at the risk of curbing economic growth. Only one in five (20%) would favor policies that might spur the economy but harm the environment.

Nearly nine in ten households (86%) now report voluntarily recycling newspapers, glass, or aluminum, which may explain why 78% of respondents consider themselves environmentalists. Nearly three quarters (73%) claim to have cut down on their household's use of energy, although this may be for economic as well as environmental reasons. Reducing the use of water (68%), replacing an inefficient automobile (67%), or avoiding aerosol sprays (68%) are activities reported by about two thirds of all households; one half (49%) would specifically avoid buying a product that is not recyclable. Another one half (51%) has given

money to an environmental cause, but only 18% have donated time.

About two thirds (62%) of those polled think that not enough progress has been made over the last twenty years in dealing with environmental problems; even fewer (60%) are optimistic that we will have them under control in the next two decades. There has been little change in either of these two measures over the past year. Perhaps to ensure that progress is made, more than one half (57%) favor taking immediate, drastic action. About eight out of ten favor a ban on chlorofluorocarbons (79%) and also support taxing manufacturers or consumers of environmentally harmful products (78%), as proposed by the Worldwatch Institute as an alternative to explicit government bans or controls.

The vast majority also continues to believe that the general public (72%), government (75%), and business and industry (85%) are not worried enough about environmental problems. Less than one in five thinks that the amount of concern shown by these three groups is at the right level. However, despite media coverage of environmental groups lobbying for dolphin-safe tuna, laws against disposable diapers, or the banning of pesticides and growth hormones, less than one in three (28%) has boycotted a company because of its environmental record.

Not surprisingly, respondents express the greatest amount of concern about environmental problems that affect them directly. About two thirds worry a great deal about the contamination of drinking water (67%), pollution of lakes and rivers (67%), air pollution (59%), and contamination of soil and water (62%).

Even though the depletion of the earth's ozone layer and the resulting "greenhouse effect" have been in the news recently, the percentage of those who worry about this issue has not changed in the last two years. The status of the earth's ozone layer concerns 49%, and the resulting warming effect is of serious concern to only 35%. Of even lesser concern are threats that are limited to another geographical area. The loss of tropical rain forests (42%) and the damage from acid rain (34%) are worries for only four Americans in ten.

There has been one encouraging trend over the past year. The percentage of those who say their community requires recycling has risen from 30% in 1990 to 41% this year.

APRIL 20
PERSONAL FINANCES

Interviewing Date: 4/11–14/91
Survey #GO 122022

We are interested in how people's financial situation may have changed. Would you say that you are financially better off now than you were a year ago, or are you financially worse off now?

Better...29%
Worse...33
Same (volunteered)..............................37
No opinion...1

Selected National Trend

	Better	Worse	Same	No opinion
1991				
March 21–24	30%	37%	32%	1%
Feb. 28–				
March 3	37	28	34	1
Feb. 14–17	37	28	35	*
Jan. 11–13	26	33	39	2
Jan. 3–6	35	32	32	1

*Less than 1%

Looking ahead, do you expect that at this time next year you will be financially better off than now or worse off than now?

Better...56%
Worse...17
Same (volunteered)..............................18
No opinion...9

Selected National Trend

	Better	Worse	Same	No opinion
1991				
March 21–24	56%	18%	20%	6%

Feb. 28–				
March 3	64	9	20	7
Feb. 14–17	57	15	20	8
Jan. 11–13	41	25	21	13
Jan. 3–6	52	18	20	10

Note: Consumer confidence, which soared after news of the Persian Gulf victory, has now returned to a level slightly below that at the beginning of 1991, before the war began. A new Gallup Business Poll finds only 29% of consumers saying that they are better off financially now than a year ago.

It is always true that the proportion expecting to be better off in the future is larger than the proportion saying that they are better off than a year ago. At present, however, this difference (56% versus 29%) is unusually large.

Surveys of economic attitudes conducted between mid-January and early March, both by Gallup and by others, were probably not very meaningful. During the white heat of war, few people's thoughts were on the economy. Now that the dust has had a chance to settle and consumer attitudes are more stable, it is significant to find more people saying that they are worse off financially (33%) than better off (29%). These data from the April 11–14 survey are fairly close to those from a poll conducted three weeks earlier (March 21–24).

Consumer attitudes and expectations have been extraordinarily volatile during the past nine months. Gallup measures of personal financial confidence (probably the most crucial at this stage of the business cycle) plunged in mid-October 1990, more because of perceived economic problems than because of the Middle East situation. After climbing most of the way back by late 1990, confidence plunged again (although not quite so deeply) in mid-January, as the war approached. Then came the quick victory in the Gulf and a sharp rise in confidence at the end of February.

APRIL 24
CANADA AND MEXICO

Interviewing Date: 3/7–10/91
Survey #GO 122020

Can you tell me what country is America's largest trading partner—that is, with what country the United States conducts the greatest amount of foreign trade?

Japan 49%
Canada (correct) 8
Soviet Union.....................................5
United Kingdom.................................3
Mexico..*
Other...5
No opinion..30

*Less than 1%

Do you happen to know the name of the prime minister of Canada? (If "yes") Who is he?

Brian Mulroney (correct) 13%
Incorrect; no opinion 87

Do you happen to know the name of the president of Mexico? (If "yes") Who is he?

Carlos Salinas/Salinas de Gortari (correct)... 3%
Incorrect; no opinion 97

Can you tell me the name of Canada's capital city? (If "yes") What is it?

Ottawa (correct)..................................16%
Montreal...14
Toronto 8
Other...23
No opinion..39

Can you tell me the name of Mexico's capital city? (If "yes") What is it?

Mexico City (correct) 54%
Incorrect; no opinion 46

Note: At a time of great interest in a proposal to create a North American free-trade zone comprised of Canada, Mexico, and the United States (Gallup has shown that 72% of Americans favor the proposed trade agreement), many Americans exhibit a profound lack of basic knowledge about their neighbors to the north and south. A recent Gallup Poll reveals that they are unaware of Canada's importance as a trading partner of the United States and have very little knowledge of the political leaders of either country.

Only 8% can correctly identify Canada as America's leading trade partner; nearly one half (49%) incorrectly thinks that Japan is our largest trading partner, while others mention such countries as the Soviet Union and Great Britain. Only 13% can identify Canadian Prime Minister Brian Mulroney, and only a handful (3%) can name Mexico's President Carlos Salinas de Gortari. Moreover, 54% can name the capital of Mexico (Mexico City), but only 16% correctly name Ottawa as the capital of Canada.

MAY 1
PRESIDENT BUSH'S EDUCATION PLAN

Interviewing Date: 4/25–28/91
Survey #GO 122027

Let's compare the United States to Japan, Great Britain, Germany, and other major Western countries in the world on a number of factors. Would you say that the United States is very strong, strong, weak, or very weak compared to other countries in the following areas:

System of public education?

	1991	1987
Very strong	6%	10%
Strong	29	38
Weak	53	40
Very weak	10	7
No opinion	2	5

Production of quality products?

	1991	1987
Very strong	8%	9%
Strong	49	47
Weak	37	37
Very weak	4	4
No opinion	2	3

Technical innovation?

	1991	1987
Very strong	13%	19%
Strong	57	51
Weak	22	21
Very weak	2	2
No opinion	6	7

Overall standard of living?

	1991	1987
Very strong	23%	35%
Strong	61	51
Weak	13	10
Very weak	1	1
No opinion	2	3

The Bush administration proposed last week a new plan designed to improve the quality of education in this country. Here are several of the highlights of the plan. Please tell me if you favor or oppose a voluntary national test which would be used to measure and compare abilities of students by school districts across the country.

Favor	68%
Oppose	26
No opinion	6

	Favor	Oppose	No opinion
By Education			
College Graduate	66%	32%	2%
College Incomplete	71	26	3
High-School Graduate	68	26	6
Less Than High-School Graduate	64	23	13

Now please tell me, if this step were taken, how much—if at all—would it improve the quality of education children receive in this country? Would it improve it a great deal, somewhat, not too much, or not at all?

Great deal	23%
Somewhat	42
Not too much	15

Not at all	14
No opinion	6

	Great deal	Some- what	Not too much	Not at all*
By Education				
College Graduate	15%	38%	20%	24%
College In- complete	28	40	14	14
High-School Graduate	21	48	16	10
Less Than High-School Graduate	31	39	8	9

*"No opinion" has been omitted.

Would you favor or oppose a program which would allow parents to send their children to the public, parochial, or private school of their choice and use state and local tax dollars to pay for all or part of it?

Favor	50%
Oppose	45
No opinion	5

	Favor	Oppose	No opinion
By Education			
College Graduate	49%	48%	3%
College Incomplete	54	42	4
High-School Graduate	51	44	5
Less Than High-School Graduate	47	45	8

And if this step were taken, how much—if at all—would it improve the quality of education children receive in this country? Would it improve it a great deal, somewhat, not too much, or not at all?

Great deal	29%
Somewhat	34
Not too much	17
Not at all	14
No opinion	6

	Great deal	Some- what	Not too much	Not at all*
By Education				
College Graduate	25%	33%	17%	19%
College In- complete	33	32	19	11
High-School Graduate	30	35	17	13
Less Than High-School Graduate	28	34	13	12

*"No opinion" has been omitted.

Would you favor or oppose a program which would encourage schools to pay teachers more if they went beyond regular teaching duties by teaching core subjects, teaching in dangerous or challenging settings, or serving as mentors for new teachers?

Favor 76%
Oppose..19
No opinion.......................................5

	Favor	Oppose	No opinion
By Education			
College Graduate	84%	13%	3%
College Incomplete	80	16	4
High-School Graduate	77	17	6
Less Than High-School Graduate	80	13	7

And if this step were taken, how much—if at all—would it improve the quality of education children receive in this country? Would it improve it a great deal, somewhat, not too much, or not at all?

Great deal 38%
Somewhat..43
Not too much.....................................9
Not at all..6
No opinion...4

	Great deal	Some- what	Not too much	Not at all*
By Education				
College Graduate	35%	49%	8%	6%
College In- complete	41	45	6	5
High-School Graduate	41	41	10	5
Less Than High-School Graduate	32	39	11	10

*"No opinion" has been omitted.

Would you favor or oppose the use of government grants and contributions from business and industry to invent new and different types of public schools across the country?

Favor 73%
Oppose..22
No opinion...5

	Favor	Oppose	No opinion
By Education			
College Graduate	79%	17%	4%
College Incomplete	75	21	4
High-School Graduate	75	21	4
Less Than High-School Graduate	61	29	10

And if this step were taken, how much—if at all—would it improve the quality of education children receive in this country? Would it improve it a great deal, somewhat, not too much, or not at all?

Great deal 38%
Somewhat..40
Not too much.....................................9
Not at all..6
No opinion...7

	Great deal	Some- what	Not too much	Not at all*
By Education				
College Graduate	41%	41%	8%	6%

College In- complete....41	40	6	7
High-School Graduate.....39	42	9	5
Less Than High-School Graduate.....30	37	12	7

*"No opinion" has been omitted.

Note: The majority of Americans says that the U.S. system of public education does not measure up to those in other Western nations and Japan. Furthermore, their attitudes toward public education vis-à-vis these other nations have become increasingly negative over the past four years. At the same time, the latest Gallup Poll shows substantial support for most elements of the proposed national education program unveiled by the Bush administration last week, with one exception: Support is mixed for a system whereby parents could use tax dollars to send their child to the public or private school of their choice.

Almost two thirds (63%) say that our system of public education is weak compared to Japan, Great Britain, Germany, and other major Western countries. Only 35% today think that our system is strong compared to these nations.

The quality of public education in the United States comes off much worse than in three other areas in which we are sometimes unfavorably compared with other nations. The United States is weak vis-à-vis Japan and Western countries in terms of product quality (41%), technical innovation (24%), and our overall standard of living (14%).

This perception of the quality of U.S. public education has dropped significantly since the same questions were asked in a Gallup/Times-Mirror survey in 1987. At that time, 48% thought that our system was strong compared to the other countries, with only 47% saying that it was weak. In fact, education was the only one of the four elements tested which has declined since 1987.

Respondents support most of the key elements of the education plan announced last week by President George Bush and his new secretary of education, Lamar Alexander. Seventy-six percent favor paying teachers more if they perform unusual duties, such as teaching core courses or teaching in dangerous settings; 81% say that implementation of this step would improve a great deal or somewhat the quality of education in this country. Seventy-three percent favor creating "new" schools, funded by both the government and business and industry; 78% say that this would improve education. Another 68% support a voluntary national test to be taken by students across the country; 65% say that such a test would make a difference in the quality of education.

Support is significantly lower for the controversial recommendation that parents be allowed to use state and local tax dollars to send their children to the school of their choice—either public, private, or parochial. Fifty percent favor this plan, while 45% oppose it. And 63% say that this parental choice system would improve the quality of education.

MAY 3
U.S. CENSUS

Interviewing Date: 4/25–28/91
Survey #GO 122027

It has been suggested that parts of certain groups in America, particularly minorities and the poor in inner cities, are missed and not counted by the census. The suggestion has been made that the government estimate how many people are missed and add these estimates into the final census count. Other people say that the census should only include the actual number of people counted. Which of these views comes closer to your own?

Add estimates into count.......................48%
Only include actual number counted..........43
No opinion...9

	Add estimates	Include actual number	No opinion
By Sex			
Male 40%		49%	11%
Female.................55		37	8

By Ethnic Background

White	46	45	9
Nonwhite	63	27	10
Black	56	32	12

Note: The 1990 decennial U.S. Census is now more than a year old, and initial population counts for states, counties, and cities have been released. One controversial aspect of the census lingers on, however—the issue of whether or not the actual figures should be adjusted to reflect estimates of people missed by the census. It is generally agreed that it does, in fact, miss some percentage of the population, most particularly minority, urban, homeless, and more transitory individuals who are less likely to fill out mailed forms or to be contacted in person by census takers.

The Census Bureau conducts surveys and gathers other data that can be used to "adjust" the basic census statistically to factor in estimates of the undercounts. The results would change the census enough in some instances to affect the number of congressmen representing certain states and also to affect federal funds distributed on the basis of population. There has been a great deal of debate about whether the use of these estimates goes beyond the constitutional mandate to conduct an actual census.

The public remains split on this complex but highly important issue. About one half (48%) say that they favor using the estimates to adjust the census, while 43% think that it should use actual counts only. Despite recent publicity surrounding the estimate issue, these attitudes essentially have not changed from a Gallup Poll conducted immediately before the census, in March 1990, when the vote was 48% versus 45%.

MAY 3
RECESSION

Interviewing Date: 4/25–28/91
Survey #GO 122027

In your opinion, has the bottom of the current recession been reached, or not?

	Yes
National	30%

	Yes
By Sex	
Male	33%
Female	28

By Ethnic Background	
White	31
Black	26

By Household Income	
$50,000 and Over	33
$30,000–$49,999	35
$20,000–$29,999	27
Under $20,000	28

Selected National Trend

	Yes
1991	
April 11–14	33%
March	42

Note: Despite some evidence from a new Federal Reserve report that the economic recession may be bottoming out, a new Gallup Poll shows that less than one third of Americans thinks the worst is over. Only 30% say that the recession has bottomed out, while 59% say that it has not. Respondents are slightly less optimistic now than in an early April poll, when 33% said that the recession had bottomed out and 53% replied that it had not.

These measures are also down from the more optimistic thinking that prevailed in March, shortly after the Persian Gulf victory. At that point, 42% thought that the bottom had been reached, while 47% said that it had not.

MAY 3
ALASKA OIL SPILL

Interviewing Date: 4/25–28/91
Survey #GO 122027

As a result of the 1989 Exxon Valdez oil spill in Alaska, the Exxon Corporation agreed to pay a $100 million criminal fine as well as a $1 billion civil penalty. On

Tuesday [April 23], a federal judge rejected the agreement for the $100 million fine, saying it was too lenient. Do you agree with the judge's ruling that the fine was not enough, or do you think the amount agreed upon was adequate?

Not enough.......................................56%
Adequate..35
No opinion.. 9

	Not enough	Adequate	No opinion
By Sex			
Male	59%	34%	7%
Female	53	36	11
By Education			
College Graduate	60	35	5
College Incomplete	65	27	8
High-School Graduate	55	35	10
Less Than High-School Graduate	42	42	16
By Region			
East	52	40	8
Midwest	58	31	11
South	52	36	12
West	60	32	8
By Age			
18–29 Years	63	33	4
30–49 Years	59	32	9
50 Years and Over	48	33	14

Note: A majority of Americans agrees with the recent decision of a federal judge that a criminal fine of $100 million is too lenient for an environmental disaster of the magnitude of the *Exxon Valdez* spill in Alaska. The judge overturned an agreement by which the Exxon Corporation was to pay $100 million in criminal penalties for the spill. (Exxon also had agreed to pay $1 billion in civil costs.)

A little over one half of respondents (56%) say that the $100 million fine was too small, while only one third (35%) thinks that the size of the fine was adequate. Younger people and those who live in the West are most likely to

think that the size of the fine was inadequate. Two thirds (63%) of those under the age of 29 find the fine too small, compared to only 48% of those over the age of 50. In addition, 60% of those in the West find the fine too small, compared to 52% of residents in the South and the East.

MAY 4
MOST IMPORTANT PROBLEM

Interviewing Date: 4/25–28/91
Survey #GO 122027

What do you think is the most important problem facing this country today?

	April 1991	March 1991
Economy in general	20%	24%
Poverty; homelessness	13	10
Drugs; drug abuse	10	11
Unemployment	8	8
Federal budget deficit	6	8
Education	6	2
Ethics, morals	4	2
Kuwait, Gulf crisis	3	4
Environment	3	2
Other;* no opinion	27	29

*None of the "other" replies drew more than 3%.

Which political party do you think can do a better job of handling the problem you have just mentioned—the Republican party or the Democratic party?

	April 1991	March 1991
Republican	32%	40%
Democratic	27	27
No difference (volunteered); no opinion	41	33

Note: The big boost that Operation Desert Storm's success gave to the Republican party's image is no longer evident. One month ago, in the afterglow of victory in the Persian Gulf, the Gallup Poll found 40% of Americans viewing the GOP as the party better able to handle the country's most important problem. Currently, only 32% see the Republicans as clearly superior to the Democrats.

The Republican party still maintains a slight edge (32% versus 27%) over the Democratic party on this key measure of strength. The current figures, however, suggest that the public's high regard for President George Bush's handling of foreign affairs may not improve its confidence in his handling of domestic affairs.

Since the Gulf war ended, many expected the economy to replace the war as the dominant concern of the public. This has not proved to be true, as the biggest shift has been toward other domestic problems. Today, respondents are as likely to cite poverty, drugs, education, ethics, or the environment (36% total) as they are to cite the economy, unemployment, or the federal budget deficit (34% total).

MAY 4
DEMOCRATIC PRESIDENTIAL CANDIDATES

Interviewing Date: 4/25–28/91
Survey #GO 122027

Asked of registered Democrats and those who lean Democratic: Please tell me whether you have a favorable or unfavorable opinion of each of the following Democrats who might run for president in 1992:

	Favor-able	Unfavor-able*
Richard Gephardt	49%	16%
Mario Cuomo	48	22
Jesse Jackson	42	52
Albert Gore	41	16
Lloyd Bentsen	40	25
George McGovern	36	39
George Mitchell	26	13
Douglas Wilder	25	14
Charles Robb	17	11
Bill Clinton	15	12
Paul Tsongas	15	12

Stephen Solarz	12	12
Dave McCurdy	7	12

*The missing remainder for each man is "No opinion (heard of)" and "Total percent heard of," which do not add to 100% and are not strictly part of this question.

Also asked of registered Democrats and those who lean Democratic: Please tell me which one of these persons you would like to see nominated as the Democratic party's candidate for president in 1992. And who would be your second choice?

	First choice	Second choice	First & second choices combined
Cuomo	23%	10%	33%
Jackson	14	13	27
Bentsen	9	13	22
Gephardt	11	9	20
Gore	9	10	19
McGovern	8	11	19
Robb	4	3	7
Wilder	3	3	6
Mitchell	3	2	5
Tsongas	1	3	4
Clinton	1	2	3
Solarz	1	1	2
McCurdy	–	–	–
No opinion	13	30	–

Asked of registered voters: If George Bush runs for reelection in 1992, in general are you more likely to vote for Bush or for the Democratic party's candidate for president?

Bush	51%
Democratic candidate	30
Undecided; no opinion	19

	Bush	Democratic candidate	Undecided; no opinion
By Politics			
Republicans	85%	2%	13%
Democrats	20	67	13
Independents	45	25	30

Selected National Trend

	Bush	Democratic candidate	Undecided; no opinion
1991			
March	67%	17%	16%
February	54	33	13

Also asked of registered voters: If you knew that a Democratic presidential candidate voted against the resolution allowing President Bush to use military force in the Persian Gulf war, would that make you more likely or less likely to vote for him, or would it not much affect your vote?

More likely	11%
Less likely	23
Not much affect vote	61
No opinion	5

	More likely	Less likely	Not much affect vote	No opinion
By Politics				
Republicans	8%	32%	58%	2%
Democrats	14	15	65	6
Independents	11	23	60	6

Asked of the entire sample: Over the next few years, would you like to see the Democratic party and its candidates move in a more conservative direction, a more liberal direction, or stay about the same?

Conservative	34%
Liberal	20
Same	35
No opinion	11

	Conservative	Liberal	Same	No opinion
By Politics				
Republicans	44%	14%	32%	10%
Democrats	31	24	39	6
Independents	29	21	35	15

I'm going to read some criticisms that have been made about the Democratic party and its candidates. Please tell me whether you generally agree or disagree with the following statements:

The Democrats are too supportive of racial quotas as a way to improve conditions for minorities?

Agree	48%
Disagree	40
No opinion	12

	Agree	Disagree	No opinion
By Politics			
Republicans	62%	25%	13%
Democrats	32	60	8
Independents	45	40	15

The Democrats are too weak on foreign policy and national defense?

Agree	50%
Disagree	38
No opinion	12

	Agree	Disagree	No opinion
By Politics			
Republicans	71%	19%	10%
Democrats	32	57	11
Independents	46	40	14

The Democrats rely too much on increasing taxes and government spending to deal with problems?

Agree	61%
Disagree	33
No opinion	6

	Agree	Disagree	No opinion
By Politics			
Republicans	76%	19%	5%
Democrats	40	54	6
Independents	61	31	8

Note: Democratic officials attempting to push their party in a more conservative direction can find encouragement in the results of a new Gallup Poll, which finds the public generally in agreement with some of the major criticisms that moderate-to-conservative Democrats have leveled at the party's more liberal establishment. Unlike the last two presidential election years, 1992 may present a real opportunity for a Democratic candidate who is not a traditional liberal.

The Democrats' ability to mount an effective challenge to George Bush in 1992 may well hinge on the state of the economy. But even if economic conditions create an opportunity for the Democrats, they still must overcome several negative perceptions. First, a solid majority (61%) of the public, including four in ten (40%) self-described Democrats, thinks that the party relies too much on raising taxes and increasing government spending. The tax issue seems particularly damaging to the Democrats among middle-income Americans, many of whom drifted toward the GOP over the past decade. Unless the party can increase its appeal among middle-income people, its prospects for recapturing the White House will not improve.

Second, the Democrats lack credibility on foreign policy and defense. By a margin of 50% to 38%, the public sees them as too weak on foreign policy and national defense. And third, close to one half (48%) agrees that the Democrats are too supportive of racial quotas; 40% disagree. This racially divisive issue puts Democratic candidates in a no-win situation—defending quotas risks alienating white voters who otherwise might be inclined to vote Democratic, but backing away from quotas risks turning off black supporters and depressing voter turnout among a solidly pro-Democratic group.

When asked in which direction the Democratic party should move over the next few years, the public prefers a conservative tilt over a liberal one by 34% to 20% (35% say that the party should not change ideologically and 11% have no opinion). Both self-identified Democrats and independents are more inclined to want to see the party move to the right than to the left.

Now that the euphoria over the Persian Gulf victory has subsided, Gallup Poll results provide a more realistic picture of Democratic prospects for defeating Bush in 1992. Roughly one half (51%) of registered voters now expects to vote for Bush, while 30% see themselves supporting the yet-unnamed Democratic party's candidate. One in five voters (19%) declares no preference one way or the other. These results certainly speak better for the party's chances than did a March poll, which showed Bush with a 67%-to-17% lead.

With the field of Democratic 1992 presidential candidates still far from certain, polls of voter preferences for the Democratic nomination largely reflect name recognition. Two well-known liberal politicians lead the pack: New York Governor Mario Cuomo and civil rights activist Jesse Jackson. Cuomo is the first or second choice of 33% of Democratic voters, Jackson of 27%. While Jackson is second only to Cuomo in terms of nomination preferences, a majority (52%) of Democratic voters has an unfavorable opinion of him. (The Democratic Leadership Council chose not to invite Jackson to speak at its convention in May.)

Three potential candidates who are not traditional liberals—Texas Senator Lloyd Bentsen (22%), House Majority Leader Richard Gephardt (20%), and Tennessee Senator Albert Gore (19%)—share third place in the poll with George McGovern (19%). Each of the three is well liked among Democratic voters and scores favorability ratings on a par with Cuomo's.

Virginia Governor Douglas Wilder, a moderate black politician who many think will become a presidential candidate, also receives generally favorable reviews, as does Virginia Senator Charles Robb, despite recent allegations about past misconduct in his personal life. Both men, however, are not yet widely known and rank well below the leaders in support for the nomination.

In addition to Robb, two other politicians prominent in the Democratic Leadership Council—Arkansas Governor Bill Clinton and Oklahoma Congressman Dave McCurdy—have been mentioned by Washington insiders as potential presidential candidates. However, both men have very low name recognition and rank at the bottom of the list along with New York Congressman Stephen Solarz, whose pro-force stand on the Gulf war helped make him a presidential prospect in the aftermath of Operation Desert Storm's success.

Paul Tsongas, the former Massachusetts senator who already has declared himself a candidate, seems a long shot. The self-described pro-business liberal's favorability ratings are mixed (15% versus 12%). Only 4% of Democratic voters say that Tsongas is their first or second choice.

In the race for the Democratic presidential nomination, a vote against authorizing Bush to use force in the Gulf war may not seriously hurt a candidate's chances. A candidate who went on record against the military option, however, might find the issue to be a liability in November. By a margin of 2 to 1 (23% versus 11%), independent voters say that they are less rather than more likely to support a Democrat who opposed force.

MAY 5
AMERICANS AND THEIR AUTOMOBILES

Interviewing Date: 3/28–30/91
Survey #GO 122023

Do you drive a car or other vehicle?

	Yes
National	89%

The following questions were asked of those who drive a car or other vehicle:

Do you have a driver's license?

	Yes
National	99%

About how much time did you spend in your car yesterday?

Less than 30 minutes	10%
30 to 59 minutes	13
1 to 2 hours	25
2 to 3 hours	16
3 to 4 hours	7
4 to 5 hours	7
5 to 6 hours	4
6 to 7 hours	2
7 to 8 hours	1
8 hours or more	2

None; no opinion	13

Mean: 2 hours, 24 minutes

About how many miles would you say you drive in an average week?

Under 25	10%
25 to 50	18
51 to 100	20
101 to 150	10
151 to 200	10
201 to 400	17
401 to 750	7
Over 750	3
None; no opinion	5

Mean: 190 miles

Do you think of your car as just a means of transportation, or as something special— more than just a way to get around?

Just transportation	56%
Something special	43
No opinion	1

How often do you think you can tell what someone is like from the kind of car he or she drives—almost always, usually, sometimes, not very often, or never?

Almost always	6%
Usually	21
Sometimes	35
Not very often	22
Never	14
No opinion	2

If price were no object, what car would you like to own?

Mercedes-Benz	10%
Cadillac	5
Corvette	5
Jaguar	5
Lamborghini	4
Porsche	4
BMW	3
Buick	3
Ferrari	3
Ford	3

Rolls-Royce..3
Lexus..2
Lincoln Continental..............................2
Lincoln Town Car.................................2
Chevrolet Caprice................................1
Honda..1
Volvo..1
Infiniti ....*
Other..37
None...2
No opinion...4

*Less than 1%

If price were no object, what antique or classic car would you like to own?

1957 Chevy Bel Air 8%
Rolls-Royce...7
Corvette...5
Model T Ford.......................................4
1957 T-Bird...3
Ford Mustang 3
1955 Chevy..2
Cadillac 2
Mercedes-Benz.......................................2
Model A Ford.......................................2
Duesenberg..1
Jaguar...1
Roadster...1
1956 Chevy..1
Other..31
None...12
No opinion...15

What is the fastest speed that you have ever driven an automobile?

	All drivers	Men	Women
55 or less	3%	2%	4%
56 to 60	1	1	2
61 to 70	17	7	27
71 to 80	20	14	28
81 to 90	18	16	20
91 to 100	12	14	8
101 to 110	6	9	4
111 to 120	7	11	2
121 to 130	4	6	2
131 to 140	5	10	1
Over 140	5	8	1
No opinion	2	2	1

Mean: 93.9 miles per hour

Selected National Trend
(Fastest Speed Driven—1953)

	All drivers
Less than 45	7%
45 to 54	11
55 to 64	17
65 to 74	21
75 to 84	19
85 to 94	13
95 or more	12

How many miles per hour over the posted speed limit do you think you can drive on a highway before you get a ticket?

None...5%
One to four..9
Five...32
Six to nine...10
Ten..23
Eleven to fourteen.......................................1
Fifteen..6
More than fifteen...6
It varies; it depends (volunteered)..............2
No opinion...6

Is there an age at which you think a person should no longer be permitted to drive? (If "yes") What age?

No age; none..67%
Under 70 9
71 to 75...11
76 to 80...6
81 to 85...3
86 to 90...1
91 to 95...*
96 to 100..*
Over 100...*
No opinion...3

*Less than 1%

Would you rather ride in a car driven by a man or a woman?

	All drivers	Men	Women
With a man	43%	46%	39%
With a woman	16	10	22
No difference; no opinion	41	44	39

Selected National Trend

	With man	With woman	No difference; no opinion
1949	49%	5%	46%
1946	66	12	22
1939	60	8	32

Which, in your opinion, are the safer drivers—men or women?

	All drivers	Men	Women
Men are safer	37%	49%	26%
Women are safer	38	24	51
No opinion	25	27	23

Do you like to drive, or do you consider it a chore?

Like to drive	79%
Consider it a chore	20
No opinion	1

How much do you like to drive—a great deal, a fair amount, not too much, or not at all?

Great deal	29%
Fair amount	51
Not too much	16
Not at all	3
No opinion	1

When several people are available to drive, do you try to be the driver, or do you try to avoid the driving?

Try to be the driver	46%
Try to avoid driving	39
It depends (volunteered)	15
No opinion	*

*Less than 1%

Which of the following have you ever done:

	Yes
Slept overnight in your car?	36%
Lived in your car for more than twenty-four hours?	8
Sung in the car when driving alone?	81
Shouted, cursed, or made gestures to other drivers whose driving upset you?	67
Transacted business by car telephone?	10

Does your car have a name—that is, have you named your car?

	Yes
National	15%

Does your car have any of the following:

	Yes
Vanity license plates with your name, initials, or message?	8%
Customized body parts like mag wheels?	17
Custom engine equipment?	11
Special paint job, striping, ornamentation, numbers, or name painted on?	14
Tinted windows?	38
Custom undercarriage that raises car high off the ground?	4
Items hanging from mirror or in rear window or stuck to windows?	24

Do you have any of the following in your car:

	Yes
Car telephone?	7%
Television set?	3
Burglar alarm?	14
Audio cassette or CD player?	65
Radar detector?	13

Which of the following do you or your spouse do, in order to take care of your car:

	Yes
Wash or wax car?	89%
Minor engine maintenance or tune-ups?	57

Major repairs to engine or
  transmission or other parts of car? 28
Change oil? 69
Body work?..22
Paint car? 13

*Within the last twelve months have you,
yourself, attended any of the following:*

	Yes
Auto show?....................................	20%
Tractor or truck pull?	9
Stock car race?.................................	7
Drag race?.....................................	7
Demolition derby?..............................	5
Sports car rally?...............................	4

*Do you subscribe to or regularly read any
automobile magazine?*

	Yes
National..	12%

*Do you belong to any car club, such as
antique or classic car clubs or specialty car
clubs?*

	Yes
National..	3%

*During the last twelve months have any of
these happened to you:*

	Yes
Your car broken into?	8%
Your car vandalized?............................	8
Your car stolen?	2
Something stolen from your car?	10

*Within the last twelve months have you
done any of the following while you were
driving behind the wheel:*

	Yes
Personal grooming such as combing your hair or putting on makeup?	28%
Eaten breakfast, lunch, or dinner?	42
Read a newspaper, book, or magazine?.......	8
Fallen asleep?....................................	7

*How many vehicles are currently owned by
you and the others in your household?*

None.. 1%
One...24
Two 43
Three..16
Four 8
Five or more...................................... 7
No opinion.. 1

*In your opinion, which cars—Japanese,
American, or German:*

	Japan-ese	Amer-ican	German	No opinion
Are best in overall quality?......	27%	46%	19%	8%
Are best value for the money?......	39	46	6	9
Are best for workman-ship, crafts-manship? ...	26	41	23	10
Offer best exterior, styling, looks?.......	18	58	14	10
Offer best mechanical technology and are best engineered?	29	39	21	11
Are most economical to operate?..	55	34	2	9
Are most fun to drive?.....	22	47	16	15
Have most comfortable, roomy interiors?	6	73	12	9
Are safest to drive?.....	11	57	21	11
Have most stylish, best-looking interiors? ...	12	59	17	12
Are most res-ponsive, best perform-ing, and best handling?...	23	44	22	11
Have best re-sale value?..	29	36	23	12

Are most likely to come out with technological innovations?	46	34	10	10
Are most likely to come out with advanced and innovative exterior styling?	29	50	9	12
Need fewest repairs and least maintenance and are most dependable and trouble free?	38	40	11	11
Are most luxurious?	7	61	23	9
Are most prestigious?	7	42	41	10

Just your own opinion or impression— over the last five years, do you think American cars have improved, gotten worse, or remained about the same in terms of:

	Improved	Worse	Same	No opinion
Overall quality, workmanship, and craftsmanship?	67%	10%	21%	2%
Exterior styling and looks?	74	7	17	2
Economy of operation?	68	6	21	5
Safety?	82	3	12	3
Needing fewer repairs, less maintenance?	51	10	30	9

Note: The automobile, next to family and home, is Americans' most important possession. On average we spend more than two hours per day in our cars. We eat in them, sleep in them, and occasionally live in them. We even give them pet names.

A recent Gallup Mirror of America Poll shows that 89% of respondents age 18 and older drive. (This may not sound surprising, but as recently as 1965 only 71% drove a car.) On average, they drive about 190 miles per week. All but a handful (1%) interviewed by Gallup say that they have a legal driver's license.

Three quarters of respondents live in households with more than one car. Forty-three percent own two cars, 16% have three, and another 15% have four or more cars at their disposal.

Respondents persist in saying that they would rather ride in a car driven by a man than a woman—the same as fifty years ago, even though they say that men are probably no safer than women behind the wheel. (And no wonder! The average American male has clocked more than 100 miles per hour at some point in his driving career.) Feminism and the insurance industry notwithstanding, 43% would prefer a man as driver, while only 16% say that their choice would be a woman.

This preference continues a trend first measured by Gallup more than fifty years ago, although Americans are somewhat less sexist now. In 1939, 60% said that they would rather ride with a male driver but by 1946, immediately after World War II, the male preference figure rose to 66%. Women themselves prefer a male driver to one of their own sex, 39% to 22%. Only 10% of men say that they would prefer a woman to drive, while 46% opt for a man.

Overall, the dream car of 42% of Americans is something foreign: German cars (Mercedes-Benz, Porsche, and BMW) are the clear winners at 17%, Japanese finish second with 8%, and all other foreign cars together capture the fancy of 17%. American-made vehicles are the dream car of only 33%. Twenty-two percent do not specify any particular car, and 3% have no choice.

Drivers also were asked which antique or classic car they would most like to own. Two distinctly different vehicles hold a clear edge over all others. Eight percent opt for the 1957 Chevy Bel Air, while 7% choose a Rolls-Royce. Interestingly, the affection for the '57 Chevy seems to be the result of movie-induced nostalgia rather than genuine remembrance.

One fact of life relating to ownership of an automobile is crime. Slightly less than one in ten has had their car broken into or vandalized

(8% each), and 2% have had their car stolen within the past twelve months. These are about the same levels recorded by Gallup in previous surveys.

MAY 8
PUBLIC OFFICIALS' PRIVATE LIVES

Interviewing Date: 5/2–5/91
Survey #GO 122032

Do you think that the increased attention being given to the private lives of public officials and candidates is a good thing or a bad thing for politics and government in this country?

Good..43%
Bad..47
No opinion......................................10

	Good	Bad	No opinion
By Sex			
Male 49%		43%	8%
Female...................38		50	12
By Education			
College Graduate 43		50	7
College Incomplete...47		45	8
High-School Graduate..............44		47	9
Less Than High-School Graduate 37		44	19
By Age			
18–29 Years............47		43	10
30–49 Years............43		48	9
50 Years and Over.....41		47	12
By Politics			
Republicans............40		50	10
Democrats 45		45	10
Independents...........44		47	9
By Political Ideology			
Liberal...................44		50	6
Moderate...............43		50	7
Conservative..........45		46	9

Selected National Trend

	Good	Bad	No opinion
1989			
June* 44%	47%	9%
March*..................49	39	12

*Gallup Poll conducted for *Newsweek*

Do you think news organizations have gone too far in the way they have reported the following stories about the private lives of public figures, or not:

	Yes	No	No opinion
Content and allegations in Kitty Kelley's new book about Nancy Reagan?..............58%	27%	15%
Possible involvement of Massachusetts Senator Edward Kennedy in Palm Beach rape case?....48	43	9
Virginia Senator Charles Robb's alleged involvement with beauty queen and attendance at drug parties in early 1980s? 43	36	21
White House Chief of Staff John Sununu's use of military aircraft for personal trips without fully reimbursing government?........27	67	6

For each of the following stories about public officials, please tell me whether you feel it should almost always be reported, whether it should sometimes be reported depending on the circumstances, or whether it should almost never be reported. When a public official:

	Almost always	Some-times	Almost never	No opinion
Used military aircraft for personal trips without fully reimbursing the government?........76%	16%	7%	1%
Is found to have not paid federal income tax one time in the past? 69	21	9	1
Is found to have exaggerated his record of military service? 65	22	11	2
Is found to have exaggerated his academic record?.......62	25	11	2
Is having an extramarital affair?........39	22	37	2
Is a homo-sexual? 33	21	43	3
Attended a party years ago at which cocaine was used?....29	29	41	1
Is found to have been arrested for marijuana possession when he was a college student? 26	23	50	1
Had an extra-marital affair six or seven years ago? ..18	22	59	1

Note: A new Gallup Poll shows that Americans strongly support press coverage of the circumstances surrounding White House Chief of Staff John Sununu's use of military aircraft for personal trips. However, they are somewhat less certain about the appropriateness of other recent press revelations, including coverage of a new book about Nancy Reagan and reports about the personal life of Virginia Senator Charles Robb.

The poll suggests that people make clear distinctions about the types of revelations that they think proper for the media to expose. They view stories that focus on financial malfeasance or evidence of lying as fair game, but they are less sure about public officials' private lives.

Only 27%, for example, say that the press went too far in covering reports that Sununu abused the privilege of using military aircraft for personal trips, while 67% say that it did not. Public reaction to the coverage of a rape accusation against the nephew of Massachusetts Senator Edward Kennedy at the family compound in Palm Beach is more mixed: 48% say that the press went too far, while 43% say that it did not.

The public is mildly sympathetic to Senator Robb's arguments that the press overstepped its bounds in dredging up old reports of his personal improprieties from the early 1980s. More respondents say that the press went too far in its coverage of Robb (43%) than say it did not (36%), although 21% have no opinion on the issue. The strongest disapproval is reserved for media coverage of Kitty Kelley's new book about Nancy Reagan: 58% think that the press went too far. (Despite these sentiments, the Kelley book has become one of the fastest selling in publishing history.)

In more general terms, a substantial majority agrees that the press almost always should report stories about a public official's use of military aircraft for personal use (76%), not paying income tax (69%), exaggerating a record of military service (65%), and exaggerating college records (62%). There is much weaker support for the contention that the press should always cover stories about a public official's having a current extramarital affair (39%), being a homosexual (33%), having attended a party years ago where cocaine was used (29%), having been arrested for marijuana possession in college (26%), or having an extramarital affair six or seven years ago. For the latter, only 18% say that it almost always should be reported, while a majority (59%) says that it almost never should be reported.

MAY 9
VICE PRESIDENT QUAYLE

Interviewing Date: 5/6–7/91
Survey #GO 122037

There have been a number of important stories in the news recently. Which one story would you say you have been following most closely?*

Bush's health, heart	39%
Kurds in Iraq	9
Typhoon in Bangladesh	4
Dan Quayle	2
Economy; recession	1
All other stories	26
No story	15
No opinion	4

*Volunteered responses

Do you approve or disapprove of the way Dan Quayle is handling his job as vice president?

Approve	50%
Disapprove	25
No opinion	25

	Approve	Dis-approve	No opinion
By Sex			
Male	54%	25%	21%
Female	46	24	30
By Ethnic Background			
White	51	25	24
Nonwhite	38	32	30
Black	44	23	33
By Education			
College Graduate	48	26	26
College Incomplete	47	26	27
High-School Graduate	51	25	24
Less Than High-School Graduate	53	20	27
By Region			
East	50	20	30
Midwest	51	28	21
South	50	21	29
West	46	32	22
By Age			
18–29 Years	49	24	27
30–49 Years	49	28	23
50 Years and Over	51	22	27
By Politics			
Republicans	62	16	22
Democrats	39	33	28
Independents	46	29	25

Selected National Trend

	Approve	Dis-approve	No opinion
1990			
November	47%	33%	20%
August	47	23	30
July	44	30	26
May	48	27	25
February	46	27	27
1989			
November	43	29	28

Based on what you know about Vice President Dan Quayle, do you think he is qualified to serve as president if it becomes necessary, or not?

Yes	43%
No	46
No opinion	11

	Yes	No	No opinion
By Quayle Approval			
Approve	68%	23%	9%
Disapprove	6	91	3

Selected National Trend

	Yes	No	No opinion
1990			
November	33%	59%	8%
March	31	54	15

May....................34   52   14
1988
October.................46   42   12
September 34   47   19
August..................41   40   19

If President Bush runs for reelection in 1992, do you think he should keep Dan Quayle as his vice presidential running mate or choose someone else?

Keep Quayle	39%
Choose someone else	51
No opinion	10

	Keep Quayle	Choose someone else	No opinion
By Sex			
Male	45%	48%	7%
Female	34	54	12
By Ethnic Background			
White	40	51	9
Nonwhite	37	54	9
Black	36	51	13
By Education			
College Graduate	38	56	6
College Incomplete	34	52	14
High-School Graduate	43	48	9
Less Than High-School Graduate	40	49	11
By Region			
East	40	51	9
Midwest	40	53	7
South	43	47	10
West	30	56	14
By Age			
18–29 Years	33	58	9
30–49 Years	40	50	10
50 Years and Over	41	49	10
By Politics			
Republicans	46	46	8
Democrats	30	60	10
Independents	37	53	10

Selected National Trend

	Keep Quayle	Choose someone else	No opinion
1990			
November	36%	55%	9%
March	35	49	16

I'd like you to rate Vice President Dan Quayle using a scale that goes from the highest possible rating of +5 for someone you have a very favorable opinion of, all the way down to the lowest position of -5 for someone you have a very unfavorable opinion of. How far up or down the scale would you rate Vice President Dan Quayle?

Highly favorable (+5, +4)	18%
Mildly favorable (+3, +2, +1)	46
Mildly unfavorable (-1, -2, -3)	18
Highly unfavorable (-4, -5)	13
No opinion	5

Selected National Trend

	Highly, mildly favorable	Mildly, highly unfavorable	No opinion
1990			
November	50%	28%	22%
March	46	27	27

Please tell me which word or phrase better describes your impression of Dan Quayle. If you feel neither phrase describes Quayle, please say so.

Steady, reliable	61%
Undependable	23
Neither; no opinion	16

Intelligent	39%
Only average	54
Neither; no opinion	7

Confident	46%
Insecure	43
Neither; no opinion	11

Warm, friendly	71%
Cold, unfriendly	12
Neither; no opinion	17

Strong...34%
Weak...44
Neither; no opinion 22

A leader...21%
A follower 63
Neither; no opinion 16

Here is a list of terms that have been used to describe the qualities of a president. For each, tell me whether or not it applies to Dan Quayle:

	Applies	Does not apply	No opinion
Understands complex issues	44%	44%	12%
Would display good judgment in crisis	43	43	14
Experienced in government	52	40	8
Communicates effectively with American people	36	58	6
Knowledgeable about foreign affairs	45	42	13
Knowledgeable about national issues	61	31	8
Stands up for what he believes	65	24	11

How much confidence do you have in Dan Quayle [George Bush] to handle the job of president, should the situation arise—a great deal, a fair amount, only a little, or no confidence?*

	Quayle 1991	Bush 1985*
Great deal	13%	27%
Fair amount	37	36
A little	24	17
No confidence	25	14
No opinion	1	6

*Gallup Poll conducted for Newsweek

Note: A new Gallup Poll indicates that President George Bush's recent heart problem, which reinitiated speculation about the possibility of Vice President Dan Quayle as president, may have increased at least temporarily Americans' convictions that Quayle is qualified to hold that office. Forty-three percent now say that he is qualified to serve as president, while 46% say that he is not. In two separate surveys in 1990, only 31% and 33% thought Quayle qualified, with 54% and 59% saying that he was not. Additionally, the percentage who have a favorable opinion of Quayle is also higher now (64%) than it was last November (50%).

The latest Gallup Poll was conducted after it became clear that President Bush's condition was not as serious as originally thought and after he had returned to the White House. To some degree, this upsurge in Quayle's perceived qualifications may represent an immediate reaction to an emotional event, with Americans rallying behind him when the possibility of his becoming their leader seemed real. In the weeks ahead, Quayle's ratings may return to previous levels as Bush's health leaves the front pages.

Quayle inspires significantly less confidence as a potential president than Bush did in 1985 when President Ronald Reagan was undergoing cancer surgery. Fifty percent now say that they have a great deal or a fair amount of confidence in Quayle's ability to handle the job of president, while 49% have only a little or no confidence. When the same question was asked by Gallup/Newsweek in 1985, 63% said that they had confidence in then Vice President Bush's ability to handle the job, with only 31% showing little or no confidence.

The poll also reveals little change in other Quayle measures since last year. About one half (50%) approves of the job he is doing as vice president, essentially unchanged from the 1990 results. Additionally, 51% say that President Bush should choose someone else as his running mate in 1992, again not significantly different from similar findings reported last year.

What is behind the problems with Quayle's image? He does least well in terms of being seen as a leader, strong, and intelligent, but the public gives him much more credit for being warm and friendly and steady and reliable.

The current poll also shows that a majority gives Quayle credit for only three presidential qualities: that he would stand up for what he believes (65%), that he is knowledgeable about national affairs (61%), and that he is experienced in government (52%). However, less than one half says that he is knowledgeable about foreign affairs (46%), that he understands complex issues (44%), that he would use good judgment in a crisis (43%), and that he could communicate effectively with the American people (36%).

MAY 10
U.S. SPACE PROGRAM

Interviewing Date: 5/2–5/91
Survey #GO 122032

I am going to ask you several questions about government spending. In answering, please bear in mind that sooner or later all government spending has to be taken care of out of the taxes that you and other Americans pay. As I mention each program, tell me whether the amount of money now being spent for that purpose should be increased, kept at the present level, reduced, or ended altogether:

The U.S. space program?

Increased...21%
Kept same...44
Reduced..28
Ended 3
No opinion...4

Selected National Trend

	Increased	Kept same	Reduced	Ended*
1989	27%	42%	22%	4%
1986**	26	50	14	5
1984**	21	48	23	5

*In this and the next four parts to this question, "no opinion"—at 5% or less—has been omitted.
**In this and the next four parts to this question, the 1986 and 1984 polls were conducted by Gallup for *Newsweek*.

Improving medical and health care for Americans generally?

Increased...80%
Kept same...16
Reduced..2
Ended ....*
No opinion...2

*Less than 1%

Selected National Trend

	Increased	Kept same	Reduced	Ended
1989	73%	18%	4%	1%
1986	64	27	5	1
1984	63	28	5	1

Providing food programs for low-income families?

Increased...55%
Kept same...34
Reduced..7
Ended 2
No opinion...2

Selected National Trend

	Increased	Kept same	Reduced	Ended
1989	51%	35%	9%	1%
1986	46	35	11	3
1984	48	37	12	1

Total spending for defense and military purposes?

Increased...18%
Kept same...49
Reduced..30
Ended 1
No opinion...2

Selected National Trend

	Increased	Kept same	Reduced	Ended
1989	17%	39%	38%	2%
1986	21	41	31	2
1984	18	43	35	2

Federal money to improve the quality of public education?

Increased 76%
Kept same..18
Reduced 4
Ended 1
No opinion 1

Selected National Trend

	Increased	Kept same	Reduced	Ended
1989	72%	19%	5%	1%
1986	63	26	7	1
1984	65	27	5	1

How would you rate the job being done by NASA, the space agency? Would you say it is doing an excellent, good, only fair, or poor job?

Excellent..16%
Good..48
Fair..24
Poor... 6
No opinion... 6

On the whole, do you feel our investment in space research is worthwhile, or do you think it would be better spent on domestic programs such as health care and education?

Investment is worthwhile 40%
Better spent on domestic programs...........56
No opinion... 4

	Worth-while	Domestic programs	No opinion
By Sex			
Male	48%	46%	6%
Female	33	64	3
By Ethnic Background			
White	42	53	5
Nonwhite	35	63	2
Black	24	73	3
By Education			
College Graduate	52	45	3
College Incomplete	47	48	5
High-School Graduate	34	63	3
Less Than High-School Graduate	30	62	8
By Region			
East	42	53	5
Midwest	37	58	5
South	38	57	5
West	44	53	3
By Age			
18–29 Years	38	57	5
30–49 Years	41	55	4
50 Years and Over	41	54	5
By Household Income			
$50,000 and Over	54	43	3
$30,000–$49,999	46	50	4
$20,000–$29,999	36	60	4
Under $20,000	30	64	6
By Politics			
Republicans	53	44	3
Democrats	30	65	5
Independents	39	56	5
By Political Ideology			
Liberal	37	60	3
Moderate	39	57	4
Conservative	47	49	4
By Bush Approval			
Approve	43	53	4
Disapprove	32	63	5

Selected National Trend

	Worth-while	Domestic programs	No opinion
July 1990	39%	59%	4%
July 1989	43	52	5

How important do you think it is for the United States to be the first country to land a person on Mars? Would you say this is very important, somewhat important, not too important, or not at all important?

Very important 8%
Somewhat important 27

Not too important.................................32
Not at all important.............................32
No opinion...1

Some people feel that the U.S. space program should concentrate on unmanned missions like Voyager 2, *which sent back information from planets such as Neptune. Others say we should concentrate on maintaining a manned space program like the space shuttle. Which comes closer to your view?*

Unmanned missions.............................39%
Manned missions 49
Both (volunteered)...............................*
No opinion..12

*Less than 1%

Selected National Trend

	Unmanned missions	Manned missions	Both	No opinion
July 1990	34%	48%	6%	12%
July 1989	40	43	9	8

All in all, would you say the U.S. space shuttle program has been a worthwhile and important program for this country, or would the money have been better spent in some other way?

Worthwhile program 61%
Better spent some other way...................36
No opinion...3

	Worth-while program	Better spent some other way	No opinion
By Sex			
Male	67%	31%	2%
Female	55	41	4
By Ethnic Background			
White	63	34	3
Black	36	62	2

By Education			
College Graduate	71	27	2
College Incomplete	65	31	4
High-School Graduate	60	38	2
Less Than High-School Graduate	43	52	5
By Region			
East	60	37	3
Midwest	57	41	2
South	60	36	4
West	67	31	2
By Age			
18–29 Years	60	39	1
30–49 Years	64	34	2
50 Years and Over	57	37	6
By Political Ideology			
Liberal	55	42	3
Moderate	62	36	2
Conservative	68	29	3

Would you, yourself, like to be a passenger on a space shuttle flight sometime in the future?

	Yes
National	34%

	Yes
By Age	
18–29 Years	45%
30–49 Years	39
50 Years and Over	21

Note: In the wake of two successful space shuttle missions in the past month, the latest Gallup Poll shows a significant increase in the number of Americans who give NASA—the space agency—a positive rating. However, the public continues to think that money spent on space research could be better applied to domestic programs such as education and health care.

Nearly two thirds of respondents (64%) describe the job being done by NASA as excellent or good, up significantly from the 46% who thought that way last July. Similarly, NASA's negative ratings have dropped from

49% last year to only 30% now. (Last summer's lower ratings probably reflected the problems that the space program was encountering at that time, including the grounding of the space shuttle program and the technical problems with the Hubble telescope.) Perhaps as a result of these feelings of space supremacy, the race to be first on Mars has become significantly less important. About one third (35%) now thinks that it is important for the United States to be the first country to land an astronaut on Mars, down from 51% who thought that way two years ago.

Not all respondents, however, favor a continuation of manned space activities. Only 49% think that the United States should focus on manned missions, while 39% favor unmanned projects. Still, the lure of space maintains its appeal to some: 34% would like to be a passenger on a space shuttle flight at some point in the future.

Despite the improvement in NASA's ratings, space exploration remains a low priority for most people's tax dollars in comparison to other government programs. Overall, more than one half (56%) think that the money invested by this country in space research would have been better spent on programs such as health care and education. This mind-set has remained substantially the same over the past two years.

Additionally, when given a list of five areas on which government money can be spent, less than one in five say that they would like to see an increase in spending on space (21%). Forty-four percent want it kept the same, while 28% say that it should be decreased. In contrast, large majorities favor increasing government spending on public education (76%) and health-care programs (80%), and about one half (55%) would like to see an increase in spending on food programs to assist low-income families. The only other program that gets as low marks as space is defense; only 18% favor an increase in government spending.

MAY 15
AIDS

Interviewing Date: 5/2–5/91
Survey #GO 122032

What would you say is the most urgent health problem facing this country at the present time?

AIDS	45%
Cancer	16
Lack of or high cost of health care, insurance for elderly and the poor	10
Drug abuse	4
The elderly; problems of aging	4
Malnutrition; hunger	2
No national health-care program	2
Heart disease	2
Childhood diseases; child abuse	2
Pollution	1
Lack of knowledge; education	1
Obesity	1
Alcohol abuse	*
Smoking	*
Other	6
None; no opinion	4

*Less than 1%

Those responding AIDS

By Sex

Male	46%
Female	43

By Ethnic Background

White	44
Black	50

By Education

College Graduate	47
College Incomplete	51
High-School Graduate	42
Less Than High-School Graduate	39

By Region

East	47
Midwest	40
South	44
West	49

By Age

18–29 Years	60
30–49 Years	44
50 Years and Over	35

In your opinion, which of the following groups of people should be tested for AIDS:

	Should be tested
Doctors?	87%
Dentists?	87
Nurses?	84
All patients as they are being admitted to hospitals?	79
Couples applying for marriage licenses?	82
Immigrants applying for permanent residence in the United States?	81
Inmates of federal prisons?	78
Members of the armed forces?	67
Visitors from foreign countries?	62
All American citizens?	46

As I read off some statements about AIDS, would you tell me whether you agree or disagree with each one:

	Agree	
	May 1991	Oct. 1987
AIDS sufferers should be treated with compassion?	91%	87%
The government is not doing enough about the problem of AIDS?	60	53
People with the AIDS virus should be made to carry a card to this effect?	59	54
Everyone should have a blood test to see if they have AIDS?	58	48
I sometimes think that AIDS is a punishment for the decline in moral standards?	34	43
In general, it's people's own fault if they get AIDS?	33	51

Employers should have the right to dismiss an employee because that person has AIDS?	21	25
I would refuse to work alongside someone who has AIDS?	16	25
People with AIDS should be isolated from the rest of society?	10	21
Landlords should have the right to evict a tenant from an apartment or a house because that person has AIDS?	10	17

Note: With the 1991 International AIDS Conference just weeks away, a substantial majority of Americans continues to favor AIDS testing for a number of at-risk populations. And in the case of health-care professionals, virtually everyone backs such testing. At the same time, a comparison of findings between today and October 1987 reveals increased compassion and tolerance for AIDS victims.

Despite protests from civil libertarians and gay-rights activists, 87% favor AIDS testing for doctors and dentists, 84% favor testing for nurses, and 79% say that all patients should be tested for AIDS as they are admitted to the hospital.

There have, however, been some declines in the numbers of those who favor testing of other populations. Still, a majority continues to favor testing for couples applying for marriage licenses (82%), immigrants applying for permanent status in the United States (81%), inmates of federal prisons (78%), members of the armed forces (67%), and visitors from foreign countries (62%). In fact, 46% think that all American citizens should be tested. And for those who test positive for AIDS, six in ten (59%) say that victims should carry a card to this effect.

On several other measures relating to AIDS, the Gallup Poll shows the public displaying increased sensitivity and compassion for those who have contracted the disease. In 1987, 51% agreed with the statement "in general, it's people's own fault if they get AIDS." Today only 33% agree. Again, in 1987, 87% agreed that AIDS sufferers should be treated with compassion; today the percentage is 91%.

Forty-three percent agreed with the statement "I sometimes think that AIDS is a punishment for the decline in moral standards" in 1987, while today 34% agree. In 1987, 25% agreed that employers should have the right to dismiss an employee because that employee had AIDS; today the comparable figure is 21%. Only 16% agree with the statement that they would refuse to work alongside someone with AIDS today, but in 1987 the percentage agreeing was 25%. And finally, in 1987, 21% agreed that people with AIDS should be isolated from society, compared to only 10% today.

While there has been some decline in the last four years in the percentage of those who name AIDS as the nation's most urgent health problem, it still ranks number one by a wide margin (45%). Cancer, in second place, is named by only 16%. At the same time, six out of ten (60%) think that the government is not doing enough about the problem of AIDS, an increase from 53% who thought that way in 1987.

MAY 22
HONESTY AND ETHICAL STANDARDS

Interviewing Date: 5/16–19/91
Survey #GO 122034

How would you rate the honesty and ethical standards of the people in these different fields—very high, high, average, low, or very low?

	Very high, high	Average	Low, very low	No opinion
Druggists, pharmacists	60%	32%	5%	3%
Clergy	57	31	8	4
Medical doctors	54	37	8	1
Dentists	50	41	6	3
College teachers	45	35	7	13
Engineers	45	39	4	12
Policemen	43	42	13	2
Funeral directors	35	43	11	11
Bankers	30	52	14	4
Television reporters, commentators	29	49	19	3
Journalists	26	52	16	6
Newspaper reporters	24	54	17	5
Lawyers	22	43	30	5
Business executives	21	55	16	8
Building contractors	20	49	22	9
Senators	19	48	30	3
Local political office-holders	19	54	23	4
Congressmen	19	44	32	5
Real estate agents	17	54	22	7
State political office-holders	14	53	28	5
Stockbrokers	14	46	21	19
Insurance salesmen	14	47	33	6
Labor union leaders	13	41	34	12
Advertising practitioners	12	46	32	10
Car salesmen	8	37	49	6

Selected National Trend
(*Percent Saying Very High or High*)

	1990	1988	1985	1983
Druggists, pharmacists	62%	66%	65%	61%
Clergy	55	60	67	64
Medical doctors	52	53	58	52
Dentists	52	51	56	51
College teachers	51	54	53	47
Engineers	50	48	53	45
Policemen	49	47	47	41

Funeral directors	35	24	32	29
Bankers	32	26	38	38
Television reporters, commentators	32	22	33	33
Journalists	30	23	31	28
Newspaper reporters	24	22	29	26
Lawyers	22	18	27	24
Business executives	25	16	23	18
Building contractors	20	22	21	18
Senators	24	19	23	16
Local political office-holders	21	14	18	16
Congressmen	20	16	20	14
Real estate agents	16	13	15	13
State political office-holders	17	11	15	13
Stockbrokers	14	13	20	19
Insurance salesmen	13	10	10	13
Labor union leaders	15	14	13	12
Advertising practitioners	12	7	12	9
Car salesmen	6	6	5	6

Note: Pharmacists and the clergy receive the highest ratings for honesty and ethical standards from the public, according to the latest Gallup Poll. Six in ten (60%) think that druggists have very high or high standards, and 57% similarly rate the clergy. This poll marks the third consecutive time that druggists have edged out members of the clergy for the top position. (However, the 3-percentage point difference between the two ratings in 1991 is not statistically meaningful.) The clergy's current rating is down 10 percentage points from their all-time record (67%) set in 1985.

Among the professions whose image has suffered the most over the past year are policemen and U.S. senators, whose ratings have declined 6 and 5 percentage points respectively since last year. Since the well-publicized police beating of a black motorist in Los Angeles, only 43% give policemen a positive rating, down from 49%. Interestingly, the current rating of 19% for senators is identical to that measured in 1988 when Senator Gary Hart was involved in a highly publicized affair with Donna Rice. The 5-percentage point decline for senators from 1991 to 1990 probably can be attributed to the recent controversies involving Senators Edward Kennedy and Charles Robb.

Other professions whose public images have become less favorable in the past year are engineers (from 50% to 45%) and college teachers (from 51% to 45%). Ratings for journalists and business executives both lost 4 percentage points in the last year. The public's perception of the rest of the other professions on the list did not differ by more than 1 or 2 percentage points from last year's ratings.

When the ratings of all twenty-five professions are considered, they seem to reflect a more pessimistic attitude about the state of honesty and ethics in our society today. In 1991 none of those listed saw its ratings increase significantly. Indeed, fourteen professions saw their ratings decline, five had small increases, and six remained constant. This overall feeling of pessimism stands in sharp contrast to 1985, when no profession's rating declined significantly. In fact, in the aftermath of the Reagan reelection and economic good times, many of the professions on the list recorded all-time highs for honesty and ethical standards.

MAY 29
HANDGUN OWNERSHIP

Interviewing Date: 5/16–19/91
Survey #GO 122034

Do you have a gun in the house?

	Yes
National	46%

	Yes
By Sex	
Male	52%
Female	40

By Ethnic Background
White..49
Nonwhite...32
Black..28

By Education
College Graduate..........................36
College Incomplete.......................50
High-School Graduate...................44
Less Than High-School Graduate..............43

By Region
East..29
Midwest..47
South...58
West..47

By Age
18–29 Years....................................44
30–49 Years....................................47
50 Years and Over..........................46

By Household Income
$50,000 and Over...........................48
$30,000–$49,999............................55
$20,000–$29,999............................42
Under $20,000................................42

By Politics
Republicans.....................................53
Democrats..38
Independents...................................48

By Political Ideology
Liberal..40
Moderate..46
Conservative....................................49

Selected National Trend

	Yes
March 1991	46%
1990	47
1985	44
1980	45
1975	44
1968	50
1959	49

Do you have a gun anywhere else on your property such as in your garage, barn, shed, or in your car or truck?

	Yes
National	8%

Asked of those who replied in the affirmative: Is it a pistol, shotgun, rifle, or what?

Pistol..47%
Shotgun..51
Rifle...50
Assault gun.....................................*
Other..2
No opinion.......................................3

*Less than 1%

Selected National Trend

	Pistol	Shotgun	Rifle
March 1991	55%	53%	55%
1989	52	60	65
1985	49	55	60
1975	41	58	55
1972	36	61	60

The following questions were asked of pistol owners:

Thinking now just about your pistol or handgun—Is this gun yours, or does it belong to someone else in the household?

My gun...66%
Someone else in household..................27
Both own jointly (volunteered)...............5
Someone outside (volunteered)..............1
No opinion..1

Do you happen to know where your handgun(s) is (are) located right now?

	Yes
National	94%

Do you ever carry your handgun on your person, or not?

	Yes
National	23%

Do you ever carry your handgun in your car or your truck?

	Yes
National	39%

Is your gun loaded right now, or not?

	Yes
National	43%

Would you know how to use your gun if you had to, or not?

	Yes
National	92%

Have you ever fired the gun under any circumstances?

	Yes
National	78%

Have you ever used your handgun to defend yourself, your home, or family or possessions, either by firing it or threatening to fire it?

	Yes
National	8%

Has a handgun ever been used to threaten you in a robbery, mugging, or some other situation?

	Yes
National	16%

Would you happen to know, is the right to own a gun guaranteed by the Constitution, or not?

Yes	77%
No	9
Depends on interpretation (volunteered)	4
No opinion	10

Note: The most recent Gallup survey shows that as many as one household in four owns a handgun, virtually all owners (92%) know how to use it, three quarters (78%) have fired it, and four in ten (43%) say that their handgun is loaded now. Moreover, nine in ten (94%) know the current location of their weapon, and for many handgun owners it is usually close at hand. Four in ten (39%) have their gun in their car or truck, while one quarter (23%) carry it on their person.

Eight percent of owners claim to have used or threatened to use their gun to protect themselves or their property, and 16% claim that they themselves have been threatened by someone with a handgun. Perhaps as a justification for gun ownership, most handgun owners (77%) believe that their right to own a weapon is guaranteed by the Constitution.

JUNE 5
ABORTION

Interviewing Date: 5/30–6/2/91
Survey #GO 122036

Do you think abortions should be legal under any circumstances, legal only under certain circumstances, or illegal in all circumstances?

Legal, any circumstances	32%
Legal, certain circumstances	50
Illegal, all circumstances	17
No opinion	1

	Legal, any	Legal, certain	Illegal, all*
By Sex			
Male	30%	53%	14%
Female	34	47	19
By Ethnic Background			
White	32	50	17
Nonwhite	24	53	16
Black	38	43	17
By Education			
College Graduate	39	49	11
College Incomplete	39	45	15
High-School Graduate	29	51	18
Less Than High-School Graduate	19	53	25
By Region			
East	34	50	16
Midwest	27	54	17

South	30	48	20
West	39	47	12

By Age

18–29 Years	39	42	19
30–49 Years	30	52	16
50 Years and Over	30	53	15

By Household Income

$50,000 and Over	44	46	10
$30,000–$49,999	29	55	14
$20,000–$29,999	31	49	18
Under $20,000	29	46	23

By Politics

Republicans	24	54	21
Democrats	36	48	16
Independents	38	47	13

By Religion

Protestants	30	51	16
Catholics	28	52	19

By Political Ideology

Liberal	46	42	11
Moderate	39	53	7
Conservative	20	57	21

By Bush Approval

Approve	29	53	16
Disapprove	45	38	17

*"No opinion"—at 7% or less—has been omitted.

Selected National Trend

	Legal, any	Legal, certain	Illegal, all*
1990	31%	53%	12%
July 1989	29	51	17
April 1989	27	50	18
1988	24	57	17
1983	23	58	16
1981	23	52	21
1980	25	53	18
1979	22	54	19
1977	22	55	19
1975	21	54	22

*"No opinion"—at 5% or less—has been omitted.

Do you approve or disapprove of the recent Supreme Court ruling that the government can prohibit family-planning clinics receiving federal funding from providing patients with any information about abortion?

Approve	25%
Disapprove	66
No opinion	9

	Approve	Dis- approve	No opinion

By Sex

Male	27%	64%	9%
Female	24	67	9

By Ethnic Background

White	25	66	9
Nonwhite	31	64	5
Black	28	64	8

By Education

College Graduate	22	73	5
College Incomplete	24	70	6
High-School Graduate	28	62	10
Less Than High-School Graduate	26	59	15

By Region

East	19	72	9
Midwest	29	61	10
South	32	59	9
West	18	74	8

By Age

18–29 Years	24	69	7
30–49 Years	27	67	6
50 Years and Over	24	63	13

By Household Income

$50,000 and Over	19	76	5
$30,000–$49,999	28	66	6
$20,000–$29,999	30	62	8
Under $20,000	24	64	12

By Politics

Republicans	33	58	9
Democrats	22	70	8
Independents	22	69	9

By Religion
Protestants 26	65	9
Catholics 28	65	7

By Political Ideology
Liberal..................17	75	8
Moderate...............16	80	4
Conservative..........35	57	8

By Bush Approval
Approve.................28	63	9
Disapprove.............16	79	5

Some people feel that if the government helps pay for family-planning services, it has the right to prohibit any discussion of abortion as a family-planning option. Others feel that, no matter what the government says, health-care professionals in government-funded clinics have the right to discuss abortion with their patients under the free-speech guarantees of the Constitution. Which comes closer to your view?

Government has right to prohibit discussion............................19%	
Health-care professionals have right to discuss..........................74	
No opinion...7	

	Govern-ment	Health-care profes-sionals	No opinion
By Sex			
Male 20%	74%	6%
Female...................19	74	7
By Ethnic Background			
White...................17	80	3
Nonwhite 30	67	3
Black 8	85	7
By Education			
College Graduate 18	80	2
College Incomplete...17	79	4
High-School Graduate...............19	73	8
Less Than High-School Graduate 26	62	12

By Region
East 16	79	5
Midwest.................20	74	6
South 24	67	9
West 16	77	7

By Age
18–29 Years...........19	77	4
30–49 Years...........19	75	6
50 Years and Over.....19	72	9

By Household Income
$50,000 and Over.....13	83	4
$30,000–$49,999....17	78	5
$20,000–$29,999....25	70	5
Under $20,000........23	70	7

By Politics
Republicans............25	68	7
Democrats 17	75	8
Independents...........15	82	3

By Religion
Protestants 20	73	7
Catholics 18	75	7

By Political Ideology
Liberal..................12	85	3
Moderate...............11	85	4
Conservative..........26	67	7

By Bush Approval
Approve.................21	73	6
Disapprove.............11	83	6

Would you favor or oppose Congress passing a law that would allow federally funded clinics to provide information about abortion?

Favor 66%	
Oppose...28	
No opinion...6	

	Favor	Oppose	No opinion
By Sex			
Male 66%	28%	6%
Female...................68	26	6

By Ethnic Background

White	64	29	7
Nonwhite	70	27	3
Black	80	14	6

By Education

College Graduate	73	22	5
College Incomplete	68	27	5
High-School Graduate	68	27	5
Less Than High-School Graduate	51	35	14

By Region

East	69	24	7
Midwest	65	29	6
South	61	32	7
West	72	22	6

By Age

18–29 Years	75	23	2
30–49 Years	67	29	4
50 Years and Over	60	29	11

By Household Income

$50,000 and Over	75	21	4
$30,000–$49,999	67	29	4
$20,000–$29,999	66	29	5
Under $20,000	63	30	7

By Politics

Republicans	58	34	8
Democrats	71	24	5
Independents	73	23	4

By Religion

Protestants	63	30	7
Catholics	67	28	5

By Political Ideology

Liberal	79	19	2
Moderate	75	18	7
Conservative	58	35	7

By Bush Approval

Approve	66	28	6
Disapprove	72	25	3

Thinking about how this issue might affect your vote for the U.S. Congress, would you:

Only vote for candidates who favor allowing federally funded clinics to provide abortion information?..........11%

Never vote for candidates who take this position?........................8

Consider this as one of many important issues when voting?.............64

Or would you not see this as an important issue?........................12

No opinion..5

In 1973 the Supreme Court ruled that states cannot place restrictions on a woman's right to an abortion during the first three months of pregnancy. Would you like to see this ruling overturned, or not?

Yes..42%
No..52
No opinion..6

	Yes	No	No opinion
By Sex			
Male	41%	53%	6%
Female	43	51	6
By Ethnic Background			
White	42	52	6
Nonwhite	45	52	3
Black	37	53	10
By Education			
College Graduate	30	66	4
College Incomplete	40	56	4
High-School Graduate	43	50	7
Less Than High-School Graduate	56	35	9
By Region			
East	42	50	8
Midwest	43	52	5
South	46	47	7
West	33	63	4
By Age			
18–29 Years	38	59	3
30–49 Years	41	54	5
50 Years and Over	46	44	10

By Household Income

$50,000 and Over....30	68	2
$30,000–$49,999....42	52	6
$20,000–$29,999....44	48	8
Under $20,000........48	46	6

By Politics

Republicans............47	48	5
Democrats 40	55	5
Independents..........37	56	7

By Religion

Protestants 42	52	6
Catholics 47	47	6

By Political Ideology

Liberal.................34	61	5
Moderate...............31	59	10
Conservative..........49	45	6

By Bush Approval

Approve................42	52	6
Disapprove............40	54	6

Selected National Trend

	Yes	No	No opinion
July 1989..............34%	58%	8%
April 1989*...........39	51	10
December 1988.......37	57	6

*Gallup Poll conducted for *Newsweek*

Do you generally favor or oppose using federal funds to enable poor women to have abortions?

Favor 50%
Oppose...42
No opinion...8

	Favor	Oppose	No opinion
By Sex			
Male.....................52%	40%	8%
Female...................47	45	8
By Ethnic Background			
White....................49	44	7
Nonwhite 48	40	12
Black 64	25	11

By Education

College Graduate 58	34	8
College Incomplete...54	40	6
High-School Graduate..............47	46	7
Less Than High-School Graduate 41	50	9

By Region

East 56	38	6
Midwest................44	45	11
South 44	49	7
West 57	35	8

By Age

18–29 Years............54	41	5
30–49 Years............50	42	8
50 Years and Over.....48	43	9

By Household Income

$50,000 and Over.....60	33	7
$30,000–$49,999....52	42	6
$20,000–$29,999....49	44	7
Under $20,000.........48	44	8

By Politics

Republicans............41	51	8
Democrats 60	34	6
Independents..........51	41	8

By Religion

Protestants 47	44	9
Catholics 49	44	7

By Political Ideology

Liberal...................63	30	7
Moderate...............59	30	11
Conservative..........42	52	6

By Bush Approval

Approve................47	46	7
Disapprove............65	29	6

Which political party better reflects your views on abortion—the Republicans or the Democrats?

	May-June 1991	July 1989
Republicans.........................30%	34%
Democrats 35	37

Neither (volunteered)............... 12		8
Both (volunteered).................... 1		1
No opinion........................... 22		20

Do you approve or disapprove of the way George Bush has handled the abortion issue?

Approve...35%
Disapprove...34
No opinion..31

	Approve	Dis-approve	No opinion
By Sex			
Male.....................39%	35%	26%
Female..................32	34	34
By Ethnic Background			
White...................36	33	31
Nonwhite...............37	28	35
Black...................23	50	27
By Education			
College Graduate......35	44	21
College Incomplete...36	37	27
High-School Graduate.............37	29	34
Less Than High-School Graduate....29	32	39
By Region			
East......................30	41	29
Midwest.................40	29	31
South...................40	29	31
West.....................28	40	32
By Age			
18–29 Years............33	37	30
30–49 Years............36	32	32
50 Years and Over.....34	36	30
By Household Income			
$50,000 and Over.....34	39	27
$30,000–$49,999...36	34	30
$20,000–$29,999....41	29	30
Under $20,000........31	39	30
By Politics			
Republicans............54	21	25
Democrats...............24	46	30
Independents...........26	39	35
By Religion			
Protestants.............36	31	33
Catholics...............41	33	26
By Political Ideology			
Liberal...................25	51	24
Moderate................33	35	32
Conservative...........48	25	27
By Bush Approval			
Approve.................44	23	33
Disapprove.............. 7	81	12

Selected National Trend

	Approve	Dis-approve	No opinion
1989			
November...............38%	45%	17%
July 43	35	22

Note: The recent Supreme Court decision upholding a restrictive federal regulation on abortion is opposed by two thirds (66%) of the public, according to a new Gallup Poll. In the aftermath of *Rust v. Sullivan*, the poll also finds an equally high level of public support (66%) for congressional action to overturn the regulation, which bars family-planning clinics that receive federal money from providing patients with any information about abortion.

The poll finds no increase in the ranks of the so-called pro-choice side of the abortion debate: 32% take the most extreme position, that abortion should be legal under any circumstances. This is statistically equal to the 31% found both last year and in 1989, immediately after the *Webster v. Reproductive Services* decision. Prior to *Webster*, fewer Americans favored unrestricted abortions; one quarter (24%) took this position during the presidential election year of 1988.

In fact, the poll suggests that the so-called pro-life constituency has recovered some of the support lost after the *Webster* decision. The percentage who say that abortion should never be legal has returned to its 1989 level (17%) after falling to 12% in 1990. Moreover, respondents are now somewhat more likely to say that *Roe v. Wade*—the 1973 Supreme Court decision establishing the legal right to an abortion—should be overturned. Four in ten (42%) currently support reversing *Roe*, compared with 34% last year.

Gallup's analysis would suggest that opinion on the Court's decision is not based exclusively on views of the legal status of abortion. Thus, the group opposing the *Rust v. Sullivan* decision includes both those with strongly pro-choice views and those with more restrictive views on abortion, who appear to oppose the ruling as an unfair government restriction on free speech. When the issue is framed as a choice between the government's right to dictate policy when providing financial aid versus the rights of individual health-care practitioners to advise their patients as they see fit, the public overwhelmingly gives priority to an individual's right to free speech (74%) over the government's right to set policy (19%).

The Republican party and President George Bush appear to have avoided serious political consequences from the unpopular ruling, at least for the time being, and the poll shows no signs that the Democrats have gained any political advantage. Three in ten (30%) think that the Republican party best represents their view on abortion, while one third (35%) chooses the Democrats. Both of these proportions are down slightly from those recorded in 1989.

Like the abortion issue in general, federal restrictions on aid to family-planning clinics are not a strong enough factor on their own to determine most people's vote for Congress. About one in five say that they definitely would vote for or against a candidate, depending on his position on this issue. This group is split fairly evenly: 11% would only vote for a candidate who supports eliminating the rule barring abortion advice in federally funded clinics, and 8% would never vote for a candidate taking this position. For the great majority (64%), a candidate's stand on this issue ranks as only one of many important factors to consider when deciding how to vote.

The poll results make it clear, however, that the issue could present problems in the future for Bush and the GOP. Congressional Democrats are discussing legislation that would overturn the ruling by authorizing federally

funded clinics to discuss abortion. Were such legislation to pass, the Bush administration would face the choice of vetoing it and thus mobilizing opposition from pro-choice elements within both parties, or signing it at the risk of alienating pro-life activists within the GOP. Currently, the public is divided on Bush's handling of the abortion issue: 35% approve, 34% disapprove, with 31% having no opinion.

JUNE 12
SATISFACTION INDEX

Interviewing Date: 5/16–19/91
Survey #GO 122034

In general, are you satisfied or dissatisfied with the way things are going in the United States at this time?

Satisfied...49%
Dissatisfied.......................................49
No opinion..2

Selected National Trend

1991	Satisfied	Dis-satisfied	No opinion
March 21–24	52%	43%	5%
February 28–March 3	66	31	3
February 14–17	54	40	6
January 17–20	62	33	5
January 3–6	32	61	7
1990			
December 13–16	33	64	3
November 1–4	31	64	5
October 25–28	31	66	3
October 11–14	29	67	4

Interviewing Date: 5/23–26/91
Survey #GO 122035

In your opinion, has the bottom of the current recession been reached, or not?

Yes...33%
No..53
No opinion..14

	Yes	No	No opinion
1991			
May 16–19.............26%	65%	9%
April 25–28...........30	59	11
April 11–14...........33	53	14
March 21–24..........42	47	11

What do you think is the most important problem facing this country today?

Economy in general 21%
Poverty; homelessness 12
Drugs; drug abuse.................................10
Unemployment....................................... 9
Federal budget deficit............................ 6
Education 5
Recession.. 4
Other;* no opinion..............................37

*None of the "other" replies drew more than 5%.

Note: Dissatisfaction with the way things are going in the United States is increasing, apparently signaling a return to the more negative national mood recorded in the days before the Persian Gulf war. The latest poll shows that, for the first time since before the war began, as many Americans are now dissatisfied with the way things are going as are satisfied (49% each). The level of national dissatisfaction was particularly high last fall at a time when Congress and the president were unable to agree on a budget bill. When the war began in January there was a sharp drop in dissatisfaction, and the current level is midway between these two extremes.

The cause for this dissatisfaction appears to be the economy. When asked to name the most important problem facing this country, 46% of respondents give answers that relate to economic issues: the economy in general (21%), unemployment (9%), the federal budget deficit (6%), the recession (4%), and other specific economic problems (6%).

This worry over the economy contrasts sharply with the concerns of Americans during the fall of 1989 and spring of 1990. At those times, they apparently were fairly satisfied with the economy and instead named drugs, drug abuse, and other noneconomic problems as their most pressing concerns. Last fall and winter they were most likely to be worried about the budget deficit and the war.

The latest Gallup Poll shows no strong signs that respondents expect the nation's economic problems to get better. Only one third (33%) says that the bottom of the current recession has been reached. While these numbers are slightly more optimistic than those obtained in a Gallup Poll a few weeks earlier, they continue to lag behind the optimism noted in March, shortly after the war was over.

JUNE 15
PERSIAN GULF SITUATION

Interviewing Date: 5/23–26/91
Survey #GO 122035

As you may know, the economic sanctions imposed against Iraq by the United Nations are still in place. These sanctions prohibit Iraq from selling its oil or other products to other countries. Would you favor leaving the sanctions in place as long as Saddam Hussein remains in power, allowing Iraq to sell some oil if the money goes to pay for food and medical supplies, or lifting the sanctions to allow Iraq to resume normal trade?

Leave sanctions in place........................52%
Allow conditionally..............................39
Lift completely.................................... 5
No opinion.. 4

All in all, was the current situation in the Mideast worth going to war over; or not?

Yes...72%
No..23
No opinion.. 5

Selected National Trend

	Yes	No	No opinion
1991			
April 25–28............70%	24%	6%
April 4–6 71	22	7

February 28– March 3 80	15	5
January 30– February 2 71	24	5
January 11–13........46	44	10
January 3–6 47	44	9
1990		
December 13–16 49	44	7
December 6–9..........47	45	8
November 29– December 2..........51	41	8
November 15–18......46	45	9
September 27–30 49	41	10
August 30– September 2........45	44	11
August 23–26.........49	41	10

Note: Three months after the end of the Persian Gulf war, Americans want the UN economic sanctions against Iraq continued. Despite press reports of the heavy toll that the sanctions are taking on the Iraqi economy, slightly over one half (52%) surveyed in a new Gallup Poll favors leaving the sanctions in place as long as Saddam Hussein remains in power. Another 39% would favor allowing Iraq to sell some of its oil if the proceeds are designated only for the purchase of food and medical supplies—a proposal that so far has been rejected by the United States. Very few Americans (5%) say that the sanctions should be completely lifted, to allow Iraq to resume normal trade.

Meanwhile, there has been little decline in respondents' positive opinions about the U.S. involvement in the war. More than seven in ten (72%) believe that the Iraqi situation was worth going to war over, essentially the same number measured by the Gallup Poll shortly after the war ended.

JUNE 19
RACIAL QUOTAS

Interviewing Date: 6/13–16/91
Survey #GO 222002

Do you think the United States currently has enough federal laws and regulations aimed at reducing race, religion, and sex discrimination, or does Congress need to pass additional laws and regulations aimed at reducing this type of discrimination?

Has enough laws....................................55%
Needs additional laws.............................37
No opinion...8

	Has enough	Needs additional	No opinion
By Ethnic Background			
White.................58%	34%	8%
Black 30	62	8

Generally speaking, do you think that companies should be required to hire about the same proportion of blacks and other minorities as live in the surrounding community, or not?

Yes...45%
No..50
No opinion...5

	Yes	No	No opinion
By Ethnic Background			
White.................41%	54%	5%
Black 78	17	5

Have you seen, heard, or read anything about the civil rights bill now before Congress?

	Yes
National..40%

	Yes
By Ethnic Background	
White..40%
Black 49

The following questions were asked of those who had seen, heard, or read about the civil rights bill:

Congress is currently considering one civil rights bill sponsored by congressional Democrats and another by the Bush administration. Which of the two bills would you like to see Congress pass, or would you like to see neither bill pass?

Democrats' bill.....................................24%
Bush administration's bill 25

Neither 27
No opinion 24

By Ethnic Background

	White	Black
Democrats' bill	20%	45%
Bush administration's bill	28	8
Neither	28	25
No opinion	24	22

Based on what you have heard or read about the two bills, which do you think requires racial quotas in hiring and promotion—the Democrats' bill, the Bush administration's bill, neither, or both?

Democrats' bill 41%
Bush administration's bill 10
Neither 20
Both 10
No opinion 19

By Ethnic Background

	White	Black
Democrats' bill	43%	28%
Bush administration's bill	11	8
Neither	18	32
Both	9	17
No opinion	19	15

Why do you think congressional Democrats are supporting new civil rights legislation at this time? Do you think it is:

Mostly for partisan
political advantage? 61%
Mostly because they feel
new laws are needed to
protect civil rights? 32
Both (volunteered) 4
Neither (volunteered) .... *
No opinion 3

By Ethnic Background

	White	Black
Partisan political advantage	65%	30%
New laws are needed	29	54

Both 4   7
Neither ....*   3
No opinion 2   6

*Less than 1%

Why do you think President Bush has refused to support the Democratic version of the civil rights bill? Is it:

Mostly for partisan
political advantage? 28%
Mostly because he feels the
Democrats' bill goes too far
in encouraging racial quotas? 61
Both (volunteered) 3
Neither (volunteered) 1
No opinion 7

By Ethnic Background

	White	Black
Partisan political advantage	27%	34%
Democrats' bill goes too far	63	50
Both	3	4
Neither	*	2
No opinion	7	10

*Less than 1%

Note: President George Bush has the upper hand in the controversy over quotas and the civil rights legislation now before Congress. A new Gallup Poll finds only limited support for the Democrats' civil rights bill, which would make it easier for women and minorities to win job discrimination suits. Most who do not favor the bill agree with Bush that its passage would lead to quotas in hiring and promotion.

The Democratic bill is a revision of legislation passed by Congress last year but vetoed by Bush as a quota bill; it would have effectively overturned a 1989 Supreme Court decision placing the burden of proof in job discrimination cases on employees. This time, Bush has proposed an alternative bill of his own, which he claims will help reduce discrimination without encouraging employers to set up quotas.

Looking beyond the specifics now being debated in Washington, the public divides sharply along racial lines on the key issue. While more than three quarters of blacks (78%) say that companies should be required to have the same proportion of blacks and minorities on their payroll as live in surrounding communities, fewer than one half of whites (41%) share this view.

The quotas issue creates a no-win situation for the Democratic party. While it needs to find ways to counteract growing disaffection with the party among blacks, pushing the civil rights bill risks further alienating white Democrats, many of whom have made a habit of voting Republican in presidential elections.

Despite extensive coverage by the national press, only 40% claim to have heard or read something about the bill. Blacks are more likely than whites to say that they have paid attention, but even among blacks awareness is fairly low (49% versus 40% of whites).

A majority of Americans (55%) generally does not see a need for new federal legislation aimed at reducing racial, religious, and gender discrimination. Those who do see such a need, however, are now at 37%, up from last fall's 33%.

Given a choice of bills currently being considered, the public is as likely to opt for the Bush bill (25%) or no bill at all (27%) as it is to favor the Democratic version (24%); another 24% have no opinion. Blacks, who might be expected to benefit most, give less than overwhelming support to the Democratic version: fewer than one half (45%) of those who have followed the debate have a clear preference for it.

Democratic efforts to deflect Bush's criticisms by adding language to the bill explicitly barring quotas have not worked thus far. Now, 41% believe that the Democratic bill, but not the Bush alternative, would require quotas, while another 10% think that both bills would require quotas.

A majority (61%) of those aware of the legislation believes that congressional Democrats are playing politics with the racial issue rather than making a serious attempt to reduce discrimination. Bush's role in the quotas debate, on the other hand, is viewed more positively: six in ten (61%) think that he opposes the Democratic bill for substantive reasons—his assertion that it would lead to

quotas in hiring and promotions—rather than for political reasons.

JUNE 26
DEATH PENALTY

Interviewing Date: 6/13–16/91
Survey #GO 222002

Are you in favor of the death penalty for persons convicted of murder?

Yes...76%
No...18
No opinion...6

	Yes	No	No opinion
By Sex			
Male	81%	14%	5%
Female	72	21	7
By Ethnic Background			
White	78	16	6
Nonwhite	74	22	4
Black	59	31	10
By Education			
College Graduate	70	25	5
College Incomplete	78	17	5
High-School Graduate	78	15	7
Less Than High-School Graduate	75	17	8
By Region			
East	73	19	8
Midwest	73	18	9
South	76	20	4
West	82	13	5
By Age			
18–29 Years	75	20	5
30–49 Years	77	18	5
50 Years and Over	75	17	8
By Household Income			
$50,000 and Over	73	23	4
$30,000–$49,999	75	17	8

$20,000–$29,999....86	12	2
Under $20,000........72	20	8

By Politics
Republicans............83	13	4
Democrats.............67	23	10
Independents...........79	17	4

By Religion
Protestants.............77	17	6
Catholics...............77	16	7

By Political Ideology
Liberal..................71	24	5
Moderate................72	16	12
Conservative...........82	13	5

By Bush Approval
Approve.................79	16	5
Disapprove.............70	25	5

Selected National Trend

	Yes	No	No opinion
1988.....................79%	18%	3%
1986.....................70	22	8
1985.....................72	20	8
1981.....................66	25	9
1978.....................62	27	11
1976.....................65	28	7
1972.....................57	32	11
1971.....................49	40	11
1969.....................51	40	9
1966.....................42	47	11
1965.....................45	43	12
1960.....................51	36	13
1953.....................68	25	7
1937.....................65	35	*
1936.....................61	39	*

*Not included in these surveys

Asked of those who favor the death penalty: Why do you favor the death penalty for persons convicted of murder?

Revenge; an "eye for an eye"...................50%
Acts as deterrent....................................13
Keeps them from killing again.................19
Costly to keep them in prison..................13

Judicial system is too lenient....................3
Other..11
No opinion..2

	White	Black

By Ethnic Background
	White	Black
Revenge; an "eye for an eye".... 50%	48%
Acts as deterrent.................... 13	16
Keeps them from killing again.. 18	23
Costly to keep them in prison... 14	2
Judicial system is too lenient...... 3	2
Other.................................. 10	16
No opinion........................... 2	2

*Multiple responses were given.

Asked of those who oppose the death penalty: Why do you oppose the death penalty for persons convicted of murder?

Wrong to take a life................................41%
Punishment should be left to God..............17
Persons may be wrongly convicted............11
Does not deter crime...............................7
Possibility of rehabilitation....................6
Unfair application of penalty...................6
Other...16
No opinion...6

	White	Black

By Ethnic Background
	White	Black
Wrong to take a life............... 40%	44%
Punishment should be left to God..... 17	20
Persons may be wrongly convicted.............. 10	16
Does not deter crime.................8	7
Possibility of rehabilitation.......6	4
Unfair application of penalty......5	5
Other.................................. 18	8
No opinion........................... 6	7

*Multiple responses were given.

What do you think should be the penalty for murder—the death penalty or life imprisonment, with absolutely no possibility of parole?

Death penalty....................................53%
Life imprisonment.............................35
Neither (volunteered)...........................3
No opinion...9

	White	Black

By Ethnic Background

	White	Black
Death penalty	56%	26%
Life imprisonment	32	62
Neither (volunteered)	3	2
No opinion	9	10

Do you feel that the death penalty acts as a deterrent to the commitment of murder— that it lowers the murder rate, or not?

Yes..51%
No...41
No opinion...8

By Ethnic Background

	White	Black
Yes	53%	38%
No	40	53
No opinion	7	9

Selected National Trend

	1986	1985
Yes	61%	62%
No	32	31
No opinion	7	7

Asked of those who favor the death penalty: Suppose new evidence showed that the death penalty does not act as a deterrent to murder—that it does not lower the murder rate. Would you favor or oppose the death penalty?

Favor...69%
Oppose...26
No opinion...5

By Ethnic Background

	White	Black
Favor	71%	58%
Oppose	24	38
No opinion	5	4

Selected National Trend

	1986	1985
Favor	73%	71%
Oppose	19	21
No opinion	8	8

Asked of those who oppose the death penalty: Suppose new evidence showed that the death penalty acts as a deterrent to murder—that it lowers the murder rate. Would you favor or oppose the death penalty?

Favor...25%
Oppose...65
No opinion..10

By Ethnic Background

	White	Black
Favor	27%	14%
Oppose	62	81
No opinion	11	5

Selected National Trend

	1986	1985
Favor	18%	18%
Oppose	71	67
No opinion	11	15

As I read off each of these statements, would you tell me if you agree or disagree with it:

A black person is more likely than a white person to receive the death penalty for the same crime?

Agree...45%
Disagree...50
No opinion...5

	Agree	Dis-agree	No opinion
By Sex			
Male	46%	47%	7%
Female	44	52	4

By Ethnic Background
	Agree	Disagree	No opinion
White	41	54	5
Nonwhite	64	32	4
Black	73	20	7

By Education
College Graduate	54	40	6
College Incomplete	49	48	3
High-School Graduate	41	54	5
Less Than High-School Graduate	39	53	8

By Region
East	45	51	4
Midwest	45	47	8
South	40	55	5
West	52	44	4

By Age
18–29 Years	41	55	4
30–49 Years	50	46	4
50 Years and Over	43	50	7

By Household Income
$50,000 and Over	49	48	3
$30,000–$49,999	39	55	6
$20,000–$29,999	56	40	4
Under $20,000	42	51	7

By Politics
Republicans	33	63	4
Democrats	52	42	6
Independents	52	44	4

By Political Ideology
Liberal	49	48	3
Moderate	57	35	8
Conservative	41	55	4

By Bush Approval
Approve	41	55	4
Disapprove	59	36	5

A poor person is more likely than a person of average or above average income to receive the death penalty for the same crime?

Agree		60%
Disagree		36
No opinion		4

	Agree	Disagree	No opinion
By Sex			
Male	64%	32%	4%
Female	57	39	4
By Ethnic Background			
White	59	37	4
Nonwhite	63	42	5
Black	72	22	6
By Education			
College Graduate	70	28	2
College Incomplete	70	29	1
High-School Graduate	55	42	3
Less Than High-School Graduate	47	41	12
By Region			
East	59	39	2
Midwest	62	33	5
South	58	35	7
West	64	35	1
By Age			
18–29 Years	54	44	2
30–49 Years	67	31	2
50 Years and Over	57	35	8
By Household Income			
$50,000 and Over	65	34	1
$30,000–$49,999	58	40	2
$20,000–$29,999	71	27	2
Under $20,000	56	36	8
By Politics			
Republicans	54	43	3
Democrats	64	30	6
Independents	64	34	2
By Political Ideology			
Liberal	61	36	3
Moderate	85	14	1
Conservative	58	40	2
By Bush Approval			
Approve	57	40	3
Disapprove	73	25	2

Apart from your own opinion about the death penalty, what form of punishment do you consider to be the most humane—the electric chair, the gas chamber, lethal injection, firing squad, or hanging?

Lethal injection 66%
Electric chair 10
Gas chamber 6
Firing squad 3
Hanging 3
None (volunteered) 6
No opinion 6

	White	Black
By Ethnic Background		
Lethal injection	69%	44%
Electric chair	9	19
Gas chamber	6	6
Firing squad	3	3
Hanging	3	6
None (volunteered)	5	13
No opinion	5	9

Note: Public support for the death penalty remains high, with three quarters of Americans now favoring capital punishment as an option in murder cases. The current level of support is only marginally lower than the half-century high of 79% recorded by Gallup in 1988.

The present one-sided division—76% in favor, 18% opposed, and 6% with no opinion—reflects a quarter century of steady growth in support for capital punishment. The low point occurred in 1966 when Gallup found 42% in favor of the death penalty and 47% opposed. This marks the only time in fifty-five years of Gallup polling that opponents of capital punishment outnumbered supporters. Interestingly, support for the death penalty would decline from 76% to 53% if life in prison with no possibility of parole were a certainty for those convicted of murder.

Six in ten (60%) now agree that the poor are more likely than those of average or above average income to receive the death penalty for the same crime. Blacks are substantially more likely to agree—72% to 22%, compared to 59% and 37% among whites. The public is more evenly divided on whether blacks are more likely than whites to be sentenced to death for the same crime—45% agree and 50% disagree. (This is up slightly from 1986 when 39% agreed.) Black perceptions on this issue stand in sharp contrast to those of whites. Blacks believe by almost a 4-to-1 ratio (73% to 20%) that persons of their race are more likely than whites to receive the death penalty. Among whites, only 41% agree.

Arguments over the death penalty often focus on the issue of whether or not it serves as a deterrent to murder. The Gallup Poll suggests that deterrence is not the most significant factor. Only a bare majority (51%) cites it, while 41% say that it has no effect on the murder rate. Rather, when those who favor the death penalty are asked why they favor it, fully one half (50%) says for revenge—the Biblical "eye for an eye"—while only 13% say that they favor capital punishment because it acts as a deterrent.

Additionally, when those who favor the death penalty are asked whether they would continue to favor the measure if it were proved conclusively that it did not deter murder, only a small percentage (26%) would switch to the opposing position. Similarly, only one quarter of those who oppose the death penalty (25%) would favor it if it were shown to serve as a deterrent.

In addition to revenge (50%) and deterrence (13%), those who favor capital punishment explain their position by saying that it would keep a murderer from killing again (19%) and cite the cost of keeping murderers in prison (13%). On the other hand, those who oppose the death penalty give the following reasons: it is wrong to take a life (41%), punishment should be left to God (17%), the person could have been wrongly convicted (11%), the death penalty does not deter crime (7%), there is always the possibility of rehabilitation (6%), and the penalty may have been unfair (6%).

Once the death penalty is determined, lethal injection is increasingly favored by the public as the most humane method of execution. Two thirds (66%) opt for lethal injection, with the electric chair a distant second (10%). (In 1985 comparable figures were 56% for lethal injection and 16% for the electric chair.) Only small percentages now favor the gas chamber, firing squad, or hanging as the most humane way for the state to take a life.

JULY 3
SOUTH AFRICA

Interviewing Date: 6/27–30/91
Survey #GO 222004

How closely have you followed recent events in South Africa—very closely, fairly closely, not too closely, or not at all closely?

	June 1991	February 1990
Very closely	7%	22%
Fairly closely	32	46
Not too closely	37	22
Not at all closely	24	9
No opinion	*	1

*Less than 1%

Asked of those who have followed the situation in South Africa very or fairly closely: Do you think the South African government has made significant progress during the last year in trying to resolve its racial problems, or not?

Yes	51%
No	45
No opinion	4

	Yes	No	No opinion
By Sex			
Male	58%	38%	4%
Female	43	54	3
By Ethnic Background			
White	54	42	4
Nonwhite	35	53	12
Black	34	64	2
By Education			
College Graduate	63	35	2
College Incomplete	46	52	2
High-School Graduate	47	50	3
Less Than High-School Graduate	36	49	15
By Region			
East	62	36	2
Midwest	51	48	1
South	45	50	5
West	46	49	5
By Age			
18–29 Years	43	56	1
30–49 Years	52	46	2
50 Years and Over	55	38	7
By Household Income			
$50,000 and Over	66	32	2
$30,000–$49,999	46	52	2
$20,000–$29,999	46	47	7
Under $20,000	45	50	5
By Politics			
Republicans	53	42	5
Democrats	46	52	2
Independents	54	41	5
By Religion			
Protestants	48	48	4
Catholics	47	50	3
By Political Ideology			
Liberal	50	48	2
Moderate	66	30	4
Conservative	46	48	6
By Bush Approval			
Approve	54	43	3
Disapprove	48	48	4

Selected National Trend

	Yes	No	No opinion
February 1990	59%	36%	5%
September 1986	22	72	6

Also asked of those who have followed the situation in South Africa very or fairly closely: Some people feel that economic sanctions against South Africa should be lifted as a result of the changes that are taking place there now. Others think the economic sanctions should be maintained to pressure the government to make further changes. Which view comes closer to your own?

Lift sanctions.....................................26%
Maintain sanctions............................62
No opinion...12

	Lift sanctions	Maintain sanctions	No opinion
By Sex			
Male.....................32%	60%	8%
Female..................18	65	17
By Ethnic Background			
White....................27	60	13
Nonwhite 27	69	4
Black 19	72	9
By Education			
College Graduate 28	65	7
College Incomplete...23	71	6
High-School Graduate..............25	60	15
Less Than High-School Graduate 27	43	30
By Region			
East.....................32	55	13
Midwest................18	68	14
South 28	61	11
West....................23	65	12
By Age			
18–29 Years...........30	61	9
30–49 Years...........24	69	7
50 Years and Over.....26	55	19
By Household Income			
$50,000 and Over.....33	62	5
$30,000–$49,999....26	67	7
$20,000–$29,999....14	72	14
Under $20,000........29	58	13
By Politics			
Republicans............33	54	13
Democrats 22	66	12
Independents..........24	64	12
By Religion			
Protestants 25	61	14
Catholics 24	66	10
By Political Ideology			
Liberal..................22	71	7
Moderate..............20	68	22
Conservative..........29	68	13
By Bush Approval			
Approve................28	58	14
Disapprove............22	68	10

As you may know, the International Olympic Committee has banned South Africa from participation in the Olympic Games for the last thirty years. Do you favor or oppose lifting the ban to allow South Africa's participation in the 1992 Olympics?

Favor 67%
Oppose...25
No opinion...8

Note: By a margin of 62% to 26%, aware Americans strongly favor maintaining economic sanctions against South Africa, despite the repeal of the Population Registration Act that racially classified all South Africans at birth. However, they divide 51% to 45% on whether that country has made significant racial progress in the last year.

Even at the time of Nelson Mandela's release from prison in February 1990, when greater attention was focused on the changes taking place in South Africa, similar proportions in the aware group (66% versus 27%) favored maintaining sanctions. With the exception of releasing all political prisoners, the Pretoria government has fulfilled the conditions for lifting the international sanctions. However, most respondents seem to agree with black leaders in this country who think it is too early to take such action. Nevertheless, the Bush administration is considering lifting sanctions if the South African government releases its remaining political prisoners.

Surprisingly, many Americans do not think that significant racial progress has been made in South Africa in the past year. At the time of Mandela's release, more than one half (59%) of the aware group thought that the Pretoria government had made such progress. Today the number has declined slightly to 51%, despite the dismantling of the legal structure of apartheid with the abolition of the Population Registration Act, the Land Act, and the Group Areas Act.

Far fewer respondents have kept as current with these recent legal developments as they did with the release of Mandela from jail. Only 39% now are following news of South Africa very or fairly closely, compared with 68% at the time of his release. Still, 67% favor lifting the ban that has kept that country out of the Olympic Games for more than three decades.

JULY 10
DEMOCRATIC PRESIDENTIAL CANDIDATES

Interviewing Date: 6/27–30/91
Survey #GO 222004

Asked of registered Democrats and those who lean Democratic: So far, only former Massachusetts Senator Paul Tsongas has declared himself a candidate for the Democratic presidential nomination. Which other Democrats, if any, would you like to see enter the race for their party's presidential nomination?

	Total*	Liberals	Conser- vatives
Mario Cuomo	9%	15%	3%
Albert Gore	6	5	8
Jesse Jackson	4	5	5
Edward Kennedy	4	4	4
Jay Rockefeller	3	4	1
Bill Clinton	2	1	4
Richard Gephardt	2	2	1
Lloyd Bentsen	2	2	1

*No others were mentioned by more than 1% of Democratic respondents.

Also asked of registered Democrats and those who lean Democratic: Suppose that you, yourself, were able to select the Democratic party's candidate for president in 1992. Which of the following would be important considerations in selecting a candidate:

	Total	Liberals	Conser- vatives
His views on national health-care policy?	93%	96%	90%
His support for new taxes to solve certain problems?	86	85	88
His views on protecting women and minorities from job discrimination without using quotas?	85	86	85
His views on gun control?	79	82	79
His views on abortion?	74	76	73
His views on trade policies toward Japan?	67	67	69
Whether he is liberal or conservative?	66	76	64
His views on the death penalty?	65	62	77
Whether he supported Bush's decision to go to war against Iraq?	61	58	70
His views on government assistance to private and parochial school parents?	55	51	65

Also asked of registered Democrats and those who lean Democratic, who rated an issue as "important" in the previous question: When choosing a Democratic presidential candidate, would you prefer a candidate who:

	Total*	Liberals	Conser- vatives
Favors a national health-care system?	65%	70%	63%
Favors stricter gun-control laws?	59	67	54
Would support new taxes to solve certain problems?	56	64	50

Opposes making abortions more difficult to obtain?...............46	60	30
Favors the death penalty in murder cases?.................46	40	59
Favors new trade restrictions against Japan?................43	42	44
Opposes quotas in hiring and promotion?..........40	40	38
Favors quotas in hiring and promotion?..........40	39	43
Supported Bush's decision to go to war against Iraq?....36	32	48
Has liberal views?.....35	59	10
Favors government assistance to private and parochial school parents?.....32	28	42
Has conservative views?................26	15	49
Opposes increasing federal taxes?........26	18	33
Favors making abortions more difficult to obtain?...............25	14	41

*No other positions on issues were considered important by more than 20% of Democratic respondents.

Note: With the Democratic party's nominating convention now just one year away, the latest Gallup Poll finds that Democrats and Democratic-leaning independents most often cite New York Governor Mario Cuomo (9%) and Tennessee Senator Albert Gore (6%) when asked which other Democrats besides the only declared candidate, former Massachusetts Senator Paul Tsongas, should run for president in 1992. Although fewer (3%) come up with the name of West Virginia Senator Jay Rockefeller, his advocacy of health-care issues might help boost his prospects as a candidate. Health-care policy (65%) rates at the top of a list of issues

considered important by Democratic respondents when selecting a presidential candidate.

Cuomo is clearly the most wanted candidate among Democratic respondents who describe themselves as liberals: 15% cite Cuomo, compared with 5% for Gore, 5% for Jesse Jackson, 4% for Edward Kennedy, and 4% for Rockefeller. These liberal Democrats essentially want the candidate to be an activist who will speak up for traditional liberal causes. When asked about the kinds of political views they would like to see represented in a Democratic candidate, solid majorities cite support for a government-funded national health-care system (70%), support for stricter gun-control laws (67%), a willingness to support new federal taxes for certain government programs in areas such as crime prevention, the environment, and education (64%), opposition to new laws that would further restrict abortion (60%), and generally liberal views on most issues (59%).

As seen in the 1988 presidential primaries, the more liberal segment of the Democratic party is likely to play the more important role in selecting the eventual nominee. However, in 1992 it is widely expected that there will be no presidential race on the Republican side, since George Bush runs unopposed for his party's nomination. This may boost the influence of the more conservative Democrats, especially in open primaries, who will be less tempted to cross over and vote in the Republican primary.

Even though many voters with more conservative political views have switched their allegiance from the Democrats to the Republicans over the past two decades, the Democratic party's rank and file still includes a sizable proportion of conservatives. Gore (8%) tops the list of potential candidates whom conservative Democrats would like to see enter the race, followed by Jackson (5%), Kennedy (4%), Arkansas Governor Bill Clinton (4%), and Cuomo (3%). Gore's support for President Bush's decision to use military force against Iraq helps his chances among conservative Democrats, one half (48%) of whom says that it is important for the party's presidential candidate to have backed Bush on Iraq.

While Rockefeller does not make conservatives' short list, the health-care issue may give him an opportunity to win support outside of the party's more liberal mainstream. Conservative Democrats, like their liberal counterparts, rate health care their top priority—63% say that it is important for the candidate to support a national health-care system funded by the government.

Conservative Democrats, like liberals, also prefer a candidate who supports stricter gun-control laws (54%). And 50% would go along with liberal Democrats in wanting a nominee willing to propose new federal taxes to fund in critical areas such as crime prevention, the environment, and education. Democratic liberals and conservatives part company, however, on social issues such as opposing laws to make abortions more difficult to obtain (60% versus 30%) and favoring the death penalty (40% versus 59%).

JULY 13
ALLEGED 1980 HOSTAGE DEAL

Interviewing Date: 6/27–30/91
Survey #GO 222004

Would you favor or oppose having Congress investigate charges that the Reagan-Bush campaign made a deal with Iran to delay the release of U.S. hostages until after the November 1980 election?

Favor 63%
Oppose..32
No opinion.. 5

	Favor	Oppose	No opinion
By Politics			
Republicans............	48%	48%	4%
Democrats	78	17	5
Independents..........	65	31	4
By Political Ideology			
Liberal..................	77	21	2
Moderate...............	69	25	6
Conservative..........	54	42	4

Note: Six in ten (63%) Americans favor a congressional investigation into allegations that the Reagan-Bush campaign struck a deal in

1980 with the Iranian government to delay the release of U.S. hostages until after the November presidential election. About one third (32%) opposes such an investigation. As might be expected, support is greatest among those with a political or ideological perspective different from that of Ronald Reagan and George Bush. Three quarters (78%) of Democrats and one half (48%) of Republicans also favor such action.

JULY 17
CLARENCE THOMAS

Interviewing Date: 7/11–14/91
Survey #GO 222006

President Bush recently nominated a new justice to the Supreme Court. Can you tell me what his name is?

Clarence Thomas (correct)......................31%
Other names.. 6
No opinion..63

In its recent rulings, do you think the Supreme Court has been too liberal, too conservative, or just about right?

Too liberal..20%
Too conservative................................25
About right..39
No opinion..16

	Too liberal	Too conservative	About right	No opinion
By Sex				
Male	23%	27%	38%	12%
Female..........	18	24	39	19
By Ethnic Background				
White...........	21	26	37	16
Nonwhite	17	22	45	16
Black	18	24	42	16
By Education				
College Graduate.....	17	38	37	8
College In-complete....	19	28	40	13

High-School Graduate.....20	23	41	16
Less Than High-School Graduate.....26	16	32	26

By Region

East.............21	30	33	16
Midwest........20	24	40	16
South...........22	20	41	17
West............18	28	41	13

By Age

18–29 Years...14	24	43	19
30–49 Years...18	34	37	11
50 Years and Over.....27	18	36	19

By Household Income

$50,000 and Over..........17	34	39	10
$30,000– $49,999.....22	26	40	12
$20,000– $29,999.....18	25	39	18
Under $20,000.....22	20	35	23

By Politics

Republicans...21	21	46	12
Democrats.....21	31	32	16
Independents..19	25	37	19

By Religion

Protestants....23	19	41	17
Catholics......21	29	38	12

By Political Ideology

Liberal..........14	38	36	12
Moderate.......15	36	38	11
Conservative..29	18	41	12

By Bush Approval

Approve........22	21	43	14
Disapprove....17	40	26	17

Please tell me whether you generally approve or disapprove of the Supreme Court's rulings over the past two years in each of the following areas:

In cases where the rights of prisoners or people charged with committing crimes are an issue?

Approve	33%
Disapprove	44
No opinion	23

In cases where abortion is an issue?

Approve	32%
Disapprove	50
No opinion	18

In cases where racial discrimination, affirmative action, or racial quotas are an issue?

Approve	39%
Disapprove	37
No opinion	24

Clarence Thomas is the federal judge nominated to serve on the Supreme Court. Would you like to see the Senate vote in favor of Clarence Thomas serving on the Supreme Court, or not?

Yes	52%
No	17
No opinion	31

	Yes	No	No opinion
By Ethnic Background			
White.................52%		16%	32%
Black...................57		18	25

From what you may have heard or read about Bush's decision, do you think Clarence Thomas was selected:

Mostly because Bush considered him to be best qualified for the position?	37%
Mostly because he is black?	32
Mostly for other reasons?	19
No opinion	12

	Best qualified	Black	Other	No opinion
By Ethnic Background				
White...........38%		31%	18%	13%
Black...........32		37	20	11

From what you know about Clarence Thomas, as a Supreme Court justice do you think he would be too liberal, too conservative, or just about right?

Too liberal..7%
Too conservative.................................20
About right...46
No opinion..27

In 1973 the Supreme Court ruled that states cannot place restrictions on a woman's right to an abortion during the first three months of pregnancy. Would you like to see this ruling overturned, or not?

Yes..37%
No..56
No opinion..7

Selected National Trend

	Yes	No	No opinion
May 1991	42%	52%	6%
July 1989	34	58	8
April 1989*	39	51	10
December 1988	37	58	5

*Gallup Poll conducted for *Newsweek*

When the U.S. Senate holds hearings on the Clarence Thomas nomination, do you think senators should insist that he explain his views on abortion before confirming him, or should he be allowed to refuse to answer questions about abortion?

Insist he explain his views.....................54%
Allow him to refuse to answer.................39
No opinion..7

Note: A new Gallup Poll finds that over one half of the American public supports President George Bush's nomination of Federal Judge Clarence Thomas to the Supreme Court. Fifty-two percent would like to see him confirmed by the Senate, while only one in six (17%) opposes his confirmation and one third (31%) has no opinion.

Thomas's conservative views contrast sharply with those of Thurgood Marshall, the man he would replace. The retirement of Marshall, the former civil rights attorney who became the Court's first black justice in 1967, allowed Bush to make his second nomination to the high court. Thus far, neither Thomas's conservatism nor his differences with civil rights leaders appear to have adversely affected his image as an acceptable candidate. Among both blacks and whites, supporters of confirmation outnumber opponents by a 3-to-1 margin.

The public regards the Thomas nomination much more favorably than it viewed that of another outspoken conservative, Robert Bork, after Ronald Reagan proposed him in 1987. A Gallup/*Newsweek* Poll taken shortly after Bork's nomination found public opinion on his confirmation to be closely divided—31% in favor, 25% opposed, and 44% with no opinion. Bork's nomination was eventually rejected by the Senate.

Despite President Bush's statements that he would appoint the best qualified person to the Court, most respondents think that Thomas's race or his political views were the more important considerations. Fewer than four in ten (37%) believe that he was chosen as the best qualified candidate, while one third (32%) says that he was selected because he is black and 19% say that other, mostly political, factors played the major role. On balance, the Thomas selection has been received positively in the black community, but not overwhelmingly so. Opinion on whether he should be confirmed, however, does not differ significantly between blacks (57% favor versus 18% oppose) and whites (52% favor versus 16% oppose).

Thomas's conservatism is not a liability in a country that has been moving to the right for two decades. When asked specifically about the suitability of his political views for the high court, only 20% say that he would be too conservative. Indeed, the poll provides no indication that the public sees a problem with the ideological direction of the Court. Nearly as many say its recent decisions have been too liberal (20%) as say they have been too conservative (25%). These results suggest that public perceptions of the institution of the

Court still owe much to the legacies of the Warren and Burger Courts and less to the more recent Rehnquist Court.

Abortion is the one issue that may be an obstacle to Thomas's confirmation. A majority (54%) says that he should explain his views on abortion before being confirmed by the Senate; four in ten (39%) would allow him to decline to answer questions on this issue. Should he decide to air his views on abortion, however, he faces a divided public. Those who oppose overturning *Roe v. Wade* outnumber supporters of such a change by 56% to 37%.

JULY 18
PERSIAN GULF SITUATION

Interviewing Date: 7/11–14/91
Survey #GO 222006

Do you approve or disapprove of the way George Bush has handled the situation in Iraq since the war in the Persian Gulf ended?

Approve...63%
Disapprove.......................................30
No opinion.. 7

	Approve	Dis-approve	No opinion
By Sex			
Male......................63%	32%	5%
Female..................63	28	9
By Ethnic Background			
White....................63	30	7
Nonwhite...............55	38	7
Black....................53	42	5
By Education			
College Graduate.....58	35	7
College Incomplete...64	32	4
High-School		
Graduate.............65	29	6
Less Than High-		
School Graduate....60	28	12
By Region			
East.....................59	36	5
Midwest................60	30	10
South....................68	26	6
West.....................64	29	7
By Age			
18–29 Years............66	28	6
30–49 Years............64	30	6
50 Years and Over.....58	33	9
By Household Income			
$50,000 and Over.....71	26	3
$30,000–$49,999....61	34	5
$20,000–$29,999....64	28	8
Under $20,000........55	34	11
By Politics			
Republicans............78	18	4
Democrats 48	44	8
Independents...........60	31	9
By Religion			
Protestants 64	29	7
Catholics 63	31	6
By Political Ideology			
Liberal...................57	39	4
Moderate...............64	30	6
Conservative..........70	26	4
By Bush Approval			
Approve.................77	18	5
Disapprove.............24	70	6

All in all, was the current situation in the Mideast involving Iraq and Kuwait worth going to war over, or not?

Yes..66%
No...28
No opinion... 6

	Yes	No	No opinion
By Sex			
Male....................71%	24%	5%
Female..................62	30	8
By Ethnic Background			
White....................71	24	5
Nonwhite...............40	48	12
Black....................37	50	13

By Education

College Graduate 70	26	4
College Incomplete...68	28	4
High-School Graduate..............67	26	7
Less Than High-School Graduate 59	31	10

By Region

East 62	33	5
Midwest................68	26	6
South 69	24	7
West 63	28	9

By Age

18–29 Years............64	34	2
30–49 Years............71	24	5
50 Years and Over.....63	26	11

By Household Income

$50,000 and Over.....79	19	2
$30,000–$49,999....72	26	2
$20,000–$29,999....67	27	6
Under $20,000........53	36	11

By Politics

Republicans............80	16	4
Democrats 54	37	9
Independents...........64	29	7

By Religion

Protestants 69	24	7
Catholics 67	27	6

By Political Ideology

Liberal...................61	33	6
Moderate................67	23	10
Conservative...........75	22	3

By Bush Approval

Approve.................75	19	6
Disapprove............37	56	7

Selected National Trend

	Yes	No	No opinion
1991			
May 23–26.............72%	23%	5%
April 25–28............70	24	6
April 4–6 71	22	7
February 28–March 3 80	15	5
January 30–February 2 71	24	5
January 11–13........46	44	10
January 3–6 47	44	9
1990			
December 13–16 49	44	7
December 6–9.........47	45	8
November 29–December 2..........51	41	8
November 15–18......46	45	9
September 27–30 49	41	10
August 30–September 2........45	44	11
August 23–26.........49	41	10

Would you favor or oppose the United States resuming military action against Iraq if the Iraqis refuse to observe the UN resolution calling for destruction of their nuclear weapons capability?

Favor 74%
Oppose..18
No opinion..8

If the United States does resume military action against Iraq, what should be our objective:

To destroy Iraq's nuclear weapons capability?..........................6%
To remove Saddam Hussein from power?...................................14
Both 77
No opinion...3

Note: Seventy-four percent of Americans favor renewing military action against Iraq unless President Saddam Hussein conforms with United Nations resolutions calling for the destruction of his country's nuclear weapons capability. These and other findings emerge from the latest Gallup Poll. Despite the extensive allied bombing of Iraq's nuclear sites during the Persian Gulf war, it was disclosed recently that Baghdad retains nuclear weapons-making materials.

Respondents' willingness to resume military action against Iraq apparently reflects ongoing concern over Hussein's continued influence in the region. Almost eight out of ten (77%) say that the aim of further military action, if undertaken, should be both to destroy Iraq's nuclear capability and to remove Hussein from power.

Despite his influence and the accusations against the restored Kuwaiti government of human rights violations, retrospective support for U.S. involvement in the Gulf war continues to be high. Sixty-six percent think that the situation was worth going to war over, while 28% do not. This level of support is down, however, from a high of 80% in early March, immediately after victory was declared. It is also down slightly from Gallup's last measurement in May (72%). Another 63% approve of the way that President George Bush has handled the situation in Iraq since the war ended, while 30% disapprove.

JULY 24
SOUTH AFRICA

Interviewing Date: 7/11–14/91
Survey #GO 222006

Do you approve or disapprove of President Bush's decision to remove economic sanctions against South Africa?

Approve..45%
Disapprove..30
No opinion..25

	Approve	Dis-approve	No opinion
By Sex			
Male	54%	30%	16%
Female	37	30	33
By Ethnic Background			
White	47	27	26
Nonwhite	33	51	16
Black	32	56	12
By Education			
College Graduate	54	32	14
College Incomplete	45	33	22
High-School Graduate	43	31	26
Less Than High-School Graduate	40	25	35
By Region			
East	41	34	25
Midwest	47	25	28
South	47	29	24
West	45	34	21
By Age			
18–29 Years	43	35	22
30–49 Years	44	34	22
50 Years and Over	47	24	29
By Household Income			
$50,000 and Over	52	30	18
$30,000–$49,999	47	33	20
$20,000–$29,999	43	33	24
Under $20,000	39	30	31
By Politics			
Republicans	56	22	22
Democrats	35	39	26
Independents	45	31	24
By Religion			
Protestants	45	28	27
Catholics	46	31	23
By Political Ideology			
Liberal	41	41	18
Moderate	44	30	26
Conservative	54	25	21
By Bush Approval			
Approve	52	24	24
Disapprove	26	54	20

Note: Last week George Bush joined his European allies in announcing an end to the economic sanctions against South Africa, in place since 1986. The president's action is supported by 45% of Americans and opposed by 30%, while 25% have no opinion. Major differences in support for removing the sanctions occur by gender, political party, and race. Men are significantly more likely to approve than women, Democrats more than Republicans, and whites more than blacks.

JULY 24
SOVIET UNION

Interviewing Date: 7/18–21/91
Survey #GO 222007

I'd like your overall opinion of Mikhail Gorbachev. Is your overall opinion of him very favorable, mostly favorable, mostly unfavorable, or very unfavorable?

Very favorable	14%
Mostly favorable	60
Mostly unfavorable	14
Very unfavorable	5
No opinion	7

By Political Ideology

	Very, mostly favorable	Mostly, very un- favorable	No opinion
Liberal	80%	17%	3%
Moderate	78	12	10
Conservative	73	22	5

Selected National Trend

	Very, mostly favorable	Mostly, very un- favorable	No opinion
January 1991	70%	23%	7%
October 1990	74	17	9
September 1990	70	21	9
May 1990	68	21	11
December 1989	77	15	8
December 1988	72	21	7

Do you think relations between the United States and the Soviet Union are getting better, getting worse, or staying about the same?

Better	62%
Worse	3
Same	34
No opinion	1

By Political Ideology

	Better	Worse	Same	No opinion
Liberal	70%	2%	28%	*
Moderate	70	*	29	1
Conservative	59	3	36	2

*Less than 1%

Selected National Trend

	Better	Worse	Same	No opinion
Jan. 1991	41%	12%	46%	1%
Oct. 1986	24	60	13	3

From what you have heard or read, how serious do you think the Soviet Union's economic problems are—very serious, somewhat serious, not too serious, or not at all serious?

Very serious	71%
Somewhat serious	23
Not too serious	2
Not at all serious	1
No opinion	3

By Political Ideology

	Very serious	Some- what serious	Not too, not at all serious	No opinion
Liberal	74%	22%	3%	1%
Moderate	74	17	*	9
Conservative	70	24	5	1

*Less than 1%

Now, what are your expectations for the Soviet Union? Do you think President Gorbachev's attempts to restructure the Soviet economy are likely to succeed or likely to fail?

Succeed	47%
Fail	35
No opinion	18

By Political Ideology

	Succeed	Fail	No opinion
Liberal	56%	30%	14%
Moderate	46	35	19
Conservative	45	40	15

Selected National Trend

	Succeed	Fail	No opinion
January 1991	46%	42%	12%
June 1989	65	21	14

As you may know, last December President Bush approved up to one billion dollars in federal loans to help ease food shortages in the USSR. Do you approve or disapprove of that decision?

Approve	54%
Disapprove	42
No opinion	4

	Approve	Dis-approve	No opinion
By Political Ideology			
Liberal	60%	37%	3%
Moderate	55	41	4
Conservative	54	43	3

Do you favor or oppose the following types of U.S. aid to the Soviet Union:

Providing technical assistance, advice, and expertise?

Favor	69%
Oppose	26
No opinion	5

	Favor	Oppose	No opinion
By Political Ideology			
Liberal	75%	21%	4%
Moderate	76	18	6
Conservative	66	30	4

Donating American grain and other farm products?

Favor	58%
Oppose	38
No opinion	4

	Favor	Oppose	No opinion
By Political Ideology			
Liberal	61%	36%	3%
Moderate	58	33	9
Conservative	59	38	3

Providing financial loans?

Favor	48%
Oppose	48
No opinion	4

	Favor	Oppose	No opinion
By Political Ideology			
Liberal	59%	38%	3%
Moderate	46	52	2
Conservative	44	51	5

Providing cash that would not have to be paid back?

Favor	6%
Oppose	92
No opinion	2

	Favor	Oppose	No opinion
By Political Ideology			
Liberal	8%	90%	2%
Moderate	5	93	2
Conservative	4	96	*

*Less than 1%

Do you think the United States is doing too much, not enough, or about the right amount to help the Soviet Union in its current economic crisis?

Too much	20%
Not enough	9
About right	64
No opinion	7

	Too much	Not enough	About right	No opinion
By Political Ideology				
Liberal	19%	13%	63%	5%
Moderate	11	4	76	9
Conservative	22	7	66	5

Have you heard or read about the proposed nuclear arms-reduction agreement between the United States and the Soviet Union?

	Yes
National	73%

Asked of those who replied in the affirmative: Everything considered, would you like to see the U.S. Congress vote in favor of this proposed nuclear reduction treaty, or not?

	Yes
National	84%

	Yes
By Political Ideology	
Liberal	84%
Moderate	86
Conservative	83

Note: The majority of Americans approves of the way in which the United States and its allies have come to the aid of the Soviet Union to help ease its current economic crisis. About two thirds (64%) of those interviewed in a new Gallup Poll say that our response to the Soviet economic crisis has been about right, while one in five (20%) thinks that we have done too much and 9% say that we have done too little.

In terms of specific measures, seven out of ten (69%) favor the recently announced program of providing the Soviets with technical assistance, advice, and expertise. For programs aimed directly at the Soviet food shortage, 58% favor donating grain and other farm products, while 54% approve of the U.S. loan of $1 billion last December to ease food shortages. Support for financial loans is split, however: 48% approve and 48% disapprove. And there is virtually no support for our providing the Soviet Union with cash that would not have to be paid back; only 6% would approve, while 92% would not.

Most Americans are well aware of the seriousness of the Soviet economic crisis: 94% agree that the USSR's economic problems are either very (71%) or somewhat (22%) serious. Moreover, they have lost some faith over the last two years in the ability of Soviet President Mikhail Gorbachev to solve the economic crisis: less than one half (47%) says that he will succeed in restructuring his country's economy, while 35% say that he will fail. These numbers are significantly more pessimistic than two years ago when, in the initial flush of excitement over *perestroika*, two thirds of Americans (65%) thought that Gorbachev would succeed in his economic reform efforts.

On another front, there is overwhelming support for the recently announced nuclear arms-limitation treaty between the United States and the USSR. Seventy-three percent say that they have heard or read about the treaty; and of these, 84% favor congressional ratification.

Perhaps as a result of the announcement of the treaty, the majority of Americans is now convinced that U.S. relations with the Soviets are on the upswing. The Gallup Poll shows that 62% find that relationships between the two superpowers are getting better, while only 3% say that they are getting worse. This is a dramatic turnaround from 1986, when 60% thought that relations were getting worse, and it also marks a significant upswing from this past January, in the middle of the Persian Gulf war, when only 41% thought that relationships between the two countries were getting better.

JULY 25
PERSONAL FINANCES/RECESSION

Interviewing Date: 7/11–14/91
Survey #GO 222006

We are interested in how people's financial situation may have changed. Would you say that you are financially better off now than you were a year ago, or are you financially worse off now?

Better	34%
Worse	32
Same (volunteered)	33
No opinion	1

	Better	Worse	Same	No opinion
By Sex				
Male	37%	30%	32%	1%
Female	31	34	34	1

By Ethnic Background

White..........32	32	35	1
Nonwhite 41	34	25	*
Black 41	33	26	*

By Education

College Graduate.....37	27	36	*
College In-complete....37	30	33	*
High-School Graduate.....35	33	31	1
Less Than High-School Graduate.....22	41	36	1

By Region

East 28	39	32	1
Midwest........30	33	36	1
South 39	28	32	1
West 36	28	34	2

By Age

18–29 Years...47	31	21	1
30–49 Years...37	30	32	1
50 Years and Over..........21	34	44	1

By Household Income

$50,000 and Over..........48	24	28	*
$30,000–$49,999.....34	29	36	1
$20,000–$29,999.....33	32	34	1
Under $20,000.....23	43	34	*

By Politics

Republicans...39	25	35	1
Democrats 30	36	33	1
Independents..30	36	33	1

By Political Ideology

Liberal..........33	33	34	*
Moderate.......30	26	42	2
Conservative..36	32	31	1

By Bush Approval

Approve........37	28	34	1
Disapprove....21	46	32	1

*Less than 1%

Selected National Trend

	Better	Worse	Same	No opinion
1991				
May 16–19....32%	32%	33%	3%
April 11–14...29	33	37	1
March 21–24..30	37	32	1
Feb. 28–March 3 37	28	34	1
Feb. 14–17....37	28	35	*
Jan. 11–13 26	33	39	2
Jan. 3–6........35	32	32	1
1990				
Dec. 13–16....38	36	26	*
Oct. 25–28 38	35	26	1
Oct. 18–21 27	41	30	2
Oct. 11–14 32	41	26	1
September 40	27	32	1
August..........43	27	29	1
July 44	28	27	1
February........49	24	26	1

*Less than 1%

Looking ahead, do you expect that at this time next year you will be financially better off than now or worse off than now?

Better...57%
Worse...15
Same (volunteered).............................19
No opinion..9

Selected National Trend

	Better	Worse	Same	No opinion
1991				
May 16–19....57%	16%	19%	8%
April 11–14...56	17	18	9
March 21–24..56	18	20	6
Feb. 28–March 3 64	9	20	7
Feb. 14–17....57	15	20	8
Jan. 11–13 41	25	21	13
Jan. 3–6........52	18	20	10
1990				
Dec. 13–16....58	18	17	7
Oct. 25–28 50	27	15	8
Oct. 18–21 41	34	16	9
Oct. 11–14 48	30	13	9
September 51	17	20	12

August..........57	16	20	7
July.............58	17	18	7
February........65	13	16	6

How would you describe business conditions in your community—would you say they are very good, good, not too good, or bad?

Very good..	5%
Good..	43
Not too good......................................	37
Bad..	12
No opinion...	3

Selected National Trend

	Very good, good	Not too good, bad	No opinion
1991			
May......................49%	49%	2%
March....................44	55	1
1990			
July......................57	41	2

Right now, do you think that economic conditions in the country as a whole are getting better or getting worse?

Better..	34%
Worse..	51
Same (volunteered)...............................	9
No opinion...	6

In your opinion, has the bottom of the current recession been reached, or not?

Yes..	42%
No..	48
No opinion...	10

Selected National Trend

	Yes	No	No opinion
1991			
May 23–26..............33%	53%	14%
May 16–19..............26	65	9
April 25–28............30	59	11
April 11–14............33	53	14
March 21–24..........42	47	11

Note: Fully one half of Americans remain pessimistic about the short-run outlook for the economy. Although an increasing proportion now believes that the bottom of the recession may have been reached, consumer confidence remains at a relatively low level and has improved only slightly during the last two or three months. Therefore, consumers are unlikely to play a major role in driving the economy up from recession in the months ahead.

One half of all consumers (51%) believes that economic conditions in the country as a whole are now getting worse. Only one third (34%) says that conditions are getting better. Similarly, one half (48%) thinks that the bottom of the recession has not yet been reached. On a somewhat brighter note, those believing that the bottom has been reached has increased from 26% in May to 42% now.

When people were asked how they would describe current business conditions in their own communities, opinions also were evenly divided, with 48% saying good or very good and 49% saying not too good or bad. These perceptions have not changed in the last two months.

In the current survey, 34% claim to be better off financially now than they were a year ago, while a nearly equal 32% say that they are worse off. As is almost always the case, a majority (57%) expects to be better off financially a year from now, while a much smaller proportion expects to be worse off (15%). None of these measures of general consumer confidence has changed significantly during the last two months.

On three different occasions during the last year and one half, consumer confidence has shown great volatility. In October 1990 confidence was driven down by the double whammy of recession and the Persian Gulf crisis. In mid-January 1991 confidence slumped as war appeared imminent, and at the end of February confidence soared as victory became apparent.

If one disregards these three periods when fast-moving events had an extraordinary but temporary impact on consumer confidence, a clear picture of slow and steady change emerges. A Gallup consumer confidence index based on personal financial attitudes and expectations showed steady decline from February 1990 to late March-early April 1991, one month after the Gulf victory had been won. Since then, this index has regained less than one quarter of its lost ground, which leaves consumer attitudes about as they were at the beginning of the year, before the war heated up.

JULY 25
PARTY BETTER FOR PEACE AND PROSPERITY

Interviewing Date: 7/18–21/91
Survey #GO 222007

Looking ahead for the next few years, which political party do you think would be more likely to keep the United States out of World War III—the Republican or the Democratic party?

Republican 42%
Democratic 33
No difference; no opinion.....................25

Selected National Trend

	Repub-lican	Demo-cratic	No difference; no opinion
1990			
October..................34%	36%	30%
August* 36	34	30
1988			
September*............43	33	24
July*.....................39	36	25
May* 31	39	30
January* 36	35	29
1984			
August..................36	40	24
April....................30	42	28
1983			
September 26	39	35
1982			
October..................29	38	33
1981			
April....................29	34	37

*Asked of registered voters

Which political party—the Republican or the Democratic—will do a better job of keeping the country prosperous?

Republican 49%
Democratic 32
No difference; no opinion.....................19

Selected National Trend

	Repub-lican	Demo-cratic	No difference; no opinion
1990			
October.................37%	35%	28%
August* 45	30	25
1988			
September*............52	34	14
July*.....................46	39	15
May* 41	39	20
January* 42	35	23
1984			
August..................48	36	16
April....................44	36	20
1983			
September 33	40	27
1982			
October..................34	43	23
1981			
April....................41	28	31

*Asked of registered voters

Note: Despite the recession of the past year, a new Gallup Poll shows that the Republicans are riding high as the party of prosperity. One half (49%) of respondents now sees the GOP as the party better able to keep the country prosperous, while only one third (32%) says that the Democrats can do a better job. Since Gallup first began asking this question in 1951, the party holding the White House generally has lost ground on the prosperity measure during economic downturns; given today's economic climate, the Republicans' current advantage is especially impressive.

The latest results are comparable to those recorded last summer, before most Americans began to feel the effects of the recession. In an August 1990 Gallup Poll, the GOP enjoyed a 45%-to-30% advantage on the prosperity question. Two months later in October, as the recession took hold, the Democrats drew about even as the party of prosperity (37% Republican versus 35% Democratic). Now that the Republicans have retaken the lead, it is apparent that the Democrats have been unable to capitalize on the political opportunities created by the recession.

The GOP also holds an advantage on another key Gallup barometer of party strength. The Republicans lead by 42% to 33% as the party more likely to keep the United States out of World War III. Most likely a reflection of public support for President George Bush's decision to use military force against Iraq, these latest results are a significant improvement in the GOP's standing since Iraq's invasion of Kuwait last August. Both the August and October polls found the two parties to be about even on the peace measure.

During the last recession, in Ronald Reagan's first term, the Republicans saw their image as the party of prosperity suffer. In 1981 they lost their advantage on this measure and subsequently suffered heavy losses in the 1982 off-year congressional elections. The GOP did not reclaim its image as the party of prosperity until the presidential election of 1984. Improved economic conditions played no small part in Reagan's sweeping victory over Walter Mondale that year. Barring a major scandal or other unforeseen developments during the next year, only the state of the economy seems to stand between Bush and reelection in 1992.

JULY 31
PERSIAN GULF SITUATION

Interviewing Date: 7/18–21/91
Survey #GO 222007

Looking back, do you approve or disapprove of the U.S. decision last January to go to war with Iraq in order to drive the Iraqis out of Kuwait?

Approve...78%
Disapprove..21
No opinion..1

	Approve	Dis-approve	No opinion
By Sex			
Male	82%	17%	1%
Female	74	24	2
By Ethnic Background			
White	82	16	2
Nonwhite	46	52	2
Black	37	61	2
By Education			
College Graduate	76	23	1
College Incomplete	79	18	3
High-School Graduate	79	20	1
Less Than High-School Graduate	75	21	4
By Region			
East	74	24	2
Midwest	79	19	2
South	82	16	2
West	75	24	1
By Age			
18–29 Years	77	21	2
30–49 Years	80	18	2
50 Years and Over	76	23	1
By Household Income			
$50,000 and Over	86	14	*
$30,000–$49,999	80	19	1
$20,000–$29,999	81	18	1
Under $20,000	69	29	2
By Politics			
Republicans	91	8	1
Democrats	67	32	1
Independents	74	24	2
By Religion			
Protestants	80	19	1
Catholics	79	18	3
By Political Ideology			
Liberal	68	31	1
Moderate	80	18	2
Conservative	85	15	*

By Bush Approval
Approve.................90   9   1
Disapprove............43   55   2

*Less than 1%

Do you approve or disapprove of the way the following people handled the situation in the Persian Gulf region: Soviet Premier Mikhail Gorbachev; Allied commander General Norman Schwarzkopf; Chairman of the Joint Chiefs of Staff General Colin Powell; Secretary of State James Baker; the U.S. news media covering the war; the U.S. Congress; the U.S. military; George Bush?

	Approve	Dis-approve	No opinion
Military	94%	5%	1%
Schwarzkopf	89	7	4
Powell	83	8	9
Bush	80	18	2
Baker	78	11	11
Congress	63	26	11
News media	60	37	3
Gorbachev	53	32	15

In view of the developments since we first sent our troops to the Persian Gulf region, do you think the United States made a mistake in sending troops to the Persian Gulf region, or not?

Yes..15%
No..82
No opinion.. 3

Selected National Trend

	Yes	No	No opinion
1991			
February 28–March 3	10%	87%	3%
February 7–10	21	76	3
January 30–February 2	18	80	2
January 23–26	18	77	5
January 17–20	16	80	4
January 11–13	29	65	6
January 3–6	31	61	8
1990			
December 6–9	28	66	6

November 29–December 2	29	66	5
November 15–18	27	65	8
November 8–11	27	68	5
November 1–4	25	67	8
October 25–28	24	71	5
October 18–21	26	67	7
October 11–14	26	68	6
October 3–4	21	71	8
September 27–30	20	73	7
September 14–16	18	73	9
September 10–11	19	76	5
August 30–September 2	16	76	8
August 23–26	18	76	6
August 16–19	17	75	8

Do you feel that the United States and its allies should have continued fighting until Saddam Hussein was removed from power, or not?

Yes..76%
No..20
No opinion.. 4

Selected National Trend

	Yes	No	No opinion
1991			
April 4–6	56%	36%	8%
February 28–March 3	46	49	5

How concerned are you that Saddam Hussein will again pose a military threat to the Middle East region?

Very concerned 52%
Somewhat concerned 32
Not too concerned...............................10
Not at all concerned.............................5
No opinion.. 1

As you may know, the economic sanctions imposed against Iraq by the United Nations are still in place. These sanctions prohibit Iraq from selling its oil or other products to other countries. Would you favor leaving the sanctions in place as long as Saddam Hussein remains in power, allowing Iraq to sell some oil if the money goes to pay for food and medical supplies, or lifting the sanctions to allow Iraq to resume normal trade?

	July 1991	May 1991
Leave sanctions in place	52%	52%
Allow conditionally	37	39
Completely lift	6	5
No opinion	5	4

If Saddam Hussein is removed from power in Iraq, should the United States offer economic aid to help rebuild Iraq, or not?

	July 1991	March 1991
Yes	44%	37%
No	49	58
No opinion	7	5

Do you feel you have a clear idea of what the U.S. military involvement in the Iraqi situation is all about—that is, why our troops are in Saudi Arabia?

Yes	81%
No	18
No opinion	1

Selected National Trend

	Yes	No	No opinion
1990			
December 13–16	74%	24%	2%
November 29–December 2	73	26	1
November 15–18	69	29	2
September 27–30	75	23	2
August 30–September 2	76	23	1
August 23–26	70	28	2
August 16–19	74	24	2

As a result of the Persian Gulf war, do you think that:

The prestige and influence of the United States has increased around the world?

Yes	79%
No	16
No opinion	5

Nations are less likely to invade other nations than they were before the war?

Yes	60%
No	33
No opinion	7

Iraq is less likely to threaten its neighbors in the future?

Yes	54%
No	40
No opinion	6

The world's access to Middle East oil is now more secure?

Yes	47%
No	40
No opinion	13

The prospects for peace between Israel and its Arab neighbors have improved?

Yes	42%
No	46
No opinion	12

The Middle East is a more stable region?

Yes	34%
No	59
No opinion	7

How much longer do you think the United States should maintain military forces in and around the Persian Gulf to maintain peace and stability in the region?

Up to six months	16%
Six months to one year	22
More than one year	14
More than two years	31
No opinion	17

If you knew that a Democratic presidential candidate voted against the resolution allowing President Bush to use military force in the Persian Gulf war, would that make you more likely or less likely to vote for him, or would it not much affect your vote?

	July 1991	April 1991
More likely	8%	11%
Less likely	35	23
Not much affect vote	53	61
No opinion	4	5

Note: One year after the Iraqi invasion of Kuwait, a new Gallup Poll shows that Americans remain solidly supportive of the U.S. response to Saddam Hussein's aggression, including the decision to go to war against Iraq last January. While the proportion who says that the United States should have continued fighting until Hussein was removed from power has significantly increased, a majority nonetheless believes that Operation Desert Storm served to increase our prestige abroad and to discourage further invasions elsewhere in the world.

Looking back, 78% approve of the U.S. decision to go to war against Iraq; only 21% disapprove. On another measure, only 15% say that we made a mistake in committing military forces to the Persian Gulf region. Additionally, five months after the war was won, there appears to be little confusion about its aims: 81% have a clear idea of what the U.S. military involvement in the Iraqi situation was all about, while only 18% do not.

Respondents are most likely to agree that the war increased the prestige and influence of the United States around the world (79%). A majority also agrees that, as a result of the war, nations are less likely now to invade other nations (60%) and that Iraq is less likely to threaten its neighbors in the future (54%). However, there is no consensus on three other consequences of the war: 47% agree that the world's access to Middle East oil is more secure, but 40% disagree; 42% agree that the prospects for peace between Israel and its neighbors has improved, but 46% disagree; and only 34% agree that the Middle East is a more stable region as a result of the war, while 59% say that it is not.

The positive effect of the war on George Bush has been undeniable. His approval rating has not dropped below 70% since fighting began in the middle of January, peaking at an historic high of 89% in March (his current rating is 70%). Other winners include the U.S. military (94% approval); General Norman

Schwarzkopf (89%, unchanged from 88% who approved in March); Chairman of the Joint Chiefs of Staff General Colin Powell (83%, down only slightly from 87% in March); and Secretary of State James Baker (78%, down from 84% in March).

The images of those who opposed or criticized the conflict are less favorably perceived now than at the end of the war. Sixty-three percent now approve of the role of Congress in the crisis, compared to 79% who approved of its performance in the immediate aftermath of the victory in March. Congress is seen only slightly more favorably than the press: 60% approve of the news media's handling of the war, down significantly from March, when 71% approved.

Despite respondents' generally positive feelings about the conflict, they have one regret: 76% say that the United States and its allies should have continued fighting until Hussein was removed from power, up from 46% who thought that way immediately after the war ended and 56% who thought that way in April. Thus, it is not surprising that 52% say that the economic sanctions against Iraq should be left in place as long as Hussein remains in power. Another 37% would allow some Iraqi oil sales if the proceeds are designated only for food and medical supplies (a proposal similar to one recently made by President Bush), but only 6% say that the sanctions should be lifted entirely.

With an election year coming up, there is increasing evidence that their votes on the war could come back to haunt some Democratic candidates for president. One third (35%) of respondents say that they would be less likely to vote for a Democratic candidate if they knew that he voted against the resolution allowing President Bush to use military force in the Persian Gulf. This backlash sentiment is growing rather than subsiding; in late April, only 23% said that they would be less likely to vote for such a candidate.

AUGUST 1
HEALTH CARE: U.S. VERSUS CANADIAN

Interviewing Date: 7/11–14/91 (United States); 7/10–13/91 (Canada)
Survey #GO 222006 (United States)

Is it your impression that Canada* or the United States has a better system of health care?

	U.S. respondents	Canadian respondents
Canada better	43%	91%
United States better	26	3
Both are equal	2	1
No opinion	29	5

*The Canadian poll was conducted by Gallup Canada of Toronto, Ontario.

Considering the quality and efficiency of services delivered, in general do you think the costs that Americans [in Canada: Canadians] pay for health care and prescription drugs through direct fees, insurance premiums, and taxes are very high, high, about right, low, or very low?

	U.S. respondents	Canadian respondents
Very high	57%	19%
High	33	37
About right	6	34
Low	1	7
Very low	1	1
No opinion	2	2

Overall, how would you rate the quality of health care available to residents of your community—excellent, good, fair, or poor?

	U.S. respondents	Canadian respondents
Excellent	22%	23%
Good	37	48
Fair	24	21
Poor	14	7
No opinion	3	1

Percent saying "Excellent" or "Good"

	U.S. respondents	Canadian respondents
By Household Income		
$50,000 and Over	74%	77%
$30,000–$49,999	62	70
$20,000–$29,999	63	70
Under $20,000	43	60

Note: While the majority of Americans sees medical costs as excessive and the quality of health care as low, Canadians give their own system a ringing endorsement: 91% prefer the Canadian system to the one in the United States. And when Gallup asks Americans which country's health-care system is superior, Canada's wins by a margin of 43% to 26%.

Escalating medical costs are at the root of American unhappiness with the state of health care. The special U.S.-Canada Gallup Poll finds close to three in five Americans (57%), compared with only one in five Canadians (19%), regarding health-care costs in their country as very high. According to *Newsweek* magazine, the United States spends twice as much on health care today as it did eight years ago: our annual expenditures per capita ($2,354 in 1989) are significantly greater than those in Canada ($1,683).

The U.S. system also loses out to the Canadian one on perceptions of quality. When Americans are asked to rate the quality of health care available in their local community, three in five (59%) rate it as excellent or good, while two in five (38%) rate it as fair or poor. Canadians are significantly more likely to evaluate local health-care quality favorably (71% excellent or good versus 28% fair or poor).

The gap in perceptions of quality between Americans and Canadians widens as one moves down the income scale. Only the most affluent segment of the U.S. population is as happy with the quality of health care as is its Canadian counterpart. At the $50,000-plus income level, three quarters of both Americans (74%) and Canadians (77%) rate local health-care quality positively. Below the $20,000 income level, however, the situation is very different. Among this least affluent group, the percentage rating quality as excellent or good is 17 points lower among Americans than it is among Canadians (43% versus 60%).

Unlike Canada, the United States does not have government-provided universal medical coverage. Employers pay the bulk of the costs for health insurance. As health-care costs have soared, Americans of low-to-moderate incomes have been most affected. Most companies have reduced benefits or asked employees to pay a greater share of their health insurance costs.

AUGUST 3
LABOR UNIONS

Interviewing Date: 7/18–21/91
Survey #GO 222007

Do you approve or disapprove of labor unions?

Approve..60%
Disapprove...30
No opinion...10

	Approve	Dis-approve	No opinion
By Sex			
Male.....................60%	33%	7%
Female.................61	27	12
By Ethnic Background			
White...................59	31	10
Nonwhite 66	26	8
Black 78	16	6
By Education			
College Graduate 60	33	7
College Incomplete...58	34	8
High-School		
Graduate..............63	28	9
Less Than High-		
School Graduate 56	26	18
By Region			
East 62	28	10
Midwest.................68	21	11
South 54	37	9
West 58	34	8
By Age			
18–29 Years............68	22	10
30–49 Years............55	35	10
50 Years and Over.....60	31	9
By Household Income			
$50,000 and Over.....51	40	9
$30,000–$49,999....62	31	7
$20,000–$29,999....66	28	6
Under $20,000.........63	26	11

By Politics			
Republicans............50	38	12
Democrats 76	18	6
Independents..........59	32	9
By Religion			
Protestants 60	31	9
Catholics 62	28	10
By Political Ideology			
Liberal...................74	21	5
Moderate................52	35	13
Conservative..........53	38	9
By Bush Approval			
Approve.................57	33	10
Disapprove.............68	24	8

Selected National Trend

	Approve	Dis-approve	No opinion
1985.....................58%	27%	15%
1981.....................55	35	10
1979.....................55	33	12
1978.....................59	31	10
1973.....................59	26	15
1967.....................66	23	11
1965.....................70	19	11
1963.....................67	23	10
1961.....................63	22	15
1959.....................68	19	13
1957.....................76	14	10
1953.....................75	18	7
1949.....................62	22	16
1947.....................64	25	11
1941.....................61	30	9
1939.....................68	24	8
1936.....................72	20	8

A bill is now before Congress that would ban companies from hiring permanent replacement workers during strikes, guaranteeing employees the right to claim their jobs after the strike. Would you favor or oppose Congress passing this bill banning the hiring of permanent replacement workers?

Favor 47%
Oppose..45
No opinion...8

	Favor	Oppose	No opinion
By Sex			
Male	47%	49%	4%
Female	47	41	12
By Ethnic Background			
White	47	45	8
Nonwhite	49	43	8
Black	47	44	9
By Education			
College Graduate	45	47	8
College Incomplete	47	45	8
High-School Graduate	52	41	7
Less Than High-School Graduate	37	50	13
By Region			
East	53	42	5
Midwest	48	46	6
South	42	47	11
West	46	42	12
By Age			
18–29 Years	52	40	8
30–49 Years	49	45	6
50 Years and Over	42	48	10
By Household Income			
$50,000 and Over	42	53	5
$30,000–$49,999	50	43	7
$20,000–$29,999	50	46	4
Under $20,000	49	39	12
By Politics			
Republicans	41	51	8
Democrats	57	35	8
Independents	45	48	7
By Religion			
Protestants	43	48	9
Catholics	53	41	6
By Political Ideology			
Liberal	56	39	5
Moderate	44	44	12
Conservative	41	52	7
By Bush Approval			
Approve	44	48	8
Disapprove	56	37	7

In 1981, President Reagan fired all the air traffic controllers when their union staged an illegal strike. Looking back, do you think President Reagan made the right decision, or not?

Yes	39%
No	50
No opinion	11

Asked of those who replied "yes": Why do you think it was the right decision?

Strike was illegal	27%
Had to stand up to unions who were too powerful; wouldn't negotiate and were unreasonable; had to break stranglehold	24
Air travel is vital; had to keep flying	16
I don't like unions	8
Safer	3
Other	10
None	5
No opinion	7

Asked of those who replied "no": Why do you think it was the wrong decision?

They had the right to strike	16%
Hurt safety of air travel; afraid to fly	14
Fired a lot of good people and put in unskilled people	13
Shouldn't have stepped in; took too much power	11
Put people out of work; hurt economy	10
Should have negotiated a settlement	9
Attempt to bust unions	8
Other	9
None	3
No opinion	7

Note: On the tenth anniversary of the air traffic controllers' strike, a new Gallup Poll finds that more Americans (50%) now believe President Ronald Reagan erred in firing the strikers than believe he acted correctly (39%). In contrast, respondents in 1981 backed Reagan's handling of the strike by a margin of 2 to 1 (59% to 30%). Even among union households, a 49% plurality supported the president, reflecting people's opposition to strikes by government employees whose absence would undermine public safety.

The new poll also finds that over the last decade the image of labor unions has improved: 60% now approve of unions in general, compared with 55% during the 1981 strike when approval reached an all-time low. However, Gallup finds the public sharply divided on a key labor-management issue of 1991: whether Congress should bar companies from hiring permanent replacements for striking workers. The proposed federal legislation (recently passed by the House but not yet acted upon by the Senate) is supported by 47%, while a statistically equal 45% oppose it; 8% express no opinion

Among those who now think Reagan's firing of the air traffic controllers was wrong, concerns about air safety (as well as sympathetic views toward unions) are most often cited. Fourteen percent mention that the firings compromised air safety, and 13% cite the replacement of qualified workers by unskilled ones. Sixteen percent say that the controllers had the right to strike, while 11% think that the government exercised too much power and 9% say that a settlement should have been negotiated; 8% say that it was an attempt to bust the unions. An additional 10% think that the firings hurt the economy.

Most of those who approve of the firings express some form of negativity about labor unions: 27% cite the illegality of the strike; another 24% specify the need to curb overly powerful unions, while 8% simply dislike unions. Only 16% mention the importance of keeping the planes flying.

For fifty-five years Gallup has measured American opinion of labor unions. Support peaked in 1957, when three fourths (76%) approved; the lowest rating (55%) was posted in 1979 and again in 1981, at the time of the air traffic controllers' controversy. Today's approval rating is 60%.

AUGUST 4
HEALTH CARE

Interviewing Date: 6/27–30/91
Survey #GO 222004

In your opinion, is there a crisis in health care in this country today, or not?

Yes...91%
No.. 8
No opinion.. 1

In your opinion, what do you think is the biggest problem with health care in the United States today?

Cost; paying for care and insurance..........42%
Elderly, poor, homeless don't
   have coverage................................13
Many people don't have access
   to care; it is distributed unevenly
   and unfairly...................................... 5
Hospitals, doctors charge too much........... 5
Number of people without insurance;
   too many without insurance.................. 4
No national plan; not enough on part
   of the government; need government
   help, socialized medicine..................... 4
AIDS.. 2
Medicare; Medicaid 2
Insurance doesn't pay enough;
   high deductible 1
Facilities, hospitals are full;
   too few doctors 1
Quality of care is bad; bad hospitals;
   unknowledgeable doctors..................... 1
Cost of malpractice insurance 1
Other..13
None.. *
No opinion.. 6

*Less than 1%

In your opinion, does the health-care system in this country need reforming and change, or does it work pretty well the way it is?

Needs reforming...................................85%
Works the way it is 14
No opinion.. 1

How satisfied are you personally with:

Your ability to find appropriate medical care when you need it?

Very satisfied 50%
Somewhat satisfied 36
Not at all satisfied...............................12
No opinion.. 2

The quality of medical care you receive?

Very satisfied 51%
Somewhat satisfied 37
Not at all satisfied...........................10
No opinion.......................................2

Your ability to pay for medical care when you need it?

Very satisfied 33%
Somewhat satisfied 42
Not at all satisfied...........................23
No opinion.......................................2

I'm going to mention some reasons people have given for the rapidly increasing cost of health care in this country. As I read each one, please tell me if you think it is an important reason why health-care costs are rising, or not:

Amount hospitals are charging?

Important..86%
Not important..................................12
No opinion.......................................2

New and expensive medical equipment and technology?

Important..81%
Not important..................................17
No opinion.......................................2

Amount doctors are charging?

Important..80%
Not important..................................18
No opinion.......................................2

People without insurance whose health costs have to be paid by taxpayers?

Important..78%
Not important..................................19
No opinion.......................................3

Malpractice lawsuits and awards?

Important..77%
Not important..................................19
No opinion.......................................4

Cost of prescription drugs?

Important..74%
Not important..................................24
No opinion.......................................2

Americans are living longer, therefore requiring more health care?

Important..71%
Not important..................................27
No opinion.......................................2

Cost of treating AIDS patients?

Important..66%
Not important..................................27
No opinion.......................................7

Use of the health-care system for treatment of drug and alcohol abuse?

Important..65%
Not important..................................30
No opinion.......................................5

Using your best estimate, in total, how many times have you, yourself, visited a doctor in the last twelve months?

None..16%
One time 19
Two times..17
Three times......................................14
Four times 7
Five to ten times 16
Eleven times or more...........................10
No opinion..1

Asked of those who had visited a doctor in the last twelve months: How satisfied were you with the care, treatment, and attention you received on your last visit to a doctor? Would you say you were very satisfied, somewhat satisfied, not very satisfied, or not at all satisfied?

Very satisfied 67%
Somewhat satisfied 24
Not very satisfied 4
Not at all satisfied...............................5
No opinion.......................................*

*Less than 1%

Using your best estimate, in total, how many times have you been treated at a hospital emergency room in the last twelve months?

None...75%
One time 15
Two times..5
Three times or more..............................4
No opinion...1

Asked of those who had visited an emergency room in the last twelve months: How satisfied were you with the care, treatment, and attention you received on your last visit to the emergency room? Would you say you were very satisfied, somewhat satisfied, not very satisfied, or not at all satisfied?

Very satisfied 45%
Somewhat satisfied 28
Not very satisfied 8
Not at all satisfied..............................18
No opinion...1

Using your best estimate, in total, how many times have you spent at least one night in a hospital as a patient in the last twelve months?

None...86%
One time 7
Two times..3
Three times or more..............................4

Asked of those who had spent at least one night in the hospital in the last twelve months: How satisfied were you with the care, treatment, and attention you received on your last stay in the hospital? Would you say you were very satisfied, somewhat satisfied, not very satisfied, or not at all satisfied?

Very satisfied 58%
Somewhat satisfied 21
Not very satisfied 10
Not at all satisfied..............................11
No opinion...*

*Less than 1%

If you needed to see a doctor, how easy would it be for you to find one to treat your needs—very easy, somewhat easy, not too easy, or not at all easy?

Very easy 70%
Somewhat easy 20
Not too easy......................................5
Not at all easy....................................4
No opinion...1

Now suppose you needed to go to a hospital emergency room. How easy would it be for you to find one to treat your needs—very easy, somewhat easy, not too easy, or not at all easy?

Very easy 71%
Somewhat easy 18
Not too easy......................................6
Not at all easy....................................4
No opinion...1

Do you have a personal doctor—that is, a doctor you go to regularly for routine checkups and for basic health problems?

Yes..80%
No..20
No opinion...*

*Less than 1%

When you see a doctor, is it usually a doctor:

You selected yourself?.........................67%
In an HMO?......................................12
In a clinic or minor
    emergency health-care center?.............12
In an emergency room or hospital?...........5
In some other situation (volunteered).........3
No opinion...1

Have you ever put off going to a doctor because of the cost?

	1991	1938
Yes	40%	48%
No	60	52

Have there been times in the last twelve months when you did not have money enough to pay for medical or health care?

	1991	1977*
Yes	27%	15%
No	73	84
No opinion	**	1

*Gallup Poll conducted for the Kettering Foundation
**Less than 1%

In the past twelve months have you, or anyone in your family, experienced a catastrophic illness or had a relative who needed extensive nursing home or in-home care?

	Yes
National	24%

Asked of those who replied in the affirmative: How much of the cost of the illness did health insurance cover? Did it cover all of the costs, some of the costs, or none of the costs?

All of the costs	19%
Some of the costs	60
None of the costs	11
Not insured (volunteered)	1
No opinion	9

Asked of those who have not experienced a catastrophic family illness: How worried are you that you or someone in your family will experience a catastrophic illness or need long-term nursing home or in-home care in the next few years? Would you say you are very worried about this, somewhat worried about this, or not at all worried about this?

Very worried	20%
Somewhat worried	42
Not at all worried	38
No opinion	*

*Less than 1%

Generally, how confident are you that you have enough money or health insurance to pay for:

Routine health care, including checkups and minor illnesses?

Very confident	51%
Somewhat confident	33
Not too confident	8
Not at all confident	8
No opinion	*

*Less than 1%

A major illness or operation?

Very confident	32%
Somewhat confident	35
Not too confident	17
Not at all confident	15
No opinion	1

Long-term nursing home or in-home care?

Very confident	10%
Somewhat confident	27
Not too confident	29
Not at all confident	30
No opinion	4

Are you personally covered by health insurance that helps you pay doctor, hospital, or other kinds of medical expenses?

	Yes
National	87%

Asked of those who replied in the affirmative: Do you get your health insurance coverage through an employer, do you buy health insurance on your own, or are you insured by Medicare or Medicaid?

Through employer	69%
On my own	15
Medicare or Medicaid	14
No opinion	2

Also asked of those who are covered by health insurance: Do you pay some portion of the cost for your health-care coverage, all of the cost, or none of the cost?

Some of the cost....................................64%
All of the cost....................................14
None of the cost................................21
No opinion..1

Also asked of those who are covered by health insurance: Are you satisfied or dissatisfied with your health insurance coverage?

Very satisfied 49%
Somewhat satisfied 32
Somewhat dissatisfied...........................9
Very dissatisfied.................................. 8
No opinion.. 2

Asked of those who are dissatisfied with their health insurance: Why are you dissatisfied with your health insurance coverage?

Cost; I pay too much; they pay too
   little; high deductible 48%
Poor coverage; doesn't cover much...........32
Not personal; can't pick doctor 2
Can't get appointment........................... 1
Too long to process claims, get paid.......... 4
Other; no opinion...............................13

Do you think the government should be responsible for providing medical care for people who are unable to pay for it?

	1991	1938
Yes....................................	80%	81%
No......................................	13	19
No opinion...........................	7	–

Which one of the following three approaches to financing health care would you favor: a health-care plan in which businesses are required to either provide coverage for all their employees or contribute to a federal fund that would cover all uninsured Americans; a national health-care plan run by the federal

government, financed by taxpayers, which would cover all Americans; or leave things the way they are?

By businesses.....................................34%
By federal government.........................40
Leave as is...22
No opinion.. 4

Note: Despite the crisis atmosphere that permeates our health care, most Americans are more or less satisfied with the system. Sixty-seven percent are very satisfied with the attention and treatment they received on their last doctor's visit, and another 24% are somewhat satisfied. Satisfaction rates also are fairly high for visits to hospitals (58% are very, 21% somewhat satisfied with their last stay) and emergency rooms (45% and 28%). As for the overall quality of medical care, 88% are very or somewhat satisfied, and 86% can find appropriate medical care when they need it.

Four in five of us (80%) have a personal doctor we see regularly. Ninety percent say that it would be easy to find a doctor if needed, and 89% say that it would be easy to find a hospital emergency room if required. In fact, one in four (24%) was treated in an emergency room last year; one in twenty-five went three or more times. These patients were likely to be young, black, low income, uninsured, southern, and to have put off doctor visits because of cost, reflecting the common use of hospital emergency rooms as primary care for the poor.

Ninety-one percent tell Gallup that our country faces a health-care crisis. When asked to identify the single biggest problem in health care today, three in four name cost-related issues—reinforcing the fact that it is cost, not quality or accessibility, that worries the average American.

Asked which reasons associated with rising health-care costs were important, respondents say that hospital charges lead the list (86%), followed by new and expensive medical equipment and technology (81%), doctors' fees (80%), the financial burden of covering the health costs of those without insurance (78%), and malpractice lawsuits and awards (77%). Also cited are the cost of prescription drugs (74%), the fact that people are living longer and thus requiring more health coverage (71%), the cost of treating AIDS patients (66%), and the use of the health-care system for treatment of drug and alcohol abuse (65%).

The Mirror finds that the high cost of medical care affects the way that respondents approach their health-care needs. Forty percent have delayed a doctor's visit at some point because of the cost (although this was worse during the Depression: in a 1938 Gallup Poll, 48% reported deferring treatment). Twenty-seven percent had trouble paying for medical or health care in the last twelve months, up from 15% in a 1977 Gallup Poll for the Kettering Foundation.

While most respondents (84%) are confident that they have enough money or health insurance to pay for routine health care, that figure drops to 67% for a major illness or operation and plummets to 37% for long-term nursing home or in-home care. Moreover, six in ten (62%) are very or somewhat worried that someone in their family will have a catastrophic illness or need long-term care in the next few years. They have cause for concern: last year, costs exceeded insurance benefits for 72% of the one in four families who was in that situation.

Americans seem anxious for a change in the way health care is delivered and paid for in this country, with 85% believing that the entire system needs reform. Four in five (80%) think that the government should be responsible for providing medical care for people who are unable to pay—virtually the same percentage who thought that way during the Depression (81% in Gallup's 1938 poll). Most would opt either for government-sponsored national health insurance (40%) or for the kind of employer-backed insurance plan recently promoted by the Democrats (34%). Only 22% prefer leaving the system the way it is.

A change in national health policy is unlikely, however, before the 1992 presidential election. For now, for most Americans, their existing health insurance stands between them and the ever-rising tide of health-care costs: 87% are covered by health insurance. For those with coverage, the benefits themselves seem to be adequate. Four out of five (81%) are somewhat or very satisfied with their coverage. Those who are not satisfied complain that the coverage costs too

much or does not pay for enough. Most health insurance comes as a fringe benefit from employers (69%), although some individuals do buy their own insurance coverage (15%) and others qualify for Medicare or Medicaid (14%).

AUGUST 7
CONGRESS

Interviewing Date: 7/25–28/91
Survey #GO 222008

Do you approve or disapprove of the way Congress is handling its job?

Approve...32%
Disapprove..53
No opinion..15

	Approve	Dis-approve	No opinion
By Sex			
Male	31%	58%	11%
Female	33	48	19
By Ethnic Background			
White	32	54	14
Nonwhite	32	49	19
Black	32	53	15
By Education			
College Graduate	35	56	9
College Incomplete	34	55	11
High-School Graduate	30	54	16
Less Than High-School Graduate	31	45	24
By Region			
East	34	51	15
Midwest	34	54	12
South	32	52	16
West	29	55	16
By Age			
18–29 Years	39	43	18
30–49 Years	34	52	14
50 Years and Over	26	60	14

By Household Income

$50,000 and Over.....37	56	7
$30,000–$49,999....29	57	14
$20,000–$29,999...30	54	16
Under $20,000........33	48	19

By Politics

Republicans............35	54	11
Democrats..............37	50	13
Independents...........25	58	17

By Political Ideology

Liberal...................36	53	11
Moderate................26	59	15
Conservative..........33	57	10

By Bush Approval

Approve................38	49	13
Disapprove............18	77	5

Selected National Trend

	Approve	Dis-approve	No opinion
October 1990.........24%	68%	8%
September 1987......42	49	9
April 1983.............33	43	24
June 1982..............29	54	17
June 1981..............38	40	22
June 1979..............19	61	20
September 1978......29	49	22
May 1977..............40	40	20
June 1975..............29	54	17
August 1974...........48	35	17
April 1974.............30	47	23

The U.S. Senate has voted to increase its members' salaries from $101,900 to $125,100 per year, the same amount members of the House of Representatives now make. In exchange, senators would not be able to accept speaking fees from special-interest groups. Do you favor or oppose raising senators' salaries from $101,900 to $125,100 per year?

Favor...18%
Oppose...77
No opinion...5

	Favor	Oppose	No opinion
By Sex			
Male 21%	76%	3%
Female..................15	78	7
By Ethnic Background			
White....................19	77	4
Nonwhite 13	77	10
Black 13	79	8
By Education			
College Graduate 36	60	4
College Incomplete...19	77	4
High-School Graduate..............10	85	5
Less Than High-School Graduate 12	80	8
By Region			
East 22	73	5
Midwest.................15	81	4
South 16	78	6
West 18	77	5
By Age			
18–29 Years............18	75	7
30–49 Years............20	77	3
50 Years and Over.....15	79	6
By Household Income			
$50,000 and Over.....34	64	2
$30,000–$49,999....17	81	2
$20,000–$29,999....15	79	6
Under $20,000........10	82	8
By Politics			
Republicans............19	76	5
Democrats 17	80	3
Independents...........17	78	5
By Political Ideology			
Liberal...................17	77	6
Moderate................27	66	7
Conservative...........19	80	1
By Bush Approval			
Approve................19	76	5
Disapprove.............16	82	2

Note: As Congress begins its summer recess, members will be returning home to less than a hero's welcome. A new Gallup Poll finds that only one in three Americans (32%) approves of the way that Congress is handling its job. The low ratings contrast sharply with President George Bush's continuing high marks (71% approval in the current poll). Moreover, three out of four (77%) object to the Senate's recent pay raise, even when told that it brings senators' pay up to the same level as their House colleagues and that, in return for the increase, senators will no longer accept speaking fees.

Congress may take some comfort in the finding that fewer express disapproval today (53%) than did so last October, when the federal budget impasse provoked 68% of the public to disapprove. However, its current standing is equally low among adherents of both political parties: only 35% of Republicans and 37% of Democrats now approve. Of political independents, only 25% approve.

Since Gallup initiated this assessment in 1974, congressional approval has topped 40% only twice. A September 1987 Gallup Poll, taken after the Iran-contra affair had damaged Ronald Reagan's image, showed 42%. Congress's highest rating—in fact, the only time in the last two decades of polling when approval was higher than disapproval (48% to 35%)—was recorded in the aftermath of Watergate, before Richard Nixon's resignation in 1974.

The Democratic-controlled Senate should take note that its recently voted pay hike is at least as unpopular among Democrats (80% oppose) as it is among Republicans (76%) and independents (78%). Large majorities of all demographic and political subgroups oppose the salary increase. College graduates are considerably more sympathetic than others, but even within this group opponents outnumber supporters by 60% to 36%.

AUGUST 7
PRESIDENT BUSH

Interviewing Date: 7/25–28/91
Survey #GO 222008

Do you approve or disapprove of the way George Bush is handling his job as president?

Approve...71%
Disapprove..21
No opinion...8

	Approve	Dis-approve	No opinion
By Sex			
Male 72%	23%	5%
Female....................69	19	12
By Ethnic Background			
White.....................74	18	8
Nonwhite 55	34	11
Black 52	37	11
By Education			
College Graduate 68	26	6
College Incomplete...73	20	7
High-School Graduate..............75	17	8
Less Than High-School Graduate 64	22	14
By Region			
East 69	23	8
Midwest.................72	20	8
South 70	19	11
West 73	20	7
By Age			
18–29 Years............73	18	9
30–49 Years............74	18	8
50 Years and Over.....66	25	9
By Household Income			
$50,000 and Over.....79	16	5
$30,000–$49,999....72	20	8
$20,000–$29,999....71	22	7
Under $20,000.........67	22	11
By Politics			
Republicans............88	8	4
Democrats 61	30	9
Independents...........66	24	10
By Religion			
Protestants 73	18	9
Catholics 75	19	6

By Political Ideology

Liberal	67	25	8
Moderate	64	27	9
Conservative	81	15	4

Selected National Trend

1991	Approve	Dis-approve	No opinion
July 18–21	70%	21%	9%
June 27–30	72	22	6
May 16–19	77	15	8
April 4–6	83	12	5
March 14–17	86	9	5
February 28–March 3	89	8	3
February 7–10	79	18	3
January 17–20	82	12	6
January 11–13	64	25	11
January 3–6	58	31	11

The following table shows the average approval ratings for eight presidents during their first, second, and third years:

Presidential Performance Ratings
(Percent Approval)

	First year	Second year	Third year
Bush	64%	68%	77%*
Reagan	58	44	44
Carter	62	46	37
Ford	54	43	48
Nixon	61	57	50
Johnson	74	66	51
Kennedy	76	72	64
Eisenhower	68	66	71

*January-July

Note: George Bush continues to receive broad public support five months after victory in the Persian Gulf war boosted his approval rating to record levels. According to the most recent Gallup Poll, seven in ten (71%) approve of his handling of his job as president. His approval is down from its post-Operation Desert Storm peak of 89%, the highest presidential approval rating in Gallup's annals, but his current rating, by historical standards, remains very high.

Not since John F. Kennedy has a president's approval rating averaged significantly above 50% during his third year in office. Unless Bush's ratings fall rather sharply during the remainder of 1991, he will be the first president since Dwight Eisenhower whose average approval rating for his third year in office surpasses his first-year average.

Recent events, including the nomination of Clarence Thomas to the Supreme Court, the lifting of sanctions against South Africa, and the announcement of a new arms agreement with the Soviet Union, have not had much impact on the president's job performance ratings. Approval has ranged from 70% to 72% since mid-June. Between March and June, Bush approval declined gradually as the public came down from the emotional high of the Gulf victory.

Throughout his first three years in office, Bush has been significantly more popular than his five immediate predecessors. Ronald Reagan, Jimmy Carter, Gerald Ford, Richard Nixon, and Lyndon Johnson—each of these men was in some political trouble at this point in his term. For year three in office, average approval in the Gallup Poll ranged from a low of 37% (Carter) to a high of only 51% (Johnson). Bush, benefiting greatly from his success in the Gulf, has averaged 77% approval for the first seven months of 1991.

Of the postwar presidents, only Kennedy and Eisenhower had approval figures rivaling those of Bush for their first three years in office. Kennedy received the highest first-year approval (76%) on record and remained popular throughout his brief presidency. Even so, by his third year Kennedy's average approval rating had declined to 64%. Eisenhower, on the other hand, improved his rating from 68% to 71% between his first and third year, a feat not since duplicated.

AUGUST 8
POLITICAL AFFILIATION

Interviewing Date: January-June 1991
Several Surveys

In politics, as of today, do you consider yourself a Republican, a Democrat, or an independent? *

Republican 30%
Democrat...39
Independent 31

	Repub- lican	Demo- crat	Inde- pendent
By Age			
18–29 Years............	30%	38%	32%
30–49 Years............	29	39	32
50 Years and Over.....	32	42	26

*Those who said "don't know" or "other" are omitted.

Selected National Trend

	Repub- lican	Demo- crat	Inde- pendent
1990.....................	32%	40%	28%
1989.....................	33	40	27
1988.....................	30	42	28
1987.....................	30	41	29
1986.....................	32	39	29
1985.....................	33	38	29
1984.....................	31	40	29
1983.....................	25	44	31
1982.....................	26	45	29
1981.....................	28	42	30
1980.....................	24	46	30
1979.....................	22	45	33
1976.....................	23	47	30
1975.....................	22	45	33
1972.....................	28	43	29
1968.....................	27	46	27
1964.....................	25	53	22
1960.....................	30	47	23
1954.....................	34	46	20
1950.....................	33	45	22
1946.....................	40	39	21
1937.....................	34	50	16

Note: Gallup's most recent party identification figures, based on 4,000 personal interviews from January through June, show no significant increase in the percentage of Americans who call themselves Republicans. The latest results give the Democrats a 39%-to-30% advantage in party identification over the Republicans, while 31% call themselves independents.

Gallup has asked this question, using an in-person interviewing methodology, since 1937. The parties were about even—40% Republican, 39% Democrat—when the postwar era began in 1946. Since that time the Democrats have maintained at least a narrow advantage in the yearly totals. They held their biggest leads in 1964 (53% to 25%), the year Lyndon Johnson defeated Barry Goldwater in a landslide, and in 1975, immediately after the Watergate scandal (45% to 22%).

Party identification figures for the first half of 1991 are statistically similar to Gallup's final figures for 1990, which showed 40% of the public calling themselves Democrats and 32% Republicans. In fact, Gallup's yearly averages of Republican and Democratic party identification have varied by only a few points since 1984, when Ronald Reagan had recovered politically from the 1982 recession. Since that time, Republican identification has ranged from 30% to 33%, while Democratic identification has ranged from 38% to 41%.

These findings suggest that the GOP's post-Watergate recovery took place in the mid-1980s and that the party since has made no further gains. Despite George Bush's high approval ratings throughout his term and the boost to the GOP image from the Gulf war victory, the Republicans have not gained ground during the Bush years on this fundamental measure.

The dramatic shift seen toward the GOP among young people may be reversing itself in the 1990s. Today's figures give the Democrats a 38%-to-30% edge among people under 30 years of age. This is certainly more favorable for the Republicans than the 2-to-1 advantage seen for the Democrats in 1980 (41% to 18%) before Reagan took office. Yet the Gallup figures show that the GOP may have lost some ground to the Democrats among young people since 1986, when as many called themselves Republicans (35%) as called themselves Democrats (33%).

AUGUST 8
CIVIL RIGHTS AND DISCRIMINATION

Interviewing Date: 6/13–16/91
Survey #GO 222002

Over the past year or so, how much progress do you think has been made in the area of civil rights in this country—a lot of progress, some progress, not very much progress, or no progress at all?

A lot 11%
Some...47
Not very much 27
No progress at all 11
No opinion..4

	A lot	Some	Not very much	None*
By Sex				
Male 10%	46%	26%	18%
Female..........11	49	27	13
By Ethnic Background				
White...........11	49	26	14
Nonwhite 9	51	24	16
Black 7	31	35	27
By Education				
College Graduate......7	44	32	17
College Incomplete ..4	52	26	18
High-School Graduate.....11	52	25	12
Less Than High-School Graduate.....21	34	28	17
By Region				
East 10	50	28	12
Midwest........11	48	21	20
South 14	46	25	15
West 7	45	35	13
By Age				
18–29 Years....5	53	28	14
30–49 Years....8	46	30	16
50 Years and Over.....17	45	24	14
By Household Income				
$50,000 and Over......9	45	30	16
$30,000– $49,999......8	48	27	17
$20,000– $29,999......8	51	28	13
Under $20,000.....14	45	25	16
By Politics				
Republicans...10	61	21	8
Democrats 11	34	36	19
Independents...9	48	25	18
By Political Ideology				
Liberal...........7	43	32	18
Moderate.......15	44	19	22
Conservative..12	54	25	9
By Bush Approval				
Approve........12	54	24	10
Disapprove.....4	27	38	31

Selected National Trend

	A lot	Some	Not very much	None*
1990............. 16%	48%	23%	13%
1989............. 11	44	30	15

*"None" combines "no opinion"—at 8% or less—with "no progress at all."

Looking back over the last ten years, do you think the quality of life of blacks has gotten better, stayed about the same, or gotten worse?

Better...53%
Stayed the same................................27
Worse..15
No opinion..5

	Better	Same	Worse	No opinion
By Sex				
Male 52%	27%	16%	5%
Female..........53	28	15	4
By Ethnic Background				
White...........55	27	13	5
Nonwhite 49	39	12	*
Black 35	26	37	2

By Education

College Graduate.....44	30	20	6
College In-complete....51	30	14	5
High-School Graduate.....57	27	13	3
Less Than High-School Graduate.....55	22	16	7

By Region

East.............50	27	19	4
Midwest........48	33	15	4
South...........61	21	14	4
West...........49	31	14	6

By Age

18–29 Years...49	33	15	3
30–49 Years...52	28	16	4
50 Years and Over.....56	23	15	6

By Household Income

$50,000 and Over.....52	31	14	3
$30,000– $49,999.....52	26	16	6
$20,000– $29,999.....47	33	16	4
Under $20,000.....58	22	16	4

By Politics

Republicans...66	23	7	4
Democrats.....44	28	22	6
Independents..49	30	17	4

By Political Ideology

Liberal..........47	30	21	2
Moderate.......48	18	24	10
Conservative..59	29	9	3

By Bush Approval

Approve........58	28	10	4
Disapprove....40	25	32	3

*Less than 1%

Selected National Trend

	Better	Same	Worse	No opinion
1990				
October.........61%	21%	13%	5%
July.............61	24	8	7
1980				
December......77	13	6	4
May.............71	17	8	4

For the next few questions I'd like you to think about your own community. In general, do you think blacks have as good a chance as white people in your community to get any kind of job for which they are qualified, or don't you think they have as good a chance?

Blacks have as good a chance..................68%
Blacks do not have as good a chance.........26
No blacks/whites in this community (volunteered)....................................4
No opinion...2

	As good a chance	Not as good a chance	No blacks/ whites	No opinion
By Ethnic Background				
White...........70%	23%	4%	3%
Black...........40	58	*	2

Selected National Trend

	As good a chance	Not as good a chance	No blacks/ whites	No opinion
1990............70%	23%	3%	4%
1989............65	28	5	2
1978............67	24	*	9
1963............43	48	*	9

*Less than 1%

Do you think blacks have as good a chance as white people in your community to get any kind of housing they can afford, or don't they have as good a chance?

Blacks have as good a chance..................72%
Blacks do not have as good a chance.........23
No blacks/whites in this community (volunteered)....................................3
No opinion...2

	As good a chance	Not as good a chance	No blacks/ whites	No opinion
By Ethnic Background				
White	74%	21%	3%	2%
Black	55	42	1	2

Selected National Trend

	As good a chance	Not as good a chance	No blacks/ whites	No opinion
1990	72%	19%	3%	6%
1989	68	27	3	2

Do you think black children have as good a chance as white children in your community to get a good education, or don't you think they have as good a chance?

Black children have as good a chance.......81%
Black children do not have as good
 a chance..15
No blacks/whites in this community
 (volunteered)......................................2
No opinion..2

	As good a chance	Not as good a chance	No blacks/ whites	No opinion
By Ethnic Background				
White	83%	13%	2%	2%
Black	56	38	*	6

*Less than 1%

Selected National Trend

	As good a chance	Not as good a chance	No blacks/ whites	No opinion
1990	83%	11%	3%	3%
1989	80	15	4	1

Some people say that to make up for past discrimination, women and members of minority groups should be given preferential treatment in getting jobs and places in colleges. Others say that their ability, as determined in test scores, should be the main consideration. Which point of view comes closer to how you feel on the subject?

Give preferential treatment.....................11%
Determine by test scores.......................81
No opinion..8

	Preferential treatment	Test scores	No opinion
By Ethnic Background			
White	8%	84%	8%
Black	24	60	16

Selected National Trend

	Preferential treatment	Test scores	No opinion
December 1989	10%	84%	6%
January 1984	10	84	6
December 1980	10	83	7
October 1977	11	81	8
March 1977	10	83	7

Have you ever been a victim of discrimination or reverse discrimination in getting an education, a job, a promotion, or housing?

Yes...22%
No..77
No opinion..1

	Yes	No	No opinion
By Ethnic Background			
White	21%	78%	1%
Black	36	63	1

Do you think the United States currently has enough federal laws and regulations aimed at reducing race, religion, and sex discrimination, or does Congress need to pass additional laws and regulations aimed at reducing this type of discrimination?

Has enough laws...................................55%
Needs additional laws............................37
No opinion..8

	Has enough	Needs more	No opinion

By Ethnic Background

	Has enough	Needs more	No opinion
White	58%	34%	8%
Black	30	62	8

Here are several ways people have suggested would help improve the situation of blacks in American society today. Do you favor or oppose each of these:

New laws requiring businesses to hire blacks in the same proportion as exists in the local community?

Favor 45%
Oppose...49
No opinion... 6

Spending more money to improve schools in black communities?

Favor 73%
Oppose...21
No opinion... 6

More Head Start programs to provide preschool education?

Favor 83%
Oppose...14
No opinion... 3

Spending more federal funds on job-training programs?

Favor 72%
Oppose...24
No opinion... 4

Tougher federal laws with stiffer penalties for companies which discriminate in hiring and promoting?

Favor 64%
Oppose...29
No opinion... 7

Increasing federal assistance to blacks who want to start their own businesses?

Favor 59%
Oppose..34
No opinion..7

Note: A recent Gallup Poll on civil rights and discrimination in this country reveals a continuing and significant division between whites and blacks. While blacks are deeply concerned about their lack of opportunities and progress in society, a majority of whites thinks that blacks have the same opportunities as all other Americans. In addition, a majority of whites opposes new civil rights legislation now being considered by Congress, but a majority of blacks favors such legislation. Nonetheless, both races favor increased funding for several existing programs designed to help minorities.

Many black Americans still think that they do not have equal opportunities in terms of housing (55%), education (56%), and jobs (40%) in their community. Whites, on the other hand, do not share this perception of a lack of opportunity for blacks: they believe that blacks have as good a chance as whites in these three areas (74%, 83%, and 70%, respectively).

Blacks also say that there has been not very much or no progress at all in civil rights over the past year (60%) and that the quality of life for blacks in this country has stayed the same or gotten worse over the last ten years (26% say the same, 37% say worse). But whites say that progress is continuing to be made by blacks (60%) and that the quality of life for blacks in fact has gotten better over the last ten years (55% say improved, 27% the same, 13% worse).

Both blacks and whites, however, are significantly less likely to say that the quality of life for blacks has improved over the last ten years than has been the case in previous Gallup Poll measurements. Seventy-seven percent of all Americans said that black quality of life had gotten better over the last ten years in 1980. Now, in 1991, only 53% agree that it has improved.

Despite these attitudes, the new Gallup Poll suggests that considerably less than a majority—black or white—actually encounter discrimination in their daily lives. Thirty-six percent of blacks report having at some time been the victim of discrimination in employment, jobs, housing, or promotion. By contrast, 21% of whites have been the victim of discrimination or reverse discrimination in these same areas.

There is a substantial difference between the attitudes of black and white respondents on the perceived need for new civil rights legislation: only 34% of whites think that new federal laws are needed, compared to 62% of blacks. At the same time, there is widespread support on the part of both blacks and whites for renewed emphasis on existing programs that would help blacks and minorities help themselves, as well as for toughening laws against discrimination. For example, 83% favor spending more federal money on Head Start programs, including 93% of blacks and 82% of whites; 72% favor spending more federal funds on job-training programs for blacks (86% of blacks and 71% of whites); 73% favor more federal spending to improve schools in black communities (89% of blacks, 71% of whites); 64% favor legislation that would provide stiffer penalties for discrimination in hiring and promotion (80% of blacks, 62% of whites); and 59% favor programs providing federal assistance to blacks who want to start their own business (86% of blacks, 50% of whites).

On the other hand, only 45% support new laws that would require employers to hire proportionately based on representation of blacks in the community: 79% of blacks favor this type of law, compared with only 40% of whites. Moreover, there continues to be overwhelming rejection of the idea that minorities and women be given preferential treatment in getting jobs and college entrance, as opposed to decisions made strictly on ability. Gallup has measured this trade-off over the past fourteen years and has never found more than 11% who favor making race, rather than ability as measured by test scores, the deciding factor. Only 24% of blacks and 8% of whites in the most recent poll say that they would favor preferential treatment based on race.

AUGUST 14
CLARENCE THOMAS/ROBERT GATES

Interviewing Date: 8/8–11/91
Survey #GO 222010

Would you like to see the Senate vote in favor of Clarence Thomas serving on the Supreme Court, or not?

	Yes
National	56%

	Yes

By Sex

Male	62%
Female	50

By Ethnic Background

White	57
Nonwhite	48
Black	46

By Education

College Graduate	66
College Incomplete	59
High-School Graduate	51
Less Than High-School Graduate	51

By Region

East	56
Midwest	53
South	60
West	53

By Age

18–29 Years	57
30–49 Years	59
50 Years and Over	51

By Household Income

$50,000 and Over	67
$30,000–$49,999	59
$20,000–$29,999	51
Under $20,000	52

By Politics

Republicans	65
Democrats	45
Independents	56

By Political Ideology

Liberal	49
Moderate	48
Conservative	64

By Bush Approval

Approve	64
Disapprove	34

Would you like to see the Senate vote in favor of Robert Gates serving as CIA director, or not?

	Yes
National	35%

	Yes
By Sex	
Male	41%
Female	28
By Ethnic Background	
White	35
Nonwhite	34
Black	33
By Education	
College Graduate	33
College Incomplete	32
High-School Graduate	37
Less Than High-School Graduate	35
By Region	
East	33
Midwest	35
South	39
West	29
By Age	
18–29 Years	39
30–49 Years	34
50 Years and Over	34
By Household Income	
$50,000 and Over	39
$30,000–$49,999	32
$20,000–$29,999	35
Under $20,000	36
By Politics	
Republicans	43
Democrats	32
Independents	29
By Political Ideology	
Liberal	31
Moderate	30
Conservative	42
By Bush Approval	
Approve	39
Disapprove	26

Note: Clarence Thomas appears to be losing support among blacks since the National Association for the Advancement of Colored People (NAACP) announced its decision to oppose his nomination to the Supreme Court. In a new Gallup Poll, 56% say that the Senate should confirm him, while 23% oppose confirmation. These overall results differ little from those seen in a mid-July poll, when 52% favored Thomas and 17% opposed him.

While white support for Thomas has held steady—57% now favor his confirmation, compared with 52% in the July poll—black support may be slipping. Among the new poll's small sample of blacks, opinion divides 46% in favor, 37% opposed. Last month, however, blacks backed Thomas by a margin of 57% to 18%.

President George Bush's other recent controversial nomination, of Robert Gates as director of the Central Intelligence Agency (CIA), does not appear to have stirred much interest among the public. Close to one half (45%) expresses no opinion on whether Gates should be confirmed, including 15% who say that they have never heard of Bush's nominee, who was the agency's deputy director during the time of the Iran-*contra* arms deals.

Confirmation hearings for Gates were put on hold by the Senate last month after Iran-*contra* investigator Lawrence Walsh produced a witness whose testimony cast doubt on senior CIA officials' denials that they knew about the secret diversion of funds to the *contras*. Despite the negative publicity from Iran-*contra* and the more recent Bank of Credit and Commerce International (BCCI) scandal, however, more respondents favor (35%) than oppose (20%) Senate confirmation of Gates.

AUGUST 14
PRESIDENT BUSH

Interviewing Date: 8/8–11/91
Survey #GO 222010

Do you approve or disapprove of the way George Bush is handling his job as president?

Approve...71%
Disapprove......................................22
No opinion.......................................7

Now, let me ask you about some specific problems facing the country. As I read off each one, would you tell me whether you approve or disapprove of the way President Bush is handling that problem:

Economic conditions in this country?

Approve...33%
Disapprove......................................61
No opinion.......................................6

	Approve	Dis-approve	No opinion
By Sex			
Male.....................35%	59%	6%
Female.................31	62	7
By Ethnic Background			
White....................34	59	7
Nonwhite 24	74	2
Black 23	76	1
By Education			
College Graduate 41	56	3
College Incomplete...39	57	4
High-School Graduate...............28	64	8
Less Than High-School Graduate 29	62	9
By Region			
East 28	64	8
Midwest.................34	60	6
South 37	57	6
West.....................33	62	5
By Age			
18–29 Years............37	57	6
30–49 Years............34	61	5
50 Years and Over.....29	63	8
By Household Income			
$50,000 and Over.....43	53	4
$30,000–$49,999....33	61	6
$20,000–$29,999....31	67	2
Under $20,000........29	62	9

By Politics			
Republicans............53	42	5
Democrats 15	80	5
Independents..........30	63	7
By Political Ideology			
Liberal..................25	71	4
Moderate...............22	66	12
Conservative..........45	51	4
By Bush Approval			
Approve................45	49	6
Disapprove.............5	93	2

Selected National Trend

	Approve	Dis-approve	No opinion
1991			
July 34%	59%	7%
June.....................36	58	6
March...................37	56	7
1990			
October.................30	65	5
July 40	53	7
1989			
November..............40	51	9
March...................52	27	21

Foreign policy?

Approve...68%
Disapprove......................................25
No opinion.......................................7

	Approve	Dis-approve	No opinion
By Sex			
Male 72%	24%	4%
Female.................65	26	9
By Ethnic Background			
White....................71	22	7
Nonwhite 50	46	4
Black 44	52	4
By Education			
College Graduate 76	20	4
College Incomplete...74	22	4
High-School Graduate...............66	26	8
Less Than High-School Graduate 58	31	11

	Approve	Dis-approve	No opinion

By Region (left)

	Approve	Disapprove	No opinion
East	69	21	10
Midwest	67	25	8
South	68	27	5
West	68	29	3

By Age

	Approve	Disapprove	No opinion
18–29 Years	71	23	6
30–49 Years	69	24	7
50 Years and Over	65	27	8

By Household Income

	Approve	Disapprove	No opinion
$50,000 and Over	81	17	2
$30,000–$49,999	73	19	8
$20,000–$29,999	69	27	4
Under $20,000	56	35	9

By Politics

	Approve	Disapprove	No opinion
Republicans	85	11	4
Democrats	51	40	9
Independents	67	26	7

By Political Ideology

	Approve	Disapprove	No opinion
Liberal	60	34	6
Moderate	69	22	9
Conservative	78	19	3

By Bush Approval

	Approve	Disapprove	No opinion
Approve	82	13	5
Disapprove	32	60	8

Selected National Trend

	Approve	Dis-approve	No opinion
1991			
July	71%	19%	10%
June	64	28	8
March	79	11	10
1990			
October	61	29	10
July	62	26	12
1989			
November	65	21	14

Situation in the Middle East?

Approve	71%
Disapprove	24
No opinion	5

	Approve	Dis-approve	No opinion

By Sex

	Approve	Disapprove	No opinion
Male	75%	22%	3%
Female	67	27	6

By Ethnic Background

	Approve	Disapprove	No opinion
White	73	22	5
Nonwhite	56	42	2
Black	54	45	1

By Education

	Approve	Disapprove	No opinion
College Graduate	76	20	4
College Incomplete	72	24	4
High-School Graduate	70	25	5
Less Than High-School Graduate	64	28	8

By Region

	Approve	Disapprove	No opinion
East	69	27	4
Midwest	73	21	6
South	68	27	5
West	72	22	6

By Age

	Approve	Disapprove	No opinion
18–29 Years	74	22	4
30–49 Years	75	22	3
50 Years and Over	64	29	7

By Household Income

	Approve	Disapprove	No opinion
$50,000 and Over	80	18	2
$30,000–$49,999	78	20	2
$20,000–$29,999	73	22	5
Under $20,000	60	34	6

By Politics

	Approve	Disapprove	No opinion
Republicans	87	10	3
Democrats	54	40	6
Independents	69	26	5

By Political Ideology

	Approve	Disapprove	No opinion
Liberal	65	32	3
Moderate	69	20	11
Conservative	78	20	2

By Bush Approval

	Approve	Disapprove	No opinion
Approve	83	13	4
Disapprove	34	62	4

Selected National Trend

	Approve	Dis-approve	No opinion
1991			
July	69%	26%	5%
March	90	8	2
1989			
March	44	26	30

Note: As the 1992 presidential election year approaches, George Bush's overall approval rating in the Gallup Poll holds steady at 71%. The president's good grades have much to do with his success in the foreign policy arena. Throughout his presidency his approval rating for handling foreign affairs has never dipped below 60% and now stands at 68%.

Not since Bush first took office, however, has a majority of the public approved his handling of economic conditions. Today, only one third (33%) expresses approval, not significantly higher than his low point on this measure (30%) recorded last fall. Even immediately after victory in the Persian Gulf war, Bush approval on the economy did not reach 40% in the Gallup Poll.

The president wins majority approval for his handling of foreign policy (68%) among all major population subgroups, even Democrats (51%). On the other hand, approval on the economy only exceeds the 40% mark among Republicans (53%) and the most affluent segment of the population (43% among those with family incomes of $50,000 or more). By region, Bush's rating is lowest in the East (28%), where the effects of the recession have been especially harsh.

AUGUST 15
MIDDLE EAST SITUATION

Interviewing Date: 8/8–11/91
Survey #GO 222010

I'd like your overall opinion of some foreign countries. Is your overall opinion of [country] very favorable, mostly favorable, mostly unfavorable, or very unfavorable?

Those saying "very," "mostly favorable"

Soviet Union	66%
Egypt	63
Israel	62
Saudi Arabia	56
Jordan	30
Syria	23
Iran	13
Iraq	7

Selected National Trend
(Those Saying "Very," "Mostly Favorable")

	March 1991	Feb. 1991	Feb. 1990
Soviet Union	50%	57%	64%
Egypt	66	66	–
Israel	69	79	44
Jordan	22	–	–
Iran	14	13	7
Iraq	7	4	–

How closely would you say you have followed the recent situation in the Middle East involving Israel and the Palestinians —very closely, fairly closely, or not at all closely?

	August 1991	March 1991
Very closely	22%	40%
Fairly closely	53	45
Not at all closely	24	14
No opinion	1	1

Asked of those who are following the Middle East situation very or fairly closely: In the Middle East situation, are your sympathies more with the Israelis or more with the Palestinian Arabs?

Israelis	59%
Palestinian Arabs	21
Both; neither (volunteered)	12
No opinion	8

	Israelis	Palestinian Arabs	Both; neither	No opinion
By Sex				
Male	63%	21%	11%	5%
Female	55	21	13	11
By Ethnic Background				
White	61	20	12	7
Nonwhite	50	28	11	11
Black	48	31	9	12
By Education				
College Graduate	63	19	12	6
College Incomplete	58	24	12	6
High-School Graduate	59	22	11	8
Less Than High-School Graduate	54	22	12	12
By Region				
East	55	26	14	5
Midwest	63	17	11	9
South	65	16	10	9
West	50	30	13	7
By Age				
18–29 Years	62	27	6	5
30–49 Years	57	21	14	8
50 Years and Over	60	19	13	8
By Household Income				
$50,000 and Over	60	22	15	3
$30,000–$49,999	60	21	11	8
$20,000–$29,999	63	20	11	6
Under $20,000	58	26	9	7
By Politics				
Republicans	66	21	9	4
Democrats	55	22	13	10
Independents	58	20	14	8

	Israelis	Palestinian Arabs	Both; neither	No opinion
By Religion				
Protestants	60	18	12	10
Catholics	62	22	11	5
By Political Ideology				
Liberal	58	24	10	8
Moderate	51	24	21	4
Conservative	66	18	10	6
By Bush Approval				
Approve	63	20	10	7
Disapprove	47	28	15	10

Selected National Trend

	Israelis	Palestinian Arabs	Both; neither	No opinion
March 1991*	60%	17%	16%	7%
Feb. 1991	64	7	19	10
Oct. 1990*	48	23	19	10
Aug. 1989	50	14	15	21
Dec. 1988*	46	24	16	14
May 1986	43	20	20	17

*Based on the "aware" group

Also asked of the "aware" group: Do you think there will or will not come a time when Israel and the Arab nations will be able to settle their differences and live in peace?

	Yes
National	52%

Selected National Trend

	Yes
March 1991	54%
October 1990	46
May 1988	55

Also asked of the "aware" group: Do you think this will happen during the next five years, or not?

	Yes
National	23%

Selected National Trend

As a way to bring peace to the Middle East, it has been proposed that Israel withdraw from occupied Arab lands if Arab nations in return recognize Israel's right to exist as a nation. Do you favor or oppose this proposal?

	August 1991	March 1991
Favor	71%	73%
Oppose	19	17
No opinion	10	10

How likely do you think it is that both sides will agree to this proposal?

	August 1991	March 1991
Very likely	5%	4%
Somewhat likely	28	33
Not too likely	39	42
Not at all likely	24	17
No opinion	4	4

If Israel did give up occupied Arab lands, how likely is it that this action would bring lasting peace to the Mideast?

	August 1991	March 1991
Very likely	12%	11%
Somewhat likely	39	46
Not too likely	28	27
Not at all likely	16	12
No opinion	5	4

Note: Five months after the end of the Persian Gulf war, a new Gallup Poll finds Americans continuing to see Israel in a more favorable light than they did prior to the conflict. But while good feelings toward Israel have persisted, respondents now are more skeptical that a "land for peace" deal between Israel and its Arab neighbors might bring about lasting peace in the region. In the national euphoria after Iraq's defeat, 57% said that if Israel gave up occupied Arab lands, lasting peace was very or somewhat likely. Today, despite recent progress toward an international Middle East peace conference, only 51% say that this is likely to lead to real peace.

Sixty-two percent now express favorable views of Israel, down somewhat since the period immediately after the Gulf war ended (69% in a March poll). U.S. public opinion toward the Jewish state reached a high point in February, after Saddam Hussein launched Scud missiles against Israel. At that time Americans, sympathetic toward the Israeli people and appreciative of the restraint shown by their government, gave Israel a 79% favorability rating.

Currently, 59% of Americans following news of the Middle East side with the Israelis in their conflict with the Palestinian Arabs, while 21% side with the Palestinians. Prior to the war, in October 1990, the Israeli edge was smaller by 48% to 23%.

Besides Israel, the other nations in the postwar Middle East regarded positively by majorities of Americans are Egypt (63%) and Saudi Arabia (56%), two moderate Arab states allied with the United States in the military effort against Iraq. Despite having joined the alliance against Iraq, Syria—linked in the past with terrorist acts against the United States and other Western nations—ranks low in positive ratings (23%).

Americans remain resolute in their dislike of Iraq: only 7% have a favorable view of that country. Iran, only recently replaced as our number one villain in the region, does not fare much better: 13% hold a positive opinion. Moreover, Jordan, Iraq's lone ally in the Gulf war, also is not very well liked in the United States, with only a 30% favorability rating for Israel's neighbor to the east. Jordan's ratings, however, have improved somewhat since the Gulf victory in March, when only 22% expressed favorable views.

During the post-Gulf war euphoria, hopes were raised that Israel and its Arab neighbors finally would work out a solution to their enduring dispute. Today, Gallup finds no increase in optimism about a peaceful settlement, despite the Bush administration's apparent success in persuading Israel and the Arab nations to attend a peace conference this fall. Consistent with the results of the March poll, the "aware" public closely divides over whether Israel and the Arab nations will ever work out a peaceful settlement: 52% see it happening, but 44% do not. One quarter (23%) is optimistic that a settlement will be worked out in the next five years.

As seen in March (73%), seven in ten respondents (71%) now say that they would favor a "land for peace" agreement in the Middle East, whereby Israel would return occupied territories and the Arab nations would agree to recognize Israel's right to exist as a nation. But while people might see this as a reasonable solution, only one third (33%) thinks it very or somewhat likely that both sides would endorse it.

The Soviet Union, Syria's former patron and supplier of military arms, scores one of its highest favorability ratings on record. Two thirds (66%) of Americans say that they have a favorable opinion of the Soviet Union, up from 50% in March. At the end of the Gulf war, respondents viewed the Soviet Union in the context of President Mikhail Gorbachev's peace proposals, which many saw as interfering with allied plans for completing the military action against Iraq. Today, as Gorbachev courts President George Bush for assistance in solving his country's internal problems, the Soviets are more likely to be seen as supporting U.S. goals in the region.

AUGUST 16
INTERRACIAL MARRIAGE/
AFRICAN-AMERICANS

Interviewing Date: 6/13–16/91
Survey #GO 222002

Do you approve or disapprove of marriage between blacks and whites?

Approve	48%
Disapprove	42
No opinion	10

	Approve	Dis- approve	No opinion
By Ethnic Background			
White	44%	45%	11%
Black	70	19	11

Selected National Trend
(Entire Sample)

	Approve	Dis- approve	No opinion
1983	43%	50%	7%
1978	36	54	10
1972	29	60	11
1968	20	72	8

(By Ethnic Background)

	Those Who Approve	
	White	Black
1983	38%	76%
1978	32	66
1972	25	58
1968	17	48

Asked of blacks: Some people say the term "African-American" should be used instead of the word "black." Which term do you prefer—"African-American," or "black," or doesn't it matter to you?

	1991	1989*
African-American	18%	9%
Black	19	36
Doesn't matter	61	45
No opinion	2	10

*New York Times/CBS national sample

Note: For the first time, more Americans approve (48%) of marriage between whites and blacks than disapprove (42%), according to a recent Gallup Poll. In 1968, when Gallup first asked the public about racial intermarriage, only 20% approved, while 72% disapproved. By 1972 the percentage approving had increased to 29%; a decade later (1983), 43% said that they approved.

Interracial marriage continues to be viewed much more favorably by blacks than by whites. In the current survey, for example, seven in ten blacks (70%) approve, compared with only about four in ten whites (44%). The survey data indicate that the increased approval of marriage between whites and blacks over the last quarter century has occurred among both the white and black populations. For example, in 1968 only 17% of whites approved of interracial marriage compared to 44% today. In the case of blacks, 48% approved in 1968, while the 1991 figure is 70%.

Among the public as a whole, the most liberal attitudes about interracial marriage are held by young people, the best educated, and those outside the South. In contrast, approval is lowest among older Americans, those with less than a college education, and people residing in the South.

On a related topic, some black leaders have advocated "African-American" as the term of choice to describe persons of African descent. The recent Gallup Poll shows that for the majority of blacks today, it is not an issue. Whereas 19% prefer black and 18% like African-American, 61% say that it does not matter which term is used. In 1989, when the same question was asked by the *New York Times*/CBS poll, preference for the term black was stronger: 36% opted for black, while only 9% said African-American and 45% claimed that it did not matter.

AUGUST 20
SOVIET UNION

Interviewing Date: 8/19/91
Survey #GO 222031

I'd like your overall opinion of Mikhail Gorbachev. Is your overall opinion of him very favorable, mostly favorable, mostly unfavorable, or very unfavorable?

Very favorable.....................................22%
Mostly favorable................................54
Mostly unfavorable............................10
Very unfavorable................................. 4
No opinion...10

Selected National Trend

	Very, mostly favorable	Mostly, very un- favorable	No opinion
July 1991...............74%		19%	7%
January 1991...........70		23	7
October 1990 74		17	9
September 1990.......70		21	9
May 1990...............68		21	11
1989....................77		15	8
1988....................72		21	7

How about the Soviet Union? Is your overall opinion of it very favorable, mostly favorable, mostly unfavorable, or very unfavorable?

Very favorable.......................................5%
Mostly favorable..................................31
Mostly unfavorable..............................33
Very unfavorable..................................17
No opinion...14

Selected National Trend

	Very, mostly favorable	Mostly, very un- favorable	No opinion
August 8–11, 1991 ...66%		25%	9%
March 1991 50		42	8
January 1991...........57		35	8
May 1990...............55		32	13
February 1990 64		26	10
August 1989...........51		40	9
February 1989 62		29	9
December 1988.......44		46	10

As far as you know, is there still a "cold war" between the United States and the Soviet Union, or is the "cold war" over?

Still exists.......................................53%
Over...35
No opinion...12

Selected National Trend

	Still exists	Over	No opinion
January 1991...........38%	56%	6%
September 1990.......40	50	10
May 1990...............52	40	8

NATO recently announced a plan to reduce its forces, which would include a 50% reduction in U.S. military forces in Europe. Do you favor or oppose these reductions in NATO forces?

	August 19, 1991	May 1990
Favor	45%	54%
Oppose	46	34
No opinion	9	12

How closely have you followed the current situation [August 19, 1991] involving the replacement of President Gorbachev with new leadership in the Soviet Union?

Very closely	26%
Fairly closely	38
Not too closely	26
Not at all closely	10
No opinion	*

*Less than 1%

Do you approve or disapprove of the way President Bush is dealing with the current events in the Soviet Union [August 19, 1991] involving the change in leadership?

Approve	62%
Disapprove	15
No opinion	23

As a result of these recent changes in the Soviet Union, do you think that:

	Yes
President Gorbachev will resume power at some later point in time?	31%
Efforts at transforming the Soviet economy to a free market system will continue?	40
The Soviet Union will attempt to regain control by force of Eastern European nations such as Hungary and Poland?	46
Disturbances, rebellions, or civil war will break out within the Soviet Union?	76
Relations between the Soviet Union and the United States will go back to where they were before Gorbachev came to power?	44

Do you think the Bush administration has gone too far or not far enough in expressing American disapproval of the removal from power of Soviet President Gorbachev, or do you feel the administration's response so far has been about right?

Too far	4%
Not far enough	19
About right	66
No opinion	11

The United States and other Western nations have been encouraging Soviet President Gorbachev to make sweeping economic, social, and legal reforms over the past five years. Did the United States do too much to support Gorbachev's efforts, too little, or were the actions of the United States about right?

Too much	9%
Too little	13
About right	73
No opinion	5

As far as you are concerned, should the United States continue with its policy of economic and political cooperation with the Soviet Union, or not?

Yes	53%
No	30
It depends (volunteered)	11
No opinion	6

If the Soviet Union should seek to regain control of Poland, Hungary, Czechoslovakia, and other East European nations by force, should the United States and its NATO allies:

Send military troops?	24%
Send economic/military assistance?	35
Remain neutral?	36
No opinion	5

Please tell me whether you favor or oppose the following measures the United States could take in response to the recent changes in the Soviet Union:

	Favor
Suspend federal loans to help ease food shortages?	38%
Suspend economic and technical assistance, advice, and expertise?	46
Hold off on decision to ratify the recently agreed-upon nuclear arms treaty?	55
Provide diplomatic and economic support to democratic and reform groups within the Soviet Union?	59
Restrict American investments in the Soviet Union?	53
Recall the U.S. ambassador to the Soviet Union?	29
Break off diplomatic relations with the Soviet Union?	16

If there are disturbances, rebellions, or a civil war within the Soviet Union as a result of the recent changes, should the United States and its NATO allies:

Send military troops?	8%
Send economic/military assistance?	35
Remain neutral?	51
No opinion	6

Note: A special Gallup Poll conducted on Monday evening, August 19, after reports of the ouster of Soviet President Mikhail Gorbachev, shows that relatively few Americans favor an abrupt termination of relations between the two countries. Over one half favors continuing the U.S. policy of economic and political cooperation with the Soviet Union.

The new poll also shows little evidence of change in Americans' attitudes about the existence of the "cold war" between the two countries. On Monday night, 53% said that the Cold War still existed, a number essentially unchanged from May of last year.

Attitudes toward a wide variety of possible steps that the United States could take in reaction to the crisis are mixed. For example, only one third (29%) favors recalling the U.S. ambassador (or, in the current time frame, keeping new Ambassador Robert Strauss in Washington without sending him to his post). Despite President George Bush's declaration that we should "avoid in every possible way

actions that would lend legitimacy" to the new government, only 16% say that we should go so far as to break off diplomatic relations with the Soviet Union.

In addition, slightly more than one half (55%) favors a delay in ratification of the recently agreed-upon nuclear arms reduction treaty, while a similar number (53%) favors restricting American investments in the USSR. Less than a majority favors suspending two forms of economic aid to the Soviets: 46% say that recently promised economic and technical assistance should be suspended, while 38% say that loans to help ease Soviet food shortages should be curtailed.

There are some signs of a cautionary shift in support for reductions in U.S. troop strength in Western Europe. In May the public split 54% to 34% in favor of a proposed NATO troop reduction plan that would have cut our military forces in Europe in half. Immediately after Monday evening's events, the public is more evenly divided: 45% favor the reductions, but 46% oppose them.

Seventy-six percent are convinced that internal turmoil will manifest itself in the Soviet Union within the coming months. If rebellions or a civil war break out, one third (35%) would favor sending economic and military assistance, but no troops; 8% favor sending in U.S. troops on behalf of the democratic forces. About one half (51%) thinks that we should remain neutral.

Nearly one half (46%) also says that, as a result of the changes, the USSR will attempt to regain control of the East European countries by force. If it does so, 24% of Americans would favor sending in U.S. troops, 35% would favor economic and military assistance, while only 36% say that we should remain neutral.

There is little support for arguments that the United States and other Western nations helped cause the crisis by doing either too much or not enough in relation to Gorbachev's attempted reforms. Three quarters (73%) say that our actions in encouraging the reforms were about right. Only 13% say that we did too little, while 9% say that we went too far. As for Gorbachev himself, will he return to power, as was claimed by the new Soviet leadership on Monday night? Only 31% of Americans think that he will.

The crisis provoked an immediate drop in positive attitudes toward the Soviet Union. Favorable attitudes toward the USSR, which had peaked at 66% in early August, fell to 36% on Monday night.

The public apparently is adopting a wait-and-see attitude toward President Bush's handling of the situation: 62% approve of the job he is doing so far in handling the crisis, but 23% have no opinion. Two thirds (66%) say that the administration's response so far in expressing disapproval has been about right, while 19% say that it has not gone far enough. The president's overall approval rating has not been affected as a result of the crisis; it is at 69%, unchanged from earlier in August.

AUGUST 21
VICE PRESIDENT QUAYLE

Interviewing Date: 8/8–11/91
Survey #GO 222010

I'd like you to rate Vice President Dan Quayle using a scale that goes from the highest possible rating of +5 for someone you have a very favorable opinion of, all the way down to the lowest position of -5 for someone you have a very unfavorable opinion of. How far up or down the scale would you rate Vice President Dan Quayle?

Highly favorable (+5, +4)	15%
Mildly favorable (+3, +2, +1)	42
Mildly unfavorable (-1, -2, -3)	22
Highly unfavorable (-4, -5)	15
No opinion	6

Based on what you know about Vice President Dan Quayle, do you think he is qualified to serve as president if it becomes necessary, or not?

Yes	40%
No	54
No opinion	6

	Yes	No	No opinion
By Sex			
Male	43%	52%	5%
Female	37	55	8

By Ethnic Background			
White	40	54	6
Nonwhite	37	56	7
Black	37	57	6
By Education			
College Graduate	34	60	6
College Incomplete	38	57	5
High-School Graduate	38	56	6
Less Than High-School Graduate	53	36	11
By Region			
East	31	63	6
Midwest	36	53	11
South	51	44	5
West	40	56	4
By Age			
18–29 Years	38	57	5
30–49 Years	41	54	5
50 Years and Over	41	50	9
By Household Income			
$50,000 and Over	39	58	3
$30,000–$49,999	39	55	6
$20,000–$29,999	36	58	6
Under $20,000	45	47	8
By Politics			
Republicans	54	41	5
Democrats	28	66	6
Independents	36	57	7
By Political Ideology			
Liberal	30	65	5
Moderate	35	56	9
Conservative	47	47	6
By Bush Approval			
Approve	46	48	6
Disapprove	26	68	6

Selected National Trend

	Yes	No	No opinion
1991			
May (late)	38%	53%	9%
May (early)*	43	46	11

1990			
November..............33	59	8	
March...................31	54	15	
1989			
May.....................34	52	14	
1988			
October.................46	42	12	
September 34	47	19	
August..................41	40	19	

*Poll conducted May 6–7, 1991, immediately after President Bush's heart problems were widely reported.

If President Bush runs for reelection in 1992, do you think he should keep Dan Quayle as his vice presidential running mate or choose someone else?

Keep Quayle.......................................42%
Choose someone else 52
No opinion... 6

Selected National Trend

	Keep Quayle	Choose someone else	No opinion
1991			
May (late)...............39%	52%	9%
May (early)* 39	51	10
February.................38	53	9
1990			
November...............36	55	9
March...................35	49	16

*Poll conducted May 6–7, 1991, immediately after President Bush's heart problems were widely reported.

1992 Ticket
(Key Voter Groups)

	Keep Quayle	Choose someone else	No opinion
All registered voters			
August 1991............41%	53%	6%
February 1991 38	53	9

Registered Republicans/Those Who Lean Republican

August 1991............50	46	4
February 1991 50	43	7

Asked of registered voters: If George Bush and Dan Quayle run for reelection in 1992, in general are you more likely to vote for Bush and Quayle or for the Democratic party's candidates for president and vice president?

Bush and Quayle....................................51%
Democratic candidates...........................34
Undecided; other..................................15

Also asked of registered voters: If Dan Quayle were the Republican party's candidate for president in 1996, in general would you be more likely to vote for Quayle or for the Democratic candidate for president?

Quayle...24%
Democratic candidate...........................59
Undecided; other..................................17

Asked of registered Republicans and those who lean Republican: If George Bush decides not to run for reelection, which one of the following persons would you like to see nominated as the Republican party's candidate for president in 1992?

James Baker..18%
Jack Kemp...16
Dick Cheney 13
Dan Quayle 10
Phil Gramm... 2
Pete Wilson 1
Other... 8
Undecided...32

Note: With 1992 fast approaching, a Gallup Poll suggests that Dan Quayle is likely to be more of a liability than an asset to George Bush's expected reelection bid. The vice president's public image has improved very little during his time in office. While there are a few bright spots in the poll results, even the good news must be qualified.

Quayle is generally regarded as likeable, but Americans find him significantly less so than his two immediate predecessors. More say that they have a favorable (57%) than an unfavorable (37%) opinion of him, but at a similar point in office former Vice Presidents George Bush and Walter Mondale received much higher ratings (70% favorable, 23% unfavorable for Bush; 69% favorable, 17% unfavorable for Mondale).

More respondents say that Quayle is qualified to be president in 1991 than expressed such views during his first two years in office. Now, 40% express confidence in Quayle's ability to fill Bush's shoes; polls during 1989–90 showed that percentage fluctuating between 31% and 34%. Even so, a majority (54%) still thinks that he is not qualified. Only in the period immediately after the unsettling reports last May about President Bush's irregular heartbeat did the "not qualified" percentage drop below 50%.

A Bush-Quayle ticket beats an unspecified Democratic ticket by a healthy margin (51% versus 34%) in a trial heat of the 1992 election. Yet a majority (52%) hopes that there will be no such ticket, preferring instead that the president selects a new running mate.

As long as the president's approval ratings hold up and he remains in good health, Quayle's problems may not seriously hamper Bush's efforts to win a second term. Gallup analyses of past polling data suggest that very few people change their vote on the basis of their thoughts about vice presidential candidates. Moreover, in the context of a partisan campaign, many GOP voters are likely to rally in support of Quayle despite any reservations they may express today, more than one year away from the election.

Perhaps a more serious issue for the Republicans is what effect renominating Quayle in 1992 might have on the party's presidential prospects for 1996 and beyond. In the post-World War II era, the vice presidency has proved to be a valuable stepping stone to the White House or, at least, to a presidential nomination. In addition to Bush, former Vice Presidents Lyndon Johnson, Richard Nixon, and Gerald Ford all went on to serve as president, while Mondale, Jimmy Carter's vice president, was the 1984 Democratic candidate for president.

However, few voters appear to take Quayle seriously as a contender for the nation's top job. When Republican voters are asked whom their party should nominate for president next year—in the unlikely event that Bush bows out—only one in ten chooses Quayle from a list of six potential candidates. Secretary of State James Baker tops the list with 18%, followed by Housing and Urban Development Secretary Jack Kemp (16%), Defense Secretary Dick Cheney (13%), and then Quayle (10%).

The results of a presidential trial heat for 1996 matching Quayle against the Democratic party's yet-unknown candidate are perhaps even more discouraging for the vice president. Quayle loses by a more than 2-to-1 margin to an unspecified Democrat, 59% to 24%.

AUGUST 28
SOVIET UNION

Interviewing Date: 8/23–25/91
Survey #GO 222012

I'd like your overall opinion of Mikhail Gorbachev. Is your overall opinion of him very favorable, mostly favorable, mostly unfavorable, or very unfavorable?

Very favorable	20%
Mostly favorable	60
Mostly unfavorable	9
Very unfavorable	5
No opinion	6

How about the Soviet Union? Is your overall opinion of it very favorable, mostly favorable, mostly unfavorable, or very unfavorable?

Very favorable	9%
Mostly favorable	51
Mostly unfavorable	22
Very unfavorable	8
No opinion	10

How about Boris Yeltsin? Is your overall opinion of him very favorable, mostly favorable, mostly unfavorable, or very unfavorable?

Very favorable	21%
Mostly favorable	39

Mostly unfavorable.............................13
Very unfavorable................................ 7
No opinion...20

How about the Soviet people? Is your overall opinion of them very favorable, mostly favorable, mostly unfavorable, or very unfavorable?

Very favorable....................................32%
Mostly favorable.................................50
Mostly unfavorable.............................. 6
Very unfavorable................................. 3
No opinion... 9

As far as you know, is there still a "cold war" between the United States and the Soviet Union, or is the "cold war" over?

	Aug. 23–25 1991	Aug. 19 1991
Still exists	40%	53%
Over	53	35
No opinion	7	12

Do you think the Western countries can continue to live more or less peacefully with the Russians, or do you think there is bound to be a major war sooner or later?

	August 1991	May 1990
Can live peacefully	66%	63%
Bound to be war	26	31
No opinion	8	6

As you may know, the Soviet Union was our ally in World War II but has been our enemy during the Cold War in the years since the war. What about today—would you say the Soviet Union is an ally or an enemy of the United States?

	August 1991	May 1990
Ally	65%	39%
Enemy	19	31
Neither (volunteered)	9	21
No opinion	7	9

NATO recently announced a plan to reduce its forces, which would include a 50% reduction in U.S. military forces in Europe. Do you favor or oppose these reductions in NATO forces?

	Aug. 23–25 1991	Aug. 19 1991	May 1991
Favor	53%	45%	54%
Oppose	40	46	34
No opinion	7	9	12

Do you think the United States is doing too much, not enough, or about the right amount to help the Soviet Union in its current economic crisis?

	August 1991	July 1991
Too much	19%	20%
Not enough	15	9
About the right amount	62	64
No opinion	4	7

Do you favor or oppose the following types of U.S. aid to the Soviet Union:

Providing financial loans?

	August 1991	July 1991
Favor	43%	48%
Oppose	54	48
No opinion	3	4

Donating American grain and other farm products?

	August 1991	July 1991
Favor	60%	58%
Oppose	36	38
No opinion	4	4

Providing cash that would not have to be paid back?

	August 1991	July 1991
Favor	7%	6%
Oppose	91	92
No opinion	2	2

Providing technical assistance, advice, and expertise?

	August 1991	July 1991
Favor	68%	69%
Oppose	28	26
No opinion	4	5

In the future, which leader do you think the United States should deal with primarily: Soviet President Mikhail Gorbachev or Russian President Boris Yeltsin?

Gorbachev	61%
Yeltsin	19
Equally with both	9
No opinion	11

Do you think recent events in the Soviet Union mean the end of communism as a major force in the world, or not?

Yes	47%
No	47
No opinion	6

Note: In the aftermath of the tumultuous events of the past week [August 19–21], American opinion of President Mikhail Gorbachev and the Soviet people reached all-time highs. Gorbachev is rated favorably by 80% of the public, and the Soviet people get an even higher rating (82%). Furthermore, favorable ratings of the Soviet Union as a country have rebounded to 60% from a temporary drop last week when the coup was unfolding. And Boris Yeltsin, still a relatively new face to many Americans, also is favorably evaluated (60%) by those who know of him. Despite Yeltsin's clearly ascendant status, however, 61% say that we should deal primarily with Gorbachev, with only 19% opting for Yeltsin.

Despite these upbeat assessments, the public is no more inclined now than before the coup to favor U.S. provision of economic assistance to the Soviet Union. A new Gallup Poll shows that respondents tend to favor technical assistance (68%) and the donation of farm products to the Soviets (60%), but they hesitate to provide financial loans (43%) and are unequivocally opposed to giving direct cash aid that does not have to be paid back (only 7% favor).

Even with the rout of the perpetrators of the coup and the dramatic reform movements under way in the Soviet Union, support for these sorts of aid programs is essentially the same as it was in July. Indeed, a majority now thinks that the United States is doing what it should to aid the Soviets economically: 62% say that we are doing the right amount, while 19% say too much and 15% too little.

Despite Gorbachev's pronouncements that he was virtually eliminating the Communist party within his country, only one half (47%) says that communism is finished as a major world force. Similarly, just about one half (53%) says that the Cold War is now over (although this figure represents a turnaround from the height of the coup, when only 35% said that it was over). Moreover, two thirds (66%) now agree that the United States and USSR can live peacefully together without a major war, but almost as many (63%) thought that way in May 1990, when Gallup last asked the question. And, in what is a significant increase, 65% now consider the USSR an ally, up from 39% in 1990. Thus, support for U.S. troop reductions in Europe is back to pre-coup levels: 53% support the idea, while 40% do not.

SEPTEMBER 3
DEMOCRATIC PRESIDENTIAL CANDIDATES

Interviewing Date: 8/23–25/91
Survey #GO 222012

Asked of registered voters: If George Bush runs for reelection in 1992, in general are you more likely to vote for Bush or for the Democratic party's candidate for president?

Bush	55%
Democratic candidate	27
Undecided; no opinion	18

Selected National Trend

	Bush	Democratic candidate	Undecided; no opinion
1991			
June	53%	30%	17%
April	51	30	19

March...................67	17	16
February...............54	33	13

Agran.......................*	*	1
No opinion..............1	3	4

*Less than 1%

Asked of registered Democrats and those who lean Democratic: Please tell me whether you have a favorable or unfavorable opinion of each of the following Democrats who might run for president in 1992:

	Favor-able	Unfavor-able	No opinion	Never heard of
Jesse Jackson.....45%	47%	5%	3%
Jerry Brown.......29	35	17	19
Mario Cuomo.......42	24	12	22
Lloyd Bentsen.....43	19	13	25
Eugene McCarthy...28	29	18	25
Douglas Wilder.......18	18	18	46
Bill Clinton......21	15	16	48
Tom Harkin.......20	12	16	52
Paul Tsongas.....18	15	14	53
Larry Agran.........3	15	11	71

Also asked of registered Democrats and those who lean Democratic: Please tell me which one of these persons you would like to see nominated as the Democratic party's candidate for president in 1992. And who would be your second choice?

	First choice	Second choice	First & second choices combined
Cuomo...................22%	8%	30%
Jackson 18	11	29
Bentsen 12	17	29
Brown 6	12	18
McCarthy................ 6	4	10
Clinton................... 5	6	11
Wilder 3	5	8
Tsongas................. 4	3	7
Harkin................... 4	2	6

Selected National Trend
(First Choice)

	April 1991	February 1991
Cuomo.............................23%	18%
Jackson 14	12
Bentsen 9	6
Brown ....–	–
McCarthy..........................–	–
Clinton.............................1	2
Wilder 3	2
Tsongas............................1	–
Harkin..............................–	–
Agran...............................–	–
All others.......................37	43
No opinion......................12	17

Also asked of registered Democrats and those who lean Democratic: Thinking more generally, which of the following two kinds of presidential candidates would you rather see the Democratic party nominate?

A liberal who will run on traditional Democratic party values 30%
A moderate who will take the party in a more middle-of-the-road direction 64
Makes no difference (volunteered).............. 2
No opinion... 4

Also asked of registered Democrats and those who lean Democratic: How would you rate the Democrats' chances of defeating George Bush in 1992? Would you say they have a very good chance, a fairly good chance, not much of a chance, or no chance at all?

Very good................................10%
Fairly good...............................40
Not much..................................39
No chance at all.......................... 7
No opinion................................. 4

Also asked of registered Democrats and those who lean Democratic: I'm going to read a list of several current political issues. Please tell me which of these you think the Democrats should use as campaign issues in 1992. *

Economy in general 62%
Poverty and homelessness 50
Health-care costs 47
Unemployment rate..............................45
Tax fairness to
    middle-income people........................42
Public education.................................39
Federal budget deficit............................39
Environment......................................34
Race relations.....................................26
Children and the family.........................25
Abortion...25

*Multiple responses were given.

Note: At a time when many political insiders regard George Bush's reelection as a virtual certainty, Democratic voters are divided on whether their party can be competitive in the presidential race. One half (50%) say that their party has at least a fairly good chance of defeating Bush, while a similar proportion (46%) says that it has little or no chance. There is some consensus, however, on what should be done to avoid a fourth consecutive electoral defeat.

First, a majority (62%) thinks that the economy in general should be a critical issue in the 1992 Democratic campaign. Democratic voters rate the economy significantly higher than ten other issues tested in the poll. Next in importance are poverty and homelessness (50%), health-care costs (47%), and the unemployment rate (45%). In somewhat of a surprise, the abortion issue ranks at the bottom of Democratic voters' lists, considered important by only 25% of both men and women. Second, a majority (64%) says that the party should nominate a moderate who will take it more toward the political center, rather than a liberal who will run on traditional Democratic party values.

The poll was completed after Tennessee Senator Albert Gore announced that he would not enter the presidential race. Now that Gore has joined House Majority Leader Richard Gephardt and Senator Jay Rockefeller as a noncandidate, only three Democrats still mentioned as potential candidates have enough name recognition to attract significant support in a national poll: New York Governor Mario Cuomo (preferred by 22% of Democratic voters), civil rights activist and veteran presidential campaigner Jesse Jackson (18%), and Michael Dukakis's 1988 running mate, Lloyd Bentsen (12%).

While Cuomo remains the top choice, his support has not increased as other prominent Democrats have taken themselves out of the race. The proportion favoring Cuomo today (22%) is similar to that recorded in April (23%), when Gore, Gephardt, and Rockefeller were included. Jackson has moved up somewhat, from 14% to 18%, over the same period, but he is unpopular among white Democrats and his support may be near its maximum level.

The Democrats who have actually become candidates, or have taken steps in that direction, are not very well known nationally. These include Arkansas Governor Bill Clinton, Iowa Senator Tom Harkin, Virginia Governor Douglas Wilder, and former Massachusetts Senator Paul Tsongas. Only about one half of Democratic voters is familiar with each of these politicians. By comparison, nearly all are with Jackson, and roughly three quarters recognize Cuomo's and Bentsen's names. Least known is Larry Agran, the former mayor of Irvine, California, who recently declared himself a candidate. Agran was George McGovern's campaign manager earlier this year before McGovern decided against a 1992 presidential bid.

Both Clinton and Tsongas, the first choice of 5% and 4%, respectively, have moved up from the 1% level they drew in April. Harkin also receives 4% (he was not included in the April list). This places them at about the same level as Jerry Brown (6%) and Eugene McCarthy (6%), two veteran campaigners reported to be considering a run. Wilder receives 3% in the current poll, close to his 2% rank in April.

SEPTEMBER 7
PRESIDENT BUSH

Interviewing Date: 8/29–9/3/91
Survey #GO 222013

Do you approve or disapprove of the way George Bush is handling his job as president?

Approve..69%
Disapprove...22
No opinion...9

Now, let me ask you about some specific problems facing the country. As I read off each one, would you tell me whether you approve or disapprove of the way President Bush is handling that problem:

Economic conditions in this country?

Approve..36%
Disapprove...59
No opinion...5

Selected National Trend

	Approve	Dis- approve	No opinion
1991			
July	34%	59%	7%
June	36	58	6
March	37	56	7

Foreign policy?

Approve..74%
Disapprove...20
No opinion...6

Selected National Trend

	Approve	Dis- approve	No opinion
1991			
July	71%	19%	10%
June	64	28	8
March	79	11	10

Note: The modest rise in George Bush's approval ratings seen immediately after the collapse of the Soviet coup is no longer apparent. A Gallup Poll completed on September 3 shows 69% approving, 22% disapproving, and 9% expressing no opinion of the president's performance. A poll taken on August 23–25, after Mikhail Gorbachev returned to Moscow and Communist party offices were closed throughout the Russian republic, showed Bush approval at 74%. His pre-coup approval rating in an earlier August poll was 71%.

The current 69% approval score marks the first time since the Persian Gulf war began in mid-January that Bush's rating has dropped below 70%. Not since Dwight Eisenhower has a president's approval rating been so high during his third year in office.

While international events of the past year have allowed Bush to capitalize politically on his strength in the area of foreign affairs, the economy remains his Achilles' heel. The president's ratings for handling the economy have been roughly 40 points lower than those for foreign policy throughout 1991. Late August figures show 36% approving of Bush on the economy and 74% approving his handling of foreign affairs.

SEPTEMBER 11
ABORTION

Interviewing Date: 9/5–8/91
Survey #GO 222014

Do you think abortions should be legal under any circumstances, legal under only certain circumstances, or illegal in all circumstances?

Legal, any circumstances........................33%
Legal, certain circumstances...................49
Illegal, all circumstances.......................14
No opinion...4

Selected National Trend

	Legal, any	Legal, certain	Illegal, all	No opinion
1991				
May	32%	50%	17%	1%
1990				
April	31	53	12	4

1989				
July 29	51	17	3	
April* 27	50	18	5	

*Gallup Poll conducted for *Newsweek*

In its 1973 Roe v. Wade *decision, the Supreme Court ruled that states cannot place restrictions on a woman's right to an abortion during the first three months of pregnancy. Would you like to see this ruling overturned, or not?*

Yes...36%
No...57
No opinion..7

Selected National Trend

	Yes	No	No opinion
1991			
July 37%		56%	7%
May.......................42		52	6
1989			
July......................34		58	8
April* 39		51	10
1988			
December 37		58	5

*Gallup Poll conducted for *Newsweek*

Whatever your own position on the issue, tell me what you think of the following actions that have been taken by people who oppose abortion. First, do you think this helps or hurts the antiabortion cause:

Supporting or opposing political candidates solely on the basis of their position on abortion?

	1991	1985*
Helps 26%		22%
Hurts....................................61		57
No opinion...........................13		21

Personally confronting and lecturing pregnant women entering abortion clinics?

	1991	1985*
Helps 21%		37%
Hurts............................71		44
No opinion......................8		19

Blocking entrances to abortion clinics to prevent pregnant women from entering them?

Helps 9%
Hurts.......................................86
No opinion..................................5

*Gallup Poll conducted for *Newsweek*

Have you heard or read about the recent efforts of Operation Rescue, a group opposing abortion, to stop clinics in Wichita, Kansas, from performing abortions?

Yes......................................63%
No..36
No opinion...............................1

Asked of those who responded in the affirmative: Do you approve or disapprove of Operation Rescue's actions?

Approve..................................15%
Disapprove...............................77
No opinion................................8

Also asked of the "aware" group: Do you approve or disapprove of the way the Bush administration has responded to the situation in Wichita?

Approve..................................36%
Disapprove...............................35
No opinion...............................29

Asked of registered voters: Has George Bush's handling of the abortion issue made you more likely or less likely to vote for his reelection in 1992, or will it not much affect your vote for president?

More likely..............................12%
Less likely..............................19
Not much affect vote.....................65
No opinion................................4

Note: Despite the highly publicized campaign by a pro-life group directed against abortion clinics in Wichita, Kansas, public support for legal abortions remains firm. A recent Gallup Poll finds a majority (57%) continuing to oppose overturning the Supreme Court's *Roe v. Wade* landmark abortion decision. Fewer than four in ten (36%) believe that the Court's 1973 ruling should be reversed.

Neither the pro-choice nor the pro-life side of the abortion debate has attracted new supporters over the past two months, since Operation Rescue's Wichita campaign came to national attention. One third (33%) of respondents takes a strongly pro-choice stance, believing that abortion should be legal under all circumstances. In contrast, only one half as many (14%) says that abortion should be completely outlawed. As seen in earlier polls, the largest segment of the public (49%) continues to take the middle ground, favoring legal abortion but only under certain circumstances.

Operation Rescue's campaign against abortion clinics receives little support, even from those sympathetic to the pro-life cause. Only 15% of all those aware of events in Wichita approve of the group's actions; roughly three quarters (77%) disapprove. The specific tactic of blocking entrances to clinics is overwhelmingly viewed negatively. Close to nine in ten (86%) say that this tactic hurts rather than helps the pro-life cause. Indeed, dissatisfaction with the disruptive nature of the Wichita demonstrations may have the effect of reducing the public's tolerance of more orderly forms of antiabortion protest. In 1985 as many as 37% said that antiabortion activists helped their cause by confronting and lecturing women entering abortion clinics. Today, after events in Wichita, only 21% see this tactic as advancing their cause.

The Bush administration has been sharply criticized for trying to play to both sides of the abortion debate in responding to the Wichita demonstrations. Public opinion toward this response is mixed: 36% approve, 35% disapprove, and 29% have no opinion. For George Bush himself, abortion remains a potentially vulnerable issue in 1992. As of today, two thirds (65%) of voters say that the president's handling of the abortion issue will not much affect whether they vote to reelect him, but 19% will be less likely to vote for Bush because of the abortion issue; fewer (12%) say that the issue increases their chances of voting for him. Were abortion to flare up as an issue in the presidential campaign, the Democrats might use it to split off Bush's affluent, well-educated supporters from those at the opposite end of the socioeconomic scale.

Should the Supreme Court reverse *Roe v. Wade* before next year's presidential election, the abortion issue almost certainly would become a major issue of the campaign. With the recent retirements of liberal justices William Brennan and Thurgood Marshall, many see the Court poised to reverse *Roe* whether or not Clarence Thomas is confirmed by the Senate to replace Marshall.

The Senate hearings on the Thomas nomination may provide a preview of how the president will position himself on the issue for 1992. Senators are expected to question Bush's second Supreme Court nominee on the abortion issue, and, unlike his first Court selection, David Souter, Thomas may not have the luxury of declining comment. A Gallup Poll taken in July found 54% saying that the Senate committee should insist that Thomas answer questions about abortion before he can be confirmed.

SEPTEMBER 14
PERSONAL FINANCES

Interviewing Date: 9/5–8/91
Survey #GO 222014

We are interested in how people's financial situation may have changed. Would you say that you are financially better off now than you were a year ago, or are you financially worse off now?

Better..34%
Worse..28
Same (volunteered)..............................37
No opinion..1

Selected National Trend

	Better	Worse	Same	No opinion
1991				
July 11–14	34%	32%	33%	1%
May 16–19	32	32	33	3
April 11–14	29	33	37	1
March 21–24	30	37	32	1
Feb. 28–				
March 3	37	28	34	1
Feb. 14–17	37	28	35	*
Jan. 11–13	26	33	39	2
Jan. 3–6	35	32	32	1

*Less than 1%

Right now, do you think that economic conditions in the country as a whole are getting better or getting worse?

	September 1991	July 1991
Better	27%	34%
Worse	60	51
Same (volunteered)	10	9
No opinion	3	6

Looking ahead, do you expect that at this time next year you will be financially better off than now or worse off than now?

Better	53%
Worse	19
Same (volunteered)	22
No opinion	6

Selected National Trend

	Better	Worse	Same	No opinion
1991				
July 11–14	57%	15%	19%	9%
May 16–19	57	16	19	8
April 11–14	56	17	18	9
March 21–24	56	18	20	6
Feb. 28–				
March 3	64	9	20	7
Feb. 14–17	57	15	20	8
Jan. 11–13	41	25	21	13
Jan. 3–6	52	18	20	10

In your opinion, has the bottom of the current recession been reached, or not?

Yes	32%
No	60
No opinion	8

Selected National Trend

	Yes	No	No opinion
1991			
July 11–14	42%	48%	10%
May 23–26	33	53	14
May 16–19	26	65	9
April 25–28	30	59	11
April 11–14	33	53	14
March 21–24	42	47	11

Note: Most Americans are not convinced that the current economic recession is over. A new Gallup Business Poll finds only 27% saying that economic conditions in the United States are currently getting better, and more than twice as many (60%) think that conditions are getting worse. In a poll two months earlier in July, the balance was not quite so unfavorable, with 34% saying better and 51% saying worse.

Correspondingly, only 32% now believe that the bottom of the current recession has been reached, compared with 60% who say that it has not. Again, these attitudes are significantly less favorable now than in the July poll, when 42% said that the bottom had been reached and 48% said that it had not.

Recent measures of consumer confidence are consistent with an economy that has been sluggish and showing only weak signs of recovery. In the latest survey, 34% reply that they are better off financially now than they were a year ago, while nearly as many (28%) say that they are worse off now. These data have shown slow improvement over the last five months, as the proportion citing worse off has declined from 37% to 28%.

However, this improvement has been somewhat offset in the last two months by a decline from 57% to 53% in the proportion expecting to be better off financially a year from now. Still, this leaves a majority expecting to be better off, compared with only 19% who expect to be worse off. To put these data in perspective, they remain far below the 49% saying better off now and 65% expecting to be better off next year, measured before the current economic recession began in February 1990.

SEPTEMBER 18
CLARENCE THOMAS

Interviewing Date: 9/13–15/91
Survey #GO 222015

How closely have you followed news coverage of the Senate hearings on the nomination of Clarence Thomas to the Supreme Court? Would you say very closely, somewhat closely, or not at all closely?

Very closely..16%
Somewhat closely...............................43
Not at all closely................................40
No opinion...1

From what you may have seen, heard, or read about the hearings, what is your impression of Clarence Thomas? Is it very favorable, favorable, unfavorable, or very unfavorable?

Very favorable....................................10%
Favorable..48
Unfavorable.......................................19
Very unfavorable................................4
Haven't followed hearings (volunteered)....10
No opinion...9

Would you like to see the Senate vote in favor of Clarence Thomas serving on the Supreme Court, or not?

Yes..54%
No..25
No opinion..21

	Yes	No	No opinion
By Ethnic Background			
White	54%	23%	23%
Black	54	32	14

Selected National Trend

	Yes	No	No opinion
1991			
August	56%	23%	21%
July	52	17	31

Do you feel strongly about that, or not?

Yes, favor..54%
   Strongly 32
   Not strongly 22
No, oppose...25
   Strongly 17
   Not strongly 8
No opinion..2

By Ethnic Background

White

Yes, favor..54%
   Strongly 31
   Not strongly 23
No, oppose...23
   Strongly 16
   Not strongly 7
No opinion..23

Black

Yes, favor..54%
   Strongly 43
   Not strongly 11
No, oppose...32
   Strongly 23
   Not strongly 9
No opinion..14

Please tell me whether you think each of the following is more a reason to support Thomas's confirmation to the Court or more a reason to oppose his confirmation:

His personal character and integrity?

Support...67%
Oppose..10
Neither (volunteered)............................2
No opinion...21

His legal qualifications and experience?

Support...66%
Oppose..12
Neither (volunteered)............................ 2
No opinion...20

His political views or ideology?

Support...48%
Oppose..20
Neither (volunteered)............................ 4
No opinion...28

His views on affirmative action?

Support...45%
Oppose..19
Neither (volunteered)............................ 4
No opinion...32

His race?

Support...41%
Oppose.. 6
Neither (volunteered)............................42
No opinion...11

His views on abortion?

Support...29%
Oppose..27
Neither (volunteered)............................ 9
No opinion...35

In general, do you think the senators questioning Clarence Thomas have been too tough on him, too easy on him, or about right?

Too tough..24%
Too easy 7
About right..53
Haven't followed hearings (volunteered)....10
No opinion... 6

In responding to senators' questions about his views on political and legal issues, do you think Clarence Thomas has been too cooperative, not cooperative enough, or about right?

Too cooperative................................... 4%
Not cooperative enough 18
About right..64
Haven't followed hearings (volunteered)..... 7
No opinion... 7

From what you know about Clarence Thomas, how likely is it that if confirmed he would vote to overturn Roe v. Wade— the 1973 Supreme Court decision legalizing abortion? Would you say very likely, somewhat likely, not too likely, or not at all likely?

Very likely 15%
Somewhat likely 28
Not too likely....................................21
Not at all likely.................................11
No opinion..25

If your senator voted in favor of Clarence Thomas serving on the Supreme Court, would that make you more likely or less likely to vote for his reelection, or would it not much affect your vote?

More likely.......................................12%
Less likely.......................................10
Not much affect vote............................72
No opinion... 6

	More likely	Less likely	Not much affect vote	No opinion
By Ethnic Background				
White...........	12%	9%	73%	6%
Southern White........	17	8	71	4
Black...........	10	10	75	5
Northern Black	11	9	74	6

Note: The first week of Senate hearings on the Supreme Court nomination of Clarence Thomas had little apparent impact on the public's support for his confirmation. A new Gallup Poll shows that respondents favor his nomination by a 54%-to-25% margin, not significantly different from an earlier poll conducted in August before the hearings began. While Thomas's position on abortion (or lack thereof) creates some negative reaction, there is general agreement that his legal and personal qualifications are reasons to support his nomination.

While Democratic members of the Senate Judiciary Committee complain that Judge Thomas has not been forthcoming enough in response to their questioning, only one in five respondents (18%) agrees with the senators' complaints; even more (24%) say that the senators themselves have been too tough in their questioning. A majority thinks that both the questioning and Thomas's responses are about right (53% and 64%, respectively).

Despite generally positive views about his openness during the hearings, Thomas's evasiveness on the abortion issue has created some misgivings. In a July Gallup Poll, 54% said that the senators should insist that he explain his views on abortion. In the current poll, when given a list of measures on which to evaluate Thomas, abortion causes the greatest dissonance among respondents; 29% say that his position on abortion makes them more likely to support his nomination, but 27% say less likely. (About four in ten, 43%, say that it is at least somewhat likely that Thomas would vote to overturn *Roe v. Wade*, if confirmed, while 32% say that it is not likely and 25% have no opinion.)

However, opinion on five other measures is positive. Two thirds say that Thomas's personal character and integrity (67%) and his legal qualifications and experience (66%) make them more likely to support his nomination; only one in ten says that these two factors make them more likely to oppose Thomas (10% and 12%, respectively). Forty-one percent think that his race is a reason to support his nomination; only 6% say that it is not. Forty-eight percent say that Thomas's political views or ideology are reasons to support him; 20% say that they are reasons to oppose his nomination. And 45% find that Thomas's views on affirmative action constitute a reason for support; 19% say that they are a reason to oppose him.

The Senate vote on Thomas, to be scheduled later in September, appears to be an issue with relatively low salience for Americans. Over seven out of ten (72%) say that their senator's vote for Thomas would not affect their vote for the senator's reelection either way (12% say

that it would make them more likely to vote for their senator, while 10% say less).

SEPTEMBER 25
PRESIDENT BUSH/DEMOCRATIC PRESIDENTIAL CANDIDATES

Interviewing Date: 9/13–15/91
Survey #GO 222015

Do you approve or disapprove of the way George Bush is handling his job as president?

Approve..68%
Disapprove...22
No opinion...10

Selected National Trend

	Approve	Dis-approve	No opinion
1991			
September 5–8	70%	21%	9%
August 29–September 3	69	22	9
August 23–25	74	18	8
August 8–11	71	22	7

Now, let me ask you about some specific problems facing the country. As I read off each one, would you tell me whether you approve or disapprove of the way President Bush is handling that problem:

Economic conditions in this country?

Approve..32%
Disapprove...60
No opinion...8

Selected National Trend

	Approve	Dis-approve	No opinion
1991			
August 29–September 3	36%	59%	5%
July	34	59	7
June	36	58	6
March	37	56	7

October	30	65	5
July	40	53	7
1989			
November	40	51	9
March	52	27	21

Foreign policy?

Approve	70%
Disapprove	21
No opinion	9

Selected National Trend

	Approve	Dis-approve	No opinion
1991			
August 29–			
September 3	74%	20%	6%
July	71	19	10
June	64	28	8
March	79	11	10
1990			
October	61	29	10
July	62	26	12
1989			
November	65	21	14
March	62	15	23

Asked of registered voters: If George Bush runs for reelection in 1992, in general are you more likely to vote for Bush or for the Democratic party's candidate for president?

Bush	51%
Democratic candidate	29
Undecided; no opinion	20

Selected National Trend

	Bush	Democratic candidate	Un-decided; no opinion
1991			
September 5–8	52%	29%	19%
August	55	27	18
June	53	30	17
April	51	30	19
March	67	17	16
February	54	33	13

Asked of registered Democrats and those who lean Democratic: Please tell me whether you have a favorable or unfavorable opinion of each of the following Democrats who might run for president in 1992:

	Favorable	Unfavor-able	No opinion	Never heard of
Jesse Jackson	35%	54%	8%	3%
Jerry Brown	36	27	19	18
Mario Cuomo	50	17	12	21
Douglas Wilder	26	11	22	41
Tom Harkin	24	7	21	48
Bob Kerrey	22	8	20	50
Paul Tsongas	20	13	15	52
Bill Clinton	21	10	16	53
Dave McCurdy	11	4	16	69
Larry Agran	5	10	12	73

Selected National Trend
(August 1991)

	Favorable	Unfavor-able	No opinion	Never heard of
Jackson	45%	47%	5%	3%
Brown	29	35	17	19
Cuomo	42	24	12	22
Wilder	18	18	18	46
Harkin	20	12	16	52
Kerrey	–	–	–	–
Tsongas	18	15	14	53
Clinton	21	15	16	48
McCurdy	–	–	–	–
Agran	3	15	11	71

Also asked of registered Democrats and those who lean Democratic: I am going to read through the list of names once more. This time please tell me which one of these persons you would most like to see nominated as the Democratic party's candidate for president in 1992. And if Mario Cuomo and Jesse Jackson choose not to run, which of the following potential candidates would you most like to see nominated?

	All candidates	Without Cuomo, Jackson
Cuomo	31%	–
Jackson	14	–
Brown	11	21
Harkin	5	6
Wilder	4	10
Kerrey	4	5
Clinton	3	6
McCurdy	3	5
Tsongas	2	5
Agran	*	1
All others	*	1
None; undecided	23	40

*Less than 1%

Also asked of registered Democrats and those who lean Democratic: Thinking more generally, which of the following two kinds of presidential candidates would you rather see the Democratic party nominate?

	Sept. 1991	Aug. 1991
A liberal who will run on traditional Democratic party values	32%	30%
A moderate who will take the party in a more middle-of-the-road direction	58	64
Makes no difference (volunteered)	3	2
No opinion	7	4

Also asked of registered Democrats and those who lean Democratic: How would you rate the Democrats' chances of defeating George Bush in 1992? Would you say they have a very good chance, a fairly good chance, not much of a chance, or no chance at all?

	Sept. 1991	Aug. 1991
Very good	11%	10%
Fairly good	32	40
Not much	41	39
No chance at all	10	7
No opinion	6	4

Note: As the field of Democratic presidential candidates finally begins to take shape, Mario Cuomo's off-stage presence looms large. A new Gallup Poll finds that one third (31%) of registered Democrats and those who lean Democratic prefer the New York governor when his name is included on a list of presidential candidates. No other potential Democratic candidate gets even one half as much support. Placing second, with only 14%, is civil rights leader Jesse Jackson, who ran in 1984 and 1988. Now that another black—Virginia Governor Douglas Wilder—has entered the race, most observers expect Jackson to sit it out in 1992.

When Cuomo and Jackson are removed as options and the choice is limited to a probable field of eight candidates, the clear winner is "undecided" (40%). Former California Governor Jerry Brown, the only one of the eight likely candidates with high name recognition nationally, attracts the highest level of support (21%). But Brown, who has already run for president twice, must overcome an image for flakiness that many think helped defeat him the last time he ran for elective office (in a 1982 Senate race against Pete Wilson). The man who earned the nickname "Governor Moonbeam" is viewed unfavorably by close to three in ten (27%) Democratic voters.

In this same test—without Cuomo and Jackson—Wilder is second to Brown in overall support (10%). Wilder may have received an assist from the poll's timing since he announced his presidential bid on the day the survey began.

Five other candidates tie for third place in Democratic voter preferences. Iowa Senator Tom Harkin, the only traditional liberal in the group, is backed by 6%, as is Arkansas Governor Bill Clinton (6%), followed by Nebraska Senator Bob Kerrey (5%), Oklahoma Congressman Dave McCurdy (5%), and former Massachusetts Senator Paul Tsongas (5%). Former Irvine, California, mayor Larry Agran trails the field with 1%.

The Democratic race is starting at a time when the effects of the Gulf war victory on George Bush's approval ratings are finally fading. The latest approval figure, 68%, is within 4 percentage points of the 64% recorded in early January, immediately before the air war with Iraq began. The president's vulnerability on economic issues is apparent. Currently, only 32% approve of Bush's handling of the economy, a figure statistically equal to his low of 30% recorded last October.

Slightly over one half (51%) of registered voters polled say that they expect to vote for Bush next year, while 29% say that they will probably vote Democratic. One in five (20%) declares no preference. These results are similar to those seen in June, before events in the Soviet Union elevated support for Bush in the Gallup Poll. But even as poll results suggest an opening for the Democrats, the party's rank and file are becoming more pessimistic about their chances for victory in 1992. Currently, fewer than one half of Democratic voters (43%) say that the party has a very good or fairly good chance of unseating Bush, down from 50% in late August.

SEPTEMBER 25
MOST IMPORTANT PROBLEM/ REPUBLICAN AND DEMOCRATIC PARTIES

Interviewing Date: 9/5–8/91
Survey #GO 222014

What do you think is the most important problem facing this country today?

Economy...16%
Poverty; homelessness 12
Drugs; drug abuse.................................12
Unemployment......................................11
Education 8
Federal budget deficit............................7
Crime..4
Health care; Medicare............................3
Ethics, morals 2
Recession...2
All other economic problems...................2
All other noneconomic problems.............14
No opinion..7

Which political party do you think can do a better job of handling the problem you

have just mentioned—the Republican party or the Democratic party?

Republican 34%
Democratic 32
No difference (volunteered); no opinion.....34

I'd like you to rate the Republican party on a scale. If you have a favorable opinion of it, name a number between +1 and +5—the higher the number, the more favorable your opinion. If you have an unfavorable opinion of it, name a number between -1 and -5—the lower the number, the more unfavorable your opinion. How would you rate the Republican party on this scale?

Highly favorable (+5, +4).......................17%
Mildly favorable (+3, +2, +1) 52
Mildly unfavorable (-1, -2, -3)................16
Highly unfavorable (-4, -5) 8
No opinion..7

Selected National Trend
(Favorable Opinion)

	Highly favorable (+5, +4)	Mildly favorable (+3, +2, +1)
September 1984	27%	39%
March 1981	30	44
October 1980	18	47
May 1980	17	50
November 1975	15	47
August 1973	19	40
October 1972	29	43
October 1970	25	47
December 1968	25	42
September 1968	30	47
July 1968	27	43
May 1968	27	46
October 1967	34	39
April 1967	33	44
December 1966	28	41
August 1966	29	44
May 1965	26	39
October 1964	21	33
October 1956	33	29
February 1956	27	31

And how would you rate the Democratic party on the same scale?

Highly favorable (+5, +4) 16%
Mildly favorable (+3, +2, +1) 47
Mildly unfavorable (-1, -2, -3) 21
Very unfavorable (-4, -5) 8
No opinion 8

Selected National Trend
(Favorable Opinion)

	Highly favorable (+5, +4)	Mildly favorable (+3, +2, +1)
September 1984	26%	39%
March 1981	34	41
October 1980	27	46
May 1980	28	48
November 1975	30	48
August 1973	29	43
October 1972	30	44
October 1970	35	44
December 1968	41	33
September 1968	32	38
July 1968	36	37
May 1968	42	36
October 1967	31	35
April 1967	40	37
December 1966	33	37
August 1966	36	40
May 1965	44	34
October 1964	45	29
October 1956	38	25
February 1956	43	26

In general, which party do you associate more with political favoritism and corruption—the Republicans or the Democrats?

Republicans 44%
Democrats 29
Both equally (volunteered) 15
Neither (volunteered) 3
No opinion 9

In your opinion, which of the following is more to blame for the nation's current economic problems—President Bush or Congress?

Bush 15%
Congress 62
Both equally (volunteered) 13
Neither (volunteered) 4
No opinion 6

Which political party—the Republican or the Democratic—do you think would do a better job of dealing with:

Relations with the Soviet Union?

	September 1991	February 1982
Republican	67%	34%
Democratic	17	36
No difference; no opinion	16	30

Foreign policy?

	September 1991	February 1982
Republican	62%	34%
Democratic	22	37
No difference; no opinion	16	29

National defense?

	September 1991	February 1982
Republican	57%	44%
Democratic	26	33
No difference; no opinion	17	23

Economic conditions in this country?

	September 1991	February 1982
Republican	45%	34%
Democratic	39	43
No difference; no opinion	16	23

Crime?

Republican 43%
Democratic 32
No difference; no opinion 25

Federal budget deficit?

Republican 42%
Democratic 33
No difference; no opinion 25

Unemployment?

	September 1991	February 1982
Republican	34%	22%
Democratic	49	56
No difference; no opinion	17	22

Abortion issue?

Republican	34%
Democratic	39
No difference; no opinion	27

Environmental issues?

	September 1991	February 1982
Republican	33%	19%
Democratic	47	50
No difference; no opinion	20	31

Race relations?

Republican	30%
Democratic	47
No difference; no opinion	23

Health-care policy?

Republican	29%
Democratic	54
No difference; no opinion	17

Poverty and homelessness?

Republican	25%
Democratic	57
No difference; no opinion	18

As of today, which political party—the Republican or the Democratic—do you think serves the interests of the following groups best:

People like yourself?

	September 1991	October 1990
Republican	39%	38%
Democratic	45	44
No difference (volunteered)	9	10
No opinion	7	8

Poor people?

	September 1991	October 1990
Republican	18%	18%
Democratic	68	64
No difference (volunteered)	7	9
No opinion	7	9

Wealthy people?

	September 1991	October 1990
Republican	76%	70%
Democratic	12	16
No difference (volunteered)	6	5
No opinion	6	9

Middle-income people?

Republican	37%
Democratic	47
No difference (volunteered)	9
No opinion	7

Note: The Democratic party may have exhausted its reserves of public goodwill that have given it majority status throughout the post-World War II era. A new Gallup Poll shows the Democrats' public image at an historic low: 63% give the party a favorable rating today, down from 65% in 1984 and 75% in 1981. Additionally, for the first time since Watergate sent the GOP's image into a tailspin, significantly more people now have a favorable opinion of the Republican party (69%) than the Democratic party (63%).

Despite an edge in overall favorability, the Republican party is not significantly more likely than the Democratic party to be highly regarded. Only 17% now give a highly favorable rating to the GOP on Gallup's scalometer question; a statistically equal percentage (16%) so rate the Democratic party. Ten years ago, when Ronald Reagan first took office, roughly twice as many respondents reported highly favorable opinions of both the

Democratic (34%) and Republican parties (30%).

The decline of the Democratic party's image, as reflected in the public's decreasing tendency to give the party a highly favorable rating, is striking. From 1956 to 1984 the Democratic party's highly favorable rating averaged 35%. Prior to 1980 it had fallen below 30% only once, but the last two measures are well below historic norms. In 1984, 26% reported a highly favorable opinion of the Democrats; today's figure is yet another 10 percentage points lower (16%). Highly favorable scores for both parties today match the lows seen for the GOP in the post-Watergate years of 1973 to 1980.

In terms of the foreign policy and defense issues handled primarily by the executive branch—in recent years by Republican presidents—respondents prefer the GOP over the Democratic party by huge margins. Specifically, the Republicans have a 50-point advantage on dealing with the Soviets (67% versus 17%), a 40-point advantage on handling foreign affairs generally (62% versus 22%), and a 31-point advantage on maintaining the nation's defenses (57% versus 26%).

However, on domestic issues that are more often associated with Congress, the public has a clear preference for the Democratic party on poverty and homelessness (57% versus 25%), health-care policy (54% versus 29%), race relations (47% versus 30%), unemployment (49% versus 34%), and the environment (47% versus 33%).

The parties are closer on several issues that are expected to be key in next year's presidential campaign. The Republicans have a narrower edge over the Democrats as the party better able to deal with crime (43% versus 32%), the federal budget deficit (42% versus 33%), and economic conditions (45% versus 39%). The Democrats are preferred by an equally small margin on the abortion issue (39% versus 34%).

The Democrats' failure to be more competitive on the economy does not bode well for their chances of defeating George Bush in 1992. The poll shows that, after declining somewhat over the summer, economic issues are increasingly perceived as the nation's top problem. However, respondents persist in saying that the Democrats better serve the interests of middle-income people (47%) and "people like yourself" (45%) than the Republicans (37% and 39%, respectively).

OCTOBER 2
MIDDLE EAST SITUATION

Interviewing Date: 9/26–29/91
Survey #GO 222017

I'd like your overall opinion of Israel. Is your overall opinion of Israel very favorable, mostly favorable, mostly unfavorable, or very unfavorable?

Very favorable.....................................11%
Mostly favorable.................................45
Mostly unfavorable..............................25
Very unfavorable................................. 9
No opinion...10

Selected National Trend

	Very, mostly favorable	Mostly, very un- favorable	No opinion
1991			
August...................62%		26%	12%
March....................69		23	8
February................79		13	8
1990			
October.................48		39	13
February................44		39	17
1989			
August...................45		45	10
February-March........49		38	13

As a way to bring peace to the Middle East, it has been proposed that Israel withdraw from occupied Arab lands if Arab nations in return recognize Israel's right to exist as a nation. Do you favor or oppose this proposal?

Favor..70%
Oppose..19
No opinion...11

Selected National Trend

	Favor	Oppose	No opinion
1991			
August	71%	19%	10%
March	73	17	10

Do you think Israel or the Arab countries is more to blame for the lack of progress in settling their differences?

Israel	22%
Arab countries	37
Both equally (volunteered)	23
Neither (volunteered)	2
No opinion	16

Note: The controversy over U.S. loan guarantees to Israel appears to have hurt the Jewish state's image among the American public. According to a new Gallup Poll, 56% have favorable views of Israel, while 34% have unfavorable views. In August, before Jerusalem's request for $10 billion in U.S. loan guarantees to resettle Soviet Jews met with strong opposition from President George Bush, Israel's ratings were significantly more positive (62% favorable versus 26% unfavorable).

Greater numbers of Americans blame the Arab countries (37%) than the Israelis (22%) for holding up progress on peace in the Middle East, but a significant proportion (23%) blames both sides. While respondents differ on who is to blame, they solidly support the idea of land for peace as a solution to Israeli-Arab conflict over the occupied territories. Seventy percent now say that they favor a proposal in which Israel would withdraw from the territories in exchange for formal recognition as a nation from the Arab countries. Only one in five (19%) opposes the land-for-peace solution. Current results are virtually identical to those recorded in August.

OCTOBER 5
METRIC SYSTEM

Interviewing Date: 8/8–11/91
Survey #GO 222019

Do you know what the metric system is?

Yes	80%
No	20

Asked of those who replied in the affirmative: Would you like to see the United States adopt the metric system, or not?

Yes	26%
No	51
Not aware of system	20
No opinion	3

Selected National Trend

	Yes	No	Not aware	No opinion
Oct. 1977	25%	45%	26%	4%
Jan. 1977	29	40	25	6
1973	29	19	46	6
1971	19	19	56	6

Note: National Metric Week sponsors can take slight comfort in discovering that four out of five Americans (80%) now claim to know what the metric system is, compared to twenty years ago when only 44% knew. However, as awareness of the metric system has grown, so has opposition to its adoption here in the United States. Since 1971 support has risen only 7 points (19% to 26%), while opposition has more than doubled, from 19% to 51%.

Fourteen years ago, when Gallup last asked about metrics, President Gerald Ford had committed the nation to abandoning its stance voluntarily as the last major holdout against the nearly universal system of weights and measures. But even as Gallup surmised that "the metrication of America is under way," the poll noted then that "resistance ... has grown as familiarity has increased." (In late 1977 three quarters claimed familiarity, but only 25% backed the metric initiative; opposition had risen to 45%.) Now, even the harbingers of metrication that Gallup noted then—distances given in kilometers, weathermen providing Celsius temperature readings—have largely disappeared.

OCTOBER 9
FEDERAL BUDGET DEFICIT

Interviewing Date: 10/3–6/91
Survey #GO 222018

There is much discussion as to the amount of money the government in Washington should spend for national defense and military purposes. How do you feel about this? Do you think we are spending too little, about the right amount, or too much?

Too little...10%
About right...36
Too much 50
No opinion.. 4

Selected National Trend

	Too little	About right	Too much	No opinion
1991				
August..........	10%	38%	47%	5%
March*.........	10	60	26	4
1990				
August..........	15	40	41	4
January.........	10	35	50	5
1987.............	14	36	44	6
1986.............	13	36	47	4
1985.............	11	36	46	7
1983.............	21	36	37	6
1982.............	16	31	41	12
1981.............	51	22	15	12
1976.............	22	32	36	10
1973.............	13	30	46	11
1971.............	11	31	50	8
1969.............	8	31	52	9

*Gallup survey conducted for *Newsweek*

If the U.S. defense budget is cut sharply, money might become available for other purposes. In which of the following areas, if any, would you like to see some of this additional money used?

Increase spending on domestic
problems such as homelessness,
drug abuse, education, and health care.....90%
Reduce federal budget deficit 80

Reduce amount of federal taxes
that Americans now pay 71
Provide financial aid to help
Soviet Union shift to free-
market economy...............................23

In which one of these areas would you like to see most of the money used?

Domestic problems.............................67%
Federal budget deficit............................16
Reduce taxes.......................................15
Aid to Soviet Union 1
No opinion... 1

How important is reducing the federal budget deficit? Would you say it is very important, somewhat important, not too important, or not at all important?

	October 1991	May 1990
Very important	58%	70%
Somewhat important	34	20
Not too important..................	5	3
Not at all important................	2	3
No opinion..........................	1	4

If George Bush vetoes [bill], would that make you more likely or less likely to vote for his reelection in 1992, or would it not have much effect on your vote:

The bill extending unemployment benefits?

More likely...14%
Less likely..19
Not have much effect 63
No opinion.. 4

The bill requiring companies to give unpaid leave?

More likely...10%
Less likely..17
Not have much effect 70
No opinion.. 3

Note: As the United States scales down its nuclear arsenal, the public overwhelmingly favors increased domestic spending over deficit reduction or tax relief as the best way to use any peace dividend. In the latest Gallup Poll, two thirds (67%) say that if sharp cuts in military spending make funds available for other purposes, this "new" money should go mainly toward increased spending on domestic problems such as homelessness, drug abuse, education, and health care. Although large majorities favor using some of the savings to help reduce the federal budget deficit or cut taxes, relatively few would use it for either of these purposes (16% and 15%, respectively).

At a time when our own economy has been in recession, there is little public sentiment for shifting funds to help the Soviets deal with their economic problems. Only one quarter (23%) would support sending any money obtained through a peace dividend to the Soviets; only 1% would devote most of the money to Soviet aid.

Public support for cutting the military budget today is as high as it was in the early 1970s, when the United States began to withdraw from Vietnam. One half (50%) of Americans now thinks that we are spending too much money on defense. Only one in ten (10%) says that the defense budget is too low, while the remainder (36%) says that it is about right. Current results are statistically similar to those recorded in early 1990 before Iraq's invasion of Kuwait but after the opening of the Berlin Wall.

OCTOBER 10
PRESIDENT BUSH

Interviewing Date: 10/3–6/91
Survey #GO 222018

Do you approve or disapprove of the way George Bush is handling his job as president?

Approve..65%
Disapprove....................................27
No opinion..................................... 8

Selected National Trend

	Approve	Dis- approve	No opinion
1991			
September 26–29	66%	25%	9%
September 13–15	68	22	10
September 5–8	70	21	9
August 24– September 3	69	22	9
July 25–28	71	21	8
June 27–30	72	22	6
May 30–June 2	74	17	9
April 25–28	76	15	9
March 28–30	82	11	7
February 28– March 3	89	8	3

Do you approve or disapprove of the reductions in U.S. nuclear arms that President Bush announced last week?

Approve..71%
Disapprove....................................20
No opinion..................................... 9

As far as you know, is there still a "cold war" between the United States and the Soviet Union, or is the "cold war" over?

Still exists....................................33%
Over..60
No opinion..................................... 7

Now, let me ask you about some specific problems facing the country. As I read off each one, would you tell me whether you approve or disapprove of the way President Bush is handling that problem:

Economic conditions in this country?

Approve..29%
Disapprove....................................64
No opinion..................................... 7

Foreign policy?

Approve..70%
Disapprove....................................25
No opinion..................................... 5

Note: Although President George Bush's recent announcement of a unilateral reduction in nuclear forces was hailed as an epoch-ending breakthrough, it apparently has had little positive impact on the public's overall opinions about his presidency. Seventy-one percent approve of Bush's nuclear reduction plan, while 20% disapprove. But a new Gallup measurement shows that Bush's overall job approval rating is now at 65%, not statistically different from the weeks before the September 27 announcement. It continues a gradual decline from his historic high of 89% in early March immediately after the Operation Desert Storm victory.

The poll shows that 70% approve of Bush's handling of foreign policy, also statistically no different from measures of his foreign policy performance in September, August, or July. The public continues to give significantly lower approval ratings to Bush's handling of the economic situation in this country, currently at a new low: 29% approval, with 64% disapproval.

The recent political changes in the Soviet Union and the announcement by both the Soviets and the Americans of massive nuclear weapons cuts have largely convinced respondents that the decades-old Cold War is over. As recently as mid-August of this year, over one half (53%) thought that the Cold War still existed. That number dropped to 40% in late August and is now at a new low of only 33%.

OCTOBER 12
CHRISTOPHER COLUMBUS

Interviewing Date: 10/3–6/91
Survey #GO 222018

Here's a different question that people find interesting to answer. Can you please tell me who first discovered America?

	Oct. 1991	Oct. 1990
Christopher Columbus	59%	55%
Leif Eriksson, the Vikings	14	14
Indians, Native Americans	7	7
Other	10	13
No opinion	10	11

Columbus Day will be observed on Monday, October 14. Do you happen to know the year that Christopher Columbus first sailed to the New World?

Year 1492..60%
Other...13
No opinion..27

Do you happen to know where in the New World Columbus first landed—that is, the name of the place?

San Salvador, Watling Island...................2%
Bahamas 2
Caribbean, West Indies 11
Other...39
No opinion..46

Do you happen to know what Columbus's nationality was?

Italian; Genoese; Genoan.......................35%
Spanish 22
Other..18
No opinion..25

Do you happen to know which country's flag Columbus sailed under?

Spain..48%
Italy..4
Other..21
No opinion..27

Some people feel Columbus doesn't deserve credit for discovering America because native peoples and possibly the Vikings arrived here centuries earlier. Others feel that although Columbus may not have been first, the impact his explorations had on world history earned him credit for discovering America. Which comes closer to your view?

Doesn't deserve credit...........................14%
Impact on history earned him credit..........79
No opinion...7

Some people say that because of his personal character and the way his voyages affected the Native American peoples, Columbus should be regarded as a villain rather than a hero. How do you see Columbus—as a hero, a villain, or a little of both?

Hero...41%
Villain..1

Both 49
Neither (volunteered) 5
No opinion 4

Note: As the year-long commemoration of the 500th anniversary of Christopher Columbus's voyage to the New World approaches, a new Gallup Poll shows that Americans are woefully uninformed about the basic facts surrounding the explorer and his voyage of discovery. Only 60% know the date (1492) when Columbus first set forth, and less than one half (48%) can recall what flag he sailed under (Spain). Only one third (35%) can correctly identify his nationality as Italian, or, more precisely, as a citizen of the northern Italian city-state of Genoa. Almost as many (22%) incorrectly identify him as Spanish.

Americans score lowest on their knowledge about where in the New World Columbus landed on his first voyage. Only 15%, for example, know that he did not reach either the North or South American continent and correctly identify his initial landfall as somewhere in the West Indies or Caribbean. Only a small fraction (4%) are aware that he actually touched land in the Bahamas. To narrow it further, even fewer (2%) can name the specific island regarded as the official landfall, San Salvador or Watling Island.

Most respondents, however, see good reason for honoring Columbus. Six in ten (59%) say that he discovered America, compared to only 14% who credit Leif Eriksson or the Vikings and 7% Native Americans or Indians. Even when reminded that others might have been in America before Columbus, an even larger number (79%) says that he should be given credit for his achievement because of its historical impact.

On the other hand, reflecting recent revisionist criticism of Columbus's role in history, more (49%) say that he should be regarded as both a hero and a villain than accord him total hero status (41%). Only 1%, however, think that he should be seen only as a villain.

OCTOBER 14
CLARENCE THOMAS

Interviewing Date: 10/10–13/91
Survey #GO 222019

How closely have you followed news coverage of the Senate hearings on the nomination of Clarence Thomas to the Supreme Court? Would you say very closely, somewhat closely, or not at all closely?

Very closely 30%
Somewhat closely 47
Not at all closely; no opinion 23

	Very closely	Some- what closely	Not at all closely; no opinion
By Sex			
Male 32%		46%	22%
Female..................27		48	25
By Ethnic Background			
White...................28		48	24
Black 49		28	23

Selected National Trend

	Very closely	Some- what closely	Not at all closely; no opinion
1991			
September 13–15 .....16%		43%	41%

From what you may have seen, heard, or read about the hearings, what is your impression of Clarence Thomas? Is it very favorable, favorable, unfavorable, or very unfavorable?

Very favorable 14%
Favorable 43
Unfavorable 23
Very unfavorable 7
Haven't followed hearings 5
No opinion 8

	Very favor- able	Favor- able	Unfavor- able	Very unfa- vorable*
By Sex				
Male 17%	44%	21%	7%
Female.........13	42	24	7

By Ethnic Background

White...........14	42	24	7
Black 14	55	14	8

By Education

College.........14	42	25	9
College In- complete....16	48	24	7
High-School Graduate.....14	44	21	7
Less Than High-School Graduate.....15	38	20	6

By Politics

Republicans...19	47	17	3
Democrats 11	39	30	8
Independents..13	43	23	10

By Bush Approval

Approve........18	49	17	4
Disapprove.....7	33	36	14

Selected National Trend

	Very favor-able	Favor-able	Unfavor-able	Very unfa-vorable*
1991				
Oct. 10–13 ....14%	43%	23%	7%
Sept. 13–15...10	48	19	4

*"Haven't followed hearings" and "no opin-
ion" have been omitted.

Would you like to see the Senate vote in favor of Clarence Thomas serving on the Supreme Court, or not? And do you feel strongly about that, or not?

Yes, favor...53%	
Strongly 37	
Not strongly 16	
No, oppose..30	
Strongly 21	
Not strongly 9	
No opinion...17	

	Yes, favor	No, oppose	No opinion
By Sex			
Male 58%	28%	14%
Female..................49	32	19
By Ethnic Background			
White....................52	31	17
Black 67	24	9

Daily Results

	Yes, favor	No, oppose	No opinion
Thursday, Oct. 10 .....52%	29%	19%
Friday, Oct. 11.........51	34	15
Saturday, Oct. 12– Sunday, Oct. 13.....59	30	11

Selected National Trend

	Yes	No	No opinion
1991			
September 13–15 ....54%	25%	21%
August 8–11...........56	23	21
July 11–14 52	17	31

Do you approve or disapprove of the Senate's decision to delay their vote on whether to confirm Thomas until next Tuesday [October 15]?

Approve..60%	
Disapprove...32	
No opinion...8	

	Approve	Dis-approve	No opinion
By Sex			
Male 58%	33%	9%
Female..................61	31	8
By Ethnic Background			
White....................60	32	8
Black 62	34	4

University of Oklahoma Professor Anita Hill charges Clarence Thomas with sexually harassing her when she worked for him in the early 1980s. Thomas denies

Hill's charges. From what you have heard or read, whom do you believe more—Anita Hill or Clarence Thomas?

Hill	29%
Thomas	48
Neither (volunteered)	6
No opinion	17

	Hill	Thomas	Neither	No opinion
By Sex				
Male	27%	51%	7%	15%
Female	31	46	5	18
By Ethnic Background				
White	28	48	6	18
Black	34	57	5	4

Daily Results

	Hill	Thomas	Neither	No opinion
Thursday, Oct. 10	26%	48%	7%	19%
Friday, Oct. 11	38	44	6	12
Saturday, Oct. 12–Sunday, Oct. 13	27	55	5	13

Some people feel the all-male Senate Judiciary Committee mishandled Hill's charges about sexual harassment by not investigating the matter more thoroughly before the Thomas hearings ended. Others feel that Hill's unwillingness to come forward publicly during the hearings kept the committee from doing more than it did. Which comes closer to your view?

Mishandled charges	41%
Kept by Hill from doing more	42
Neither (volunteered)	4
No opinion	13

	Mishandled	Kept from doing more	Neither	No opinion
By Sex				
Male	40%	44%	4%	12%
Female	42	41	4	13

By Ethnic Background

White	40	43	4	13
Black	51	37	4	8

Have you ever personally been the victim of sexual harassment on the job, or not?

Yes	14%
No	85
Never worked; no opinion	1

	Yes	No	Never worked; no opinion
By Sex			
Male	6%	93%	1%
Female	21	78	1

Note: A majority of the public continues to back Clarence Thomas for the Supreme Court despite law professor Anita Hill's allegations that Thomas sexually harassed her. A poll completed on Thursday, October 10, through Sunday, October 13, finds 53% supporting Thomas's confirmation, with 30% opposed and 17% undecided. Gallup's last poll on Thomas, taken in mid-September before Hill's charges surfaced, found a similar level of support (54%) but less opposition (25%) to the nominee.

As the hearings progressed over the weekend, public opinion on Thomas shifted back and forth as the nominee, his accuser, and other witnesses before the Senate Judiciary Committee made their cases on national television. This is most apparent on the key question of whether Thomas or Hill—who give contradictory stories—is telling the truth about the alleged sexual harassment.

On Thursday, before the hearing started, twice as many respondents found Thomas credible (51%) as they did Hill (27%). On Friday, after Hill took the stand to tell her story, opinion shifted to a point where nearly as many (38%) said that she was telling the truth as said so about Thomas (44%). But opinion shifted back again, after he had the opportunity to testify a second time late Friday and Saturday. Among those interviewed on Saturday and Sunday, 55% believed Thomas more, while only 27% believed Hill more.

Too few interviews were completed on Sunday to analyze separately. Thus, any effects on public opinion brought about by Sunday's testimony before the committee or from the announcement that Hill had taken and passed a polygraph test are largely unreflected in the poll.

Not surprisingly, there is a gender gap in opinion about Thomas. Men are more likely than women to favor his confirmation (58% to 49%). Moreover, blacks have come to the embattled nominee's defense. Two thirds (67%) of blacks now say that he should be confirmed, compared to 54% in the last poll, taken before Hill went public with her accusations. Whites are now less likely than blacks to support Thomas.

OCTOBER 15
CLARENCE THOMAS

Interviewing Date: 10/14/91*
Survey #GO 222033

Did you, yourself, happen to watch any part of the televised Senate hearings on Anita Hill's sexual harassment charges against Supreme Court nominee Clarence Thomas?

	Yes
National	86%

	Yes
By Sex	
Male	84%
Female	88

Asked of those who replied in the affirmative: About how many hours, in total, did you spend watching the hearings on television since Friday [October 11]?

	Total	Male	Female
Less than one hour	9%	11%	7%
One hour	11	12	9
Two to four hours	29	30	28
Five to nine hours	18	17	19
Ten hours or more	18	13	22

*It should be noted that polls conducted during a single evening can contain errors or bias not found in polls that spread their interviewing over several days.

Didn't watch	14	16	12
Can't say	1	1	3

From what you may have seen, heard, or read about the hearings, what is your impression of Clarence Thomas? Is it very favorable, favorable, unfavorable, or very unfavorable?

Very favorable	20%
Favorable	42
Unfavorable	17
Very unfavorable	9
Haven't followed hearings	3
No opinion	9

	Very favor- able	Favor- able	Unfavor- able	Very unfa- vorable*
By Sex				
Male	23%	43%	16%	7%
Female	17	42	18	10
By Ethnic Background				
White	20	41	18	9
Black	18	55	10	5
By Education				
College	18	55	10	5
College In-complete	29	43	14	6
No College	17	42	17	9
By Age				
18–29 Years	22	48	14	2
30–49 Years	20	43	20	7
50 Years and Over	18	39	15	14
By Politics				
Republicans	27	49	11	4
Democrats	14	41	22	11
Independents	18	39	20	11

Selected National Trend

	Very favor- able	Favor- able	Unfavor- able	Very unfa- vorable*
1991				
Oct. 10–13	14%	43%	23%	7%
Sept. 13–15	10	48	19	4

*"Haven't followed hearings" and "no opinion" have been omitted.

And what is your impression of Anita Hill?

Very favorable	6%
Favorable	29
Unfavorable	36
Very unfavorable	13
Haven't followed hearings; no opinion	16

	Very favorable	Favorable	Unfavorable	Very unfavorable*
By Sex				
Male	6%	28%	36%	14%
Female	7	29	35	13
By Ethnic Background				
White	7	29	35	12
Black	3	26	39	20
By Education				
College	7	33	35	12
College Incomplete	4	26	41	17
No College	7	28	34	12
By Age				
18–29 Years	2	19	45	15
30–49 Years	5	32	37	13
50 Years and Over	11	31	29	13
By Politics				
Republicans	4	21	44	16
Democrats	9	33	30	13
Independents	7	33	34	10

*"Haven't followed hearings" and "no opinion" have been omitted.

Would you like to see the Senate vote in favor of Clarence Thomas serving on the Supreme Court, or not?

Yes	58%
No	30
No opinion	12

	Yes	No	No opinion
By Sex			
Male	60%	29%	11%
Female	57	30	13

By Ethnic Background			
White	57	31	12
Black	69	20	11

Selected National Trend

1991	Yes	No	No opinion
October 10–13	53%	30%	17%
September 13–15	54	25	21
August 8–11	56	23	21
July 11–14	52	17	31

University of Oklahoma Professor Anita Hill charges Clarence Thomas with sexually harassing her when she worked for him in the early 1980s. Thomas denies Hill's charges. From what you have heard or read, whom do you believe more—Anita Hill or Clarence Thomas?

Hill	27%
Thomas	54
Neither (volunteered)	8
No opinion	11

	Hill	Thomas	Neither	No opinion
By Sex				
Male	23%	55%	9%	13%
Female	31	53	7	9
By Ethnic Background				
White	28	53	8	11
Black	19	61	8	12

Selected National Trend

1991	Hill	Thomas	Neither	No opinion
Oct. 10–13	29%	48%	6%	17%

All in all, do you think these hearings were a good thing or a bad thing for the country?

Good	31%
Bad	59
Both (volunteered)	5
No opinion	5

	Good	Bad	Both	No opinion
By Sex				
Male	28%	61%	4%	7%
Female	33	56	7	4
By Ethnic Background				
White	30	58	6	6
Black	36	63	*	1

*Less than 1%

As a result of the Thomas hearings, do you have more confidence or less confidence in each of the following:

Congress?

More	21%
Less	48
Same (volunteered)	22
No opinion	9

President Bush?

More	31%
Less	28
Same (volunteered)	33
No opinion	8

The nomination process for the Supreme Court?

More	26%
Less	47
Same (volunteered)	18
No opinion	9

Asked of those who watched at least an hour of the televised hearings: From what you saw and heard on television, please tell me whether you had a favorable or unfavorable opinion of each of the following senators on the committee:

Democratic Senator Joseph Biden, the committee chairman?

Favorable	63%
Unfavorable	19
Neutral (volunteered)	5
No opinion	13

Republican Senator Orrin Hatch?

Favorable	50%
Unfavorable	20
Neutral (volunteered)	5
No opinion	25

Republican Senator Arlen Specter?

Favorable	48%
Unfavorable	18
Neutral (volunteered)	7
No opinion	27

Republican Senator Alan Simpson?

Favorable	41%
Unfavorable	17
Neutral (volunteered)	10
No opinion	32

Republican Senator Strom Thurmond?

Favorable	41%
Unfavorable	21
Neutral (volunteered)	9
No opinion	29

Democratic Senator Patrick Leahy?

Favorable	38%
Unfavorable	16
Neutral (volunteered)	10
No opinion	36

Democratic Senator Howell Heflin?

Favorable	31%
Unfavorable	25
Neutral (volunteered)	9
No opinion	35

Democratic Senator Howard Metzenbaum?

Favorable	29%
Unfavorable	31
Neutral (volunteered)	9
No opinion	31

Democratic Senator Edward Kennedy?

Favorable	22%
Unfavorable	54
Neutral (volunteered)	9
No opinion	15

Which of the following statements about the recent hearings do you agree with more:

It was important to hold open
  hearings because the public has
  a right to know all the facts?................42%
Hearings should have been
  held behind closed doors to
  protect the privacy of the
  individuals involved? 55
No opinion.......................................3

	Open hearings	Closed hearings	No opinion
By Sex			
Male......................42%	55%	3%
Female...................41	55	4

The hearings included some discussion of graphic sexual language. Were you personally offended or embarrassed to hear such language on television, or not?

Yes...26%
No..64
Didn't hear..9
No opinion..1

	Yes	No	Didn't hear	No opinion
By Sex				
Male............17%	74%	8%	1%
Female..........34	55	10	1

Note: With the Senate vote today [October 15] on whether to confirm Clarence Thomas to the Supreme Court, a special Gallup Poll finds public opinion dividing by a 2-to-1 margin in his favor (58% versus 30%). The interviewing was conducted on Monday evening [October 14] and thus reflects the full impact of the three-day Senate hearings on Anita Hill's accusations of sexual harassment against Thomas. Current results are more favorable for him than those seen in Gallup's last poll, taken while the hearings were still in progress.

Now, respondents are twice as likely to believe Thomas's version of what happened as they are to believe Hill's (54% versus 27%).

Women are only slightly more likely than men to find Hill more credible. Moreover, both men and women regard Thomas more favorably than Hill. About two thirds (66%) of men and six in ten women (59%) have a favorable opinion of Thomas, but only 34% of men and 36% of women regard Hill favorably. However, consistent with Gallup's earlier poll, seven in ten blacks support Thomas's confirmation (69%).

Close to nine in ten adults (86%) say that they watched some of the televised hearings. A majority (59%) thinks that the hearings were bad, rather than good, for the country. Although they are said to have focused public attention on the issue of sexual harassment of women in the workplace, women are not much more likely than men to think that the hearings were a good thing (33% versus 28%).

A majority (55%) of those surveyed state that the hearings on Hill's accusations should have been held behind closed doors—that protecting the privacy of those involved should have been more important than the public's right to know. Thomas's supporters and opponents divide on this issue; his backers say that the hearings should not have been public, while his opponents disagree.

Somewhat surprisingly, the vulgarity and graphic descriptions of sex that came out in the testimony did not produce a strong reaction among the public. Only one fourth (26%) of all respondents (and 34% of women) say that they were personally embarrassed or offended by hearing such language on television.

The hearings caused many respondents to lose confidence in both Congress and the Supreme Court nomination process. Close to one half now have less confidence in Congress (48%) and in the process (47%). President George Bush fares somewhat better; as many say that they gained confidence in him (31%) as lost confidence (28%).

The viewing public—those who watched at least an hour of the televised hearings over the weekend—have sharply differing views of the performances of members of the Senate Judiciary Committee. Chairman Joseph Biden made the best impression: 63% had a favorable impression of him, while 19% had an unfavorable one. The other big winners were the Republicans' two chief interrogators, Orrin

Hatch and Arlen Specter; each was seen favorably by one half of the viewers (50% and 48%, respectively). Only one in five had an unfavorable opinion of Hatch (20%) and Specter (18%).

In general, Republicans came off better than Democrats. Strom Thurmond and Alan Simpson, while not scoring quite as high as Hatch and Specter, nonetheless had a 2-to-1 ratio of positive-to-negative evaluations. Among the Democrats, only Patrick Leahy did well (38% favorable, 16% unfavorable). The biggest loser, however, was Edward Kennedy. Over one half (54%) expressed unfavorable views of the Massachusetts senator, even though his role in the hearings was somewhat limited, while only 22% had a favorable view of him.

OCTOBER 16
CONFIDENCE IN INSTITUTIONS

Interviewing Date: 10/10–13/91
Survey #GO 222019

I am going to read you a list of institutions in American society. Please tell me how much confidence you, yourself, have in each one—a great deal, quite a lot, some, or very little:

The military?

Great deal	35%
Quite a lot	34
Some	20
Very little	7
None (volunteered)	1
No opinion	3

Selected National Trend

	Those saying "great deal" or "quite a lot"
March 1991	85%
1990	68
1989	63
1988	58
1987	61
1986	63

1985	61
1984*	58
1983	53
1981	50
1979	54
1977	57
1975	58

*In this and the following trends, the 1984 survey was conducted for *Newsweek* by the Gallup Organization.

Church and organized religion?

Great deal	31%
Quite a lot	25
Some	27
Very little	12
None (volunteered)	2
No opinion	3

Selected National Trend

	Those saying "great deal" or "quite a lot"
March 1991	59%
1990	56
1989	52
1988	59
1987	61
1986	57
1985	66
1984	64
1983	62
1981	64
1979	65
1977	64
1975	68
1973	66

Presidency?

Great deal	21%
Quite a lot	29
Some	32
Very little	14
None (volunteered)	3
No opinion	1

U.S. Supreme Court?

Great deal	16%
Quite a lot	23

Some..39
Very little.....................................15
None (volunteered).....................2
No opinion....................................5

Selected National Trend

	Those saying "great deal" or "quite a lot"
March 1991	48%
1990	47
1989	46
1988	56
1987	52
1986	54
1985	56
1984	51
1983	42
1981	46
1979	45
1977	46
1975	49
1973	44

Public schools?

Great deal 14%
Quite a lot..................................21
Some..38
Very little.....................................22
None (volunteered).....................2
No opinion....................................3

Selected National Trend

	Those saying "great deal" or "quite a lot"
March 1991	44%
1990	45
1989	43
1988	49
1987	50
1986	49
1985	48
1984	47
1983	39
1981	42
1979	53
1977	54
1973	58

Newspapers?

Great deal 10%
Quite a lot..................................22
Some..44
Very little.....................................20
None (volunteered).....................2
No opinion....................................2

Selected National Trend

	Those saying "great deal" or "quite a lot"
March 1991	37%
1990	39
1988	36
1987	31
1986	37
1985	35
1984	34
1983	38
1981	35
1979	51
1973	39

Banks?

Great deal 9%
Quite a lot..................................21
Some..44
Very little.....................................23
None (volunteered).....................2
No opinion....................................1

Selected National Trend

	Those saying "great deal" or "quite a lot"
March 1991	32%
1990	36
1989	42
1988	49
1987	51
1986	49
1985	51
1984	51
1983	51
1981	46
1979	60

Television?

Great deal	10%
Quite a lot	14
Some	46
Very little	26
None (volunteered)	3
No opinion	1

Selected National Trend

	Those saying "great deal" or "quite a lot"
March 1991	32%
1990	25
1988	27
1987	28
1986	27
1985	29
1984	25
1983	25
1981	25
1979	38
1973	37

Organized labor?

Great deal	10%
Quite a lot	12
Some	39
Very little	33
None (volunteered)	2
No opinion	4

Selected National Trend

	Those saying "great deal" or "quite a lot"
March 1991	25%
1990	27
1988	26
1987	26
1986	29
1985	28
1984	30
1983	26
1981	28
1979	36
1977	39
1975	38
1973	30

Big business?

Great deal	7%
Quite a lot	15
Some	42
Very little	30
None (volunteered)	2
No opinion	4

Selected National Trend

	Those saying "great deal" or "quite a lot"
March 1991	26%
1990	25
1988	26
1987	26
1986	29
1985	28
1984	30
1983	26
1981	28
1979	36
1977	39
1975	38
1973	30

Congress?

Great deal	7%
Quite a lot	11
Some	43
Very little	33
None (volunteered)	3
No opinion	3

Selected National Trend

	Those saying "great deal" or "quite a lot"
March 1991	30%
1990	24
1989	32
1988	35
1986	41
1985	39
1984	29
1983	28
1981	29
1979	34
1977	40

1975...40
1973...42

Note: Americans' confidence in the U.S. Congress and Supreme Court is at an all-time low. Fewer respondents today than at any time in the last two decades say that they have a great deal or quite a lot of confidence in these institutions which, along with the presidency, help form the foundation for our political life.

At the bottom is Congress, with the lowest confidence ratings of any institution tested in the new Gallup Poll and the lowest drawn by any institution in Gallup history: only 18% say that they have a great deal or quite a lot of confidence in Congress. These low ratings may reflect the overall economic recession, the recent House "perks" and check-bouncing revelations, and the Senate hearings on the nomination of Clarence Thomas to the Supreme Court.

The Thomas hearings also may have affected confidence in the Supreme Court; at 39%, the Court also receives its lowest rating ever, at a full 9 percentage points below Gallup's last measurement in March of this year. In fact, every institution measured by Gallup also registers lower levels of confidence than in March.

The poll finds the presidency to have the highest public confidence of the three main branches of government. Fifty percent say that they have a great deal or quite a bit of confidence in the presidency. However, it is down markedly from a high of 72% recorded immediately after the Persian Gulf victory in March of this year.

Overall, the institution with the highest level of confidence continues to be the U.S. military. Although down from its extremely high levels immediately after its successes in March, at 69% it is substantially above the next highest institution measured. Organized religion ranks second at 56%, roughly the same rating as recent measurements but still below the historic high levels of confidence generated before the televangelism scandals of the 1980s.

Only 30% now have a great deal or quite a lot of confidence in banks, not much change from the 32% of last March but still significantly below the high ratings of confidence given

banks before the recent Savings and Loan scandals. The drop in banking's legitimacy in American society has been the most dramatic of all: from a 60% confidence rating in 1979 to 30% today.

OCTOBER 23
CONFIDENCE IN POLITICAL PARTIES/CLARENCE THOMAS

Interviewing Date: 10/17–20/91
Survey #GO 222020

I'd like you to rate the Republican party on a scale. If you have a favorable opinion of the party, name a number between +1 and +5—the higher the number, the more favorable your opinion. If you have an unfavorable opinion of the party, name a number between -1 and -5—the lower the number, the more unfavorable your opinion. How would you rate the Republican party on this scale?

Highly favorable (+5, +4).....................18%
Mildly favorable (+3, +2, +1)................47
Mildly unfavorable (-1, -2, -3)...............17
Highly unfavorable (-4, -5)....................11
No opinion....................................... 7

Selected National Trend

	Highly favorable (+5, +4)
September 1991	17%
September 1984	26
March 1981	30
October 1980	18
May 1980	17
November 1975	15
August 1973	19
October 1972	29
October 1970	25
December 1968	25
September 1968	30
July 1968	27
May 1968	27
October 1967	34
April 1967	33
December 1966	28

August 1966......................................29
May 1965......................................26
October 1964 21
October 1956 33
February 1956 27

And how would you rate the Democratic party on the same scale?

Highly favorable (+5, +4).......................16%
Mildly favorable (+3, +2, +1) 42
Mildly unfavorable (-1, -2, -3) 22
Highly unfavorable (-4, -5) 13
No opinion...7

Selected National Trend

	Highly favorable (+5, +4)
September 1991...................................16%
September 1984.................................26
March 1981 34
October 1980 27
May 1980......................................28
November 1975 30
August 1973....................................29
October 1972 30
October 1970 35
December 1968..................................41
September 1968.................................32
July 1968.......................................36
May 1968.......................................42
October 1967 31
April 1967 40
December 1966..................................33
August 1966....................................36
May 1965.......................................44
October 1964 45
October 1956 38
February 1956 43

Asked of registered voters: If your senator voted in favor of Clarence Thomas serving on the Supreme Court, would you be more likely or less likely to vote for his reelection, or would it not much affect your vote?

More likely...25%
Less likely...20
Not much affect vote.............................52
No opinion...3

	More likely	Less likely	Not much affect vote	No opinion
By Sex				
Male	27%	18%	54%	1%
Female..........	24	23	50	3
By Ethnic Background				
White...........	25	21	52	2
White Southerners........	31	23	44	2
Black...........	32	12	52	4

Selected National Trend

	More likely	Less likely	Not much affect vote	No opinion
September 1991.........	12%	10%	72%	6%

Also asked of registered voters: If your senator voted against Clarence Thomas serving on the Supreme Court, would you be more likely or less likely to vote for his reelection, or would it not much affect your vote?

More likely...17%
Less likely...23
Not much affect vote.............................57
No opinion...3

	More likely	Less likely	Not much affect vote	No opinion
By Sex				
Male	13%	26%	59%	2%
Female..........	22	20	54	4
By Ethnic Background				
White...........	17	24	56	3
White Southerners........	20	24	52	4
Black...........	21	18	57	4

As a result of Anita Hill's charges of sexual harassment against Clarence Thomas and the recent Senate hearings, do you think each of the following is more likely or less likely, or things will not change much:

That women will report cases of sexual harassment?

More likely	....	60%
Less likely	....	19
Not change much	....	19
No opinion	....	2

	More likely	Less likely	Not change much	No opinion
By Sex				
Male	63%	17%	17%	3%
Female	57	20	21	2
By Ethnic Background				
White	60	19	19	2
Nonwhite	62	19	18	1
Black	61	19	19	1
By Education				
College Graduate	65	17	17	1
College Incomplete	61	20	18	1
High-School Graduate	60	18	21	1
Less Than High-School Graduate	54	20	19	7
By Region				
East	62	14	21	3
Midwest	61	21	15	3
South	57	23	19	1
West	62	14	22	2
By Age				
18–29 Years	67	16	15	2
30–49 Years	59	21	18	2
50 Years and Over	57	17	23	3

That companies will take strong steps against sexual harassment?

More likely	....	60%
Less likely	....	13
Not change much	....	25
No opinion	....	2

	More likely	Less likely	Not change much	No opinion
By Sex				
Male	65%	9%	23%	3%
Female	55	16	27	2
By Ethnic Background				
White	59	14	26	1
Nonwhite	70	9	17	4
Black	75	10	13	2
By Education				
College Graduate	63	9	27	1
College Incomplete	54	16	29	1
High-School Graduate	63	14	20	3
Less Than High-School Graduate	56	12	30	2
By Region				
East	58	14	25	3
Midwest	54	14	30	2
South	61	14	24	1
West	69	9	20	2
By Age				
18–29 Years	65	9	24	2
30–49 Years	59	13	26	2
50 Years and Over	58	15	25	2

Note: Congressional Democrats have had a bad month. A new Gallup Poll, conducted after the Senate confirmed Clarence Thomas to the Supreme Court, shows sharp declines in the public's ratings of the Democratic party since the Thomas hearings began in early September. Currently, the party's image, already at a historical low point, fell further: 58% now have a favorable opinion of the Democratic party, compared with 63% in September.

The declining image of Congress and the Democratic party cannot be attributed entirely to the Thomas hearings and the controversy over Anita Hill's charges of sexual harassment. In the past month, members of Congress have come under fire for bouncing checks at the House bank and other questionable practices.

However, the political fallout from the Thomas confirmation may be less severe than many political observers have been predicting. Majorities say that their senator's vote in favor (52%) or against (57%) Thomas will have little bearing on whether they vote to reelect him. If the senator voted in favor of Thomas, 25% say that they are more likely to support him, while 20% are less likely. If a senator voted against Thomas, 17% say that they are more likely to support him, while 23% are less likely.

That is not to say that the televised hearings have failed to make Thomas a salient issue among the electorate. In mid-September, well before Hill came forward with her allegations, three quarters (72%) said that a senator's vote on Thomas would not affect their voting behavior. The balance of opinion among voter subgroups has shifted little over the past month, with two notable exceptions: since Hill's charges and the subsequent hearings, blacks and men have become more sympathetic toward Thomas. Black voters and male voters are now more inclined to say a pro-Thomas confirmation vote increases, rather than decreases, their chances of casting their ballot for the senator.

Women voters, a focus of much media attention since the hearings, remain sharply divided on the Thomas confirmation. One quarter (24%) of female voters now say that they are more likely to support a senator who backed Thomas, while a similar proportion (23%) is less likely to do so. Both college-educated and less well-educated women are about evenly divided on this issue.

Although most Americans ended up believing that Hill's charges were untrue, the public thinks that the resulting publicity will lead to progress in combating sexual harassment. A majority (60%) says that, because of the Thomas-Hill hearings, more women will report cases of sexual harassment. In addition, a similar majority (60%) says that companies are likely to take stronger steps against sexual harassment now that the issue has been so well publicized.

OCTOBER 25
PRESIDENTIAL TRIAL HEATS

Interviewing Date: 10/17–20/91
Survey #GO 222020

Asked of registered voters: If George Bush runs for reelection in 1992, in general are you more likely to vote for Bush or for the Democratic party's candidate for president?

Bush 49%
Democratic candidate...........................32
Undecided; no opinion.........................19

Selected National Trend

	Bush	Demo- cratic candidate	Unde- cided; no opinion
1991			
September 13–15 .....51%		29%	20%
September 5–8.........52		29	19
August...................55		27	18
June.....................53		30	17
April.....................51		30	19
March...................67		17	16
February................54		33	13

Also asked of registered voters: Suppose the 1992 presidential election were being held today. If George Bush were the Republican candidate and Mario Cuomo were the Democratic candidate, whom would you vote for? [Those undecided were then asked: As of today, do you lean more to Bush, the Republican, or to Cuomo, the Democrat?]

	October 1991	March 1991
Bush	63%	78%
Cuomo...............................	29	16
Undecided; no opinion..............	8	6

Note: If Mario Cuomo relishes the role of underdog, he should be pleased with the results of a new Gallup Poll. Matched against President George Bush in a test election, Cuomo draws less than one half as many votes (29%) as Bush (63%). The New York governor makes a better showing against Bush today than he did in March, when victory in the Persian Gulf war helped boost the president's margin, 78% to 16%. Nonetheless, in his ability to attract votes at the national level, Cuomo fails to live up to his image as the man who can recapture the White House for the Democrats in 1992.

Should he become a candidate and take his case to the voters, Cuomo's fortunes might change. At this point, however, he lacks a solid political base on which to build support. The only major voter subgroup that now gives majority support to Cuomo in a race against Bush is self-identified Democrats (53%), but four in ten Democrats spurn Cuomo in favor of Bush. Moreover, Bush wins a majority of the vote among large-city residents (55%) and political liberals (52%), two groups that might seem to be natural Cuomo constituencies.

OCTOBER 26
PERSONAL FINANCES/RECESSION

Interviewing Date: 10/17–20/91
Survey #GO 222020

We are interested in how people's financial situation may have changed. Would you say that you are financially better off now than you were a year ago, or are you financially worse off now?

Better...35%
Worse...42
Same (volunteered)..............................22
No opinion... 1

Selected National Trend

	Better	Worse	Same	No opinion
1991				
September	34%	28%	37%	1%
July	34	32	33	1
May	32	32	33	3
April	29	33	37	1
March	30	37	32	1

Looking ahead, do you expect that at this time next year you will be financially better off than now or worse off than now?

Better..55%
Worse...23
Same (volunteered)..............................16
No opinion... 6

Selected National Trend

	Better	Worse	Same	No opinion
1991				
September	53%	19%	22%	6%
July	57	15	19	9
May	57	16	19	8
April	56	17	18	9
March	56	18	20	6

Right now, do you think that economic conditions in the country as a whole are getting better or getting worse?

Better...25%
Worse...64
Same (volunteered)............................... 8
No opinion... 3

Selected National Trend

	Better	Worse	Same	No opinion
1991				
September	27%	60%	10%	3%
July	34	51	9	6

In your opinion, has the bottom of the current recession been reached, or not?

Yes..31%
No...62
No opinion... 7

Selected National Trend

	Yes	No	No opinion
1991			
September 5–8	32%	60%	8%
July 11–14	42	48	10
May 23–26	33	53	14
May 16–19	26	65	9
April 25–28	30	59	11
April 11–14	33	53	14
March 21–24	42	47	11

Do you think it is especially important now for you to try and add to your savings and reserve funds, or is now a time when it would be okay to use some of your savings if there were a major purchase you wanted to make?

Important to add to savings....................65%
Okay to use savings 29
No opinion...6

If there were a major purchase you wanted to make, would you feel okay about buying it on credit, or is now a time when you would be especially reluctant to take on new debt?

Okay about buying on credit....................26%
Reluctant to take on new debt..................71
No opinion...3

Thinking of your own financial situation just now, do you feel you are in a good position to buy some of the things you would like to have, or is now a rather bad time for you to spend money?

In good position to buy things................30%
Bad time to spend money......................67
No opinion...3

During the next twelve months, do you think unemployment in the country will go up, go down, or stay about the same?

Go up...37%
Go down..21
Stay about the same............................40
No opinion...2

Which of the following applies to you:

A member of my family has been laid off or fired recently?

	Oct. 1991	Oct. 1990*
Applies	23%	17%
Does not apply	77	83
No opinion	**	**

I know people outside of my family who have been laid off or fired recently?

	Oct. 1991	Oct. 1990*
Applies	54%	50%

Does not apply	46	49
No opinion	**	1

*Gallup survey conducted for *Newsweek*
**Less than 1%

Asked of those who are employed: Thinking about the next twelve months, how likely do you think it is that you will lose your job or be laid off—very likely, fairly likely, not too likely, or not at all likely?

Very likely 6%
Fairly likely.......................................8
Not too likely....................................26
Not at all likely.................................59
No opinion...1

Selected National Trend

	Very, fairly likely	Not too, not at all likely	No opinion
1991			
July	15%	84%	1%
March	12	87	1
1990			
October	16	83	1
July	12	86	2
1982			
November	19	77	4
June	15	81	4
January	15	82	3
1980			
May	14	84	2
1975			
April	12	85	3
January	15	81	4

Note: The confidence of consumers, as they head into the all-important Christmas retail season, continues to decline. About two thirds of respondents believe that economic conditions are getting worse (64%), that now is a rather bad time to spend money for things they would like to have (67%), and that they now would be especially reluctant to take on new debt (71%).

A new Gallup Business Poll finds that opinions about the U.S. economic outlook have become steadily less favorable since mid-July. Now, 62% say that the bottom of the current recession has not yet been reached, up from 48% in July. Similarly, those saying that economic conditions are getting worse has increased from 51% to 64%.

The latest poll also finds many people feeling financially strapped. Fully 42% say that they now are worse off financially than they were a year ago, sharply up from 28% in an early September poll. This gain has more than erased the slow but steady decrease in these negative perceptions since the 37% measured in early April after the Persian Gulf victory.

Most Americans (55%) remain optimistic that this time next year they will be financially better off than now. However, here too there has been an increase since July in the proportion expecting to be worse off, from 15% to 23%.

Still, relatively few people (only 14% of all those currently employed) think that it is at least fairly likely that they will lose their job during the next twelve months. The great majority (85%) says that this is not likely to happen to them. However, 23% say that a member of their family has been laid off or fired recently, and 54% know people outside their family who have been laid off or fired.

These data go far to explain why worries about the economy have begun to translate into more specific worries about one's own personal financial situation, the use of credit, and willingness to spend money. More and more people are turning their attention to the economic problems facing the nation. Therefore, consumers are likely to keep especially close watch on their wallets this Christmas season.

OCTOBER 30
PRESIDENT BUSH

Interviewing Date: 10/24–27/91
Survey #GO 222021

Do you approve or disapprove of the way George Bush is handling his job as president?

Approve..62%
Disapprove...29
No opinion...9

Selected National Trend
(Approval Rating)

	Approve	Dis-approve	No opinion
1991			
Oct. 17–20 (Post-Thomas Confirmation)......66%		26%	8%
Oct. 3–6 (Pre-Thomas-Hill Hearings).......65		27	8
Sept. 5–8 (Pre-Thomas Hearings)............70		21	9
June 27–30 (Pre-Thomas Nomination)........72		22	6
Feb. 28–March 3 (Gulf War Victory)..............89		8	3
Jan. 17–20 (Air Strikes Begin against Iraq)........82		12	6
Jan. 11–13 (Pre-Desert Storm)................64		25	11

(Approval Rating by Groups)

	Oct. 24–27	Oct. 17–20	Oct. 3–6
Sex			
Male......................64%		69%	65%
Female...................61		63	64
Ethnic Background			
White....................67		68	68
Nonwhite 36		55	44
Education			
College..................63		68	73
College Incomplete...65		67	70
High-School Graduate..............65		66	61
Less Than High-School Graduate 53		62	54
Region			
East 54		61	55
Midwest.................64		65	66
South 68		72	68
West 62		62	70
Age			
18–29 Years...........69		75	67
30–49 Years...........65		68	70
50 Years and Over.....56		58	56

	Politics		
Republicans	85	87	86
Democrats	42	50	45
Independents	64	61	65
	Political Ideology		
Liberal	50	54	55
Moderate	52	63	50
Conservative	77	76	78

Note: The decrease in President George Bush's approval ratings seems part of a gradual downturn observed since early September. The Gallup Poll, which monitors public opinion of the president on a weekly basis, showed approval of Bush edging downward between Labor Day weekend (70%) and early October (65%), before Anita Hill's allegations of sexual harassment against Clarence Thomas captured the nation's attention.

In mid-October, when Thomas and Hill dominated the news, two successive Gallup Polls found Bush approval at 66%. Now that the focus has shifted to the economy and other issues, however, the slide has resumed: only 62% approve, while 29% disapprove and 9% have no opinion.

The stability in overall Bush approval figures in polls taken as the Thomas-Hill drama unfolded hides shifts in opinion taking place below the surface. While the national totals did not change by more than 1 percentage point, there were significant shifts in opinion among nonwhites and some other population subgroups. Between early and mid-October, Bush approval among nonwhites increased from 44% to 55%, possibly reflecting support for Thomas, the president's Supreme Court nominee. Approval increased by 4 to 13 percentage points among the following groups: men, young people, the less-well educated, Democrats, political moderates, and easterners. Over the same period, Bush approval fell among the college educated and westerners.

In the latest poll, nearly all of these increases in Bush approval by subgroups have been reversed, while the decreases have been maintained. The most dramatic reversal in opinion is seen among nonwhites. The 55% approval figure among nonwhites recorded after Thomas's confirmation fell to 36% in the latest poll.

OCTOBER 30
DAVID DUKE

Interviewing Date: 10/24–27/91
Survey #GO 222021

Have you heard or read anything about David Duke, who is one of the Republican candidates running for governor of Louisiana?

Yes	58%
No	41
No opinion	1

Asked of those who replied in the affirmative: In general, do you have a favorable or unfavorable opinion of David Duke?

Favorable	10%
Unfavorable	67
No opinion	23

	Favorable	Unfavorable	No opinion
By Sex			
Male	13%	64%	23%
Female	7	69	24
Southern White Males	26	54	20
Southern White Females	15	68	17
By Ethnic Background			
White	12	67	21
Black	2	65	33
By Education			
College Graduate	7	79	14
College Incomplete	12	70	18
High-School Graduate	10	63	27
Less Than High-School Graduate	19	38	43
By Region			
East	6	67	27
Midwest	9	64	27
South	17	63	20
West	7	72	21

By Age
18–29 Years	6	70	24
30–49 Years	11	70	19
50 Years and Over	12	61	27

By Household Income
$50,000 and Over	8	76	16
$30,000–$49,999	13	72	15
$20,000–$29,999	10	68	22
Under $20,000	11	55	34

Asked of those familiar with Duke: Duke calls himself a Republican, but Republican party officials refuse to recognize him as a Republican. Do you approve or disapprove of the Republican party's refusal to recognize Duke?

Approve...62%
Disapprove...24
No opinion...14

	Approve	Dis- approve	No opinion
By Region			
East	61%	22%	17%
Midwest	68	15	17
South	55	35	10
West	68	21	11
By Politics			
Republicans	64	22	14
Democrats	59	28	13
Independents	66	23	11

Note: As many as six in ten Americans (58%) have heard or read about the controversial David Duke, the former Ku Klux Klan leader who is a Republican candidate in the runoff election for governor of Louisiana. Despite this surprisingly high name awareness, a new Gallup Poll shows that at the national level he apparently is not tapping into any wellspring of support, fed by latent racism or economic frustration. Indeed, few respondents are willing to express positive feelings toward Duke. Of those who are familiar with him, only 10% say that their opinion is favorable, while 66% say that it is unfavorable and another 23% have no opinion.

There are, however, several population groups where Duke generates somewhat higher levels of support: men, those with low levels of education, and those in the South. His highest favorable ratings come from southern white males (26%).

The Republican party has refused to recognize Duke as a "regular" candidate, and he has been repudiated by President George Bush. There is widespread, if not overwhelming, support across the country for this decision: 62% of those familiar with Duke approve, while 24% disapprove. His candidacy has prompted press speculation about the national implications and repercussions of a person with an overtly racist background running as a legitimate contender for major political office.

OCTOBER 31
PARTY BETTER FOR PROSPERITY

Interviewing Date: 10/24–27/91
Survey #GO 222021

Which political party—the Republican or the Democratic—will do a better job of keeping the country prosperous?

Republican 44%
Democratic 41
No difference; no opinion......................15

Selected National Trend

	Repub- lican	Demo- cratic	No differ- ence; no opinion
1991			
July	49%	32%	19%
1990			
October	37	35	28
August*	45	30	25
1988			
September*	52	34	14
July*	46	39	15
May*	41	39	20
January*	42	35	23
1984			
August	48	36	16
April	44	36	20

*Asked of registered voters

Note: A new Gallup Poll provides more evidence that the recession is taking a political toll on President George Bush and his party. The GOP's advantage on a key Gallup political barometer, the party-of-prosperity question, has all but disappeared. Now, 44% name the Republican party as better able to keep the country prosperous, while 41% name the Democratic party—a statistical tie. This past July, in the afterglow of the Gulf war victory, the Republicans had a 17-point edge, 49% to 32%. The last time the parties were statistically tied was one year ago, at the beginning of the current recession.

Gallup has asked the party-of-prosperity question on a regular basis since 1951. Over four decades it has proved to be a reliable barometer of the parties' presidential prospects. In the absence of war or an international crisis, presidential elections usually turn on economic issues. The voters have elected a Democratic president three times during the postwar era—in 1960, 1964, and 1976. In those years the Democratic party held a significant advantage over the GOP as the party of prosperity. In all other postwar presidential years, when Republican candidates were victorious, the GOP equalled or surpassed the Democrats on this measure.

NOVEMBER 6
DEMOCRATIC PRESIDENTIAL CANDIDATES

Interviewing Date: 10/31–11/3/91
Survey #GO 222022

Asked of registered voters: If George Bush runs for reelection in 1992, in general are you more likely to vote for Bush or for the Democratic party's candidate for president?

Bush 49%
Democratic candidate 32
Undecided; no opinion 19

Selected National Trend

	Bush	Demo-cratic candidate	Unde-cided; no opinion
1991			
September 13–15	51%	29%	20%
September 5–8	52	29	19
August	55	27	18
June	53	30	17
April	51	30	19
March	67	17	16
February	54	33	13

Also asked of registered voters: As I read a list of issues, please tell me whether each is important or not important in determining which presidential candidate you will vote for in next year's elections:

	Important
Economic conditions	97%
Education	96
Crime	93
Unemployment	93
Federal budget deficit	92
Poverty and homelessness	91
Health-care policy	91
Tax policy	90
Environmental issues	85
National defense	76
Foreign policy	73
Race relations	70
Abortion	65

Also asked of registered voters: Which one of these issues will be most important?

	Most important
Economic conditions	22%
Unemployment	12
Education	11
Health-care policy	9
Federal budget deficit	9
Poverty and homelessness	6
Abortion	6
Crime	6
Tax policy	5
Environmental issues	5
National defense	2
Foreign policy	2
Race relations	1
None; no opinion	4

Asked of registered Democrats and those who lean Democratic: Please tell me whether you have a favorable or unfavorable opinion of each of the following Democrats who might run for president in 1992:

Jerry Brown?

Favorable......................................38%
Unfavorable...................................37
No opinion.....................................13
Never heard of..............................12

Selected National Trend

	Favorable	Unfavorable	No opinion	Never heard of
1991				
September	36%	27%	19%	18%
August	29	35	17	19

Mario Cuomo?

Favorable......................................51%
Unfavorable...................................22
No opinion.....................................11
Never heard of..............................16

Selected National Trend

	Favorable	Unfavorable	No opinion	Never heard of
1991				
September	50%	17%	12%	21%
August	42	24	12	22
April	48	22	12	18
February	42	19	17	22

Douglas Wilder?

Favorable......................................29%
Unfavorable...................................19
No opinion.....................................17
Never heard of..............................35

Selected National Trend

	Favorable	Unfavorable	No opinion	Never heard of
1991				
September	26%	11%	22%	41%
August	18	18	18	46
April	25	14	20	41
February	14	12	20	54

Tom Harkin?

Favorable......................................30%
Unfavorable...................................14
No opinion.....................................17
Never heard of..............................39

Selected National Trend

	Favorable	Unfavorable	No opinion	Never heard of
1991				
September	24%	7%	21%	48%
August	20	12	16	52

Bob Kerrey?

Favorable......................................32%
Unfavorable...................................12
No opinion.....................................16
Never heard of..............................40

Selected National Trend

	Favorable	Unfavorable	No opinion	Never heard of
1991				
September	22%	8%	20%	50%
August	14	12	17	57

Paul Tsongas?

Favorable......................................24%
Unfavorable...................................18
No opinion.....................................18
Never heard of..............................40

Selected National Trend

	Favorable	Unfavorable	No opinion	Never heard of
1991				
September	20%	13%	15%	52%
August	18	15	14	53
April	15	12	15	58

Bill Clinton?

Favorable......................................25%
Unfavorable...................................16

No opinion...17
Never heard of...............................42

Selected National Trend

1991	Favorable	Unfavorable	No opinion	Never heard of
September	21%	10%	16%	53%
August	21	15	16	48
April	15	12	18	55
February	13	12	18	57

Also asked of registered Democrats and those who lean Democratic: I am going to read through the list of names once more. This time please tell me which one of these persons you would most like to see nominated as the Democratic party's candidate for president in 1992:

Cuomo..33%
Brown...15
Wilder..9
Kerrey..8
Harkin..7
Clinton...6
Tsongas..4
Undecided; others 18

Asked of those who selected Cuomo: If Mario Cuomo chooses not to run, which of the others would you like to see nominated?

Brown...21%
Wilder...12
Kerrey...10
Harkin...10
Clinton...9
Tsongas..7
Undecided; others 31

Note: The troubled economy has revived Democratic hopes for a competitive race against George Bush in 1992. With the presidential election only one year away, a Gallup Poll shows less than one half (49%) of registered voters saying they would reelect him. One third (32%) would be inclined to support whomever the Democrats nominate, while the remaining 19% express no preference. The president's current 17-percentage point lead over an unspecified Democratic candidate is down from the 22-point advantage he held in mid-September, when he led by 51% to 29%.

A key factor in the improved Democratic prospects for 1992 is the precedence voters now give to economic and domestic issues over national defense and foreign affairs. Eight months after the end of the Persian Gulf war, only 4% of voters say that foreign policy or defense is the issue they will consider most important when voting for president next year. Instead, rated as the top issues affecting presidential voting preferences are economic conditions (22%), unemployment (12%), and education (11%).

This economic discontent appears to translate into support for a Democrat in 1992. Voters more likely to have personal economic concerns tend to be Democrats or political independents. The shift toward the Democratic party's candidate in Gallup's test election against Bush has occurred among Democrats and independents, while the president has held his ground among his fellow Republicans.

Until Mario Cuomo makes his decision on a presidential bid, the Democratic race remains wide open. When Democratic voters are given the choice of Cuomo and the six major declared candidates, the New York governor is the clear leader, with 33% of the vote overall. Running second to Cuomo, with 15%, is former California Governor Jerry Brown, the only declared candidate who is as widely recognized as Cuomo.

When Cuomo is removed from the field, the undecided category expands from 18% to 31%. While Brown at 21% receives a higher level of support than the other five candidates, his failure to attract more of the Cuomo vote, despite his advantage in name recognition, reflects his unpopularity among a large proportion of Democratic voters. About as many Democrats have an unfavorable opinion of him (37%) as a favorable one (38%). (For the other candidates, positive evaluations outnumber negative ones.)

All of the lesser-known candidates have seen their national name recognition rise steadily over the last three months. Roughly six in ten Democratic voters now indicate that they are familiar with the names of Tom Harkin, Paul Tsongas, Bob Kerrey, and Bill Clinton. About two thirds have heard of Doug Wilder. None of those declared candidates, however, has been able to break out of the pack. There is a statistical four-way tie for second place among Wilder (12%), Kerrey (10%), Harkin (10%), and Clinton (9%). Tsongas draws 7% support.

NOVEMBER 7
CAMPAIGN ISSUES: REPUBLICAN AND DEMOCRATIC PARTIES

Interviewing Date: 10/31–11/3/91
Survey #GO 222022

Which political party—the Republican or the Democratic—do you think would do a better job of dealing with each of the following:

Poverty and homelessness?

	Nov. 1991	Sept. 1991
Republican	26%	25%
Democratic	60	57
No difference; no opinion	14	18

Health-care policy?

	Nov. 1991	Sept. 1991
Republican	27%	29%
Democratic	56	54
No difference; no opinion	17	17

Unemployment?

	Nov. 1991	Sept. 1991
Republican	30%	34%
Democratic	55	49
No difference; no opinion	15	17

Race relations?

	Nov. 1991	Sept. 1991
Republican	29%	30%
Democratic	53	47
No difference; no opinion	18	23

Environmental issues?

	Nov. 1991	Sept. 1991
Republican	32%	33%
Democratic	49	47
No difference; no opinion	19	20

Education?

Republican	35%
Democratic	48
No difference; no opinion	17

Tax policy?

Republican	40%
Democratic	45
No difference; no opinion	15

Abortion issue?

	Nov. 1991	Sept. 1991
Republican	33%	34%
Democratic	44	39
No difference; no opinion	23	27

Economic conditions?

	Nov. 1991	Sept. 1991
Republican	41%	45%
Democratic	44	39
No difference; no opinion	15	16

Federal budget deficit?

	Nov. 1991	Sept. 1991
Republican	40%	42%
Democratic	41	33
No difference; no opinion	19	25

Crime?

	Nov. 1991	Sept. 1991
Republican	42%	43%
Democratic	38	32
No difference; no opinion	20	25

National defense?

	Nov. 1991	Sept. 1991
Republican	57%	57%
Democratic	29	26
No difference; no opinion	14	17

Foreign policy?

	Nov. 1991	Sept. 1991
Republican	60%	62%
Democratic	26	22
No difference; no opinion	14	16

Note: The Gallup Poll showed the Democratic party's public image for handling key issues improving significantly prior to Tuesday's elections [November 5]. National polls taken over the course of the fall campaign saw movement toward the Democrats on the pivotal issue of the economy as well as on a wide array of other concerns.

A poll completed Sunday [November 3], in the campaign's final days, finds the Democrats moving ahead of the Republicans, 44% to 41%, as the party better able to handle economic conditions. That is a significant improvement since September, when the GOP held a 45%-to-39% lead. Over the same period, the Democrats managed to pull even on the federal budget deficit (41% versus 40%) and to expand their advantage on the unemployment issue to a 25-point lead (55% versus 30%). They also gain 5 to 6 points on the issues of race relations, abortion, and crime.

However, the Democrats have one of their largest leads over the Republicans on the issue of health-care policy (56% versus 27%). Campaigning on the health-care issue in next year's presidential election may be an effective way for the Democrats to appeal to a middle class that is worried about its financial future.

While they historically have been perceived as caring more about people, this image has not always been a clear asset. This Democratic compassion is often associated with an overreliance on social programs and higher taxes for the middle class. Unlike welfare and aid to the homeless, however, national health care may be one Democratic social program that will translate into votes in 1992. Indeed,

Harris Wofford, a relatively unknown Democrat, made national health care a key issue and defeated former Governor Richard Thornburgh by a surprisingly large margin in Pennsylvania's special election for the U.S. Senate.

The Democrats suffered their biggest losses on Tuesday in New Jersey, where voters expressed their discontent with Governor Jim Florio's tax hikes. Despite their sweep of both houses of the New Jersey legislature, Republicans do not have an advantage on the tax issue nationally. When it comes to tax policy, 45% prefer the Democrats, compared with 40% for the Republicans.

NOVEMBER 13
PRESIDENT BUSH

Interviewing Date: 11/7–10/91
Survey #GO 222023

Do you approve or disapprove of the way George Bush is handling his job as president?

Approve	56%
Disapprove	36
No opinion	8

Selected National Trend

1991	Approve	Dis- approve	No opinion
Oct. 31–Nov. 3 (Pre-Election)	59%	33%	8%
Oct. 17–20 (Post-Thomas Confirmation)	66	26	8
Oct. 3–6 (Pre-Thomas-Hill Hearings)	65	27	8
Sept. 5–8 (Pre-Thomas Hearings)	70	21	9
June 27–30 (Pre-Thomas Nomination)	72	22	6
Feb. 28–March 3 (Gulf War Victory)	89	8	3

Jan. 17–20
(Air Strikes Begin
against Iraq).........82   12   6
Jan. 11–13
(Pre-Desert
Storm)................64   25   11
Jan. 3–6
(First 1991
Measure).............58   31   11
1990
Oct. 18–21
(Low Point)..........53   37   10

How strongly would you say you approve or disapprove? Would you say very strongly or not so strongly?

Approve...56%
   Very strongly....................30
   Not so strongly..................26
Disapprove......................................36
   Very strongly....................24
   Not so strongly..................12
No opinion..8

Decline in Presidential Approval Ratings from High Points

	High point (date)	Rating eight months later
Bush	89% (March 1991)	56%
Reagan		
(2d term)	68 (May 1986)	48
(1st term)	68 (May 1981)	47
Carter	75 (March 1977)	56
Ford	71 (Aug. 1974)	38
Nixon		
(2d term)	67 (Jan. 1973)	33
(1st term)	67 (Nov. 1969)	61
Johnson	79 (March 1964)	70
Kennedy	83 (May 1961)	77
Eisenhower	79 (Dec. 1956)	63
Truman	87 (June 1945)	63

Note: The steady decline in President George Bush's approval ratings continues. A new Gallup Poll shows 56% of Americans approving of the way that he is handling his job, with 36% disapproving and 8% offering no opinion. Bush's approval rating in the Gallup Poll has fallen 3 points in the past week, 10 points in the last month, and 14 points since the Labor Day weekend.

This slide in approval is part of a long-term decline in Bush's rating from the historic high of 89%, recorded in March, immediately after the conclusion of the Persian Gulf war. Even more dramatic than these declining approval figures is respondents' increasing tendency to express highly critical views of the president. Today, nearly as many adults strongly disapprove (24%) as strongly approve (30%) of Bush's performance. In March, only 5% strongly disapproved, while 74% strongly approved.

The 33-percentage point decline in Bush's ratings over the past eight months is one of the sharpest slides on record. Since Gallup introduced the presidential approval question, only Gerald Ford and Richard Nixon have suffered declines of such magnitude in a similar period of time after their approval rating reached a peak.

Ford took office in 1974 with a 71% approval score, as the nation looked to the new president to heal the wounds of the Watergate scandal. Eight months later, however, his approval had fallen 33 percentage points to 38%, paralleling the fall in Bush approval since the Gulf war. Ford was hurt by an economic recession and the unpopularity of his pardon of Nixon.

In January 1973, Nixon reached for the second time his high point in popularity—67% approval—when he announced his plan to "Vietnamize" the war in Southeast Asia. Soon afterward, however, it became apparent that the Watergate affair was more than a "third-rate burglary." Eight months into his second term, Nixon approval took a 34-percentage point drop to 33%.

While the recent decline in Bush's approval ratings puts him in the company of former presidents Ford and Nixon, his ratings are still above average by historical standards. Only one other president, Harry Truman, scored as high, in statistical terms, as Bush's 89% in early March. At the end of World War II the public gave Truman an 87% rating in the Gallup Poll. While Truman's ratings did not fall quite so far as Bush's have in the first eight months (24 versus 33 percentage points), the Truman slide continued for another eight months to reach a low of 32% in September 1946—55 percentage points below his high point.

Bush may not suffer the same fate as Truman, however. At 56%, the president's approval is now within 3 percentage points of his low point in the Gallup Poll, recorded in October 1990. At a time of economic pessimism, the president's high ratings on foreign policy are not enough to hold up his overall approval rating. If people begin to see improvement in the economy, however, the slide in Bush approval is likely to bottom out or even reverse itself.

NOVEMBER 13
DAVID DUKE

Interviewing Date: 11/7–10/91
Survey #GO 222023

Have you heard or read anything about David Duke, who is a candidate for governor of Louisiana?

	November 1991	October 1991
Yes	65%	58%
No	34	41
No opinion	1	1

Asked of those who replied in the affirmative: In general, do you have a favorable or unfavorable opinion of David Duke?

	November 1991	October 1991
Favorable	16%	10%
Unfavorable	69	67
No opinion	15	23

	November 1991 Favorable	October 1991 Favorable
By Sex		
Male	19%	13%
Female	14	7
By Politics		
Republicans	21	12
Democrats	12	12
Independents	17	8
By Region		
South Only	20	17

Asked of those familiar with David Duke: Is David Duke the kind of man you could see yourself voting for if he were to run for political office in your state?

	Yes
National	13%

	Yes
By Sex	
Male	15%
Female	10
By Ethnic Background	
White	14
Nonwhite	6
Black	5
By Education	
College Graduate	8
College Incomplete	8
High-School Graduate	19
Less Than High-School Graduate	17
By Region	
East	10
Midwest	15
South	19
West	5
By Age	
18–29 Years	17
30–49 Years	9
50 Years and Over	15
By Household Income	
$50,000 and Over	6
$30,000–$49,999	16
$20,000–$29,999	15
Under $20,000	15
By Politics	
Republicans	16
Democrats	10
Independents	14

By Religion
Protestants 14
Catholics 12

By Political Ideology
Liberal...9
Moderate..7
Conservative..16

Also asked of those familiar with David Duke: Is David Duke the kind of man you could see yourself voting for if he were to run for president?

Yes...6%
No..86
No opinion 8

Also asked of those familiar with David Duke: Some people say that the travel and convention business in New Orleans and other parts of Louisiana will be hurt if David Duke is elected governor. Thinking about your own travel and vacation plans—if David Duke is elected governor, would you personally be more likely to visit or vacation in New Orleans or other parts of Louisiana, less likely, or would it not have much effect on your travel plans?

More likely..2%
Less likely..23
Not have much effect 74
No opinion 1

I'm going to read you some proposals that are being discussed around the country today. As I read each proposal, please tell me whether you would favor or oppose it:

Requiring all able-bodied people on welfare, including women with small children, to do work for their welfare checks?

Favor 79%
Oppose..18
No opinion 3

A death penalty for persons convicted of murder?

Favor 73%
Oppose..21
No opinion 6

Reducing the size and budget of all government agencies, except for law enforcement?

Favor 67%
Oppose..28
No opinion 5

Reducing income and sales taxes across the board?

Favor 65%
Oppose..32
No opinion 3

Requiring people who live in public housing to take drug tests?

Favor 49%
Oppose..47
No opinion 4

Busing children to achieve better racial balance in the public schools?

Favor 38%
Oppose..58
No opinion 4

Giving blacks preferences over equally qualified whites in such matters as getting into college or getting jobs, because of past discrimination against blacks?

Favor 20%
Oppose..76
No opinion 4

Note: Despite strong personal disapproval for Louisiana gubernatorial nominee David Duke, the public expresses support for many of the themes he has been promoting in his campaign. A new Gallup Poll shows that a majority favors many elements of Duke's populist, antigovernment platform: across-the-board reductions in all government agencies, taxes and fees; elimination of such practices as busing and quotas; and requiring welfare recipients to work for their benefit checks.

The Gallup Poll tested elements of Duke's campaign statements taken from recent interviews and speeches. These elements were not directly identified with him in the survey and were read to respondents before any specific questions about Duke were asked. (Many of his more extreme, racist, and neo-Nazi statements were made in earlier years and thus are not now an official or overt part of his campaign.)

The key finding is that most of Duke's current positions strike a chord with Americans. He has picked up on what appears to be a populist sentiment across the country for less government, lower taxes, and less intrusion. Accordingly, 79% favor Duke's position that all able-bodied welfare recipients, including women with children, must work in order to collect welfare checks. Another 76% support his position against giving blacks preferences over equally qualified whites to make up for past discrimination.

Moreover, 73% favor the death penalty, which Duke supports, and 67% favor his blanket promise to reduce the size and budget of all government agencies, except for law enforcement. Almost as many (65%) favor an across-the-board reduction in all income and sales taxes, as advocated by Duke. And 58% favor his position of opposition to busing in order to achieve racial balance in the public schools.

The only Duke position that does not generate majority support is his advocacy of requiring residents of public housing to undergo drug testing. This issue, which some believe would violate individuals' rights to privacy, divides the public; 49% favor it, but 47% are opposed.

As for the man himself, Duke continues to have a largely unfavorable image. Sixty-five percent say that they have heard of him, and of those, while 69% have an unfavorable opinion, 16% have a favorable one, up slightly from three weeks ago when only 10% of those who knew him thought favorably of him. Duke's most favorable image is among whites in the South, particularly those with lower levels of education.

Thirteen percent of those who know of him say that they could find themselves voting for Duke for political office in their state. There has been some speculation that Duke ultimately would like to run for president. Only 6% of those who are familiar with him, however, say that he is the kind of man whom they could support for the highest office.

Finally, the poll indicates that those business leaders in New Orleans who say that a Duke governorship would hurt tourism may be right. About one in four familiar with Duke (23%) indeed would be less likely to vacation in New Orleans or other parts of Louisiana if Duke becomes governor.

NOVEMBER 20
VICE PRESIDENT QUAYLE

Interviewing Date: 11/14–17/91
Survey #GO 222024

Asked of registered voters: If George Bush runs for reelection in 1992, in general are you more likely to vote for Bush or for the Democratic party's candidate for president?

Bush 48%
Democratic candidate............................36
Undecided; no opinion..........................16

Also asked of registered voters: If George Bush keeps Dan Quayle as his vice presidential running mate in 1992, would you be more likely or less likely to vote for Bush's reelection, or would it not make much difference?

More likely......................................9%
Less likely..17
No difference......................................71
No opinion..3

	More likely	Less likely	No difference	No opinion
By Politics				
Republicans...14%	9%	74%	3%	
Democrats 6	21	71	2	
Independents... 8	20	69	3	
By 1992 Presidential Preference				
Bush 15	9	75	1	
Democratic Candidate 5	27	67	1	
Undecided; No Opinion..3	13	71	13	

September 34   47   19
August.................41   40   19

If President Bush runs for reelection in 1992, do you think he should keep Dan Quayle as his vice presidential running mate or choose someone else?

Keep Quayle..43%
Choose someone else...........................46
No opinion...11

	Keep Quayle	Choose someone else	No opinion
By Politics			
Republicans............	61%	32%	7%
Democrats	31	56	13
Independents..........	35	54	11

Selected National Trend

	Keep Quayle	Choose someone else	No opinion
1991			
August..................	42%	52%	6%
May.....................	39	52	9
1990			
November..............	36	55	9
March..................	35	49	16

Based on what you know about Vice President Dan Quayle, do you think he is qualified to serve as president if it becomes necessary, or not?

Yes..37%
No...53
No opinion...10

Selected National Trend

	Yes	No	No opinion
1991			
August..................	40%	54%	6%
May.....................	38	53	9
1990			
November..............	33	59	8
March..................	31	54	15
1989			
May.....................	34	52	14
1988			
October.................	46	42	12

Over the years Dan Quayle has served as vice president, has your confidence in him as a leader increased, decreased, or stayed about the same?

Increased...22%
Decreased 13
Stayed the same..................................62
No opinion.. 3

Note: George Bush's commitment to keeping Dan Quayle as his running mate may end up costing him votes in 1992. If Quayle remains on the ticket in 1992, one in six registered voters (16%) say that they would be less likely to vote for Bush. Fewer (9%) would be more inclined to back the president if he stays with Quayle.

Attempts by the White House to improve the vice president's image have met with little success. Three in five respondents (62%) say that their confidence in Quayle as a leader has not improved during his years in office. Fewer than four in ten (37%) now say that he is qualified to serve as president if it becomes necessary, up only marginally from 34% in a Gallup Poll taken in 1989, his first year in office.

President Bush's recent decline in popularity may reopen the debate about Quayle. During the summer, before Bush approval fell from the 70s to mid-50s and support for a Democratic alternative to Bush almost doubled, the issue of a vice presidential running mate was moot. Today, while the president still holds a significant edge in a 1992 test election against an unspecified Democratic candidate, his lead has declined sharply. Bush now leads by 48% to 36%; immediately after the Gulf war victory his lead was as much as 67% to 17%. Enough voters are now undecided (16%) to give the Democrats hope of turning the election their way.

If the president were to drop Quayle as his running mate, he has an opportunity to win additional votes among Democrats and independents. One in five Democratic (21%) and independent (20%) voters say that Quayle's presence on the GOP ticket would make them less likely to vote for Bush. Fewer than one in ten Democratic (6%) and independent (8%) voters say that keeping Quayle on the ticket improves their chances of supporting Bush. However, in attempting to woo these voters, the president might alienate others within his own party. For Republican voters, Quayle is more of a plus (14% more likely to vote for Bush with Quayle) than a minus (9%).

The president's steadfast support for Quayle in his public statements may partly explain the differences in response to Quayle by party. When asked whether Bush should keep Quayle or choose someone else as a running mate for 1992, 61% of Republicans say that they want Quayle. In contrast, only one third of Democrats (31%) and independents (35%) thinks that the president should remain loyal to Quayle.

NOVEMBER 22
AIDS

Interviewing Date: 11/14–17/91
Survey #GO 222024

Do you think public education efforts to reduce the spread of AIDS among young people should focus more on encouraging them to practice safe sex or more on encouraging them to abstain from sex?

Practice safe sex	53%
Abstain	42
Both equally (volunteered)	4
No opinion	1

	Practice safe sex	Abstain	Both equally	No opinion
By Sex				
Male	56%	38%	5%	1%
Female	50	45	4	1
By Ethnic Background				
White	53	42	4	1
Nonwhite	57	36	4	3
Black	57	35	4	4
By Education				
College Graduate	59	34	6	1
College Incomplete	56	38	6	*
High-School Graduate	52	45	3	*
Less Than High-School Graduate	49	43	4	4
By Region				
East	61	35	4	*
Midwest	53	42	4	1
South	48	45	4	3
West	51	44	5	*
By Age				
18–29 Years	72	26	2	*
30–49 Years	57	38	5	*
50 Years and Over	38	55	5	2
By Household Income				
$50,000 and Over	59	36	5	*
$30,000–$49,999	56	40	4	*
$20,000–$29,999	52	43	5	*
Under $20,000	52	43	3	2
By Politics				
Republicans	50	45	3	2
Democrats	56	40	3	1
Independents	58	37	5	*
By Religion				
Protestants	49	46	3	2
Catholics	60	37	3	*
By Political Ideology				
Liberal	65	31	4	*
Moderate	59	35	5	1
Conservative	43	52	4	1
By Community Size				
Large City	61	34	5	*
Medium City	52	43	4	1
Suburbs	51	47	2	*
Small Town	54	40	5	1
Rural Area	48	47	3	2

*Less than 1%

Many people have been tested for the AIDS virus as part of routine medical screening procedures. Have you, yourself, ever had your blood tested for the AIDS virus?

	Yes
National	25%

	Yes
By Age	
18–29 Years	38%
30–49 Years	29
50 Years and Over	13

Asked of those who have been tested: The last time you had an AIDS test, was it:

Because you just wanted to know if you were infected with the AIDS virus?	37%
In order to donate blood?	12
On the advice of your doctor?	10
For a life insurance policy?	8
For a health insurance policy?	6
Other	26
No opinion	1

Do you, yourself, plan to have your blood tested for the AIDS virus in the next twelve months?

Yes	24%
No	73
No opinion	3

Do you think the major television networks should or should not accept advertising from condom manufacturers for broadcast?

	Yes, should accept
National	70%

	Yes, should accept
By Age	
18–29 Years	87%
30–49 Years	76
50 Years and Over	54

We're interested in how people might have been affected by Magic Johnson's announcement that he is infected with the AIDS virus. As a result of what you have heard or read about Johnson, are you more likely to do any of the following:

Practice safe sex?

	Yes, more likely
National	70%

	Yes, more likely
By Age	
18–29 Years	83%
30–49 Years	77
50 Years and Over	55

Talk with a son or daughter about AIDS?

	Yes, more likely
National	69%

	Yes, more likely
By Age	
18–29 Years	71%
30–49 Years	83
50 Years and Over	55

Limit the number of sex partners you have?

	Yes, more likely
National	60%

	Yes, more likely
By Age	
18–29 Years	77%
30–49 Years	65
50 Years and Over	40

Contribute to an AIDS charity?

	Yes, more likely
National	59%

	Yes, more likely
By Age	
18–29 Years	66%
30–49 Years	63
50 Years and Over	50

Have your blood tested to find out if you have the AIDS virus?

	Yes, more likely
National	41%

	Yes, more likely
By Age	
18–29 Years	58%
30–49 Years	43
50 Years and Over	30

Note: Earvin "Magic" Johnson's dramatic announcement that he is infected with the AIDS virus has captured the attention of young people, who say that they now are more likely to practice safe sex and to take specific actions to fight AIDS because of the Los Angeles Lakers star's disclosure. This finding is especially relevant because nearly three quarters of young people (72%) say that public education efforts to reduce the spread of the disease within their age group should focus more on encouraging them to practice safe sex than to abstain from sex (26%). In contrast, among adults over age 50 these opinions are reversed (38% versus 55%).

Moreover, fully 87% of young people think that the major television networks should accept and broadcast advertising from condom manufacturers. This compares to only 54% among adults over 50.

Because of Johnson, 77% of young people say that they are more likely to limit the number of sex partners they have, and 58% are more likely to have their own blood tested to find out if they have the AIDS virus. At present, 25% of all adults and 38% of young people report that they have had their blood tested. Looking ahead, 24% of all adults and 35% of young people plan to have this test within the next twelve months.

One measure of the wide apprehension generated by this disease is that nearly one half of all tested adults say that they took the test because they wanted to know if they were infected (37%) or because their doctor advised them to take it (10%). Most of the other half reply that they were tested for incidental reasons, including 14% who, like Johnson, were applying for a life or health insurance policy and 12% who were going to donate blood.

Again, reflecting the widespread impact of Johnson's announcement, 59% of all adults say that they now are more likely to contribute to an AIDS charity than before. Among people under 50 (65%) this proportion is even higher.

NOVEMBER 26
PRESIDENT BUSH

Interviewing Date: 11/21–24/91
Survey #GO 222025

Do you approve or disapprove of the way George Bush is handling his job as president?

Approve	52%
Disapprove	39
No opinion	9

	Approve	Dis- approve	No opinion
By Sex			
Male	56%	36%	8%
Female	48	42	10
By Ethnic Background			
White	54	37	9
Nonwhite	39	49	12

By Education

College Graduate	50	42	8
College Incomplete	50	39	11
High-School Graduate	59	35	6
Less than High-School Graduate	41	44	15

By Region

East	48	43	9
Midwest	50	40	10
South	59	33	8
West	48	42	10

By Age

18–29 Years	59	34	7
30–49 Years	57	33	10
50 Years and Over	41	50	9

By Politics

Republicans	75	20	5
Democrats	32	59	9
Independents	50	40	10

By Political Ideology

Liberal	41	51	8
Moderate	50	40	10
Conservative	64	29	7

By Community Size

Large City	46	44	10
Medium City	51	42	7
Suburbs	54	39	7
Small Town	54	37	9
Rural Area	55	34	11

Selected National Trend

1991	Approve	Dis-approve	No opinion
November 14–17	56%	36%	8%
November 7–10	56	36	8
October 31–November 3	59	33	8
October 24–27	62	29	9
October 17–20	66	26	8

Note: President George Bush's approval ratings have resumed their downward slide. In a new Gallup Poll, 52% approve of the way that he is handling his job. The president's ratings are down 14 percentage points since mid-October, when he drew 66% in a poll taken shortly after the Senate confirmation of Clarence Thomas to the Supreme Court.

The latest poll results show that Bush approval has fallen by 4 percentage points in one week's time. The two previous November polls had shown his approval rating stabilizing at 56%. Now, the current 52% approval statistically equals his previous low of 53%, recorded in October 1990.

Over the past month, Bush has lost support among all major population subgroups. His approval ratings have declined by 10 percentage points or more among every demographic and political subgroup analyzed, including Republicans and political conservatives. One of the most recent declines in approval, however, has occurred among women. In one week's time, Bush's rating within this group fell from 55% to 48%, while his rating among men held steady at 56%.

NOVEMBER 28
RELIGION

Interviewing Date: 11/21–24/91
Survey #GO 222025

At the present time, do you think religion as a whole is increasing its influence on American life or losing its influence?

Increasing	27%
Losing	66
No opinion	7

Selected National Trend

	Increasing	Losing	No opinion*
May 1991	34%	57%	9%
March 1991	48	43	9
1990	33	48	19
1988	36	48	16
1986	48	39	13
1984	42	39	19
1980	35	46	19
1978	37	48	15
1976	44	45	11
1974	31	56	13

1970.....................14   75   11
1968.....................18   67   15
1965.....................33   45   22
1962.....................45   31   24
1957.....................69   14   17

*In 1990 and earlier, "no opinion" was combined with "no difference."

Do you believe that religion can answer all or most of today's problems, or that religion is largely old-fashioned and out of date?

Can answer 61%
Out of date 25
No opinion...14

Selected National Trend

	Can answer	Out of date	No opinion*
May 1991...............59%		23%	18%
March 1991 60		22	18
1990.....................63		18	19
1988.....................57		20	23
1986.....................58		23	19
1985.....................61		22	17
1984.....................56		24	20
1982.....................60		22	18
1981.....................65		15	20
1974.....................62		20	18
1957.....................81		7	12

*In 1990 and earlier, "no opinion" was combined with "neither."

How important would you say religion is in your own life—very important, fairly important, or not very important?

Very important 55%
Fairly important...................................29
Not very important 15
No opinion...1

Selected National Trend

	Very important	Fairly important	Not very important	No opinion
1991				
May.............57%		30%	13%	*
March...........55		29	16	*

February........60	29	11	*
January– February.....63	28	9	*
1990...........58	29	13	*
1989...........55	30	14	1
1988...........54	31	14	1
1987...........53	32	14	1
1986...........55	30	14	1
1985...........55	31	13	1
1984...........56	30	13	1
1983...........56	30	13	1
1982...........56	30	13	1
1981...........56	29	14	1
1980...........55	31	13	1
1978...........52	32	14	2
1965...........70	22	7	1
1952...........75	20	5	*

*Less than 1%

Do you happen to be a member of a church or synagogue?

	Yes
National...69%

Selected National Trend

	Yes
1991	
May..69%
March..66
February...67
1990...69
1989...67
1988...65
1987...69
1985...71
1983...69
1982...67
1979...68
1976...71
1965...73
1952...73
1947...76
1944...75
1940...72
1937...73

Did you, yourself, happen to attend church or synagogue in the last seven days, or not?

	Yes
National...41%

1991	Yes
May	.43%
March	.43
1990	.40
1989	.42
1988	.42
1987	.40
1985	.42
1983	.40
1982	.41
1981	.41
1979	.40
1972	.40
1969	.42
1967	.43
1962	.46
1958	.49
1957	.47
1955	.49
1954	.46
1950	.39
1940	.37
1939	.41

| Yes
--- | ---
1989 | .34%
1986 | .33

After I read off three statements, please tell me which one comes closest to describing your views about the origin and development of man:

God created man pretty much in his present form at one time within the last 10,000 years.............47%
Man has developed over millions of years from less advanced forms of life. God had no part in this process.........................9
Man has developed over millions of years from less advanced forms of life, but God guided this process, including man's creation....................40
Other; no opinion................................4

Please tell me whether you agree completely, agree somewhat, disagree somewhat, or disagree completely with this statement: The only assurance of eternal life is personal faith in Jesus Christ.

Agree completely 59%
Agree somewhat...................................17
Disagree somewhat 11
Disagree completely.............................10
No opinion...3

Which of the following three statements comes closest to describing your feelings about the Bible?

The Bible is the actual word of God and is to be taken literally word for word.......................32%
The Bible is the inspired word of God, but not everything in it should be taken literally word for word 49
The Bible is an ancient book of fables, legends, history, and moral precepts recorded by man............16
No opinion...3

Would you describe yourself as a "born-again," or evangelical, Christian?

| Yes
--- | ---
National | .41%

Note: Almost one half of Americans are creationists who believe that God created man in his present form within the last 10,000 years. A new Gallup Poll shows that 47% of respondents, when offered three choices about the origin and development of man, choose this alternative, which most scientists say is not supported by concrete evidence. Only 9% choose a secular evolutionist perspective, that man has developed over millions of years from less advanced forms of life with God playing no

By Religion

| Yes
--- | ---
Protestants | .55%
Catholics | .22

part. The remaining 40% choose a modified evolutionary position, that man has developed over millions of years with God guiding this process.

The issue of the origin of man has particular relevance in light of continuing efforts by some groups to require the teaching of the creationist perspective in public schools as an alternative to evolution. Interestingly, the number of those who choose the creationist alternative has remained roughly the same over the last nine years (44% agreed in 1982). Those who are most likely to be creationists today include Evangelicals, older Americans, those living in the South, women, those living in small towns and rural areas, and those who have lower levels of education.

In response to another question about biblical literalism, only 32% believe that the Bible is the actual word of God and is to be taken literally. One half (49%) says that the Bible is the inspired word of God, but not everything in it should be taken literally. Only 16% argue that it is simply an ancient book of legends and history, recorded by man.

Americans remain strikingly orthodox in their overall religious practices and beliefs. Seventy-six percent agree that their only assurance of eternal life is a personal faith in Jesus Christ. Moreover, 69% claim to be a member of a church or synagogue—a number that has remained remarkably constant since 1937, when Gallup first asked the question (then, 73% said that they were a member). Another 61% think that religion can answer most of today's problems, while only 25% find it old-fashioned and out of date—numbers that are only slightly more negative than earlier Gallup surveys.

In terms of religion's personal relevance, Gallup's measures show little change over the last couple of decades. Now, 55% say that religion is very important in their own personal lives, while only 15% say that it is not very important. Indeed, 41% have attended church or synagogue within the last seven days. This number has been constant since the mid-1960s but is down slightly from the higher percentages who attended church in the 1950s and early 1960s. (Women, older Americans, and Catholics attend church most often.)

Some 41% consider themselves to be "born-again," or evangelical, Christians. Sections of society highest on this evangelical measure include the South, those living in rural areas, blacks, those with lower levels of education, and Baptists.

Despite the high levels of religious belief and practices, the Gallup Poll shows that respondents now are more likely than in the past to worry that religion is losing its sway in American life. Sixty-six percent now say that religion is losing its influence, while only 27% say that it is increasing. These are the most pessimistic perceptions since the Vietnam War years of 1968 and 1970, when only 18% and 14%, respectively, said that religion was increasing its influence.

DECEMBER 4
PEARL HARBOR: FIFTIETH ANNIVERSARY

Interviewing Date: 11/21–24/91
Survey #GO 222025

What is your opinion about the country of Japan? Is your overall opinion of it very favorable, mostly favorable, mostly unfavorable, or very unfavorable?

Very favorable......................................7%
Mostly favorable................................41
Mostly unfavorable............................29
Very unfavorable...............................12
No opinion...11

Selected National Trend

	Very, mostly favorable
March 1991	65%
February 1991	62
February 1990	61
August 1989	58
March 1989	69

Asked of those who have a very or mostly favorable opinion of Japan: Why do you have a favorable opinion of Japan?

Respect for Japanese work
ethic, business success.......................24%
Good products; technology;
economy...20
Respect for Japanese
intelligence, education.......................10
Other;* no opinion.............................46

*Only main reasons are specified here.

Asked of those who have a mostly or very unfavorable opinion of Japan: Why do you have an unfavorable opinion of Japan?

Unbalanced trade; banning
of imports 34%
U.S. real estate and business
buy-outs..28
World War II; Pearl Harbor 5
Other;* no opinion.............................33

*Only main reasons are specified here.

In your opinion, do you think Japan is or is not a dependable ally of the United States?

Yes...45%
No..39
No opinion......................................16

Selected National Trend*

	Yes	No	No opinion
Jan.–Feb. 1991	44%	39%	17%
1990	44	40	16
1989	50	29	21
1988	48	30	22
1987	54	24	22
1986	55	22	23
1985	56	20	24
1980	49	26	25
1975	49	39	12
1970	44	36	20
1965	39	36	25
1960	31	55	14

*American Enterprise/Japanese Foreign Ministry surveys

This coming December 7 marks the fiftieth anniversary of a significant event in American history which occurred on December 7, 1941. Do you happen to remember what that event was?

	Yes, full knowledge of place and events
National	36%

	Yes, full knowledge of place and events
By Age	
18–29 Years	26%
30–49 Years	35
50 Years and Over	43
60 Years and Over	41

Asked of those who said only "Pearl Harbor" or gave an incorrect response or no response: As you may know, this December 7 marks the fiftieth anniversary of Pearl Harbor. Would you know specifically what happened fifty years ago, relating to Pearl Harbor?

Japanese attack on Pearl
Harbor in Hawaii;
Japanese bombing.............................71%
Beginning of U.S.
involvement
in World War II 5
Other..3
No opinion;
don't remember................................21

	Japanese attack on Pearl Harbor	Beginning of U.S. involvement	Other	No opinion
By Age				
18–29 Years	60%	4%	6%	30%
30–49 Years	76	4	2	18
50 Years and Over	73	8	3	16
65 Years and Over	77	8	3	12

As you may know, the Japanese attack on U.S. ships in Pearl Harbor marked the beginning of U.S. involvement in World War II. From what you know or have read, would the United States have eventually been involved in World War II if Pearl Harbor had not been attacked, or not?

Yes...72%
No...19
No opinion...9

Some people have argued that President Franklin D. Roosevelt knew about Japanese plans to bomb Pearl Harbor but did nothing about it because he wanted an excuse to involve the United States on the side of the Allies in the war. From what you know or have read, do you agree or disagree with this point of view?

Agree 31%
Disagree..47
No opinion.......................................22

Asked of those age 55 and older: Would you happen to remember exactly where you were and what you were doing when you first heard about Pearl Harbor on December 7, 1941?

	Total	65 years and over
Yes	74%	81%
No	24	17
No opinion	2	2

Asked of men age 60 and older: Did you personally serve in the U.S. Armed Forces during World War II, or not?

Yes...49%
No...51

Asked of women age 55 and older: Did your husband serve in the U.S. Armed Forces during World War II, or not?

Yes...40%
No...58
Never married 2

Was a close family member, or someone you knew personally, killed while serving in the U.S. Armed Forces in World War II?

	Total	65 years and older
Yes	20%	47%
No	79	52
No opinion	1	1

It has been almost half a century since the war with Japan ended. What would you say your feelings are toward the Japanese people at present—friendly, unfriendly, or neutral?

	1991	1951*
Friendly	43%	51%
Unfriendly	8	25
Neutral	47	18
No opinion	2	6

*[1951 question]: It has been six years since the war with Japan ended. What would you say your feelings are toward the Japanese people at present?

Have you forgiven the Japanese for Pearl Harbor, or not?

Yes...72%
No...19
No opinion...9

Considering all you know about Japan today and in the past, how likely do you think it is that Japan will again become an aggressor nation as it was during World War II?

	1991	1986*
Very likely	16%	15%
Somewhat likely	30	32
Not at all likely	50	47
No opinion	4	6

*Gallup survey for *Newsweek*

Some people think it would be a good thing for Japan to build a bigger military complex and take on more responsibility for its own defense. Others think it would be a bad thing because they fear Japan might become an aggressor nation like it was in World War II. Which comes closer to your view?

	1991	1989*
Good thing	33%	41%
Bad thing	59	50
No opinion	8	9

*Gallup survey for *Newsweek*

As you may know, the United States dropped atomic bombs on Hiroshima and Nagasaki in August 1945 near the end of World War II. Looking back, would you say you approve or disapprove of using the atomic bomb on Japanese cities in 1945?

	1991	1990	1945*
Approve	53%	53%	85%
Disapprove	41	41	10
No opinion	6	6	5

*Wording of question differed in 1945

Here in this country, the U.S. government required many U.S. citizens of Japanese descent to leave their homes and move to relocation camps during World War II. Looking back, would you say you approve or disapprove of this action?

Approve	33%
Disapprove	62
No opinion	5

Do you consider Japan to be an economic threat to the United States today, or not?

Yes	77%
No	20
No opinion	3

Looking ahead, do you think relations between the United States and Japan will get better, get worse, or not change much over the next ten years?

Better	30%
Worse	23
Not change much	42
No opinion	5

Note: The Japanese attack on Pearl Harbor fifty years ago this week reminds Americans as much about the present-day threat posed by Japan as it does about the past. A new Gallup Poll shows that a majority has forgiven the Japanese for the December 7, 1941, attack, but almost one half says that it is at least somewhat likely that Japan again could become an aggressor nation. Overall attitudes toward the Japanese people and their country are only moderately favorable and are on the decline. The economic threat posed by Japan appears to be the main factor behind these ambivalent feelings.

The Pearl Harbor attack is etched forever in the minds of those who are now age 55 or older, 74% of whom recall exactly where they were and what they were doing when the attack began. For most Americans, it is a tragedy to be put behind them: 72% have forgiven Japan for the events of fifty years ago. But almost one in five (19%) has not forgiven the Japanese.

Indeed, favorable opinions of Japan today are lower than at any time in recent years. Only 48% say that their opinion is favorable, while 41% do not. Favorable ratings have dropped since Gallup's most recent measures in February and March of this year. Moreover, only 43% today say that their attitude toward the Japanese people is friendly. Remarkably, this is a lower percentage than in 1951, a scant six years after World War II ended, when Gallup found that 51% of Americans had friendly attitudes toward the Japanese people.

Now, 45% say that Japan is a dependable ally, while 39% say that it is not. Perhaps, most important, 77% currently consider Japan to be an economic threat to our country. This worry over economic competition is clearly evident in the reasons respondents give for their attitudes about Japan. Those who have an unfavorable opinion talk primarily about economics: 34% cite Japan's unbalanced trade policies and banning of imports, while 28% do not like its purchases of U.S. business and real estate. Those who have a favorable opinion express admiration for the Japanese people's work ethic (24%), products (20%), and intelligence and education (10%).

Aside from the concern about Japan's economic threat, the poll also reveals undercurrents of anxiety about renewed military aggression. Almost one half of respondents (46%) think it is at least somewhat likely that Japan again could become an aggressor nation as it was during World War II; only 50% say that it is not likely. In fact, there is considerable concern about the prospect of Japan developing a bigger military complex and taking on more responsibility for its own defense, even though this might put Japan on a more even footing economically with the United States. About six out of ten (59%) disapprove of this type of rearmament, while only one third (33%) approves.

In other findings, one third (31%) agrees with a conspiracy thesis that alleges that President Franklin D. Roosevelt withheld advance information about Pearl Harbor in order to let the attack provide an excuse to get our country into the war. One half (53%) still approves of the U.S. decision to drop the atomic bomb on Hiroshima and Nagasaki near the end of the war. And many believe that one of America's more shameful reactions to Pearl Harbor was the internment of U.S. citizens of Japanese descent in relocation camps: two thirds (62%) today disapprove of this action.

The refusal of many older Americans to forgive Japan is almost certainly related to the direct impact of World War II on their own lives. One half of men now at least 60 years of age (49%) say that they served in the U.S. Armed Forces during the war; 40% of women who are now 55 years of age or older say that their husband served. More dramatically, 47% of those age 65 and older were exposed to the conflict's ultimate cost: they personally knew someone who was killed during the war. (Over four hundred thousand American soldiers and sailors died from all causes during World War II.)

DECEMBER 6
MOST IMPORTANT
PROBLEM/REPUBLICAN AND
DEMOCRATIC PARTIES

Interviewing Date: 11/21–24/91
Survey #GO 222025

What do you think is the most important problem facing this country today?*

Economic problems

Economy in general 32%
Unemployment..................................23
Recession... 5
Federal budget deficit.......................... 4
Trade deficit 4
Taxes 3

Noneconomic problems

Poverty; homelessness 16
Drugs; drug abuse..............................10
Crime.. 6
Health care...................................... 6
Dissatisfaction with government.............. 5
AIDS... 5
Ethics, morals 4
Education 4
Environment..................................... 3
International problems 3

No opinion....................................... 3

*Total adds to more than 100% due to multiple responses. None of the other responses drew more than 3%.

Which political party do you think can do a better job of handling the problem you have just mentioned—the Republican party or the Democratic party?

Republican 32%
Democratic 33
No difference (volunteered);
  no opinion 35

Selected National Trend
(Problem and Party Prior to Presidential Election)

	Republican party	Democratic party
Fear of war (Apr. 1987)	29%	37%
Unemployment (Nov. 1983).....	28	35
Inflation (Oct. 1979)..............	25	33
Inflation (Oct. 1975)..............	15	42
Vietnam (June 1971)	20	30
Vietnam (Nov. 1967).............	30	26

| Keeping peace (Sept. 1963)...... 20 | 30 |
| Keeping peace (Sept. 1959)...... 27 | 29 |

Note: For the first time since the Vietnam War era, the Democrats cannot look forward to a presidential election year secure in the knowledge that the public trusts their party more than the GOP to handle the nation's top problem. In a recent Gallup Poll, one third (32%) names the Republicans and another third (33%) the Democrats when asked which party can better deal with our most pressing problem. By contrast, the Democrats enjoyed a 7 to 8-percentage point advantage on this question in polls taken prior to the 1988, 1984, and 1980 presidential elections—all of which they lost.

The last time a Democrat won a presidential election (Jimmy Carter in 1976) his party had a huge advantage on this Gallup barometer of party strength. Benefiting from the Watergate scandal, the Democrats were preferred over the Republicans by a margin of 42% to 15% in the fall of 1975. The Democrats' failure to hold an advantage on this key measure today suggests that, despite President George Bush's falling approval ratings, the Democrats are not in a strong position to defeat him in 1992.

Over the last three decades the Democrats have lost their edge to the Republicans as the party better able to handle the top problem in only three instances: intermittently during the Bush presidency; in the mid-1980s, when the Reagan recession gave way to the Reagan recovery; and in the late 1960s to early 1970s, when the Vietnam War politically polarized the nation.

Economic concerns now clearly dominate the public's list of key problems that the nation faces. Overall, about two thirds mention some type of economic problem as our top concern. One third (32%) cites the economy in general, while one fourth (23%) cites unemployment. Less often mentioned are the recession (5%), the federal budget deficit (4%), the trade deficit (4%), and taxes (3%).

Noneconomic problems, however, still are of considerable concern to the public. Six in ten volunteer something other than an economic issue when asked to name the top problem. (Poll respondents were allowed to name more than one problem.) Topping the list of noneconomic problems are the social ills of poverty and homelessness (16%) and drug abuse (10%). Also mentioned by at least 5% of those polled are crime, health care, dissatisfaction with government, and AIDS.

DECEMBER 10
PRESIDENT BUSH

Interviewing Date: 12/5–8/91
Survey #GO 222026

Do you approve or disapprove of the way George Bush is handling his job as president?

Approve...52%
Disapprove.......................................42
No opinion... 6

Selected National Trend

1991	Approve	Dis-approve	No opinion
November 21–24......52%	39%	9%
November 14–17......56	36	8
November 7–10 56	36	8
October 31–		
November 3 59	33	8
October 24–27.........62	29	9
October 17–20.........66	26	8
October 10–13.........66	28	6
October 3–6............65	27	8
September 26–29 66	25	9
September 13–15 68	22	10

Presidential Performance Ratings
(In December Prior to Second-Term Elections)

	Approve	Dis-approve	No opinion
Bush (1991)............52%	42%	6%
Reagan (1983).........54	38	8
Carter (1979)..........54	35	11
Nixon (1971)..........50	37	13
Eisenhower (1955)....75	13	12

Asked of registered voters: If George Bush runs for reelection this year, in general are

you more likely to vote for Bush or for
the Democratic party's candidate for
president?

Bush 48%
Democratic candidate............................34
Undecided; no opinion...........................18

Selected National Trend

	Bush	Democratic candidate	Undecided; No opinion
1991			
November 21–24	48%	36%	16%
October 31–November 3	46	36	18
October 10–13	49	32	19
September 13–15	51	29	20
September 5–8	52	29	19

As you may know, Samuel Skinner will
replace John Sununu as White House chief
of staff. As a result of the change in his
chief of staff, do you have more confidence
in George Bush to deal with the nation's
problems, less confidence, or about the
same amount of confidence?

More...15%
Less... 6
Same amount.....................................74
No opinion.. 5

Now, let me ask you about some specific
problems facing the country. As I read off
each one, would you tell me whether you
approve or disapprove of the way
President Bush is handling that problem:

Economic conditions in this country?

Approve..22%
Disapprove..73
No opinion.. 5

Selected National Trend

	Approve	Disapprove	No opinion
1991			
October	29%	64%	7%
September	32	60	8
August	36	59	5
July	34	59	7
June	36	58	6
March	37	56	7

Foreign policy?

Approve..64%
Disapprove..29
No opinion.. 7

Selected National Trend

	Approve	Disapprove	No opinion
1991			
October	70%	25%	5%
September	70	21	9
August	74	20	6
July	71	19	10
June	64	28	8
March	79	11	10

Domestic policy; that is, our problems in
this country?

Approve..27%
Disapprove..68
No opinion.. 5

Health-care policy?

Approve..28%
Disapprove..63
No opinion.. 9

Thinking about the problems the country
faces, do you think President Bush
[Carter*] will handle them about as well as
anyone could be expected to, or do you
think that someone else could do a better
job of dealing with these problems?

	Bush	Carter*
President	58%	43%
Someone else	38	48
No opinion	4	9

*Gallup Poll conducted for Newsweek, July
1979

Do you approve or disapprove of the way your state's governor is handling his or her job?

Approve..42%
Disapprove..48
No opinion..10

Note: Despite the recent decline in his approval ratings, George Bush still must be considered a strong favorite for reelection next year. The latest Gallup Poll finds his approval remaining above the critical 50% level: 52% currently approve of the way he is handling his duties as president, while 42% disapprove and 6% have no opinion.

Presidents with approval ratings of 50% or above are generally reelected. Eight years ago at this time, in 1983, Ronald Reagan received 54%. He went on easily to defeat Walter Mondale the following November. Similarly, Richard Nixon received a 50% approval rating twenty years ago in 1971, ten months before his one-sided victory over George McGovern.

Jimmy Carter, who lost his reelection bid to Reagan in 1980, had an approval rating of 54% in December 1979. Carter's rating at that time, however, did not reflect his true prospects for reelection; his average that year was 37%. The December rating of 54% was an aberration, reflecting a 14-percentage point increase in approval as the public rallied around him at the beginning of the Iranian hostage crisis. During the election year that followed, Carter's approval again dropped below 40%. By contrast, Bush's overall approval rating in the Gallup Poll has never fallen below 50%.

The latest Bush figures are not significantly different from those recorded in late November, before the Thanksgiving holiday. A Gallup Poll taken November 21–24 found 52% approving of his job performance (identical to the current results) and 39% disapproving (marginally lower than today's 42%). Looking back, the decline in Bush approval was most severe between mid-October and early November, when the elections replaced the Clarence Thomas hearings as the nation's top political story. In an October 17–20 Gallup Poll, Bush had a 66% approval rating. Within three weeks it fell 10 percentage points to 56%.

Over the past month the Democrats have failed to gain on Bush in Gallup's test election. Close to one half of registered voters (48%) now say that they expect to vote for Bush's reelection next November, one third (34%) expects to vote for an unspecified Democratic challenger, while one in five (18%) is undecided. These results are not statistically different from the late November and late October polls.

Although Bush has lost political clout since the end of the Persian Gulf war, his approval ratings seem very respectable, given the current economic climate. Chief executives at the state level, for example, do not fare as well in their job performance ratings. Among adults polled nationally, only 42% approve of their state governor's job performance, some 10 points lower than Bush's current rating.

The president is clearly taking a hit on the economy. His approval rating for handling economic conditions in the country has declined to 22%, a new low. Bush is also widely criticized for his failings in domestic policy, and specifically for the way he has dealt with the health-care issue. Only 27% and 28%, respectively, give him positive marks for handling domestic affairs and health-care policy.

Despite this increased criticism, Bush's strengths in foreign policy and leadership remain evident. Even though he no longer may be directly benefiting from the effects of the Gulf war, a solid majority feels comfortable with him as our leader in the world. Close to two thirds (64%) approve of his handling of foreign policy, in sharp contrast to his 27% rating on domestic policy.

However, the public has not lost faith in Bush's ability to deal with the nation's problems, as it seemed to do with Carter ten years ago. Almost six in ten (58%) think that Bush can handle the country's problems about as well as anyone. In contrast, during a national crisis of confidence in the summer of 1979, only 43% expressed such confidence in President Carter.

The replacement of John Sununu with Samuel Skinner as White House chief of staff may help to improve Bush's standing with the public, although most say that their opinion is unaffected. Overall, 15% are now more confident in Bush's ability to handle the nation's problems, while 6% are less confident and three quarters (74%) expect the change in chief of staff to make little difference.

DECEMBER 11
REPUBLICAN PRESIDENTIAL CANDIDATES

Interviewing Date: 12/5–8/91
Survey #GO 222026

Asked of registered Republicans and those who lean Republican: Please tell me whether you have a favorable or unfavorable opinion of each of the following Republicans who might run for president in 1992:

Pat Buchanan, the political commentator?

Favorable...28%
Unfavorable.......................................33
No opinion..18
Never heard of...................................21

George Bush?

Favorable...89%
Unfavorable.......................................10
No opinion.. 1
Never heard of................................... *

*Less than 1%

David Duke, state representative from Louisiana?

Favorable...13%
Unfavorable.......................................74
No opinion.. 6
Never heard of................................... 7

Also asked of registered Republicans and those who lean Republican: Which of these three men would you most like to see nominated as the Republican party's candidate for president in 1992?

George Bush.......................................86%
David Duke... 6

Pat Buchanan...................................... 5
Undecided; no opinion......................... 3

Asked of Duke and Buchanan supporters: Who would be your second choice for the Republican nomination?

	Duke supporters	Buchanan supporters
George Bush	65%	85%
David Duke	–	8
Pat Buchanan	25	–
Undecided; no opinion	10	7

Asked of registered Republicans and those who lean Republican: Do you think David Duke's political views are too extreme to consider voting for him for president, or not?

Yes...61%
No...23
No opinion..16

Also asked of registered Republicans and those who lean Republican: Do you think Pat Buchanan's political views are too extreme to consider voting for him for president, or not?

Yes...28%
No...27
No opinion..45

Note: Economic discontent among Republican voters may produce some bumps in George Bush's otherwise smooth ride to his party's nomination next year. According to a new Gallup Poll, neither of his two principal challengers for the Republican presidential nomination—maverick Louisiana politician David Duke and conservative political commentator Pat Buchanan—has a realistic chance to unseat him. In states hard hit by the recession, however, Bush's GOP challengers may attract enough support to call attention to their antigovernment, antitax themes.

In overall support for the nomination, Duke receives only 6% and Buchanan 5% to Bush's

86% among registered Republicans and those who lean Republican. But among GOP voters worried about losing a job, maintaining their standard of living, or meeting medical bills, almost one in five supports either Duke or Buchanan.

The degree to which economic dissatisfaction translates into anti-Bush votes will be tested in February, when New Hampshire holds its primary. The severity of the recession in the New England region should boost Buchanan's chances of making a strong showing there, where he will have the anti-Bush vote to himself since Duke has announced that he will not campaign in the state.

Despite his long tenure as cohost of CNN's "Crossfire," his nationally syndicated column, numerous appearances on other political talk shows, and service in both the Nixon and Reagan White Houses, Buchanan remains unknown to many Republican voters. Four in ten have never heard of him (21%) or do not know enough about him to rate him (18%).

Those Republican voters who do have an opinion of Buchanan are divided in their views. Twenty-eight percent have a favorable opinion of him, while 33% have an unfavorable opinion. And while 28% see him as too extreme in his political views, 27% disagree.

As for Duke, after the extensive national media coverage of his failed bid for the Louisiana governorship, his name is recognized by virtually all GOP voters. Only 7% say that they have never heard of him; another 6% claim to have heard of him but offer no opinion.

While Duke has the high name identification associated with a viable political candidate, his past links to the Ku Klux Klan and other extremist groups seriously limit his vote-getting potential. Six in ten (61%) GOP voters find his political views too extreme to consider him for president. National Gallup Polls taken in the weeks before the Louisiana election revealed that Duke's message—the issue positions that are an official or overt part of his campaign—appeals to a broad spectrum of voters. Once again, however, poll results suggest that most voters are not willing to overlook Duke's past in order to support his antiestablishment campaign.

DECEMBER 12
PERSONAL FINANCES/RECESSION

Interviewing Date: 12/5–8/91
Survey #GO 222026

We are interested in how people's financial situation may have changed. Would you say that you are financially better off now than you were a year ago, or are you financially worse off now?

Better...33%
Worse..40
Same (volunteered)..............................26
No opinion..1

Selected National Trend

	Better	Worse	Same	No opinion
1991				
October.........35%		42%	22%	1%
September.....34		28	37	1
July.............34		32	33	1
May.............32		32	33	3
April............29		33	37	1
March...........30		37	32	1
February–				
March........37		28	34	1
February........37		28	35	*
Mid-January...27		33	39	1
Early January..35		32	32	1
1990				
December......38		36	26	*
Late October...38		35	26	1
Mid-October...27		41	30	2
Early				
October......32		41	26	1
September.....40		27	32	1
August..........43		27	29	1
July.............44		28	27	1
February........49		24	26	1

*Less than 1%

Looking ahead, do you expect that at this time next year you will be financially better off than now or worse off than now?

Better...54%
Worse..21

Same (volunteered)...............................17
No opinion...8

Selected National Trend

	Better	Worse	Same	No opinion
1991				
October.........55%	23%	16%	6%
September.....53	19	22	6
July.............57	15	19	9
May.............57	16	19	8
April............56	17	18	9
March...........56	18	20	6
February–March........64	9	20	7
February........57	15	20	8
Mid-January...41	25	21	13
Early January..52	18	20	10
1990				
December......58	18	17	7
Late October...50	27	15	8
Mid-October...41	34	16	9
Early October......48	30	13	9
September.....51	17	20	12
August..........57	16	20	7
July.............58	17	18	7
February........65	13	16	6

Right now, do you think that economic conditions in the country as a whole are getting better or getting worse?

Better...19%
Worse...69
Same (volunteered)................................9
No opinion...3

Selected National Trend

	Better	Worse	Same	No opinion
1991				
October.........25%	64%	8%	3%
September.....27	60	10	3
July.............34	51	9	6

How much longer do you think the country's current economic recession will last?

	Dec. 1991	Feb. 1991
A few more months...................7%	10%
Up to six months...................22	25
Up to a year......................34	32
Up to two years....................16	13
Longer than that...................11	13
Already over (volunteered).........2	*
No opinion...........................8	7

*Less than 1%

Note: Americans remain deeply pessimistic about economic conditions in this country today and are not optimistic that the recession will end any time soon. Nevertheless, a new Gallup Poll shows that a majority continue to believe that their personal financial situation will improve a year from now.

Almost seven out of ten (69%) think that economic conditions in the United States are getting worse, not better. The trend on this question has been progressively more negative over the past six months; last July only 51% thought that economic conditions were getting worse.

Despite the gloom about the national outlook, respondents remain fairly optimistic about their own personal financial situation. Over one half (54%) anticipate being better off financially at this time next year, while only 21% expect to be worse off. These figures reveal a greater sense of optimism about Americans' personal financial future now than was evident in the Carter years or in the Reagan recession of the early 1980s. They are also more positive than in October 1990, in the midst of uncertainties over the federal government's inability to agree on a budget and apprehension about impending war with Iraq.

Thirty-three percent say that they are better off financially now than a year ago, while 26% say the same and 40% say worse off. This "better off" figure has remained relatively stable since the end of the Persian Gulf war.

DECEMBER 17
KENNEDY FAMILY

Interviewing Date: 12/12–15/91
Survey #GO 222027

I'd like you to rate Edward Kennedy on a scale. If you have a favorable opinion of him, name a number between +1 and +5— the higher the number, the more favorable your opinion. If you have an unfavorable opinion of him, name a number between -1 and -5—the lower the number, the more unfavorable your opinion. How would you rate Edward Kennedy on this scale?

Highly favorable (+5, +4) 12%
Mildly favorable (+3, +2, +1) 24
Mildly unfavorable (-1, -2, -3) 27
Highly unfavorable (-4, -5) 26
No opinion 11

Selected National Trend

	Highly, mildly favorable	Mildly, highly unfavorable	No opinion
October 1991	22%	54%	24%*
1990**	61	34	5
1987†	64	31	5
1985	74	23	3
1982	63	33	4
1981	61	35	4
1980	46	50	4
1979	78	20	2
1978	72	20	8
1975	67	29	4
1973	68	28	4
1970	68	30	2
1969 (July, post-Chappaquiddick accident)	75	23	2
1969 (March)	84	12	4

*"No opinion" here includes "neutral (volunteered)."
**Times Mirror survey
†Gallup/Times Mirror survey

Did you, yourself, happen to watch any part of the televised rape trial of William Kennedy Smith in West Palm Beach, Florida?

Yes 69%
No 31

Based on what you may have heard or read about the case, do you agree or disagree with the jury's verdict that William Kennedy Smith was not guilty?

Agree 61%
Disagree 25
No opinion 14

All things considered, do you think the trial should have been televised, or not?

Yes 23%
No 74
No opinion 3

Do you approve of the decision by most news organizations to keep the name of the alleged rape victim confidential, or do you think her name should have been released?

Approve of decision 64%
Name should have been released 33
No opinion 3

Do you approve of the decision not to show the alleged rape victim's face in televised coverage of the trial, or do you think her face should have been shown?

Approve of decision 60%
Face should have been shown 36
No opinion 4

As a result of the William Kennedy Smith case, do you think women will be more likely or less likely to report being raped, or will things not change much?

More likely 10%
Less likely 29
Not change much 58
No opinion 3

	More likely	Less likely	Not change much	No opinion
By Sex				
Male	12%	26%	58%	4%
Female	9	31	57	3

	Dec. 1991	Feb. 1991
Abraham Lincoln...................	40%	42%
John Kennedy........................	39	48
Franklin Roosevelt................	29	28
George Washington	21	24
Ronald Reagan......................	19	22
Harry Truman........................	17	18
George Bush..........................	18	27
Dwight Eisenhower................	14	12
Jimmy Carter........................	10	9
Richard Nixon	10	7
Theodore Roosevelt	8	9
Thomas Jefferson	6	5
Lyndon Johnson	3	3
Woodrow Wilson....................	3	2

Note: Although William Kennedy Smith's trial ended last week in a verdict of not guilty, the damage to the Kennedy family name resulting from the rape charge persists. According to a new Gallup Poll, Senator Edward Kennedy's popularity among the national public is at a record low. Fewer than four in ten respondents (36%) now have a favorable opinion of the Massachusetts senator, and a majority (53%) even regards him unfavorably.

In more than twenty years of polling, Kennedy's favorability rating has fallen below 50% only once before: in 1980, during his unsuccessful bid to wrest the Democratic presidential nomination away from Jimmy Carter. That year, Gallup found opinion on Kennedy dividing 46% favorable versus 50% unfavorable. In all other years since 1969, when Gallup first asked the public to rate him, his favorability rating has exceeded 60%.

A Gallup Poll taken last October, immediately after the conclusion of the Senate Judiciary Committee hearings on Clarence Thomas, suggested that Senator Kennedy's image had been seriously damaged. That poll found a majority (54%) of those who had watched the televised hearings saying they had an unfavorable impression of Kennedy, by far the highest negative for any of the committee members. Only 22% rated him favorably.

In the West Palm Beach trial, the public solidly backs the jury's decision to acquit Smith on the rape charges. Six in ten (61%) agree with the verdict, while fewer than one in four (25%) disagree. However, few (10%) expect the Smith case to encourage future rape victims to come forward. Three in ten (29%) say that women will be less likely to report rape, while six in ten (58%) see little change as a result of the trial's publicity.

Television viewership of the trial was high, but it was not up to the extraordinary levels seen for the Clarence Thomas-Anita Hill hearings. Seven in ten (69%) saw at least part of the televised coverage of the Smith trial; the average viewer watched for about one hour. In contrast, 86% watched some of the Thomas-Hill hearings and the average viewer watched four hours. Most of those who watched, however, have misgivings about the idea of televising such trials. Three quarters (74%) say that, all things considered, the Smith trial should not have been televised.

The practice of protecting an alleged rape victim by keeping her name and face out of the news coverage is solidly endorsed by the public. Sixty-four percent agree with most news organizations' decision not to reveal the purported victim's name, and another 60% agree with the decision not to show her face on television.

Even John F. Kennedy's image may have suffered as a result of the alleged rape in West Palm Beach. In the years since his death, his brief presidency has been idealized by many Americans. In February 1991, before the incident at the Kennedy compound, nearly one half (48%) of respondents rated JFK as one of the three greatest presidents in U.S. history. Today, that percentage has decreased to four in ten (39%). Although he still rates ahead of every president except Abraham Lincoln, these latest results represent a significant decline in his stature among the public.

DECEMBER 18
SOVIET UNION

Interviewing Date: 12/12–15/91
Survey #GO 222027

Do you think the United States is doing too much, not enough, or about the right amount to help the Soviet Union in its current economic crisis?

Too much 35%
Not enough.......................................16
About right.......................................44
No opinion.. 5

Selected National Trend

	Too much	Not enough	About right	No opinion
1991				
August	19%	15%	62%	4%
July	20	9	64	7

Some people feel it is important that the United States now increase aid to the Soviet Union or its republics to help keep the situation there from threatening international stability. Others feel we can't afford to increase Soviet aid now because of our own economic problems. Which comes closer to your opinion?

Important to increase aid 21%
Can't afford to increase aid.....................74
No opinion.. 5

Which side do you think the United States should take regarding the future of the Soviet Union and its republics? Should the United States side with Mikhail Gorbachev, who wants to keep the Soviet Union together; side with Boris Yeltsin and others who want to divide the Soviet Union into individual republics or groups of republics; or remain neutral and take neither side?

Side with Gorbachev..............................15%
Side with Yeltsin.................................12
Remain neutral....................................68
No opinion.. 5

Note: Unhappy with the economic situation here at home, the American public solidly opposes sending new aid abroad to help the disintegrating Soviet Union or its former republics. According to a new Gallup Poll, three fourths (74%) see additional aid to the Soviets as unaffordable, given our own country's economic problems. One in five (21%) takes the opposite view, that new aid is critical to help keep the situation in the former Soviet republics from threatening international stability.

Even this past summer, after the failed coup in the Soviet Union, relatively few respondents thought that the United States should be doing more to help the Soviets in their economic crisis. A Gallup Poll in August found 15% saying that we were not doing enough, 19% saying too much, and a majority (62%) saying that we were providing about the right amount of help.

Since August, the percentage who say that the United States is going too far in helping the Soviets has almost doubled, from 19% to 35%. There has been no significant increase, however, in those who say that we are not doing enough (16% now versus 15% in August). Close to one half (44%) now says that our role in helping the Soviets is about right. Past Gallup Polls suggest that cost is the major factor behind this reluctance to provide additional assistance. Surveys taken during the summer found majority support for helping out through technical assistance or by sending surplus grain and farm products to the USSR.

Even though Mikhail Gorbachev has been a popular figure in this country in recent years, few (15%) think that we should side with him in his attempts to hold the Soviet Union together. However, even fewer (12%) think that the United States should side with Russian President Boris Yeltsin, whose power seems to grow stronger every day as the central government dissolves. Indeed, more than two thirds (68%) prefer that we take a neutral stance regarding the future of the Soviet republics.

DECEMBER 28
MOST ADMIRED MAN

Interviewing Date: 12/5–8/91
Survey #GO 222026

What man whom you have heard or read about, living today in any part of the world, do you admire the most? And who is your second choice?

The following are listed in order of frequency of mention, with first and second choices combined.

George Bush
Terry Anderson
Norman Schwarzkopf
Mikhail Gorbachev
Earvin "Magic" Johnson
Pope John Paul II
Billy Graham
Ronald Reagan
Nelson Mandela
Jesse Jackson ⎫ tied
Michael Jordan ⎭

Note: Despite his current woes, President George Bush easily outdistances this year's unexpected second choice, former hostage Terry Anderson. Besides Anderson there are three other newcomers to the most admired top ten: General Norman Schwarzkopf, third; former NBA star Earvin "Magic" Johnson (whose AIDS-induced retirement occurred shortly before the poll was conducted), fifth; and pro basketball superstar Michael Jordan, in a tie with Jesse Jackson for tenth place.

As for Anderson, it should be noted that the poll was conducted December 5–8. Coincidentally, his memorable and widely disseminated press conference took place on the morning of December 6, and he received his widest support on the nights of December 6–7.

In addition to President Bush and Jackson, the repeaters from 1990—who all finish further down the list this year—are Mikhail Gorbachev, Pope John Paul II, Billy Graham, Ronald Reagan, and Nelson Mandela. Since first making the list in 1955, Graham has been in the top ten thirty-five times.

Among the also-rans is Judge Clarence Thomas, in sixteenth place. Gone, however, from the 1990 list are mogul Donald Trump, former president Jimmy Carter, and Polish leader Lech Walesa.

DECEMBER 28
MOST ADMIRED WOMAN

Interviewing Date: 12/5–8/91
Survey #GO 222026

What woman whom you have heard or read about, living today in any part of the world, do you admire the most? And who is your second choice?

The following are listed in order of frequency of mention, with first and second choices combined.

Barbara Bush
Mother Teresa of Calcutta
Margaret Thatcher
Nancy Reagan
Oprah Winfrey
Jacqueline Kennedy Onassis
Elizabeth Taylor
Queen Elizabeth II
Sandra Day O'Connor
Betty Ford

Note: For only the eighth time in the forty-five-year history of the Gallup Poll's "most admired" lists, both the president and the First Lady appear at the top. This is somewhat surprising when one notes that the president of the United States has topped the list thirty-eight times. However, an incumbent First Lady has led the way only nine times: Jacqueline Kennedy in 1962; Pat Nixon in 1972; Rosalyn Carter in 1977, 1979, and 1980; Nancy Reagan in 1981, 1985, and 1987; and Barbara Bush today. Mrs. Carter holds a unique distinction: she was the only First Lady to lead the list when her husband did not (1980). Mrs. Bush completed her ascendance to the top (from third in 1989 and second in 1990) by a somewhat narrower margin over perennial favorite Mother Teresa.

Once again, there are far fewer changes on the women's list. The first five (Mrs. Bush, Mother Teresa, former British prime minister Margaret Thatcher, Mrs. Reagan, and Oprah Winfrey) are the same, albeit in different order. Among the other five, only Queen Elizabeth and Sandra Day O'Connor were absent from last year's list, and both had made multiple past appearances. The remaining three repeaters— Jacqueline Kennedy Onassis, Elizabeth Taylor, and Betty Ford—are veterans, with Mrs. Onassis making a record twenty-seventh appearance since 1960. Cut from the 1990 top ten are Cher, Elizabeth Dole, Corazon Aquino, and Jeane Kirkpatrick. Cher, in seventh place last year, just missed the list this year; she is tied for eleventh place with Clarence Thomas's accuser, Anita Hill.

INDEX

AIDS (*continued*)
  cost of treating patients, as reason health-care
    costs are rising, 157
  couples applying for marriage licenses should be
    tested for, 114
  dentists should be tested for, 114
  doctors should be tested for, 114
  efforts to reduce spread of AIDS among young
    people should focus on safe sex, 234–35
  employers have right to dismiss employee with,
    114
  ever had your blood tested for, 235
  everyone should have blood test to see if they
    have, 114
  government is not doing enough about problem
    of, 114
  immigrants should be tested for, 114
  inmates of federal prisons should be tested for,
    114
  landlords should have right to evict tenant who
    has, 114
  last time you had AIDS test, was it [reasons
    listed], 235
  major television networks should accept
    advertising from condom manufacturers, 235
  members of armed forces should be tested for,
    114
  as most important problem facing this country
    today, 244
  as most urgent health problem, 113–14
  nurses should be tested for, 114
  people with AIDS should be isolated, 114
  people with AIDS should be made to carry card,
    114
  people's own fault if they get, 114
  plan to have your blood tested for, in next twelve
    months, 235
  as punishment for decline in moral standards, 114
  refuse to work alongside someone who has, 114
  visitors from foreign countries should be tested
    for, 114
Alaska oil spill
  agree with judge's ruling that fine for Exxon
    Corporation was not enough, 95–96
Alcohol abuse
  as most urgent health problem, 113
  use of health-care system for treatment of, as
    reason why health-care costs are rising, 157
Anderson, Terry
  as most admired man, 254
Arab nations
  as result of Persian Gulf war, prospects for peace
    between Israel and its Arab neighbors have
    improved, 151

  doing as much as they can to support United
    States in Persian Gulf, 24
  favor proposal that Israel withdraw from occupied
    Arab lands if Arab nations recognize Israel's
    right to exist, 81, 176, 200
      national trend, 201
  if Israel did give up occupied Arab lands, how
    likely is it that this would bring lasting
    peace, 81, 176
  Israel or Arab countries more to blame for lack of
    progress in settling their differences, 201
  Israel and the Arab nations will settle their
    differences, 80, 175
      national trend, 81, 175
  will this happen [Israel and the Arab nations
    settling their differences] during next five
    years, 81, 175
      national trend, 81, 176
  See also Palestine (Palestinian Arabs)
Argentina, respondents in
  1991 as peaceful or troubled year, 1
  1991 will be better or worse than 1990, 1
Australia, respondents in
  1991 as peaceful or troubled year, 1
  1991 will be better or worse than 1990, 2
Austria, respondents in
  1991 as peaceful or troubled year, 1
  1991 will be better or worse than 1990, 2
Automobiles and their drivers
  age at which person should no longer be
    permitted to drive, 101
  do you belong to any car club, 103
  do you change the oil, 103
  do you do body work, 103
  do you do major repairs to engine, 103
  do you do minor engine maintenance, 102
  do you drive, 100
  do you have driver's license, 100
  do you have in your car an audio cassette or CD
    player, 102
  do you have in your car a burglar alarm, 102
  do you have in your car a car telephone, 102
  do you have in your car a radar detector, 102
  do you have in your car a television set, 102
  do you like to drive, 102
  do you paint car, 103
  do you subscribe to any automobile magazine,
    103
  do you think of your car just as transportation or
    as something special, 100
  do you wash or wax car, 102
  does your car have custom engine equipment, 102
  does your car have custom undercarriage, 102
  does your car have customized body parts, 102

Automobiles (*continued*)
within last twelve months, have you read while driving, 103

B

Baker, James
as choice for Bush's running mate in 1992, 61
dealing with Persian Gulf crisis, 22
handling situation in Persian Gulf, 69, 150
if Bush decides not to run, would you like to see him nominated as Republican party's candidate for president, 182

Bangladesh
typhoon in, as most closely followed news story, 107

Bankers
honesty rating, 115
national trend, 116

Banks
Savings and Loan crisis, handled by Bush, 72
your confidence in, 69, 213
national trend, 69, 213

Belgium, respondents in
1991 as peaceful or troubled year, 1
1991 will be better or worse than 1990, 2

Bentsen, Lloyd
like to see him nominated as Democratic candidate for president, 62, 97, 135, 186
your opinion of, as presidential candidate, 62, 97, 186

Biden, Joseph
your opinion of, 210

Blacks
approve of marriage between blacks and whites, 177
national trend, 177
black children have as good chance as white children in your community to get good education, 168
national trend, 168
black person more likely than white person to receive death penalty for same crime, 130–31
companies should be required to hire same proportion of blacks and minorities as live in surrounding community, 126
favor giving them preference over whites, because of past discrimination, 231
favor increasing federal assistance to blacks who want to start their own businesses, 169
favor more Head Start programs, 169
favor new laws requiring businesses to hire, in same proportion as in community, 169
favor spending more on job-training programs, 169
favor spending more to improve schools in black communities, 169
favor tougher laws for companies which discriminate in hiring and promoting, 169
have as good chance as white people in your community to get housing, 167–68
national trend, 168
have as good chance as white people in your community to get job, 167
national trend, 167
prefer term "African-American" or "black," 177
quality of life has gotten better for, 166–67
national trend, 167

Bradley, Bill
like to see him nominated as Democratic candidate for president, 62
your opinion of, as presidential candidate, 62

Brazil, respondents in
1991 as peaceful or troubled year, 1
1991 will be better or worse than 1990, 1

Brown, Jerry
like to see him nominated as Democratic candidate for president, 186, 196, 226
your opinion of, as presidential candidate, 186, 195, 225
national trend, 195, 225

Buchanan, Pat
his political views too extreme to consider him for president, 248
like to see him nominated as Republican candidate for president, 248
your opinion of, 248

Budget deficit, federal
Bush making progress on reducing, 74
national trend, 75
as Democrats' campaign issue in 1992, 187
how important is reducing, 202
as important issue in determining which presidential candidate you will vote for, 224
as most important problem facing this country today, 53, 96, 125, 197, 244
reduce, if defense budget is cut, 202
reducing, as Bush's greatest achievement, 70
Republican or Democratic party better at dealing with, 198, 227

Building contractors
honesty rating, 115
national trend, 116

Bulgaria, respondents in
how does financial situation of your household compare to twelve months ago, 3
how has economic situation in this country changed, 2

Bush, George (*continued*)

happen to see or hear his address to nation [Jan. 16], 26

happen to see or hear his State of the Union address [Jan. 29], 46

his health, as most closely followed news story, 107

how closely have you followed Iraqi-Soviet proposal to end the war in the Gulf and his reaction to it, 63

how closely have you followed Iraq's proposal to end Gulf war and his reaction to it, 57

how would you rate Democrats' chance of defeating, 186, 196

if he and Quayle run for reelection, are you more likely to vote for Bush and Quayle or for Democratic party's candidates, 182

if he chooses new running mate for 1992, which [list] would you like to see him choose, 61–62

if he decides not to run for reelection, which [list] would you like to see nominated, 182

if he keeps Quayle as his running mate, would you be more likely to vote for Bush's reelection, 232

if he runs for reelection, should he keep Quayle as his running mate, 61, 108, 182, 233
> by key voter groups, 182
> national trend, 108, 182, 233

if the Democratic presidential candidate voted against resolution allowing Bush to use force in Gulf war, would you be more likely to vote for him, 98, 151–52

like to see him nominated as Republican candidate for president, 248

likely to vote for his reelection, if he vetoes bill extending unemployment benefits, 202

likely to vote for his reelection, if he vetoes bill requiring companies to give unpaid leave, 202

making progress on avoiding raising taxes, 75
> national trend, 75

making progress on getting drug crisis under control, 75
> national trend, 75

making progress on improving educational standards, 74
> national trend, 74

making progress on improving the lot of minorities and the poor, 74
> national trend, 74

making progress on improving quality of environment, 75
> national trend, 75

making progress on increasing respect for United States abroad, 74
> national trend, 74

making progress on keeping America prosperous, 74
> national trend, 74

making progress on keeping nation out of war, 73
> national trend, 74

making progress on reducing crime rate, 74
> national trend, 74

making progress on reducing federal budget deficit, 74
> national trend, 75

more likely to vote for him or for Democratic party's candidate for president, 62, 97, 185, 195, 218, 224, 232, 245–46
> national trend, 98, 185, 195, 218, 224, 246

as most admired man, 254

performance rating on his being efficient manager, 72
> national trend, 72

performance rating on his being good representative of United States, 73
> national trend, 73

performance rating on his being inspirational leader, 73
> national trend, 73

performance rating on his communicating his ideas to the public, 73
> national trend, 73

performance rating on his developing programs to address pressing problems, 72
> national trend, 72

performance rating on his following through on his ideas, 73
> national trend, 73

performance rating on his making good appointments, 72
> national trend, 72

performance rating on his working effectively with Congress, 73
> national trend, 73

should have given Hussein longer to begin withdrawal, 63

should have waited longer for Soviet and other diplomatic efforts to end Gulf war, 64

tell me name of his recent nomination to Supreme Court, 137

in trial heat with Cuomo, 218

in trial heat with Schwarzkopf, 84

when choosing Democratic presidential candidate, would you prefer one who

supported Bush's decision to go to war
against Iraq, 136

whether Democratic presidential candidate
supported Bush's decision to go to war
against Iraq, as important consideration in
selecting him, 135

why has he refused to support Democratic version
of civil rights bill, 127

willing to negotiate to end the war, 64

your confidence in, as result of change in his
chief of staff, 246

your confidence in, as result of Clarence Thomas
hearings, 210

your opinion of, 248

Bush administration

approve of way it has responded to situation in
Wichita [efforts of Operation Rescue to stop
abortion clinics], 189

cooperative in news coverage of Gulf war, 33, 61
national trend, 61

gone too far in expressing disapproval of
removal from power of Gorbachev [Aug. 19],
179

have it and U.S. military done as well as you
expected in Persian Gulf, 31, 36
national trend, 36

which civil rights bill requires racial quotas in
hiring and promotion, 127

which of two civil rights bills would you like to
see passed, 126–27

Business and industry

companies should be required to hire same
proportion of blacks and minorities as live
in surrounding community, 126

favor laws requiring businesses to hire blacks in
same proportion as in community, 169

favor tougher laws for companies which
discriminate in hiring and promoting, 169

how would you describe business conditions in
your community, 147
national trend, 147

likely to vote for Bush's reelection, if he vetoes
bill requiring companies to give unpaid
leave, 202

more likely that companies will take strong steps
against sexual harassment, as result of Anita
Hill's charges, 217

U.S. production of quality products is strong
compared to Japan, Great Britain, and
Germany, 91

U.S. technical innovation is strong compared to
Japan, Great Britain, and Germany, 92

which of two civil rights bills requires racial
quotas in hiring and promotion, 127

worried about environment, 88

your confidence in big business, 69, 214
national trend, 69, 214

Business executives

honesty rating, 115
national trend, 116

C

Cabinet

performance rating on Bush's making good
appointments to, 72

Canada

as America's largest trading partner, 91

happen to know name of prime minister of, 91

tell me name of its capital city, 91

Canada, respondents in

costs that [you] pay for health care are very high,
153

free-trade zone would be good or bad for Canada,
84–85

heard or read about free-trade zone with United
States and Mexico, 84

1991 as peaceful or troubled year, 1

1991 will be better or worse than 1990, 2

quality rating of health care in your community,
153

which country would benefit most from free-trade
zone, 85

your impression that Canada or United States has
better system of health care, 153

Cancer

as most urgent health problem, 113–14

Carter, Jimmy

approval rating compared to Bush, 39, 68, 164,
229, 245

as greatest president, 252

handling problems the country faces as well as
anyone, 246

Census, federal

government should estimate to count minorities
and the poor, 94–95

Central America

situation in, handled by Bush, 71
national trend, 71

Cheney, Dick

as choice for Bush's running mate in 1992,
62

handling situation in Persian Gulf, 69

if Bush decides not to run, would you like to see
him nominated as Republican party's
candidate for president, 182

Children

and the family, as Democrats' campaign issue in
1992, 187

Children (*continued*)
 childhood diseases and child abuse, as most
  urgent health problems, 113–14
 See also Persian Gulf war, since war began
Chile, respondents in
 1991 as peaceful or troubled year, 1
 1991 will be better or worse than 1990, 1
Civil rights
 enough federal laws aimed at reducing race,
  religion, and sex discrimination, 126, 168–
  69
 ever been victim of discrimination, 168
 how much progress has been made in, 166
   national trend, 166
 women and members of minority groups should
  be given preferential treatment, 168
   national trend, 168
 See also Blacks; Racial quotas
Civil War
 whether it is a "just" war, 57
Clergy
 honesty rating, 115
   national trend, 115
Clinton, Bill
 like to see him nominated as Democratic
  candidate for president, 62, 97, 135, 186,
  196, 226
 your opinion of, as presidential candidate, 62,
  97, 186, 195, 225–26
   national trend, 195, 226
Columbus, Christopher
 do you know what his nationality was, 204
 do you know where in the New World he first
  landed, 204
 do you know which country's flag he sailed under,
  204
 do you know the year that he first sailed to the
  New World, 204
 doesn't deserve credit for discovering America,
  202
 should be regarded as hero or villain, 204–5
 who first discovered America, 204
Congress
 approval rating, 161–62
   national trend, 162
 approve of Democratic leaders dealing with
  Persian Gulf crisis, 23
 approve of Republican leaders dealing with
  Persian Gulf crisis, 23
 Bush or it more to blame for nation's economic
  problems, 198
 enough federal laws aimed at reducing race,
  religion, and sex discrimination, 126, 168–
  69

 favor having it investigate charges that Reagan-
  Bush campaign made deal with Iran to delay
  release of U.S. hostages, 137
 favor its passing bill banning hiring of
  permanent replacement workers during
  strikes, 154–55
 favor its passing law to allow federally funded
  clinics to provide information about
  abortion, 120–21
 favor raising senators' salaries, 162
 handling situation in Persian Gulf, 69, 150
 honesty rating of congressmen, 115
   national trend, 116
 honesty rating of senators, 115
   national trend, 116
 if your senator voted against Clarence Thomas,
  would that make you more likely to vote for
  his reelection, 216
 if your senator voted in favor of Clarence
  Thomas, would that make you more likely to
  vote for his reelection, 193, 216
   national trend, 216
 like to see it vote in favor of proposed nuclear
  arms-reduction treaty, 145
 like to see Senate vote in favor of Robert Gates as
  CIA director, 171
 performance rating on Bush's working
  effectively with, 73
   national trend, 73
 role of, in determining policy in Persian Gulf
  crisis, 25
 seen or heard about civil rights bill now before it,
  126
 vote for candidates who favor allowing federally
  funded clinics to provide abortion
  information, 121
 which of two civil rights bills would you like to
  see it pass, 126–27
 why are Democrats supporting new civil rights
  legislation, 127
 why has Bush refused to support Democratic
  version of civil rights bill, 127
 your confidence in, 69, 214
   national trend, 69, 214–15
 your confidence in, as result of Clarence Thomas
  hearings, 210
Consumer products
 favor ban on chlorofluorocarbons even if it
  meant higher prices for, 88
 favor tax on corporations which produce
  environmentally harmful products, which
  might raise the cost of, 89
Costa Rica, respondents in
 1991 as peaceful or troubled year, 1

1991 will be better or worse than 1990, 2

Crime

approve of Supreme Court's rulings in cases where rights of prisoners are an issue, 138

handled by Bush, 72

as important issue in determining which presidential candidate you will vote for, 224

as most important problem facing this country today, 197, 244

Republican or Democratic party better at dealing with, 198, 227

Crime rate

Bush making progress on reducing, 74

national trend, 74

Cuomo, Mario

like to see him nominated as Democratic candidate for president, 62, 97, 135, 186, 196, 226

in trial heat with Bush, 218

your opinion of, as presidential candidate, 62, 97, 186, 195, 225

national trend, 195, 225

Czechoslovakia

if Soviet Union should seek to regain control of, should United States send troops, 179

Czechoslovakia, respondents in

how does financial situation of your household compare to twelve months ago, 3

how has economic situation in this country changed, 2

in 1991, number of unemployed will increase, 3

in 1991, strikes will increase, 3

1991 as peaceful or troubled year, 3

1991 will be better or worse than 1990, 3

1991 will be year of economic prosperity or difficulty, 3

D

Death and dying

discussed whether you should be kept on life-support systems, 5

do you believe in life after death, 5

do you believe in reincarnation, 6

do you fear death, 6

do you have "living will," 5

do you have a will, 6

had unusual experience on verge of death, 6

how often do you think about your death, 6

if you were on life-support systems, would you like to remain on life-support system or end your life, 5

is there a heaven, 5

is there a hell, 5

like to have "living will," 5

made any arrangements for your burial, 6

patient has right to stop treatment, 5

person has moral right to end his life under these circumstances [list], 4

prefer to be buried or cremated, 6

when person cannot be cured, doctors should be allowed to end patient's life, 4–5

your chances of going to Heaven, 5

your chances of going to Hell, 5–6

Death penalty

acts as deterrent to commitment of murder, 130

national trend, 130

black person more likely than white person to receive, for same crime, 130–31

Democratic presidential candidate's views on, as important consideration in selecting him, 135

favor, for persons convicted of murder, 128–29, 231

national trend, 129

favor if it acts as deterrent to murder, 130

national trend, 130

favor if it does not act as deterrent to murder, 130

national trend, 130

poor person more likely than average-income person to receive, for same crime, 131

what form of punishment do you consider most humane, 132

what should be the penalty for murder—death or life imprisonment, 129–30

when choosing Democratic presidential candidate, would you prefer one who favors, 136

why do you favor, for persons convicted of murder, 129

why do you oppose, for persons convicted of murder, 129

Defense, national

amount now being spent for, 110, 202

national trend, 110, 202

Democrats are too weak on, 98

as important issue in determining which presidential candidate you will vote for, 224

increase spending on domestic problems, if defense budget is cut, 202

provide financial aid to Soviet Union, if defense budget is cut, 202

reduce federal budget deficit, if defense budget is cut, 202

reduce taxes, if defense budget is cut, 202

Republican or Democratic party better at dealing with, 198, 228

Defense, national (*continued*)

    in which area [list] would you like to see money
used, if defense budget is cut, 202

Democratic party

    approve of Democratic congressional leaders
dealing with Persian Gulf crisis, 23

    best serves middle-income people, 199

    best serves people like yourself, 199

    best serves poor people, 199

    best serves wealthy people, 199

    better at dealing with abortion issue, 199, 227

    better at dealing with crime, 198, 227

    better at dealing with economic conditions, 198,
227

    better at dealing with education, 227

    better at dealing with environmental issues, 199,
227

    better at dealing with federal budget deficit, 198,
227

    better at dealing with foreign policy, 198, 228

    better at dealing with health-care policy, 199,
227

    better at dealing with national defense, 198,
228

    better at dealing with poverty and homelessness,
199, 227

    better at dealing with race relations, 199, 227

    better at dealing with relations with Soviet
Union, 198

    better at dealing with tax policy, 227

    better at dealing with unemployment, 199,
227

    better at handling most important problem facing
this country today, 96, 197, 244

        national trend, 244–45

    better at keeping country prosperous, 148, 223

        national trend, 148, 223

    better reflects your views on abortion, 122–23

    do you associate it more with political favoritism
and corruption, 198

    do you consider yourself a Democrat, 165

        national trend, 165

    if Bush and Quayle run for reelection, are you
more likely to vote for them or for party's
candidates, 182

    if Quayle were the Republican candidate for
president in 1996, would you be more likely
to vote for him or for the Democratic
candidate, 182

    like to see party and its candidates move more
conservative or liberal, 98

    as more likely to keep United States out of war,
148

        national trend, 148

    more likely to vote for Bush or for Democratic
candidate for president, 62, 97, 185, 195,
218, 224, 232, 245–46

        national trend, 98, 185, 195, 218,
224, 246

    as relying too much on increasing taxes and
government spending to deal with problems,
98

    as too supportive of racial quotas, 98

    as too weak on foreign policy and national
defense, 98

    which civil rights bill requires racial quotas in
hiring and promotion, 127

    which of two civil rights bills would you like to
see passed, 126–27

    why are congressional Democrats supporting new
civil rights legislation, 127

    why has Bush refused to support Democratic
version of civil rights bill, 127

    your opinion of, rated, 198, 216

        national trend, 198, 216

Democratic presidential candidates

    his support for new taxes to solve certain
problems, as important consideration in
selecting, 135

    his views on abortion, as important
consideration in selecting, 135

    his views on death penalty, as important
consideration in selecting, 135

    his views on government assistance to private
and parochial school parents, as important
consideration in selecting, 135

    his views on gun control, as important
consideration in selecting, 135

    his views on health-care system, as important
consideration in selecting, 135

    his views on protecting women and minorities
from job discrimination without using
quotas, as important consideration in
selecting, 135

    his views on trade policies toward Japan, as
important consideration in selecting, 135

    how would you rate the Democrats' chance of
defeating Bush, 186, 196

    if candidate voted against resolution allowing
Bush to use force in Gulf war, would you be
more likely to vote for him, 98, 151–52

    like to see Democratic party and its candidates
move more conservative or liberal, 98

    like to see Schwarzkopf become candidate, 84

    prefer candidate who favors death penalty, 136

    prefer candidate who favors government
assistance to private and parochial school
parents, 136

Eastern Europe (*continued*)

    if Soviet Union seeks to regain control of these nations, should United States send troops, 179

    situation in, handled by Bush, 71

        national trend, 71

Eastern Europe, respondents in. *See* Bulgaria; Czechoslovakia; Hungary; Poland; Yugoslavia

Economic conditions

    Bush or Congress more to blame for nation's problems, 198

    handled by Bush, 172, 188, 194, 203, 246

        national trend, 172, 188, 194–95, 246

    as important issue in determining which presidential candidate you will vote for, 224

    in country as a whole, getting better or worse, 147, 191, 219, 250

        national trend, 219, 250

    Republican or Democratic party better at dealing with, 198, 227

Economic situation

    how has it changed over last twelve months, asked in five East European countries, 2

    1991 will be year of economic prosperity or difficulty, asked in five East European countries, 3

Economy

    as Bush's greatest achievement, 70

    as Democrats' campaign issue in 1992, 187

    as most closely followed news story, 107

    as most important problem facing this country today, 12, 53, 96, 125, 197, 244

    protection of environment or economic growth should be given priority, 88–89

Education

    Bush making progress on improving standards, 74

        national trend, 74

    Democratic presidential candidate's views on government assistance to private and parochial school parents, as important consideration in selecting him, 135

    ever been victim of discrimination in, 168

    favor allowing parents to send children to parochial or private school and use tax dollars to pay for it, 92

    favor busing children to achieve better racial balance in public schools, 231

    favor national test to measure abilities of students across country, 92

    favor program to pay teachers more if they went beyond regular duties, 93

    favor use of government grants to invent new types of public schools, 93

    how much would it [national test for students] improve quality of, 92

    how much would it [paying teachers more if they went beyond regular duties] improve quality of, 93

    how much would it [sending children to parochial or private school paid for by tax dollars] improve quality of, 92–93

    how much would it [use grants to invent new types of schools] improve quality of, 93–94

    as important issue in determining which presidential candidate you will vote for, 224

    increase spending on, if defense budget is cut, 202

    investment in space research would be better spent on, 111

        national trend, 111

    lack of, as most urgent health problem, 113

    as most important problem facing this country today, 96, 125, 197, 244

    policy, as Bush's greatest achievement, 70

    policy, handled by Bush, 71

        national trend, 71

    public, amount now being spent to improve quality of, 111

        national trend, 111

    public, as Democrats' campaign issue in 1992, 187

    public, your confidence in, 69, 213

        national trend, 69, 213

    Republican or Democratic party better at dealing with, 227

    U.S. system is strong compared to Japan, Great Britain, and Germany, 91

    when choosing Democratic presidential candidate, would you prefer one who favors government assistance to private and parochial school parents, 136

    See also Blacks

Egypt

    your overall opinion of, 51, 80, 174

        national trend, 174

Eisenhower, Dwight

    approval rating compared to Bush, 39, 68, 164, 229, 245

    as greatest president, 252

Elderly people

    don't have coverage, as biggest problem with health care, 156

    problems of aging, as most urgent health problem, 113–14

Elizabeth II, Queen
  as most admired woman, 254
Energy situation
  handled by Bush, 72
Engineers
  honesty rating, 115
    national trend, 115
Environment
  agree with judge's ruling that fine for Exxon
    Corporation was not enough, 95–96
  American public is worried about, 87
  are you a strong environmentalist, 86
  Bush making progress on improving quality of,
    74
    national trend, 74
  business and industry are worried about, 88
  consider yourself to be an environmentalist, 86
    national trend, 86
  as Democrats' campaign issue in 1992, 187
  does your community require sorting garbage so
    that materials can be recycled, 88
  favor ban on chlorofluorocarbons even if it
    meant higher prices for consumer products,
    88
  favor tax on corporations which produce
    environmentally harmful products, 89
  government is worried about, 88
  how concerned are you that Iraq's setting fire to
    oil refineries in Kuwait will lead to major
    ecological problems, 43
  how much optimism do you have that we will
    have our environmental problems under
    control by 2011, 88
  how much progress have we made in dealing with
    environmental problems since 1970, 88
  as important issue in determining which
    presidential candidate you will vote for, 224
  life on earth will continue only if we take actions
    [list], 87
  likely that Iraqis will unleash new threats to, 47
  as most important problem facing this country
    today, 96, 244
  protection of environment or economic growth
    should be given priority, 88–89
  what have you done [list] to improve quality of,
    88
  worry about acid rain, 87
  worry about air pollution, 87
  worry about contamination by radioactivity from
    nuclear facilities, 87
  worry about contamination by toxic waste, 86–
    87
  worry about damage to ozone layer, 87
  worry about "greenhouse effect," 87

worry about loss of natural habitats for wildlife,
  87
worry about loss of tropical rain forests, 87
worry about ocean and beach pollution, 87
worry about pollution of drinking water, 86
worry about pollution of rivers, lakes, and
  reservoirs, 86
Environmental issues
  handled by Bush, 70
    national trend, 70
  Republican or Democratic party better at dealing
    with, 199, 227
Ethics
  decline in, as most important problem facing this
    country today, 12, 96, 197, 244
European nations
  doing as much as they can to support United
    States in Persian Gulf, 24

F

Financial situation
  personal, better off next year than now, 28, 68–
    69, 90, 146, 191, 219, 249–50
    national trend, 28, 69, 90, 146–47,
      191, 219, 250
  personal, better off now than a year ago, 27–28,
    68, 90, 145–46, 190, 219, 249
    national trend, 28, 68, 90, 146, 191,
      219, 249
  of your household, compared to twelve months
    ago, asked in five East European countries,
    3
  See also Recession
Finland, respondents in
  1991 as peaceful or troubled year, 1
  1991 will be better or worse than 1990, 2
Ford, Betty
  as most admired woman, 254
Ford, Gerald
  approval rating compared to Bush, 68, 164,
    229
Foreign affairs
  Quayle as knowledgeable about, 109
Foreign policy
  as Bush's greatest achievement, 70
  Democrats are too weak on, 98
  handled by Bush, 67, 70, 172–73, 188, 195,
    203, 246
    national trend, 71, 188, 195, 246
  as important issue in determining which
    presidential candidate you will vote for,
    224
  Republican or Democratic party better at dealing
    with, 198, 228

France
    your overall opinion of, 51
France, respondents in
    1991 as peaceful or troubled year, 1
    1991 will be better or worse than 1990, 2
Free trade
    free-trade zone with Canada and Mexico, as good
        or bad for United States, 85
    read or heard about North American free-trade
        zone with Canada and Mexico, 84
    which country—Canada, United States, or
        Mexico—would benefit most from free-trade
        zone, 85
Funeral directors
    honesty rating, 115
            national trend, 116

G

Gates, Robert
    like to see Senate vote in favor of, as CIA
        director, 171
Gephardt, Richard
    like to see him nominated as Democratic
        candidate for president, 62, 97, 135
    your opinion of, as presidential candidate, 62,
        97
Germany
    U.S. production of quality products is strong
        compared to, 91
    U.S. standard of living is strong compared to,
        92
    U.S. system of public education is strong
        compared to, 91
    U.S. technical innovation is strong compared to,
        92
    your overall opinion of, 51
Germany, respondents in
    1991 as peaceful or troubled year, 1
    1991 will be better or worse than 1990, 2
Gorbachev Mikhail
    as result of recent changes in leadership [Aug.
        19], he will resume power later, 179
    as result of recent changes in leadership [Aug.
        19], relations between Soviet Union and
        United States will go back to where they were
        before he came to power, 179
    Bush administration has gone too far in
        expressing disapproval of his removal from
        power [Aug. 19], 179
    getting along with, as Bush's greatest
        achievement, 70
    handling situation in Persian Gulf, 69, 150
    his attempts to restructure Soviet economy are
        likely to succeed, 52, 143

national trend, 144
    how closely have you followed his replacement
        with new leadership [Aug. 19], 179
    as most admired man, 254
    United States did too much to support his efforts
        at reform, 179
    United States should deal primarily with him or
        Yeltsin, 185
    United States should side with him or Yeltsin,
        253
    your overall opinion of, 51–52, 143, 178, 183
            national trend, 52, 143, 178
Gore, Albert
    like to see him nominated as Democratic
        candidate for president, 62, 97, 135
    your opinion of, as presidential candidate, 62,
        97
Government
    Democrats rely too much on government
        spending to deal with problems, 98
    dissatisfaction with, as most important problem
        facing this country today, 244
    favor reducing size and budget of all agencies,
        except for law enforcement, 231
Governors
    approval rating, 247
Graham, Billy
    as most admired man, 254
Gramm, Phil
    if Bush decides not to run, would you like to see
        him nominated as Republican party's
        candidate for president, 182
Great Britain
    U.S. production of quality products is strong
        compared to, 91
    U.S. standard of living is strong compared to,
        92
    U.S. system of public education is strong
        compared to, 91
    U.S. technical innovation is strong compared to,
        92
    your overall opinion of, 51
Great Britain, respondents in
    1991 as peaceful or troubled year, 1
    1991 will be better or worse than 1990, 2
Greece, respondents in
    1991 as peaceful or troubled year, 1
    1991 will be better or worse than 1990, 2
Gun control
    Democratic presidential candidate's views on, as
        important consideration in selecting him,
        135
    do you have a gun in the house, 83, 116–17
            national trend, 83, 117

favor law requiring seven-day waiting period
before purchase, 83
national trend, 83
favor law requiring that any person who carries
gun must have license, 83
national trend, 83
favor registration of all handguns, 82
national trend, 82
is it [gun in your house] a pistol, shotgun, rifle,
or what, 83
national trend, 83
law would ban possession of handguns except by
police, 82
national trend, 83
laws covering sale of firearms should be more
strict, 82
national trend, 82
total number of guns kept in your house, 83
national trend, 83
when choosing Democratic presidential
candidate, would you prefer one who favors
stricter laws, 135
See also Handgun ownership

H

Handgun ownership
ever carry your handgun in your car or truck, 117–
18
ever carry your handgun on your person, 117
ever fired the gun, 118
ever used your handgun to defend yourself, 118
has handgun ever been used to threaten you, 118
have a gun anywhere else on your property, 117
is it [gun anywhere else on your property] a
pistol, shotgun, rifle, or what, 117
national trend, 117
is this gun yours, 117
is your gun loaded now, 118
know how to use your gun if you had to, 118
know where your handgun is now, 117
right to own gun is guaranteed by Constitution,
118
See also Gun control
Harkin, Tom
like to see him nominated as Democratic
candidate for president, 186, 196, 226
your opinion of, as presidential candidate, 186,
195, 225
national trend, 195, 225
Hatch, Orrin
your opinion of, 210
Health care
Americans are living longer, as reason costs are
rising, 157

amount doctors are charging, as reason costs are
rising, 157
amount hospitals are charging, as reason costs
are rising, 157
amount now being spent for improving medical
and, 110
national trend, 110
anyone in your family experienced catastrophic
illness or needed nursing home care, 159
availability of, handled by Bush, 72
biggest problem [list] today with, 156
cost of prescription drugs, as reason costs are
rising, 157
cost of treating AIDS patients, as reason costs are
rising, 157
costs that [you] pay for, are very high, 153
crisis in, in this country today, 156
Democratic presidential candidate's views on, as
important consideration in selecting him,
135
as Democrats' campaign issue in 1992, 187
do you get your insurance through employer,
159
do you have a personal doctor, 158
do you pay portion of cost for your health
insurance, 160
does system need reforming, 156
ever put off going to doctor because of cost, 158
favor plan in which businesses provide coverage
for their employees or favor national plan
run by government, 160
government should provide medical care for
people who are unable to pay for it, 160
have there been times when you did not have
money enough to pay for, 159
how confident are you that you have enough
money for major illness, 159
how confident are you that you have enough
money for nursing home care, 159
how confident are you that you have enough
money for routine health care, 159
how many times have you been treated at hospital
emergency room, 158
how many times have you spent at least one
night in hospital, 158
how many times have you visited a doctor, 157
how much of cost of [catastrophic] illness did
health insurance cover, 159
how satisfied are you with quality of medical care
you receive, 157
how satisfied are you with your ability to find
appropriate medical care, 156
how satisfied are you with your ability to pay for
medical care, 157

Health care (*continued*)

    how satisfied were you with treatment on your last stay in hospital, 158

    how satisfied were you with treatment on your last visit to doctor, 157

    how satisfied were you with treatment on your last visit to emergency room, 158

    how worried are you that someone in your family will experience catastrophic illness or need nursing home care, 159

    if you needed to go to hospital emergency room, how easy would it be for you to find one, 158

    if you needed to see doctor, how easy would it be for you to find one, 158

    increase spending on, if defense budget is cut, 202

    investment in space research would be better spent on, 111

    malpractice lawsuits, as reason costs are rising, 157

    as most important problem facing this country today, 197, 244

    most urgent health problem [list] facing this country, 113

    new equipment and technology, as reason costs are rising, 157

    people without insurance, as reason costs are rising, 157

    personally covered by health insurance, 159

    quality rating of, in your community, 153

    satisfied with your health insurance coverage, 160

    use of system for treatment of drug and alcohol abuse, as reason costs are rising, 157

    when choosing Democratic presidential candidate, would you prefer one who favors national system, 135

    when you see doctor, is it usually one you selected yourself, 158

    why are you dissatisfied [reasons listed] with your health insurance coverage, 160

    your impression that Canada or United States has better system of, 153

Health-care policy

    handled by Bush, 246

    as important issue in determining which presidential candidate you will vote for, 224

    Republican or Democratic party better at dealing with, 199, 227

Heart disease

    as most urgent health problem, 113–14

Heflin, Howell

    your opinion of, 210

Hill, Anita

    did Senate mishandle her charges by not investigating more thoroughly, 207

    happen to watch televised Senate hearings on her charges against Clarence Thomas, 208

    how many hours did you spend watching hearings, 208

    more likely that companies will take strong steps against sexual harassment, as result of her charges, 217

    more likely that women will report cases of sexual harassment, as result of her charges, 217

    whom do you believe more—her or Clarence Thomas, 206–7, 209

            national trend, 209

    your impression of, 209

Homelessness

    as Democrats' campaign issue in 1992, 187

    handled by Bush, 71

            national trend, 71

    as important issue in determining which presidential candidate you will vote for, 224

    increase spending on, if defense budget is cut, 202

    as most important problem facing this country today, 12, 53, 96, 125, 197, 244

    Republican or Democratic party better at dealing with, 199, 227

Hong Kong, respondents in

    1991 as peaceful or troubled year, 1

    1991 will be better or worse than 1990, 2

Hungary

    as result of recent changes in leadership in Soviet Union, it will attempt to regain control of, 179

    if Soviet Union should seek to regain control of, should United States send troops, 179

Hungary, respondents in

    how does financial situation of your household compare to twelve months ago, 3

    how has economic situation in this country changed, 2

    in 1991, number of unemployed will increase, 3

    in 1991, strikes will increase, 3

    1991 as peaceful or troubled year, 1, 3

    1991 will be better or worse than 1990, 2, 3

    1991 will be year of economic prosperity or difficulty, 3

Hussein, Saddam

    Bush should have given him longer to begin withdrawal, 63

favor leaving UN sanctions against Iraq in place as long as he remains in power, 125, 150–51

favor temporary cease-fire by United States as sign of good faith and to provide time for settlement with him, 59

how concerned are you that he will again pose military threat, 150

if he agrees to withdraw from Kuwait, would you favor immediate cease-fire by United States, 59

if he holds conference for withdrawal from Kuwait, should United States postpone any action, 11–12

if he is removed from power, should United States offer aid to rebuild Iraq, 151

if United States does resume action against Iraq, should our objective be to destroy its nuclear weapons capability or remove him, 141

likely that he will remain military threat after his forces are driven from Kuwait, 65

military force is only way he will leave Kuwait, 24

United States and allies should have continued fighting until he was removed from power, 150

United States should continue military action only until Iraq withdraws from Kuwait or continue until he is removed from power, 54–55, 64

national trend, 65

United States should stop military action if Iraq pulls out of Kuwait but he remains in power, 33

United States should stop military action if Iraq pulls out of Kuwait or only if he is removed from power, 41

I

Iceland, respondents in
1991 as peaceful or troubled year, 1
1991 will be better or worse than 1990, 1
India, respondents in
1991 as peaceful or troubled year, 1
1991 will be better or worse than 1990, 2
Insurance salesmen
honesty rating, 115
national trend, 116
Iran
favor having Congress investigate charges that Reagan-Bush campaign made deal with, to delay release of U.S. hostages until after 1980 election, 137

your overall opinion of, 51, 80, 174
national trend, 174
Iraq
approve of Bush's handling Middle East situation involving, 9–10, 14–15
national trend, 10, 15
Kurds in, as most closely followed news story, 107
as most important problem facing this country today, 12, 53
when choosing Democratic presidential candidate, would you prefer one who supported Bush's decision to go to war against, 136
whether Democratic presidential candidate supported Bush's decision to go to war against, as important consideration in selecting him, 135
your overall opinion of, 51, 80, 174
national trend, 174
See also Persian Gulf war
Ireland, respondents in
1991 as peaceful or troubled year, 1
1991 will be better or worse than 1990, 2
Israel
accept Iraqi condition that it must withdraw from Palestine and occupied Arab territories, 58
accept Iraqi condition that within month of cease-fire all allied forces and equipment must be withdrawn, including weapons provided to Israel, 58
as result of Persian Gulf war, prospects for peace between Israel and its Arab neighbors have improved, 151
diplomatic solution to Gulf crisis would link Iraqi withdrawal from Kuwait to issue of Israeli occupation of West Bank, 25
if it becomes involved in the war with Iraq, will the war last longer, 38
if it strikes back by attacking Iraq, should it strike back at military targets only, 38
Israel or Arab countries more to blame for lack of progress in settling their differences, 201
Israelis should strike back at Iraq in their own defense, 43
likely that an Israeli attack on Iraq in response to Scud missile attacks will damage alliance, 47
should it refrain from attacking Iraq, 37–38
should United States urge it to refrain from attacking Iraq, 38
will it continue to refrain from striking back at Iraq, 38, 43
your overall opinion of, 51, 80, 174, 200
national trend, 80, 174, 200

Israel (*continued*)

your sympathies more with Israelis or with Palestinian Arabs, 43, 80, 174–75

national trend, 43, 80, 175

See also Middle East situation

Israel, respondents in

1991 as peaceful or troubled year, 1

1991 will be better or worse than 1990, 2

Italy, respondents in

1991 as peaceful or troubled year, 1

1991 will be better or worse than 1990, 2

J

Jackson, Jesse

like to see him nominated as Democratic candidate for president, 62, 97, 135, 186, 196

as most admired man, 254

your opinion of, as presidential candidate, 62, 97, 186, 195

national trend, 195

Japan

approve of using atomic bomb on Japanese cities in 1945, 243

Democratic presidential candidate's views on trade policies toward, as important consideration in selecting him, 135

as dependable ally of United States, 241

national trend, 241

doing as much as it can to support United States in Persian Gulf, 24

as economic threat to United States today, 243

good for it to build bigger military complex, 242–43

likely to again become aggressor nation, 242

relations between United States and, will get better, 243

U.S. production of quality products is strong compared to, 91

U.S. standard of living is strong compared to, 92

U.S. system of public education is strong compared to, 91

U.S. technical innovation is strong compared to, 92

when choosing Democratic presidential candidate, would you prefer one who favors trade restrictions against, 136

why [list] do you have favorable opinion of, 241

why [list] do you have unfavorable opinion of, 241

your feelings toward Japanese people at present, 242

your overall opinion of, 51, 240

national trend, 240

See also Pearl Harbor

Japan, respondents in

1991 as peaceful or troubled year, 1

1991 will be better or worse than 1990, 2

Jefferson, Thomas

as greatest president, 252

John Paul II, Pope

as most admired man, 254

Johnson, Earvin "Magic"

as most admired man, 254

See also AIDS

Johnson, Lyndon

approval rating compared to Bush, 39, 68, 164, 229

as greatest president, 252

Jordan

your overall opinion of, 80, 174

national trend, 174

Jordan, Michael

as most admired man, 254

Journalists

honesty rating, 115

national trend, 116

K

Kemp, Jack

as choice for Bush's running mate in 1992, 62

if Bush decides not to run, would you like to see him nominated as Republican party's candidate for president, 182

Kennedy, Edward

like to see him nominated as Democratic candidate for president, 135

news organizations have gone too far in stories about his involvement in Palm Beach rape case, 105

your opinion of, 210, 251

national trend, 251

Kennedy, John F.

approval rating compared to Bush, 39, 68, 164, 229

as greatest president, 252

Kerrey, Bob

like to see him nominated as Democratic candidate for president, 62, 196, 226

your opinion of, as presidential candidate, 62, 195, 225

national trend, 195, 225

Korean War

whether it is a "just" war, 57

Kuwait

approve of Bush's handling Middle East situation involving, 9–10, 14–15

national trend, 10, 15

as most important problem facing this country today, 12, 53, 96

See also Persian Gulf war

L

M

Mexico
    happen to know name of president of, 91
    tell me name of its capital city, 91
Mexico, respondents in
    free-trade zone would be good or bad for Mexico, 84–85
    heard or read about free-trade zone with Canada and United States, 84
    1991 as peaceful or troubled year, 1
    1991 will be better or worse than 1990, 2
    which country would benefit most from free-trade zone, 85
Middle East
    as result of Persian Gulf war, it is a more stable region, 151
    to stop aggression in, as primary reason to go to war with Iraq, 23–24
Middle East situation
    favor establishment of independent Palestinian nation within territories occupied by Israel, 80
        national trend, 80
    favor proposal that Israel withdraw from occupied Arab lands if Arab nations recognize Israel's right to exist, 81, 176, 200
        national trend, 201
    handled by Bush, 9–10, 14–15, 72, 173
        national trend, 10, 15, 174
    how closely have you followed, 80, 174
    how likely is it that both sides will agree to proposal, 176
    if Israel did give up occupied Arab lands, how likely is it that this would bring lasting peace, 81, 176
    Israel and the Arab nations will settle their differences, 80, 175
        national trend, 81, 175
    peaceful solution should be important foreign policy goal of United States, 81
    United States should not pressure Israel, 81
    will this happen [Israel and the Arab nations settling their differences] during next five years, 81, 175
        national trend, 81, 176
    your sympathies more with Israelis or Palestinian Arabs, 43, 80, 174–75
        national trend, 43, 80, 175
    See also by country; Persian Gulf war
Military
    amount now being spent for, 110, 202
        national trend, 110, 202
    approve of way it is handling situation in Persian Gulf, 31, 36, 150
        national trend, 36

Bush administration and it have done as well as you expected in Persian Gulf, 31, 36
        national trend, 36
    cooperative in news coverage of Gulf war, 33, 61
        national trend, 61
    news organizations have respected its concern about security, in Gulf war, 33
    your confidence in, 69, 212
        national trend, 69, 212
Minorities
    Bush making progress on improving the lot of, 74
        national trend, 74
    companies should be required to hire same proportion of blacks and minorities as live in surrounding community, 126
    Democratic presidential candidate's views on protecting women and minorities from job discrimination, as important consideration in selecting him, 135
    Democrats are too supportive of racial quotas to improve conditions for, 98
    government should estimate, to count in census, 94–95
    should be given preferential treatment, 168
        national trend, 168
Mitchell, George
    happen to see or hear his response to Bush's State of the Union address, 46
    like to see him nominated as Democratic candidate for president, 62, 97
    your opinion of, as presidential candidate, 62, 97
Morals
    AIDS as punishment for decline in, 114
    decline in, as most important problem facing this country today, 12, 96, 197, 244
Mother Teresa of Calcutta
    as most admired woman, 254
Movies
    going to them more often, since Gulf war began, 66
Mulroney, Brian
    happen to know name of prime minister of Canada, 91

N

NATO
    favor reductions in U.S. forces in Europe, 179, 184
Netherlands, respondents in
    1991 as peaceful or troubled year, 1
    1991 will be better or worse than 1990, 2

Pearl Harbor (*continued*)
  know specifically what happened fifty years ago, 241
  as reason for unfavorable opinion of Japan, 241
  remember exactly where you were when you first heard about, 242
  was close family member killed while serving in U.S. Armed Forces, 242
  would United States have eventually been involved in World War II if it had not been attacked, 241–42
  your feelings toward the Japanese people at present, 242
Persian Gulf war
  accept Iraqi condition that government of Kuwait be based on people's will, 58
  accept Iraqi condition that Gulf region be declared zone free of foreign presence, 58
  accept Iraqi condition that Iraq's foreign debt will be canceled, 58
  accept Iraqi condition that Israel must withdraw from Palestine and occupied Arab territories, 58
  accept Iraqi condition that United Nations must abolish boycotts against Iraq, 58
  accept Iraqi condition that United States and allies pay for reconstruction of Iraq, 58
  accept Iraqi condition that within month of cease-fire all allied forces and equipment must be withdrawn, including weapons provided to Israel, 58
  accept Iraqi condition of total cease-fire before withdrawal would begin, 58
  afraid of traveling by air now, 66
  amount of coverage news media have given to, 48
  in antiwar demonstrations, good that Americans are speaking out, 43–44
  anyone in your family who is part of U.S. operation, 34, 45
  approve of Baker's dealing with crisis, 22
  approve of Bush's handling current situation, 26, 30, 35–36, 40, 46, 54
        national trend, 26, 30, 36, 40, 46, 54
  approve of Bush's handling situation in Iraq, since war ended, 140
  approve of Bush's plan in response to Iraqi-Soviet proposal to end war, 63
  approve of Democratic congressional leaders dealing with crisis, 23
  approve of Republican congressional leaders dealing with crisis, 23
  approve of situation handled by Baker, 69, 150

  approve of situation handled by Cheney, 69, 150
  approve of situation handled by Congress, 69, 150
  approve of situation handled by Gorbachev, 69, 150
  approve of situation handled by news media, 69, 150
  approve of situation handled by Powell, 69, 150
  approve of situation handled by Schwarzkopf, 69, 150
  approve of U.S. decision to go to war with Iraq, 26–27, 31, 36, 41, 47, 149
        national trend, 36, 41, 47
  approve of U.S. decision to send troops to Saudi Arabia, 15
        national trend, 15
  approve of U.S. decision to start ground war, 64
  approve of way U.S. military is handling situation in, 31, 36
        national trend, 36
  Arab nations, Japan, European nations, and USSR are doing as much as they can to support United States in, 24
  as result of [Iraqi peace proposal], are you optimistic that there will be quick end to war, 57
  as result of threat to captured airmen, should U.S. forces stop air strikes against Iraq, 41–42
  as result of war, Iraq is less likely to threaten its neighbors, 151
  as result of war, Middle East is more stable region, 151
  as result of war, nations are less likely to invade other nations, 151
  as result of war, prestige of United States has increased, 151
  as result of war, prospects for peace between Israel and its Arab neighbors have improved, 151
  as result of war, world's access to Middle East oil is more secure, 151
  Bush administration and military have been cooperative, in news coverage, 33
  Bush administration and U.S. military have done as well as you expected, 31, 36
        national trend, 36
  Bush did good job of explaining why we are in Persian Gulf, 46
  Bush did satisfactory job of explaining military action against Iraq, 26
  Bush has been willing to negotiate to end war, 64

Bush is correct in insisting that Iraq comply with all UN resolutions relating to withdrawal from Kuwait, 63
Bush should have given Hussein longer to begin withdrawal, 63
Bush should have waited longer for Soviet and other diplomatic efforts to end war, 64
Bush was correct in dismissing Iraqi [peace] proposal, 58
as Bush's greatest achievement, 70
changed plans [and other actions listed] as result of war, 34, 66
CNN and networks should broadcast reports from Iraq even though they are censored, 61
current situation worth going to war over, 17–18, 47, 125, 140–41
    national trend, 18, 47, 125–26, 141
diplomatic solution would link Iraqi withdrawal to issue of Israeli occupation of West Bank and a Palestinian homeland, 25
favor changing U.S. policy to allow women to serve in combat roles, 60
favor law to ban peace demonstrations while U.S. troops are fighting, 44–45
favor leaving UN sanctions against Iraq in place as long as Hussein remains in power, 125, 150–51
favor military action against Iraq on January 15, 24
favor resuming action against Iraq if Iraqis refuse to observe UN resolution calling for destruction of their nuclear weapons capability, 141
favor stopping military action to give Iraqis another chance diplomatically, 41
favor temporary cease-fire by United States as sign of good faith and to provide time for settlement with Hussein, 59
favor using tactical nuclear weapons against Iraq, 42–43, 59–60
fighting will continue for days or weeks or more, 27, 33, 36–37, 40, 54
    national trend, 37, 40, 54
good achieved by military action will outweigh harm, 56
happen to see or hear Bush's address to the nation [Jan. 16], 26
happen to see or hear Bush's State of the Union address [Jan. 29], 46
have clear idea of what U.S. military involvement is all about, 151
    national trend, 151

how closely have you followed Iraqi-Soviet proposal to end war and Bush's reaction to it, 63
how closely have you followed Iraq's proposal to end war and Bush's reaction to it, 57
how closely have you followed news about, 8–9, 13–14, 30, 39–40, 53
    national trend, 9, 14, 30, 40, 53
how concerned are you that Hussein will again pose military threat, 150
how do you think war will end, 32–33
how effective can prayers be in situation like this, 34
how much effect did U.S. policies that favored Iraq or of not having alternative energy policy have on causing situation, 47–48
how much longer should United States maintain forces in Gulf to maintain peace in region, 151
how worried are you that current situation will develop into larger war, 24, 31–32, 37
    national trend, 32, 37
how worried are you that Iraq's setting fire to oil refineries in Kuwait will lead to major ecological problems, 43
if the Democratic presidential candidate voted against resolution allowing Bush to use force in Gulf war, would you be more likely to vote for him, 98, 151–52
if Hussein agrees to withdraw from Kuwait, would you favor immediate cease-fire by United States, 59
if Hussein holds conference for withdrawal from Kuwait, should United States postpone any action, 11–12
if Hussein is removed from power, should United States offer aid to rebuild Iraq, 151
if Iraq does not meet deadline [Feb. 23], should United States and allies start ground war, 63–64
if Iraq lets January 15 deadline pass, would you favor going to war with Iraq, 10–11, 21
    national trend, 11, 21
if Iraq were to withdraw from Kuwait, would you be less likely to take military action, 24
if Israel becomes involved, will war last longer, 38
if Israel strikes back by attacking Iraq, should it strike back at military targets only, 38
if situation does not change by January, would you favor going to war with Iraq, 11, 16–17
    national trend, 11, 17

Persian Gulf war (*continued*)

if United States does resume action against Iraq, should our objective be to destroy its nuclear weapons capability or remove Hussein, 141

if United States gets Iraq to leave Kuwait, should our troops stay in region indefinitely, 24

Iraq has done all it can to solve crisis diplomatically, 24

Iraqi [peace] proposal was genuine attempt to end war, 57–58

Israel should refrain from attacking Iraq, 37–38

Israel will continue to refrain from striking back at Iraq, 38, 43

Israelis should strike back at Iraq in their own defense, 43

job rating of news organizations covering war with Iraq, 33, 48

"just" cause for taking military action, 56–57

know anyone else who is part of U.S. operation, 45

likely that Hussein will remain military threat after his forces are driven from Kuwait, 65

likely that United States and allies will strike militarily on January 15, 24–25

likely that U.S. forces in Saudi Arabia will become engaged in combat, 18–20
    national trend, 20

looking ahead, how likely is it that Iran will enter the fighting in support of Iraq, 47

looking ahead, how likely is it that Iraq will use chemical or nuclear weapons, 47

looking ahead, how likely is it that Iraqis will unleash major threats to environment, 47

looking ahead, how likely is it that an Israeli attack on Iraq in response to Scud missiles will damage alliance, 47

looking ahead, how likely is it that situation will develop into bloody ground war, 47

looking ahead, how likely is it that U.S. citizens will become victims of Iraqi terrorism, 47

military action is likely to avoid harming civilians, 57

military action has been undertaken by responsible authorities, 56

military action was taken as last resort, 56

military force is only way Hussein will leave Kuwait, 24

as most important problem facing this country today, 53, 96

news organizations have respected military's concern about security, 33

news organizations have respected privacy of families of U.S. troops, 33

number of Americans killed and injured, 33, 54

postpone NFL playoffs and Super Bowl as result of war, 34

primary reason to go to war with Iraq, 23–24

reasonable likelihood that the military action will succeed, 57

role of Congress in determining policy in, 25

since war began, has your child asked to talk to you about war, 66

since war began, has your child had difficulty sleeping, 66

since war began, has your child had nightmares about war, 66

since war began, has your child told you his fears about war, 66

since war began, have you displayed U.S. flag, 66

since war began, have you displayed yellow ribbon, 66

since war began, have you limited time your child spends watching news on television, 66

since war began, have you made special effort to spend less and save more, 67

since war began, have you made special effort to talk to your child about his concerns about, 66

since war began, have you postponed buying new car, house, or major appliance, 67

since war began, have you postponed or canceled vacation or business trip, 34, 66

since war began, have you prayed more than you usually do, 66

since war began, have you signed up for cable to watch CNN's coverage, 66

since war began, have you talked seriously with friends about it [other actions listed], 66

tactical nuclear weapons are more destructive than conventional weapons, 60

think this war is Armageddon, 45

threat of war crimes trials will lead Iraqis to treat POWs better, 42

tonight [Feb. 22] are we on the brink of a peaceful settlement, 64

United States and allies are losing ground, 41, 47, 54
    national trend, 47, 54

United States and allies should have continued fighting until Hussein was removed from power, 150
    national trend, 150

United States has done all it can to solve crisis diplomatically, 24

United States made mistake in sending troops to Saudi Arabia [or Persian Gulf region], 15–16, 30, 40–41, 46, 54, 150

Poverty (*continued*)
handled by Bush, 71
national trend, 71
as important issue in determining which
presidential candidate you will vote for, 224
as most important problem facing this country
today, 12, 53, 96, 125, 197, 244
Republican or Democratic party better at dealing
with, 199, 227
See also Poor people
Powell, Colin
as choice for Bush's running mate in 1992, 61
handling situation in the Persian Gulf, 69, 150
Predictions for 1991
better or worse than 1990, asked in five East
European countries, 3
better or worse than 1990, asked in thirty-seven
countries, 1–2
number of unemployed will increase, asked in
five East European countries, 3
as peaceful or troubled year, asked in five East
European countries, 3
as peaceful or troubled year, asked in thirty-seven
countries, 1
national trend (United States), 1
as year of economic prosperity or difficulty,
asked in five East European countries, 3
Presidency
which three presidents [list] do you regard as the
greatest, 252
your confidence in, 69, 212
Presidential candidates. *See* Democratic presidential
candidates; Republican presidential
candidates
Problems, facing this country today
handled better by Republican or Democratic
party, 96, 197
handled by Bush as well as anyone, 246
most important [list], 12, 53, 96, 125, 197, 244
national trend, 244–45
Prosperity
Bush making progress on keeping America
prosperous, 74
national trend, 74
1991 will be year of economic prosperity or
difficulty, asked in five East European
countries, 3
Republican or Democratic party better at keeping
country prosperous, 148, 223
national trend, 148, 223
Public officials
increased attention given to private lives of, as
good or bad, 105
national trend, 105

should be reported when public official attended
party at which cocaine was used, 106
should be reported when public official had
extramarital affair, 106
should be reported when public official is found
to have been arrested for marijuana
possession, 106
should be reported when public official is found
to have exaggerated his academic record, 106
should be reported when public official is found
to have exaggerated his military service, 106
should be reported when public official is found
to have not paid federal income tax, 106
should be reported when public official is found
to have used military aircraft for personal
trips, 106
should be reported when public official is having
extramarital affair, 106
should be reported when public official is
homosexual, 106
See also Media; Political officeholders
Puerto Rico
support granting full independence to, 65
support its becoming fifty-first state, 65

Q

Quayle, Dan
approval rating, 107
national trend, 107
Bush should keep, as running mate, 61
communicates effectively, 109
described as confident or insecure, 108
described as intelligent or only average, 108
described as leader or follower, 109
described as steady or undependable, 108
described as strong or weak, 109
described as warm or cold, 108
experienced in government, 109
if Bush and he run for reelection, are you more
likely to vote for Bush and Quayle or for
Democratic party's candidates, 182
if Bush decides not to run, would you like to see
him nominated as Republican party's
candidate for president, 182
if Bush keeps him as his running mate, would you
be more likely to vote for Bush's reelection,
232
if Bush runs for reelection, should he keep Quayle
as his running mate, 108, 182, 233
by key voter groups, 182
national trend, 108, 182, 233
if he were Republican candidate for president in
1996, would you be more likely to vote for
him or for Democratic candidate, 182

knowledgeable about foreign affairs, 109
knowledgeable about national issues, 109
as most closely followed news story, 107
qualified to serve as president if it becomes
    necessary, 107, 181, 233
                national trend, 107–8, 181–82, 233
stands up for what he believes, 109
understands complex issues, 109
would display good judgment in crisis, 109
your confidence in, as a leader, 233
your confidence in, to handle job of president
    should occasion arise, 109
your opinion of, rated, 108, 181
           national trend, 108

R

Race relations
as Democrats' campaign issue in 1992, 187
handled by Bush, 72
as important issue in determining which
    presidential candidate you will vote for,
    224
Republican or Democratic party better at dealing
    with, 199, 227
South African government has made progress
    during last year in trying to resolve its racial
    problems, 133
           national trend, 133
Racial quotas
approve of Supreme Court's ruling in cases where
    they are an issue, 138
companies should be required to hire same
    proportion of blacks and minorities as live
    in surrounding community, 126
Democratic presidential candidate's views on
    protecting women and minorities without
    using, as important consideration in
    selecting him, 135
Democrats are too supportive of, 98
enough federal laws aimed at reducing race,
    religion, and sex discrimination, 126, 168–
    69
seen or heard about civil rights bill now before
    Congress, 126
when choosing Democratic presidential
    candidate, would you prefer one who favors,
    in hiring and promotion, 136
when choosing Democratic presidential
    candidate, would you prefer one who
    opposes, in hiring and promotion, 136
which civil rights bill requires racial quotas in
    hiring and promotion, 127
which of two civil rights bills would you like to
    see Congress pass, 126

Radio
amount of time you spent yesterday listening to,
    49
listening to news more often, since Gulf war
    began, 60–61, 66
your main source of information about war in
    Persian Gulf, 33
Reading
amount of time you spent yesterday, 49
best way to learn for you is to read books or
    watch television, 49
do you have a favorite author, 50
do you know anyone who is illiterate, 50
during past year, how many books did you read,
    50
as good use of your time, 49
happen to be reading any books or novels, 50
           national trend, 50
happen to belong to book club, 50
happen to have bookcases in your home, 50
happen to have library card, 50
how many books do you have in your home,
    50
in last seven days, have you had chance to read,
    49
in your nonworking time, do you spend too much
    time reading newspapers, magazines, and
    books, 49
looking ahead, will you find yourself reading
    more, 49–50
most enjoyable evening for you is to read books
    or watch television, 49
most relaxing for you is to read books or watch
    television, 49
most rewarding for you is to read books or watch
    television, 49
who is your favorite author [list], 50
Reagan, Nancy
as most admired woman, 254
news organizations have gone too far in stories
    on Kitty Kelley's book about, 105
Reagan, Ronald
approval rating compared to Bush, 39, 68, 164,
    229, 245
favor having Congress investigate charges
    that Reagan-Bush campaign made deal
    with Iran to delay release of U.S. hostages,
    137
as greatest president, 252
made right decision to fire air traffic controllers
    when their union staged illegal strike, 155
as most admired man, 254
why was [firing air traffic controllers] right
    decision, 155

Reagan, Ronald (*continued*)
    why was [firing air traffic controllers] wrong
        decision, 155
Real estate agents
    honesty rating, 115
        national trend, 116
Recession
    are you now in a good position to buy things,
        220
    especially important now to add to savings, 219–
        20
    has the bottom been reached, 95, 124, 147, 191,
        219
        national trend, 95, 125, 147, 191,
            219
    how much longer will it last, 53, 250
    if there were a major purchase you wanted to
        make, would you feel okay about buying it on
        credit, 220
    as most closely followed news story, 107
    as most important problem facing this country
        today, 125, 197, 244
    See also Business and industry; Economic
        conditions; Unemployment
Religion
    agree that only assurance of eternal life is
        personal faith in Jesus Christ, 239
    can it answer today's problems, 238
        national trend, 238
    describe yourself as "born-again" Christian,
        239
        national trend, 239
    enough federal laws aimed at reducing race,
        religion, and sex discrimination, 126, 168–
        69
    happen to attend church or synagogue in last
        seven days, 238
        national trend, 239
    happen to be member of church or synagogue,
        238
        national trend, 238
    how effective do you think prayers can be in
        situation like Persian Gulf, 34
    how important is it in your own life, 238
        national trend, 238
    is it increasing its influence on American life,
        237
        national trend, 237
    since Persian Gulf war began, have you prayed
        more than you usually do, 34, 66
    which [list] comes closest to your feelings about
        Bible, 239
    which [list] comes closest to your views about
        origin of man, 239

    your confidence in church and organized, 69, 212
        national trend, 69, 212
Republican party
    approve of its refusal to recognize David Duke,
        223
    approve of Republican congressional leaders
        dealing with Persian Gulf crisis, 23
    best serves middle-income people, 199
    best serves people like yourself, 199
    best serves poor people, 199
    best serves wealthy people, 199
    better at dealing with abortion issue, 199, 227
    better at dealing with crime, 198, 227
    better at dealing with economic conditions, 198,
        227
    better at dealing with education, 227
    better at dealing with environmental issues, 199,
        227
    better at dealing with federal budget deficit, 198,
        227
    better at dealing with foreign policy, 198, 228
    better at dealing with health-care policy, 199,
        227
    better at dealing with national defense, 198, 228
    better at dealing with poverty and homelessness,
        199, 227
    better at dealing with race relations, 199, 227
    better at dealing with relations with Soviet
        Union, 198
    better at dealing with tax policy, 227
    better at dealing with unemployment, 199, 227
    better at handling most important problem facing
        this country today, 96, 197, 244
        national trend, 244–45
    better at keeping country prosperous, 148, 223
        national trend, 148, 223
    better reflects your views on abortion, 122–23
    do you associate it more with political favoritism
        and corruption, 198
    do you consider yourself a Republican, 165
        national trend, 165
    as more likely to keep United States out of war,
        148
        national trend, 148
    your opinion of, rated, 197, 215
        national trend, 197, 215–16
Republican presidential candidates
    if Bush decides not to run for reelection, which
        [list] would you like to see nominated, 182
Revolutionary War
    whether it is a "just" war, 57
Robb, Charles
    like to see him nominated as Democratic
        candidate for president, 97

Soviet Union (*continued*)
    as result of recent changes in leadership [Aug. 19], relations with United States will go back to where they were before Gorbachev came to power, 179

    Bush should have waited longer for Soviet and other diplomatic efforts to end Gulf war, 64

    change of leadership [Aug. 19], dealt with by Bush, 179

    changes in, as Bush's greatest achievement, 70

    doing as much as it can to support United States in Persian Gulf, 24

    favor donating grain and farm products to, 144, 184

    favor providing cash to, that would not have to be paid back, 144, 184

    favor providing financial loans to, 144, 184

    favor providing technical assistance to, 144, 184–85

    favor reductions in U.S. forces in Europe, 179, 184

    Gorbachev's attempts to restructure Soviet economy are likely to succeed, 52, 143
        national trend, 144

    heard or read about proposed nuclear arms-reduction agreement between United States and, 145

    how closely have you followed Iraqi-Soviet proposal to end war in Gulf, 63

    how closely have you followed replacement of Gorbachev with new leadership [Aug. 19], 179

    how serious are its economic problems, 143

    if it should seek to regain control of Poland, Hungary, Czechoslovakia, and other East European nations [after Aug. 19], should United States send troops, 179

    if there are disturbances [after Aug. 19], should United States send troops, 180

    important to increase aid to, to keep from threatening international stability, 253

    in response to recent changes [Aug. 19] in, favor breaking off diplomatic relations with, 180

    in response to recent changes [Aug. 19] in, favor holding off on decision to ratify nuclear arms treaty, 180

    in response to recent changes [Aug. 19] in, favor providing support to reform groups within, 180

    in response to recent changes [Aug. 19] in, favor recalling U.S. ambassador to, 180

    in response to recent changes [Aug. 19] in, favor restricting American investments in, 180

    in response to recent changes [Aug. 19] in, favor suspending economic assistance to, 180

    in response to recent changes [Aug. 19] in, favor suspending loans to help food shortages in, 180

    like to see U.S. Congress vote in favor of proposed nuclear arms-reduction treaty, 145

    nuclear war likely between United States and, within next five years, 52

    provide financial aid to, if defense budget is cut, 202

    recent events [after Aug. 19] mean the end of communism, 185

    relations between United States and, getting better, 52, 143
        national trend, 143

    relations with, handled by Bush, 71
        national trend, 72

    relations with, Republican or Democratic party better at dealing with, 198

    still a "cold war" between United States and, 52, 184, 203
        national trend, 52

    United States did too much to support Gorbachev's efforts at reform, 179

    United States doing too much to help in current economic crisis, 144, 184, 252–53
        national trend, 253

    United States [after Aug. 19] should continue its economic and political cooperation with, 179

    United States should deal primarily with Gorbachev or Yeltsin, 185

    United States should side with Gorbachev or Yeltsin, 253

    Western countries can continue to live peacefully with Russians, 184

    your confidence in, 69

    your overall opinion of, 51, 174, 178, 183
        national trend, 51, 174, 178

    your overall opinion of Soviet people, 184

Soviet Union, respondents in
    1991 as peaceful or troubled year, 1
    1991 will be better or worse than 1990, 2

Space program
    amount now being spent for, 110
        national trend, 110

    concentrate on unmanned missions like *Voyager 2*, 112
        national trend, 112

    important for United States to be first to land person on Mars, 111–12

    investment in space research is worthwhile, 111

    job rating for NASA, 111

like to be passenger on space shuttle flight,
112

space shuttle program has been worthwhile, 112

Spain, respondents in

1991 as peaceful or troubled year, 1

1991 will be better or worse than 1990, 2

Specter, Arlen

your opinion of, 210

Standard of living

U.S. overall standard is strong compared to
Japan, Great Britain, and Germany, 92

Stockbrokers

honesty rating, 115

national trend, 116

Sununu, John

news organizations have gone too far in stories
about his use of military aircraft for personal
trips, 105

your confidence in Bush, as result of change in
chief of staff, 246

Supreme Court

approve of ruling that government can prohibit
family-planning clinics from providing
patients with information about abortion,
119–20

approve of rulings in cases where abortion is
issue, 138

approve of rulings in cases where racial quotas are
issue, 138

approve of rulings in cases where rights of
prisoners are issue, 138

Bush's appointments to, as his greatest
achievement, 70

in its recent rulings, has it been too liberal or
conservative, 137–38

like to see 1973 ruling on abortion overturned,
121–22, 139

national trend, 122, 139

nomination of Clarence Thomas to, *see* Thomas,
Clarence

tell me name of Bush's recent nomination to,
137

your confidence in, 69, 212–13

national trend, 69, 213

your confidence in nomination process, as result
of Thomas hearings, 210

Sweden, respondents in

1991 as peaceful or troubled year, 1

1991 will be better or worse than 1990, 2

Switzerland, respondents in

1991 as peaceful or troubled year, 1

1991 will be better or worse than 1990, 2

Syria

your overall opinion of, 174

T

Taiwan, respondents in

1991 as peaceful or troubled year, 1

1991 will be better or worse than 1990, 1

Taxes

avoiding raising, as Bush's greatest
achievement, 70

Bush making progress on avoiding raising, 75

national trend, 75

Democratic presidential candidate's views on
support for new taxes to solve certain
problems, as important consideration in
selecting him, 135

Democrats rely too much on increasing, to deal
with problems, 98

fairness to middle-income people, as Democrats'
campaign issue in 1992, 187

favor allowing parents to send children to
parochial or private school and use tax
dollars to pay for it, 92

favor reducing income and sales taxes across the
board, 231

favor tax on corporations which produce
environmentally harmful products, 89

it should be reported when public official is found
to have not paid federal income tax, 106

as most important problem facing this country
today, 244

reduce, if defense budget is cut, 202

tax policy, as important issue in determining
which presidential candidate you will vote
for, 224

tax policy, Republican or Democratic party better
at dealing with, 227

when choosing Democratic presidential
candidate, would you prefer one who opposes
increasing federal, 136

when choosing Democratic presidential
candidate, would you prefer one who would
support new taxes to solve certain problems,
135

Taylor, Elizabeth

as most admired woman, 254

Teachers, college

honesty rating, 115

national trend, 115

Television

amount of time you spent yesterday watching, 49

best way to learn for you is to read books or
watch, 49

do you have television set in your car, 102

honesty rating of reporters and commentators,
115

national trend, 116

U

Unemployment
    during next twelve months, will it go up, 220
    as important issue in determining which
        presidential candidate you will vote for,
        224
    in next twelve months, likely that you will lose
        your job, 220
            national trend, 220
    in 1991, number of unemployed will increase,
        asked in five East European countries, 3
    know people outside my family who have been
        laid off, 220
    likely to vote for Bush's reelection, if he vetoes
        bill extending unemployment benefits, 202
    member of my family has been laid off, 220
    as most important problem facing this country
        today, 53, 96, 125, 197, 244
            national trend, 244
    Republican or Democratic party better at dealing
        with, 199, 227
Unemployment rate
    as Democrats' campaign issue in 1992, 187
United Nations
    accept Iraqi condition that Israel must withdraw
        from Palestine or face UN sanctions, 58
    accept Iraqi condition that it must abolish
        boycotts against Iraq, 58
    Bush is correct in insisting that Iraq comply with
        all UN resolutions relating to withdrawal
        from Kuwait, 63
    favor leaving sanctions against Iraq in place as
        long as Hussein remains in power, 125, 150–
        51
    favor resuming action against Iraq if Iraqis refuse
        to observe UN resolution calling for
        destruction of their nuclear weapons
        capability, 141
    if Iraq lets UN deadline pass, would you favor
        going to war with Iraq, 10–11, 21
            national trend, 11, 21
    United States should continue military action
        against Iraq only until Iraq withdraws from
        Kuwait, in keeping with UN resolution, 54
United States
    Bush making progress on increasing respect for,
        abroad, 74
            national trend, 74
    your confidence in, 69
    your satisfaction with way things are going in,
        29, 68, 124
            national trend, 29, 68, 124
    See also Japan; Persian Gulf war; Soviet Union

Uruguay, respondents in
    1991 as peaceful or troubled year, 1
    1991 will be better or worse than 1990, 2

V

Vice president
    if Bush chooses new running mate for 1992,
        which [list] would you like to see him
        choose, 61–62
Videos
    renting more often, since Gulf war began, 66
Vietnam War
    whether it is a "just" war, 57

W

War
    Bush making progress on keeping nation out of,
        73
            national trend, 74
    fear of, as most important problem facing this
        country today, 12
    as outmoded way of settling differences or
        sometimes necessary, 56
            national trend, 56
    Republican or Democratic party more likely to
        keep United States out of, 148
            national trend, 148
    whether [list] is a "just" war, 57
    See also Persian Gulf war
Washington, George
    as greatest president, 252
Welfare
    favor requiring all able-bodied people on welfare
        to do work for their checks, 231
Wilder, Douglas
    like to see him nominated as Democratic
        candidate for president, 62, 97, 186, 196
    your opinion of, as presidential candidate, 62,
        97, 186, 195, 225
            national trend, 195, 225
Wilson, Pete
    if Bush decides not to run, would you like to see
        him nominated as Republican party's
        candidate for president, 182
Wilson, Woodrow
    as greatest president, 252
Winfrey, Oprah
    as most admired woman, 254
Women
    as result of William Kennedy Smith case, will
        they be more likely to report being raped,
        251

Women (*continued*)

Democratic presidential candidate's views on protecting women and minorities from job discrimination, as important consideration in selecting him, 135

favor changing U.S. policy to allow them to serve in combat roles, 60

favor using federal funds to enable poor women to have abortions, 122

should be given preferential treatment, 168
national trend, 168

which are safer drivers—men or women, 102

your choice for most admired woman [list], 254

World War I

whether it is a "just" war, 57

World War II

approve of government requiring U.S. citizens of Japanese descent to move to relocation camps during, 243

approve of using atomic bomb on Japanese cities, 243

whether it is a "just" war, 57

See also Pearl Harbor

Y

Yeltsin, Boris

United States should deal primarily with Gorbachev or him, 185

United States should side with Gorbachev or him, 253

your overall opinion of, 183–84

Yugoslavia, respondents in

how does financial situation of your household compare to twelve months ago, 3

how has economic situation in this country changed, 2

in 1991, number of unemployed will increase, 3

in 1991, strikes will increase, 3

1991 as peaceful or troubled year, 3

1991 will be better or worse than 1990, 3

1991 will be year of economic prosperity or difficulty, 3